A Literary Approach to the

NEW TESTAMENT

A Literary Approach to the NEW TESTAMENT

by JOHN PAUL PRITCHARD

UNIVERSITY OF OKLAHOMA PRESS NORMAN

By John Paul Pritchard

Return to the Fountains (Durham, N.C., 1942)
Criticism in America (Norman, 1956)
The Literary Wise Men of Gotham (Baton Rouge, 1963)
August Boeckh On Interpretation and Criticism (Norman, 1968)
A Literary Approach to the New Testament (Norman, 1972)

Library of Congress Cataloging in Publication Data

Pritchard, John Paul, 1902–
A literary approach to the New Testament.

Bibliography: p.
1. Bible. N. T.—Criticism, interpretation, etc. 2. Bible. N. T.—Language, style. I. Title.
BS2361.2.P75 225.6′6 72-1793

First edition, 1972; second printing, 1980.

For Ruth

ALPHA AND OMEGA

PREFACE

A few years ago one of my nephews mentioned to his pastor that his uncle was at work on a book on the New Testament. The clergyman, stopping abruptly in his tracks, demanded, "Is he a Christian?" When my nephew said that I was, the pastor replied, "Then it'll be a good book." Not long thereafter a friend whom I had not seen for many years asked me about my writing. When I explained that it was a nonreligious, literary study of the New Testament, she looked startled and asked, "Paul, have you lost your religion?" The former comment brings to mind a statement by James Russell Lowell, that a man who has been martyred for his faith did not necessarily write good verses. The latter points to the characteristics of many studies of the New Testament as literature which confuse the literary with the religious, and even the sectarian, points of view.

Some readers may question my use of the term literary for what is, in many respects, a rhetorical approach. A century and a half ago, William Ellery Channing declared that American literature included everything written in the United States. Without subscribing to Channing's patriotic inclusiveness, I take the position implicit in the famous essay ascribed to Longinus, who evidently included rhetoric and poetics in the larger art of letters. To a degree not readily to be measured, the Gospels, the Acts, and the Apocalypse are artistic creations designed to persuade.

My life has been constantly exposed to literary and religious influences. In my teaching career of forty-seven years, I have regularly taught the New Testament in Greek and later in English.

It is a stark impossibility to acknowledge all my indebtedness in this work. To the late Professor Lane Cooper, my debt is profound. Harry Caplan, emeritus professor of Classics at Cornell University and a friend for half a century, greatly assisted me with advice and bibliographical information on classical and medieval rhetoric. Herbert George Grether, D.D., a former student of mine in Greek and a linguistic scholar of wide reputation, critically read my manuscript and made invaluable comments and suggestions. James H. Sims, my colleague at the University of Oklahoma, contributed in his reading of the manuscript many literary insights and valuable suggestions. Constant encouragement has come from two other colleagues, Victor A. Elconin and Joseph H. Marshburn. Miss Helen Cline copyread the manuscript and brought to light its many minor errors of expression. My wife has encouraged me throughout the long task. It is regrettable that Emerson's statement, that the greatest genius is the most indebted man, is not conversely true as well. If it were, I should occupy a position far above any that I can claim.

The University of Oklahoma Research Institute aided me with funds to purchase needed books.

JOHN PAUL PRITCHARD

Norman, Oklahoma

CONTENTS

MAPS

A Literary Approach to the

NEW TESTAMENT

INTRODUCTION

THE LITERARY APPROACH

Year after year, century after century, the Bible remains the world's most influential and widely read book. It has been translated into more languages and studied in more detail and from more "angles" than anything else ever written. Closely studied by believers and nonbelievers, it has been subjected to endless variety of interpretation with respect to its content. Both classes of readers have contributed substantially to its understanding. The Bible is also a work of exceptional literary interest. It repays the attention of the reader to a degree equal to any other literary masterpiece. This book attempts to present to the general reader the literary qualities of the New Testament.

Other factors being equal, the literary study of the New Testament will be more rewarding to the Christian believer. In literary study as in literary creativity, intuition plays no small part. August Boeckh for the traditionalists and Benedetto Croce for the moderns both testify to this fact. The latter asserted that concepts which have become second nature to a reader serve him also as intuitions, and such insights obviously come more readily to one who has been sympathetically readied to receive them.

Paradoxically, a Christian reader of the New Testament will probably receive more significant literary insights into it if he is not a trained theologian. The theologically oriented reader focuses on what it means for religion and morals. The literary approach views form and content as one and is concerned with what the book is. Just as the literary interpreter of Chaucer requires a wealth of information and insight concerning the times of Chaucer and the influences at work in him, so the literary interpreter of the New Testament requires information about it and insights into it. Knowing what the book *is* in itself and in its relations frequently clarifies significantly what the book means. General readers will profit from the presentation of this knowledge in developing their own insights into the New Testament.

In asserting that the reader of the New Testament will find greater reward and understanding if he is a Christian, there is no intent to belittle the values of the book for non-Christian readers. Such readers should, however, exercise what Coleridge described as "the willing suspension of disbelief for a season" in order to enter, at least temporarily, into the spirit of the work. If we endeavor to read in this spirit, we shall find the work richer and more rewarding.

For literary interpretation of the New Testament, the traditional Sunday school presentation has contributed little beyond acquainting children with episodes and agents. In it books are seldom treated as wholes made by an author with specific purpose and artistic designs. Books are to be analyzed upon sound anatomical principles for study of what they are before ideas for moral and religious instruction are drawn from them.

An author plans a unified whole of which the subdivisions are each functioning parts. He has in view one or probably several specific ends. Our task is to discover, as Goethe wrote, what the author is trying to do and to judge how well he succeeds in doing that. Since external information concerning the first task is inadequate for the New Testament, we must follow the advice of Aristotle, slightly adapted (*Poetics* xxv). By reading the book itself, we seek to answer five questions: (1) who wrote the work; (2) to whom he addressed it; (3) when he wrote it; (4) in whose interest he wrote; and (5) what was his motive. The subsequent history of the New Testament books indicates that the authors succeeded in what they undertook in spite of some misunderstandings among their later readers. It is safe then to assume that the works fairly accurately indicate what the authors had in mind when they wrote; the books adequately represent their purposes.

The problem of scriptural inspiration enters here. To what extent may New Testament books be analyzed as products of the human mind? August Boeckh, a great and devout literary scholar, wrote more than a century ago: "If a sacred book is of human origin it must be understood according to human rules in the treatment usually applied to books. If it is of divine origin, it stands on a level above all human interpretation, and can be apprehended only through divine inspiration," that is, in part at least through Christian intuitions. He held the Scriptures to be partly the work of men, who performed the actual composing and writing, putting into verbal expression what had been revealed to them. "Obviously," he concluded, "every truly sacred book, like every highly gifted man's work that is the product of inspiration, may become fully intelligible only through human and divine means at once."

Undeniably a superhuman power, which the New Testament calls the Holy Spirit, was working through the pioneers of the early Church and was active in the writers of these books. However the Spirit worked—and a literary study, as Boeckh said, cannot explain the divine share in the work—the writers were human agents with human foibles and shortcomings. It would indeed seem logical to credit the Holy Spirit with having chosen men of some competence to write and some degree of training in the art of writing; but it is human to err, and these writers were free agents. Beyond accepting the activity of a divine force at work in these writers, a literary approach cannot go; its concerns are different.

With regard to scriptural inspiration, the only clear-cut position taken here is to avoid the older belief in literal verbal inspiration of the Scriptures. Such a belief relegates the writers to mere automata, not the free agents which New Testament writers declare men to be. Our approach, then, is to focus upon the books and their writers exactly as would a study of Chaucer or Shakespeare or Whitman or, to mention closer parallels, Edmund Burke or Daniel Webster.

To the best of my knowledge, this kind of approach to the books of the New Testament has not previously been developed. Several scholars who have approximated it at first and were quite competent to develop it—Henry J. Cadbury and Stephen Neill are prominent among them—have shifted their course into theological channels.

The current developing school of redaction criticism (*Redaktionsgeschichte*), which concerns itself with the New Testament books as wholes, comes closer to the approach used here, but it focuses on the theological position presented by the books rather than on their rhetorical structure.

It is my fixed belief, arrived at after long study of the New Testament as literature, that the organizing principle on which its books were constructed—the dominant structural principle—is to be found in the pervasive rhetorical teaching of the time when they were composed. So far as their form is concerned, they are rhetorical treatises in propaganda.

THE PROBLEM OF THE LANGUAGE

Early in the third century B.C., Jewish scholars in Egypt undertook to translate the Pentateuch into the Koine Greek then spoken in Mediterranean countries. Other Hebrew Scriptures were later translated, until by the time of Christian expansion into the Hellenistic world the Old Testament and part at least of the Apocrypha were available to Gentile readers. Since the translation was made by various scholars over a period of more than two centuries, the Greek dialect used and the degree of accuracy may vary considerably; but as a whole it belongs to the clear, vigorous, and vital language that served as a *lingua franca* for the Hellennistic world.

The term *koinē* is an adjective meaning "in common usage"; the collective term for this speech is the *koinē dialektos,* the commonly spoken and written language that, in spite of local peculiarities, was intelligible throughout the Roman Empire. Renaissance scholars who revered the purity of Ciceronian Latin naturally looked down upon Koine Greek as barbarous and vulgar. In the sixteenth century Cardinal Pietro Bembo, a distinguished member of this clique, advised students not to read the Greek New Testament on the ground that it would spoil their ear for classical Greek style. Similar contempt for the dialect pervaded classical scholarship for centuries; today, along with the study of ecclesiastical Latin, it receives greater respect and attention.

The importance of the Koine in the expansion of Christianity can hardly be overestimated. It crossed all frontiers and classes of men. Although Jesus no doubt generally spoke Aramaic, He probably had some acquaintance with the Koine also; Galileans, living on one of the major caravan routes, would perforce develop some acquaintance with the dialect. Even fishermen like Peter and John no doubt had some knowledge of it. When Christianity expanded beyond the limits of Palestine and among Gentiles, Jewish Christians could communicate to some extent with Gentiles. However scanty their knowledge of the Koine, they could expand it enough to express their basic message. In the mouth of a scholar like Paul, who had grown up among Gentiles, it was a fully developed medium of communication. Without such a common language, certainly the dissemination of the new faith would have been immeasurably hampered.

For Gentiles, the Septuagint, as the Greek translation of the Jewish books came to be named, provided a bridge to lead them to knowledge of Jewish beliefs and traditions. It was the standard text used in synagogues outside of Palestine. Gentiles who became interested in Judaism by way of these synagogues were thus informed of the backgrounds on which the figure of Jesus had appeared. It was no doubt these Gentiles whom Paul and other Jewish Christian missionaries first met on their journeys as they visited the synagogues. Christian teachers had thus at hand a nucleus of Gentiles competent to grasp their teachings, an improvement upon the then current Judaism. And since Christianity did not require them to submit to the despised rite of circumcision, these men, many of them adherents to the Jewish faith, were doubly open to the appeal of the new faith.

The Gospel writers took full advantage of the services offered them by the Koine and, where feasible, of the Septuagint as well. We shall see that Mark, being addressed to less educated and less philosophical Gentiles, is expressed in simple language with a minimum of reference to the Hebrew sacred books. Matthew, addressed primarily to Jews of the Dispersion, uses somewhat more complex language and frequently bases its argument on the Septuagint. Luke, seeking to attract to the new faith men from the upper and more educated classes, employs a highly polished style and assumes in its readers a knowledge of the Septuagint. With this availability of the Septuagint, Christianity had both a prepared ground and a seed planted from which its new faith could grow.

Being vernacular, the Koine presents more translation problems than does classical literary Greek. It possessed a fluidity beyond that of literary expression: it could vary, sometimes it seems capriciously, from writer to writer, from one locality to another, and from generation to generation. It lay open to the incursions of jargon and slang, which make it at times opaque in meaning. In the case of the Septuagint, a translated work, one can often check the Greek by consulting the Hebrew expression. But since the translators evidently had Hebrew texts that at times differed from those that survive, one must make the comparison with some caution.

Occasionally, too, the translators from Hebrew into the Koine encountered Hebrew conceptions which were unknown to Greek thinking and for which, consequently, there were no equivalent words. The problems faced in trying to render into Greek the concepts of Satan and of sin are well-known instances. And even fairly common concepts are not always identical in two cultures. The concept of law, for instance, was not the same for a Roman as it was for a Hebrew.

The problems of translated works lead directly to the contemporary question of which English translation of the New Testament one should read. Thomas Carlyle expressed surprise that Christian clergymen could not read their sacred books in the original tongues. For most readers today, it is regrettably impossible to read the New Testament in Greek; they must rely upon translations.

Many English versions of the New Testament are competently done. Which translation should the literary student read? Strong arguments are advanced for the Revised Standard Version (RSV) of 1946 and the New English Bible (NEB) of 1961. James Moffatt's translation (final revised edition, 1935) has long stimulated readers. The American Bible Society's *Good News for Modern Men* (1966) is in popular language and based on sound scholarly practice. These more recent versions make use of manuscripts superior to any available to the King James Version translators, show superior knowledge of Koine Greek, and are in more up-to-date English.

The King James Version (KJV), however, has for centuries held the status of an English classic, hardly viewed consciously as a translation. Since the mid-seventeenth century most English authors have owed to it their biblical citations and echoes. Its phraseology and cadences are deeply embedded in English usage. Although its vocabulary includes meanings no longer in common use, it is not difficult for today's readers. For literary study the KJV is to be used. It may be read along with a later translation as commentary, to show the readings from better manuscripts and to clarify occasional archaic usage. This comparison, as will later appear, is especially helpful in reading the Epistles.

The New Testament writers, one must constantly keep in mind, were often dealing with ideas which transcend the levels of human discourse. Vocabulary in any language expresses experience; to it, little by little, nonmaterial significations are added as the minds of men develop them. But the mystic's communicative problem remains: How can he express what eye hath not seen, ear hath not heard, what hath not even entered into the mind of man? Seeing through a glass, darkly, he must take refuge in analogies and in symbolic expression. One never becomes fully cognizant of the higher mysteries of the New Testament. Careful study and deep attention will avail much and often lead to significant intuitional discoveries; but one is in the position of the mathematical variable which can approach the constant but can never arrive at it.

THE NEW TESTAMENT AS PROPAGANDA

Writers have made much of the dramatic qualities in the New Testament. Dramatic material is certainly there: great actions, vividly portrayed agents, world-renowned scenery. Conflict is of its essence. Its dramatic qualities reside, however, in its materials, not in its form. In the Gospels, the Acts, and in most of the Epistles, the organizing form is rhetorical; behind the presentation lie the arts of persuasion rather than of mimesis. Although William A. Beardslee (1970) supports such an interpretation, he limits his work to indicating the origins of such interpretation in Aristotle's *Rhetoric*.

With the possible exception of Paul, the men traditionally credited with the authorship of the New Testament could hardly have been trained in the art magnificently displayed in the treatises of Aristotle, Cicero, and Quintilian. Except for the audiences for Luke–Acts, the refined skills of the master orator were more than was needed to sway the people aimed at in the New Testament. More popular, everyday levels of the art were suited to such audiences. Christian teachers had a message on which they sought to found a faith; how might they best and most quickly produce conviction and prompt action in their hearers? Rhetoric was to them simply a means to an end.

A significant theory advanced by Archibald M. Hunter suggests that Peter employed Paul's traveling companion Silas (or Silvanus) as a ghost-writer in writing 1 Peter. Such a theory, which the letter vaguely implies, could account for the superior language and structure of the letter, which one would not expect to have been within Peter's capacity. It is tempting to apply such an hypothesis to other works. Matthew and John, from Galilean backgrounds similar to Peter's, could hardly have written unaided the gospels bearing their names. The writers of these masterpieces were accomplished rhetoricians who knew how to appeal to their audiences.

To speak of New Testament writers as rhetoricians is not to claim for them highly specialized training in that art. Rhetoric was, if not the most highly developed Hellenistic art, certainly the art most profoundly affecting the lives of Mediterranean peoples. It related directly to everyday conversations, to business, to litigation, to politics, and to religion. In such areas of concern, a man needed to know how to persuade others to his way of thinking and believing.[1]

[1] In the fifth century B.C., Socrates attacked the sophistical rhetoricians who taught popular courses with scant attention to the principles of honesty and justice. Plato, in his creation of the Socratic dialogues, continued this attack well into the fourth century. To both philosophers the sophistical emphasis on techniques without such principles was ethically wrong and dangerous. An

Although the lower-level handbooks on this art have not survived, no doubt instruction of this sort was carefully graduated to fit the mentality and needs of pupils.

But to learn the practical uses of rhetoric, a man did not need to resort to instruction on the higher levels. The *Satyricon* of Petronius and the satires of Persius and Juvenal indicate that Rome in the first century A.D. harbored hordes of teachers who blasted the ears of people in the streets with samples of their wares in order to attract pupils. Even without taking their courses of instruction, a man could readily pick up fragments of that learning. Rome set the pattern for Alexandria, Antioch, Ephesus, and other centers of population.

Mark was evidently written for men whose cultural training was minimal; yet its readers would have some awareness of rhetorical practices and expect to find them in some of what they read or heard. The author who wrote for these people had even greater need to know something about the devices most likely to appeal to them as a class, and of course would have to possess great skill in employing them properly. What holds true of Mark holds true of all four Gospels. The writer had to know the characteristics of his audience and the materials and rhetorical devices most likely to convince them. Rhetoric, as Aristotle had defined it, is simply a study of the arts of persuasion.

Men of common sense and alert perceptions could no doubt em-

early surviving specimen of such sophistical treatises is the *Rhetorica ad Alexandrum,* a treatise falsely ascribed to Aristotle, from probably the third century B.C. This is an eminently practical handbook of methods for handling various situations in which a man might desire to forcefully support or attack his opponents.

The first century B.C. saw a wealth of rhetorical effort by competent theorists as well as practitioners. Cicero's rhetorical treatises belong to the topmost level set by Aristotle nearly three centuries earlier; and they testify to the existence of many teachers of rhetoric in Rome and throughout the Empire. Perhaps more practically useful is the pseudo-Ciceronian *Rhetorica ad Herennium,* which presumably represents the higher level of practical rhetoric for the New Testament period as well. The high ethical level implicit in these two carried over into the first century A.D. in Quintilian's *Institutio Oratoria,* the treatise *On the Sublime,* Demetrius' *On Style,* and Tacitus' *Dialogus de Oratoribus.*

ploy many rhetorical techniques without formal instruction in them. They would at the same time use these more advantageously if they had received some degree of training in their use. Experience alone is an expensive teacher. The Christian propagandist would be following the dictates of common sense if he got all the technical assistance readily available to him. If, as has been suggested, he found someone competent to aid him in his writing, he would surely have made use of this help.

The Gospels explicitly state that the Holy Spirit would tell the apostles what to say and when to say it. This promise did not include guidance always in how they should say it. Peter and Stephen, for all their faith and fervor, delivered speeches hardly calculated to win converts. Although Paul presented in his letters a message that was practically identical to theirs, his rhetorical skill taught him how to make this message, for all its adverse criticism of his readers, more palatable to their senses.

Two principal forces impelled early Christians to their herculean evangelizing program. First was Jesus' parting injunction to go into all the world and preach the Gospel to the whole creation. The second was—at least in the eyes of many leaders—the belief that this gigantic task must be performed within the span of a human lifetime. The epilogue to John partly accounts for this assumption from the mistaken notion that "that disciple whom Jesus loved" would survive on earth until the Parousia. As John points out, they mistook a conditional statement of contingent futurity for a declaration of fact—an error not uncommon today. John evidently made no such mistake, and Luke also may have come to see the Parousia as delayed. Many Christians, including Paul, felt that their message must be spread within some fifty years, from Britain on the West to the Indus River on the East, from the Rhine River on the North to the upper reaches of the Nile River on the South, if not farther. By tactics which Luke ascribes tacitly to Paul, it is not improbable that they accomplished this feat.

With such a task and deadline before them, it would have seemed pointless to write biographies or histories for future generations. As far and as long as possible, too, they preferred the spoken to the written word. When personal contact was impracticable, they resorted perforce to letters. Repeatedly in his letters Paul regrets that he cannot converse with his correspondents; once he mentions that he has reserved less pressing matters until an impending visit.

By the eighth decade of the first century, most eyewitnesses to Jesus' life on earth had died. Since it then became imperative to prepare written propaganda for the faith, the Gospels were written to provide it. These could be circulated throughout the world as bases for further teaching to take the place of the deceased eyewitnesses.

The term *propaganda,* we must remember, carries in itself no good or bad connotation. Like such words as *accident,* it has collected a pejorative significance. Etymologically it means "things that must be propagated"; Cato used the term of multiplying plants by slips or shoots rather than from seed. The Roman Catholic foreign mission office is the Sacred Congregation for Propagating the Faith (*de Propaganda Fide*), a designation surely not intended to convey any suspicion of deceit. The modern misuse of the word, to signify lies our enemies tell about us, unfortunately blackens its correct meaning.

New Testament propaganda includes nurture of those who are already Christian; it may be argued that this was its more important purpose. When the New Testament was composed, however, the minute Christian groups were faced with the wide fields of non-Christians which Christ had declared were ready for harvest. The believers, then, organized the Gospels and the Acts according to patterns that would appeal to nonbelievers and induce them to accept the Christian faith. The basic formative principle of these works is rhetorical, designed to attract readers.

CRITICISM OF THE NEW TESTAMENT

Whether the New Testament is studied in Greek or in English, several modes of interpretation and criticism must be considered. Interpretation deals with establishing as nearly as possible the words or word forms in which the work was first written and ascertaining what they mean. Criticism evaluates the work itself. The two processes must proceed side by side; and generally the term *criticism* is used to indicate both activities. In the development of New Testament criticism, four major approaches have been employed: textual or establishment of the correct text, source criticism, form criticism, and what may be termed symbolic criticism. (A fifth approach, redaction criticism, is currently receiving wide attention.) The brief description of each given here should be supplemented by study of more detailed discussions.

TEXTUAL CRITICISM

No book of the New Testament survives in the original autograph copy. What we have, then, are copies, and copies of copies, of the original. The earliest copies we have were written more than a century later than the autographs, and these exist on fragments of papyrus.[2]

Human error accompanies the copying by hand of written works. Each time a copy (or a copy of a copy) is made, error is multiplied. Consequently, one principle observed in determining the original words is that, other things being equal, the older the copy the "better" (or, at least, more reliable) it is. Papyrus being a perishable material, the life of a copy was probably brief. A copy made a century after the original could represent as many as six intervening copies. Many of the papyrus copies, the script shows, were the work of amateur copyists, likely to contain more errors than those by professional scribes.

Copies made on vellum—specially prepared sheepskin or goatskin—have been more durable than the papyri and many of them survive in fairly complete condition. Since vellum was expensive, copies made on it were done with greater care and usually by professional copyists. The earliest surviving vellum manuscripts of the New Tes-

[2] Papyrus was a cheap but perishable material made from the papyrus reed; our word *paper* is derived from it. Like paper, papyrus tends with age to become dry and brittle and to crumble where it has been folded; it is also vulnerable to dampness. Fragments found in the dry soil of Egypt are mostly quite small, although three or four are fairly extensive copies of the Gospels.

tament date from the fourth century, a century and more later than the papyri. The care in their making and the better preservation on vellum tend to counterbalance their later date and to give them textual value at least equal to the papyri.

Until the ninth century vellum manuscripts were copied in large capital letters. During the educational revival under Charlemagne, smaller writing, often with connected letters, came into use. These, having been made at least seven centuries after the autographs, naturally are less authoritative than those made in capitals. Capital manuscripts are named, while the later manuscripts, called minuscules, are numbered.

Of the capital New Testament manuscripts, Codex Vaticanus and Codex Sinaiticus have been the most highly regarded.[3] Codex Vaticanus, written in the fourth century, has been in the Vatican Library since it was first catalogued in 1475. For brevity it is designated by the capital *B*. Codex Sinaiticus, also from the fourth century, was discovered in 1844 in Saint Catherine's Monastery on Mount Sinai, and finally published by its discoverer, Constantin Tischendorf, several years later. It is designated by *Aleph,* the first letter of the Hebrew alphabet, A having been earlier assigned to another manuscript. Sinaiticus is complete, Vaticanus nearly so.

Other important capital manuscripts include Alexandrinus (A) from the fifth century; Bezae (*D*) from the fifth or sixth century, and Ephraemi (C) from the fifth century. The last is a palimpsest; that is, its early New Testament writing had been erased and works of Saint Ephraim the Syrian had been written on it. Through chemical analysis it has been possible to fade the superimposed writing and to restore much of the earlier New Testament text. These, with a number of other manuscripts, contribute heavily to the data needed by the textual critics.

Critics formerly assumed that whenever *B* and Aleph agreed and made sense, the wording was as close to that of the autograph as was attainable. When these two disagreed, other capital manu-

[3] *Codex* is the Latin term for our kind of book bound in pages as contrasted with the *volumen* or roll. The codex had quite replaced the roll early in the Christian era.

scripts were consulted in order to find the best reading. With the discovery of the papyri and the study of capital manuscripts other than those listed above, a more inclusive search has become the rule. The textual critic now evaluates these papyri and other manuscripts with greater respect. He will consider also the evidence of early translations into languages other than Greek and of citations from the New Testament in the manuscripts of the earlier Church Fathers. Having digested this evidence, he will apply to it his intuitive insight into the usage and personality of the New Testament writer which has come to him through long "acquaintance" with the writer, with the New Testament, and with early Christian ways and attitudes in their world, as well as with the Hebrew Scriptures and habits of thought and expression. The combination of all these will lead him to conclusions which, he feels, approximate the words of the author.

A successful paleographer must be a well-trained scholar in his field, but not every well-trained scholar can be a competent paleographer. The degree of success in this field is largely due, finally, to the clarity of intuition in the trained scholar. Although paleographic study has been carried on actively for more than a century, editors still work over the text of the New Testament in the hope of closer approximation to the original words.[4]

The KJV did not have the benefit of careful manuscript study. Of all the capital manuscripts, only *D* appears to have been available

[4] Paleographical problems in the reading of manuscripts need not be here discussed in detail. The student has to reconstruct gaps in the text where the letters have been made illegible by action of mildew, bookworms, or mice. When letters are partly defaced, he must determine which of several possible letters the author wrote. Sometimes letters are crowded together so that two letters may appear as one, or vice versa. Many original copies were written without division into words, in a continuous line of letters. He must decide which of the possible divisions into words the author had in mind as he wrote. He may find passages in which the copyist has thoughtlessly omitted lines of the original or duplicated them. These are but a few of the riddles he attempts to solve in order to arrive at a text as near to the author's as he can hope to reach. To this end, patient attention, long acquaintance with the author's style and vocabulary, and intuitive power must combine.

to the translators, and they apparently did not use it. The rules under which they worked forbade them from going far from the preceding Bishop's Bible of 1568, though they did make use of other translations including the Vulgate. They did, to be sure, translate also "out of the original Greek," but the Greek text of Theodore Beza which they used was a slight modification only of a hastily and at times carelessly prepared edition by Erasmus in 1516.

The KJV translators did consider carefully the signification of the Greek in the text available to them, and recent discoveries attest to their scholarly deliberations; but they were, all unaware of it, working from a defective Greek text. Obviously, no major errors involving doctrine would have escaped notice, but the myriad minor details which the editor of any author's work hopes to verify or correct appear in their work. It is amazing that their translation is, as a work of scholarship, as good as it is. In literary style it remains unsurpassed.

Once the text has been at least tentatively established, all further investigation of a literary work is called higher criticism. (In what sense these later steps are "higher" has never been determined.) We shall consider several approaches to the establishd text that have won attention by scholars. The earliest of these to be practiced is source criticism.

SOURCE CRITICISM

Early in the nineteenth century German scholars became concerned to discover if possible what prior documents had been incorporated into the extant Gospels, especially the three Synoptics. Such studies had been inaugurated a few decades earlier with the revival of questions about sources of Homer's two poems. This problem of Homeric origin had been handled as early as the second century B.C. by Alexandrian scholars, at least by implication.

Since these poems were far too long to be recited at one sitting of an audience, they had been broken up into recognized parts; even earlier these parts had been given specific titles. In the *Iliad* they vary in length from three hundred to six hundred hexameter verses. It is not clear to what extent these sections were regarded as incorporations or adaptations of earlier lays; the ancient peoples had no conception of literary property, and a poet was free to borrow anything he liked from another without any charge of plagiarism. By the time of Jesus, the geographer Strabo indicated the existence of two literary camps on questions of Homeric authorship.

Later interest in "the Homeric Question" was revived in 1795 by the publication of Friedrich August Wolf's *Prolegomena ad Homerum*. Wolf asserted that analysis of the *Iliad* indicated a core or original *Iliad* (*Urilias*), a comparatively short poem with which other lays were combined to form the longer poem that survives. His hypothesis quickly attracted wide attention.

Since the artificial distinction between sacred and secular scholarship had not yet been drawn, students of classical literature treated the New Testament as part of their subject of study. They soon began to adapt this hypothesis to the New Testament, first of all to Mark. Hypothetical versions of an original Mark (*Urmarkus*) soon appeared. Although the existence of a primitive Marcan document has not been favored by recent scholars, Wolf's *Prolegomena* had started a critical approach to the Bible in general that has long held the attention of students of both Old and New Testaments.

It had long been seen that nearly all of Mark can be reproduced from Matthew and Luke, either verbatim or in closely similar words. To express it statistically, of Mark's 661 verses Matthew includes 606, Luke 320; only 24 verses in Mark do not occur in either or both these Gospels. In both these Gospels, about one-half of Mark's verses are taken verbatim, while the other half are only slightly altered in wording. Obviously, Mark served as a major source for Matthew and Luke.

Next it was observed that a large part of Matthew and Luke—250 verses of Matthew's 1068 and Luke's 1149—which do not occur in Mark are closely similar, often identical, in wording. These similarities strongly indicated a second source; and the nearly identical wording meant that this source was written, not oral. This document (it was tacitly assumed that it was a single document on the analogy of Mark, apparently) quickly became known as the second source. Since it had no name, the German scholars who led in such critical studies called it The Source and referred to it as *Q*, the initial word of *Quelle*, the German word for source. Scholars could now speak of the two-document theory in relation to Matthew and Luke.

A third stage in such theorizing was clearly indicated. The problem that remained was the materials peculiar to Matthew and those peculiar to Luke. Where did this material come from? *Q* had plausibly been established as a written source by comparison of the passages in Matthew and Luke. Although there was no evidence to show whether these differing parts of the two Gospels were from written or oral sources, at this time written sources were generally taken for granted. The 214 verses peculiar to Matthew were accordingly assigned to a document designated *M*, and the 570 verses peculiar to Luke were assigned to a document designated *L*. Whether *M* and *L* each represented one or several documents did not enter into the consideration of this matter.

FORM CRITICISM

In the ancient world both Jewish and Hellenic education made extensive use of rote memorization. A Jewish rabbinical saying was that a good student is like a well-plastered cistern that never loses a drop. From classical Greek education came the practice of memorizing the Homeric poems. The Fathers of the Church in the centuries following the New Testament era used to cite from memory the Psalms and the entire New Testament. Private libraries were few. In the Hellenistic world a man had to rely heavily upon his memory; and since he read little by our standards, he had a much more tenacious verbal memory than is common today.

Moreover, oral accounts were preferred to written records among the Christians, as the practice of Paul attests and as the practice of Christian leaders well into the second century shows. For the first four decades or so of the Church's expansion, many of the speakers on the faith were eyewitnesses of Jesus' career or had heard eyewitness accounts of it. These accounts their retentive memories would store up and pass on with a tenacious recollection of the wording that would be almost unheard of today. Although the introduction to Luke attests the existence of earlier written accounts in some number, undoubtedly the early Church relied heavily for several decades upon word-of-mouth transmission of the Christian message.

This oral tradition had been tacitly ignored by the source critics, whose attention was fixed upon documentary records. Since the end of World War I, however, German scholars have led others to consider the characteristics presumably present in this early oral Christian tradition. Pioneers in this study were Rudolf Bultmann, who published his *Die Geschichte der synoptischen Tradition* (*History of the Synoptic Tradition*) in 1931, and Martin Dibelius, whose *Die Formgeschichte des Evangeliums* (*Form Criticism of the Gospel*) appeared in 1935. Earlier publications by these men had prepared the way for the statements of these books, and by the time they had appeared British and American scholars had already taken up their theories. ("Form criticism" is a free and not wholly happy rendering of the German *Formgeschichte,* which more accurately means "the business of form" or "matters relating to form.")

The observable differences among the synoptic Gospels in the arrangement of Jesus' actions and words indicate to the form critics that the writers of these Gospels had available to them a mass of brief oral accounts. Differences in reports of apparently identical events, together with the connecting of identical sayings by Jesus to different events, lead the form critics to conclude that early Christian teachers slightly edited their accounts to suit the circumstances in (*Sitz im Leben*) of the audience to whom they were presenting their message.

The outstanding exception to this editorial process was the Passion story, which in all the Gospels has come down to us in nearly identical form. This story, which Paul declared formed the nucleus of his message (1 Cor. 2:1–2), was the center, the form critics believe, around which clustered other events and statements which the teachers felt more free to modify to fit an immediate situation.

An instance of such modification is found in Mark 10:2–12. Here is Jesus' teaching on marriage after divorce in its strictest form: any man who remarries after divorcing his wife commits adultery, and any woman who divorces her husband commits adultery. The form critics point out that while Roman law permitted a wife to divorce her husband, Jewish law made provision only for a husband to divorce his wife. Jesus would have had no reason to mention a situation nonexistent among his hearers; but another Christian teacher, faced with a similar question from a Gentile audience, might reasonably have felt that in such a situation Jesus would have expanded his prohibition against divorce to include both sexes.

That such adaptations were made by early teachers, there is little reason to doubt. Although Peter said Jesus' words were the words of eternal life (John 6:68), they were not yet held to be so sacrosanct as to require verbally accurate quotation. Even in citations of the Old Testament, Gospel writers and letter writers exercised verbal freedom. Whether the modification occurred first in Mark or in an earlier oral source, it is of course impossible to determine.

Accepting the hypothesis that all episodes reported in the Gospels are not given precisely as they occurred, form critics undertook to classify the stories which they assume to have been circulated by early Christian evangelists. They then applied the folklorist's principle of dating the stories according to their form. Some forms being more primitive than others, they sought to discover how near to the time of each episode itself the story's form placed it. The nearer to the original, they felt, the closer it was to reproducing the actual event.

From this involved process they concluded that the manner in which Matthew and Luke edited the account of Mark indicates the pattern by which the pre-Gospel traditions developed. Luke, for example, presents parables much more complex than those reported in Mark. The ultimate intent of such study is to recover as nearly as possible the actual, unedited words of Jesus. In so doing, it is hoped, one may draw nearer to Jesus' specific teachings.

Such concepts of the Gospels present them as valuable records of Jesus' message as it was presented to the Church during the four decades before the Gospels appeared. These concepts, however, cast doubt upon the Gospels' value as records of what Jesus actually said and did.

The form critics have made valuable contributions to the interpretation of the Gospels. First, they have pointed up the error of the source critics in tacitly ignoring oral tradition about Jesus which was more acceptable to audiences than were written records. Second, they have escaped the error of assuming that first-century men held the same reverence for strict accuracy in biographical and historical reporting that we have. These are lessons which New Testament students needed to learn.

The major difficulty with the form critics themselves is one common to various activities of literary criticism. When a critic gains an important new insight into a body of literature, he is often tempted to claim for it more than it merits, much as new medical discoveries are hailed as panaceas when they first appear. The discoverer succumbs to the temptation of building an entire approach (out of what is later discovered to be only an important contribution) to knowledge of the whole field. In so doing, he may fall into serious error.

An example of such error is the form critic's adoption of methods used to analyze and classify primitive literature. To apply this method to the New Testament is to ignore the fact that the Hellenistic age was far removed from primitive society in its entire outlook. Furthermore, the application requires the telescoping into some four decades between Jesus and the first Gospel a process which folklorists see as normally covering far longer periods of time.

When an honest, intelligent, trained critic advances a new hypothesis, it is only fair to assume that it has merit and deserves earnest attention. Long ago, we learned that there is more than one approach to the truth. The new theorist must remind himself that the important object is the result hoped for, and that any method that helps to arrive at understanding and appreciation of a literary work is to be used to achieve that end. The approach presented in this study, that of considering the New Testament as made up of propagandist works which are to be examined on rhetorical principles, is but one of many valid approaches.

SYMBOLIC CRITICISM

Symbolic criticism is a term here freely used to embrace various approaches to a literary work which attempt to go beyond the literal meaning of what is expressed. Everyone knows that his words at times fail to convey what he intended either because they imply meanings he never intended or because they convey less than he had in mind. In the latter case, he sometimes feels that what he has in mind cannot be literally expressed in words. This experience in everyday communication is felt particularly in attempts to communicate ideas, emotions, and sensations.

In literature this difficulty has long been recognized. The author of the treatise "On the Sublime," written probably at the same time as the Gospels, listed as one of the tests for great literature that the work when read by a man of sound judgment and long experience of literature must convince him after repeated readings that more is implied in it than meets the eye (Longinus VII.3). If, moreover, the subject of the work includes matters far transcending human experience, as in the New Testament, the author is forced to convey through myth, allegory, or symbol matters for which words do not exist.

The modes of teaching here grouped under the term *symbolic* were well known to first-century writers, both Jewish and Gentile, and the Christian tradition naturally made use of them. In one of the earliest surviving Christian books, Galatians (4:21–31), Paul allegorizes the two wives of Abraham: Sarah, who bore Isaac, represents the covenant of grace; Hagar, the Egyptian bondwoman who bore Ishmael, stands for the covenant made at Sinai. In Hebrews 6–7 the legendary king Melchizedek mentioned in Genesis 14:18–20, the "priest of the most high God," is treated as a prototype of Jesus—an allegory developed in conjunction with Psalm 110:4.

A century or two later, when Christians felt the lack of Christian literature for educating their children, they allegorized the *Iliad*, the *Odyssey*, and the *Aeneid*. Odysseus and Aeneas, for example, symbolized the Christian soul wandering in search of its heavenly home

—an idea later allegorized differently by John Bunyan. In his *City of God,* Augustine after the fall of Rome to Alaric in 407 B.C. even further allegorized the *Aeneid* and the concept of eternal Rome: the earthly Rome is but a symbol for the heavenly, the New Jerusalem, eternal in the heavens.

Through Augustine's sermons and pamphlets the belief that the Scriptures were the husk which must be stripped off to reach the allegorical kernel of truth spread throughout Christendom and set the pattern of preaching for ensuing generations. Although present-day preaching has abandoned such excesses of allegorical interpretation in the pulpit, the sound principle advanced by Longinus in the first century still flourishes in literary and biblical study.

August Boeckh insisted that the true critic with all his training must possess also an intuitive insight into the significance of what he is interpreting. According to Bishop Stephen Neill, the outstanding nineteenth-century critics Lightfoot, Westcott, and Hort "demanded" that the biblical critic be a Christian in order to receive the intuitions necessary to sound interpretation. This requirement seems to be supported by Jesus' saying (Matt. 13:52), in comparing an instructed scribe to a householder who brings out of his storehouse things new and old.

In admonishing the Christian teacher to rightly divide the word of truth, the author of 2 Timothy (2:15) urges the values in keen analytical insight. There is also in such directions an implicit warning against carrying such interpretation to unwarranted extremes. Standards cannot mark precisely where the danger line lies. In seeking for the inner meaning of symbols, the interpreter must proceed cautiously.

Some general guiding lines may be set up here. The British scholars named above gave express warning against the critic's letting his desire to edify or his own devotional feelings interfere with consistently objective interpretation. Like warning must be issued against permitting any favorite theory or bias to intervene between the work and its interpretation to unbalance the conclusion—a counsel of perfection, yet to be heeded to the limit of one's objectivity. "Fads," such as numerology, for example, must be severely curbed; they have their place, but a minor place.

Both the values and the dangers proceeding from the interpreter's possessing theological training must be borne in mind. The secularly trained student must admit that areas exist relating to knowledge of the New Testament which his training hardly prepares him to explore. The theologically trained scholar must try to approach the work from the objective literary point of view, yet use what special enlightenment his discipline provides to elucidate what is implied in it.

Northrop Frye, in his remarkable *Anatomy of Criticism* (1957), developed a theory of symbols used as sign, image, archetype, or monad which the biblical student will find stimulating and profitable. We will use a more obvious classification of symbols. First, certain symbols have become readily identifiable through general use: in the New Testament, the cross and the Lamb of God; in secular affairs, the crescent for Islam and the hammer and sickle for communism.

Second, an author may create a private set of symbols, as did Yeats for his poetry and Tolkien for his tales. They may become fixed in the author's use of them, but require that we learn his system. A stage between these two is represented by Jewish apocalyptic writing, in which, as in Daniel 7–12 and in the Revelation, a fairly fixed set of symbols may be understood by initiates yet unintelligible to outsiders.

Third, in some writing the meaning of the symbol will fluctuate with the author's intention and among different authors. What Emerson in "The Poet" called "the manifold meaning of every sensuous fact" complicates the interpretation for the reader. He must try to penetrate the veil of the literal statement to find what the author sought to convey through it. To quote Emerson again, the author may have "builded better than he knew" and presented what lay beyond the limits of his conscious mind.

Such an instance, according to Christian interpretation, occurs in the Messianic passages in Isaiah, especially in chapter 7. The prophecy to King Ahaz in the eighth century B.C. of a child to be born must have referred to some imminent birth in order to have had any effect upon the youthful king puzzled by the international maze in which he wandered. It is improbable that Isaiah himself had any inkling of what was to happen seven centuries later. Jesus nonetheless saw himself as foretold by Isaiah and even carefully prepared his triumphal entry to Jerusalem on Palm Sunday in accord with the vision in Zechariah (9:9).

Before the reader can enter into the interpreting of this third class of symbols, he must have steeped himself in the writer's mental and literary patterns as well as in related authors' works and whatever background material is available. The reader becomes not only an instructed scribe but a sympathetic one. As German romantic critics taught a century and a half ago, the reader has wormed his way into the very personality of the author and to the best of his capacity has followed the course of his mind as he was writing. A notable example of such study is that by the late John Livingston Lowes in *The Road to Xanadu* (1927), in which he relived Coleridge's life during the many months of gestation of "The Rime of the Ancient Mariner."

The difficulties in symbolic criticism are obvious and have long been recognized. First and foremost among them is its practice by uninformed persons, who lack knowledge, training, insight. Uninformed readers may mistake what the author tried to do or the methods he followed in order to do it. Readers may lack adequate knowledge of the milieu in which the author moved or, even when they possess the knowledge, they may lack intuitive power.

In the New Testament, Paul perhaps most clearly shows his awareness of the problems of communication and interpretation for both writer and reader. In 1 Corinthians 2 he tried to explain the difficulties and how he had tried to solve them by his teaching. He had brought them true knowledge expressed in a lowly manner quite unlike that of the scholars of the day. "We speak the wisdom of God in a mystery, even a hidden wisdom, which God ordained before the world unto our glory." Then freely adapting two passages from Isaiah (64:4; 65:17), he added, "But as it is written, Eye hath not seen, nor ear heard, neither have entered into the heart of man, the things which God hath prepared for them that love him."

The highly literate, mystically endowed Paul well knew the all but insurmountable problem of putting into words what he had become aware of. For example, again in chapter 15 he attempts to explain the resurrection of the body, a challenging effort in which he had had to resort to such a paradox as "celestial bodies" and to the analogy of souls to heavenly planets and stars. In his explanation he was forced, finally, to characterize the matter in a "mystery"—a teaching comparable to those which the secret cults so numerous in Corinth were accustomed to present to initiates, often dramatically depicted—a far higher truth than those mysteries for all their earthly wisdom could present.

As Emerson remarked, a symbol presumably has more than one meaning. One who has intuitively grasped a meaning from a symbol should not presume that other men's intuitions derived from it are wrong if they differ from his or that his is incorrect for disagreeing with theirs. It is human to err, even intuitively. One must rationally test what he has intuitively discerned—as Emerson and Paul both knew—before accepting his interpretation as a valid one.

Why should the New Testament reader become acquainted with these various methods of interpretation? Obviously, we should read the most accurate edition available and know something of the problems involved in its preparation. We should know the merits and defects also of the several New Testament translations. In addition, we need to know something of the Jewish and Hellenistic backgrounds of the books as they were composed. We can learn much from prevailing theories on the sources used and how the authors made use of them. Finally, we must endeavor to learn what each author was specifically trying to do and how he proceeded in this attempt.

MYSTICISM IN THE NEW TESTAMENT

The name *New Testament* indicates that the work is a new covenant between God and man that supersedes the Old Testament. God being a partner in this covenant, it follows that this covenant treats of matters that lie beyond rational human powers of discovery or full comprehension. Such knowledge must come to man intuitively or by revelation. Men to whom such knowledge comes are known as mystics, men who undergo experiences through which they intuitively apprehend matters outside the realm of human reasoning. A large part of the prophet's message is mystically derived. He differs from the mystic chiefly in his proclaiming what he has learned, while the mystic may or may not speak out publicly.

Although in a scientific and rational (and skeptical) age like ours, men often doubt the existence of mystical powers, the evidence for them is too strong to be denied. How widespread mystical capacity may be, it is impossible to say. Emerson believed that any man who would adopt a state of passive receptivity could receive mystical messages: "If we listen, we will hear." The listening is to him the prerequisite; Emerson and Thoreau—another notable mystic—both insist on this. Whitman declared, "I loafe, and invite my soul."

A man like Emerson who was interested in representative men may have been too inclusive in asserting mystical capacity in all men. The fact remains that both inside and outside the Judaeo-Christian tradition the power is well attested. One cannot shrug off so well supported a phenomenon merely on the ground that he has had no personal contact with or awareness of it.

In *The Religious Experience of the Roman People,* Warde Fowler cited with approval Ira W. Howerth's description of religion as "the effective desire to get into right relations with the power that governs the universe." F. von Hugel in *The Mystical Element of Religion* saw religion as a tension-in-unity of three forces, the intellectual, the institutional, and the mystical. The basic Hebrew concept of a covenant with God implies a direct communication with God. Jesus' prayer (John 17:11), that his followers "may be one, as we are," coupled with his symbol of the vine and branches (John 15:4–5), implies mystical relation between man and God. For contemporary man, the intellectual and institutional forces in religion tend to overwhelm the mystical. To use the figure in the Apocalypse (3:20), man is too often unaware that Jesus stands at the door and knocks.

The reader of the New Testament will progress in his understanding of it only if he realizes the existence of the mystical force in Christianity. The more mystically receptive he is, the more profound will be his insights. Having centered his attention upon receiving intuitions, he will temporarily almost negate whatever might impair them. In the old phrase, he will have "mortified the flesh." In such a state political, social, cultural, and sensual concerns stand in abeyance. What he does afterwards, after achieving mystical insights, is another matter.

A difficulty mentioned in the discussion of symbolic interpretation strikes here with double force. The deeper the mystical insight, the less probably will the materially derived human vocabulary be adequate to convey it, and the more will the interpreter's difficulty be enhanced. No man, however great his mystical power may be, can wholly grasp what comes to him from an infinite source. He must put into words as well as he can what he has partly perceived.

Words being inadequate to state his insights, the interpreter will have recourse to metaphorical expression, which will itself be often inadequate to bear the force of his intuition. The father-son analogy which Jesus employed to point to his relation with God is not wholly satisfactory; in John's statement that Jesus had existed with God from the beginning, we have the paradox of a son coeval with his own father.

The metaphors and analogies with which the New Testament abounds, though always helpful to our understanding, are inadequate. They can be misinterpreted by an inattentive reader. Even the instructed reader must exercise extreme care not to read into the symbol what is not there, as well as to be alert to see what has been overlooked. The parable of the prodigal son, for instance, is surely inadequately so named. Luke was too good a literary artist to digress from his subject to something else at the climactic point of his story. The "good boy" who had done exactly as he had been told by his father but had learned no natural affection cannot be a mere minor afterthought.

The leading agents in the New Testament are mostly people with mystical powers. Joseph, Mary, and Zacharias all receive intimations

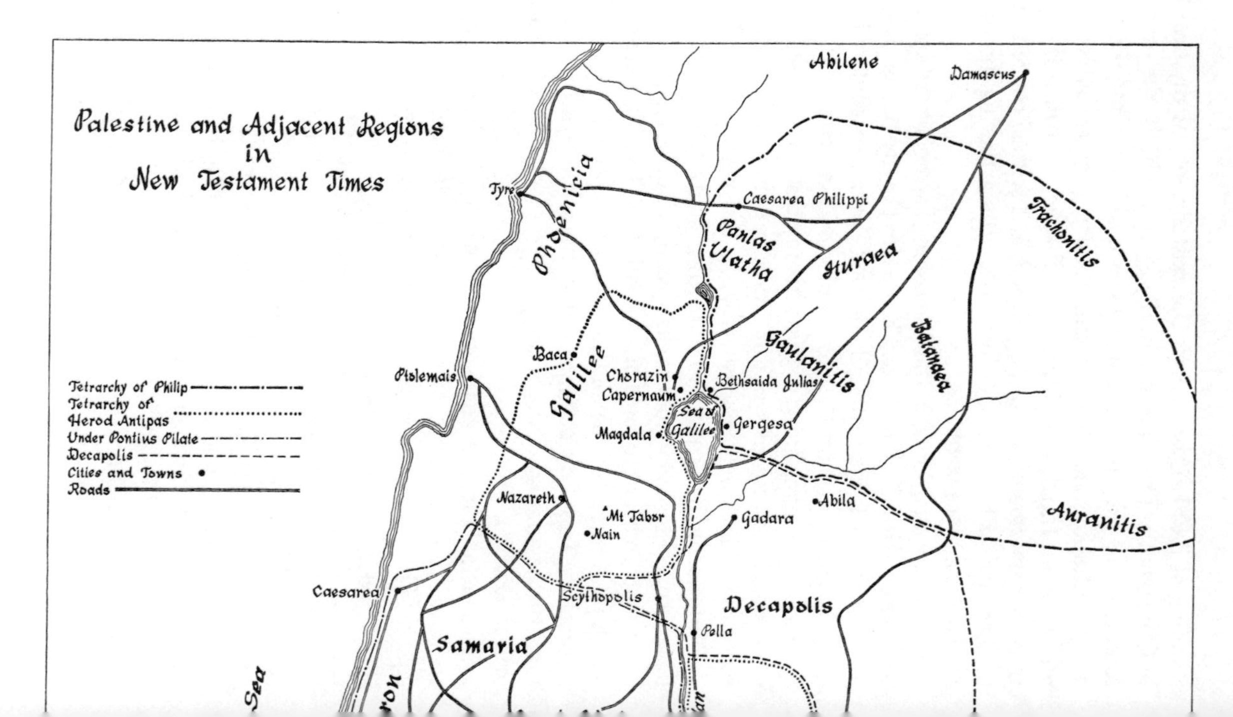

Palestine and Adjacent Regions
in
New Testament Times
Tetrarchy of Philip
Tetrarchy of
Herod Antipas
Under Pontius Pilate
Decapolis
Cities and Towns
Roads
Abilene
Damascus
Tyre
Phoenicia
Caesarea Philippi
Panias
Ulatha
Ituraea
Trachonitis
Gaulanitis
Batanaea
Auranitis
Galilee
Baca
Ptolemais
Chorazin
Capernaum
Bethsaida Julias
Sea of Galilee
Gergesa
Magdala
Nazareth
Mt Tabor
Nain
Abila
Gadara
Caesarea
Scythopolis
Decapolis
Pella
Samaria
Sea

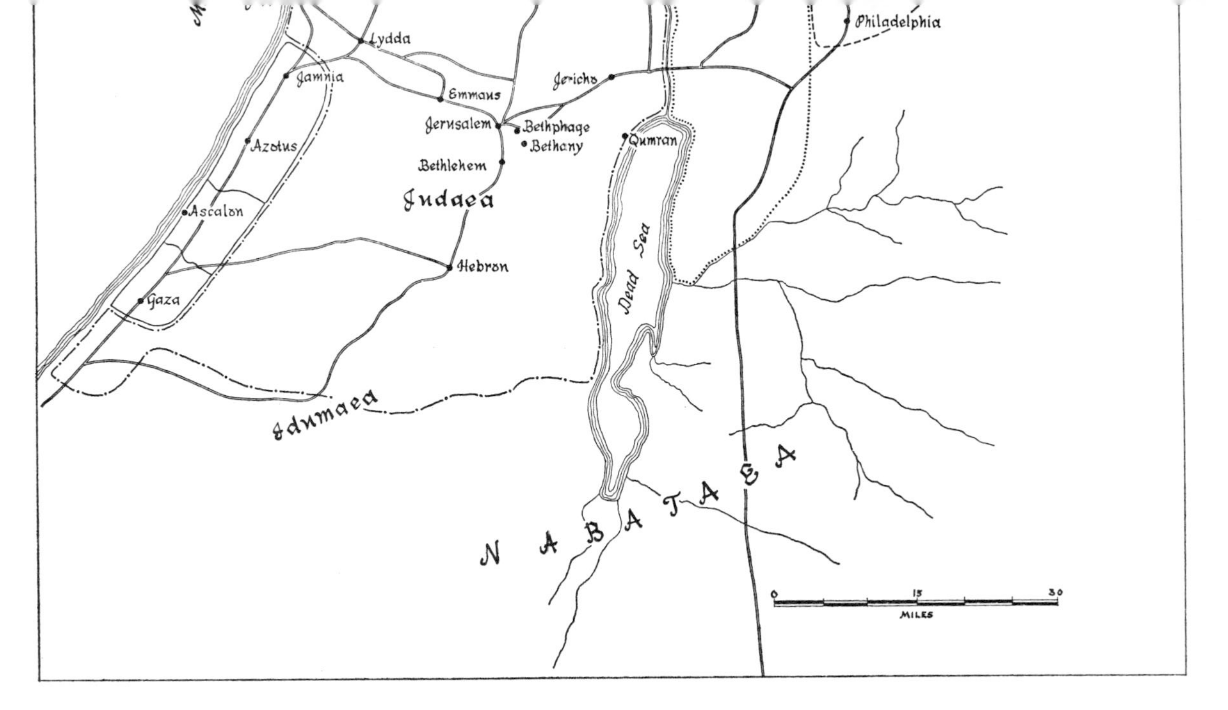

Philadelphia
Lydda
Jamnia
Emmaus
Jericho
Jerusalem
Bethphage
Bethany
Qumran
Azotus
Bethlehem
Judaea
Ascalon
Dead Sea
Hebron
Gaza
Idumaea
NABATAEA
0
15
30
MILES

—Joseph in a dream and the other two in visions. John the Baptist had received an intimation by which he should recognize the one whose forerunner he was to be. Peter, James, and John underwent a mystical experience at the transfiguration. Paul's mystical experiences were frequent after his conversion. The coming of the Holy Spirit at Pentecost and its frequent messages thereafter fall into the same category. And the apocalypse that came to John on Patmos was a series of mystical visions. Such experiences were perhaps out of the ordinary; yet they were part of the religious life of the early Church.

The ancient world, both Oriental and Hellenistic, both Jewish and Gentile, accepted such happenings as genuine. Centuries earlier, Homer had asserted that the gods used to appear frequently to men on intimate personal terms; though they now appeared less often, people believed that they could still do so; the experience of Paul and Barnabas at Lystra is a case in point. The popular cults and religions that were replacing the Olympian religion in urban centers likewise enacted or recorded epiphanies or visions of deities. The Christian teacher's problem was seldom to convince his hearers of the actuality of the supernatural and of God's relations with men, as might be the problem today; he had to convince them of the rightness of his message and of its capacity to replace what they had formerly been accepting.

General readers will readily see that mastery of all the kinds of interpretation discussed here is not requisite to their understanding the literary values of the New Testament. They should know something of the methods which scholarly interpreters use in trying to furnish as accurate a text as possible and in seeking to explain the development of the books themselves. These readers may apply the use of figures and symbols themselves as they read.

It is recommended that the Introduction be read before the discussions of the several books of the New Testament. Each book should be read at a single sitting before reading the chapter that treats of it. Each chapter should be read with the book it discusses open for reference. Terms which are not readily understood may be clarified by recourse to the Index, which lists other pages on which they occur. Such reading should be undertaken to satisfy an interested curiosity about the New Testament. The Bibliography lists works which treat more fully the topics handled in this Introduction and in the succeeding chapters.

CHAPTER 1

THE GOSPEL ACCORDING TO MARK

Ancient literary works were in most cases not given titles by their authors; these were added later by others, and not always well chosen. The ascription of the second Gospel to Mark is accordingly not necessarily correct; the Greek title (*kata Markon*) in fact does not categorically state his authorship. The translators of the King James Version (KJV) rendered it accurately as "according to Mark," which may mean nothing more than "the way Mark told it." This formula begs the question of authorship, albeit no doubt unintentionally in the minds of the translators.

It is important to establish this point, because at least two Gospels —Matthew and John—were almost certainly not composed by the men whose names they bear. However early Christians interpreted the titles of the Gospels, and they probably would have been surprised at our concern about this matter, we consider it of major importance in the study of a book to assign it to its proper author.

It is true that during the second century A.D. the authorship of the books that later formed the New Testament was extensively discussed. Already the propriety of using them in public worship and instruction apparently was debated. As the debate developed, canons began to take form, at least two of them, the Muratorian and the list made by Marcion, before the end of the second century. A criterion of acceptance was naturally the validity of the data in the book. This was increased if it could claim authorship by an eyewitness of Jesus' life on earth or at least by one who had learned from eyewitness evidence of that career. Aside from this concern for the sources of the data, little attention was devoted to such matters.

By modern standards, ancient authorship was treated with free-and-easy disregard of the author. Since the concept of a book as its author's personal property hardly existed—he could not hope to profit from its sale—he was little concerned about his claim to authorship. Downright forgery of works with their ascription to well-known authors was extensively practiced; the names of some ancient forgers have survived. Scholars still labor to establish authentic lists of works by Plato, Lysias, and Cicero.

When such forgery was committed by publishers simply to promote sales, the practice was generally disapproved. If, however, the writer's purpose was honorable, his borrowing of a well-known author's name might under some circumstances be tacitly approved. This is especially true with New Testament books. The writer of the letters to Timothy and Titus, and the writer of Jude, in using the names of Paul and the brother of Jesus as authors of second-century works, made claims patently contrary to fact. The writers evidently felt that they were writing in the spirit of the men whose names they borrowed: these men would have handled problems as the writers did if they had still been living. Such innocent forgery was accepted as proper.

In later years, when the canons were taking shape, men not greatly concerned with dates but intent upon sound doctrine possibly assumed these to be genuine apostolic documents. This lack of scholarly concern about authorship is alien to us, but was not to them.

The hint in 1 Peter (5:12) that Peter had employed Silvanus in composing his letter raises the possibility that other New Testament writers may have received similar help. One cannot rule out the existence of ghost-writers. The only demonstrably educated men whose names are attached to New Testament books were Luke and Paul. The apostles were humble, unlettered men from Galilee. They could hardly be presumed to possess fluent knowledge of Koine Greek, and surely were ignorant of the devices through which literary works are organized and embellished. If they were connected with any New Testament books, it could hardly have been as their actual writers.

Mark, who lived in Jerusalem, was apparently young enough to have gained some fluency in Greek. In Acts it is reported that he was for a time a member of Paul's first Gentile effort. Whether he could have mastered the skills in composition apparent in the Gospel is less certain. Scholars are in the main willing to accept him as its author, though the possibility that he was aided by another man better versed in literary devices cannot be ruled out.

The tradition that Mark wrote this Gospel is supported by fairly trustworthy evidence. Late second-century prologues to Mark and other Gospels which assert traditional authorship are now rejected as forgeries. On the other hand, Eusebius, a painstaking fourth-century Church historian, strongly supports his authorship. He cites from the nonextant work of the second-century writer Papias of Hierapolis that Mark wrote his gospel at the request of Peter's Roman followers to record the teaching which they had verbally received from Peter (*Ecclesiastical History* II.25). Papias, Eusebius adds, had been a companion of Polycarp, who had known the apostle John.

Another scholarly writer, Irenaeus, bishop of Lyons, in the late second century also accepted the ascription to Mark. Clement of Alexandria, a contemporary of Irenaeus, declared that Mark wrote this gospel during the lifetime of Peter. With three second-century reputable scholars attesting to it, and no strong evidence to the contrary, one may accept it as in all probability by Mark.

Ancient dates are often troublesome because there was no universally accepted calender; the Julian Calendar had been in existence for a century when the Gospels were written, but its general acceptance was slow. Scholars, however, generally agree that Mark was written between 65 and 75 A.D.

As to the place where Mark was written, many scholars have felt that its assignment to Rome may be partly the result of bias. For various reasons the church in Rome was rapidly rising into prominence by the second century, and may well have wished to be sponsor to a gospel like other important Christian centers—Ephesus, Antioch, Caesarea, and Alexandria. The wish is often quite honestly father to such a thought, which can readily crystallize into accepted fact. The tradition that Mark was heavily indebted to information from Peter bolstered the claim. Peter was widely believed to have been the first bishop of Rome; and Mark presumably worked with him as he was writing. To many Christians it, no doubt, seemed strange that so prominent a disciple and apostle as Peter should not have written a gospel—a spurious Gospel of Peter was at one time in circulation—and under this theory of Petrine influence, Mark satisfied such a wish. With such pressures supporting the choice of Rome as the place of writing, this question cannot be settled with any assurance.

Mark's possible sources must also remain unspecified. It seems that he may have gotten much from Peter; the tradition cannot be totally ignored. Irenaeus declares that Mark got much from oral sources, a possible and even likely supposition. As a boy in Jerusalem, he probably had firsthand knowledge of events during Passion Week. Since his home in Jerusalem had been a center for Christians in the first years of the Church, he no doubt heard from the Galilean followers of Jesus about the Galilean ministry. Luke's gospel mentions memorabilia about Jesus that existed well before it was written. These logia, as they were called, were possibly, in part at least, available to Mark. It is conceivable, though not demonstrable, that all these materials were at hand as Mark was written.

Important as the sources were, the literary student is still more concerned with the writer's employment of them. His work will be considered for its style, its selection of materials included, and its organization.

Stylistically, Mark is the least polished of the Gospels. Its Greek vocabulary is small—1,330 words—and all but 80 of its words occur in the other Gospels. Its words are those that a man of limited education would know. Syntactically, it betrays its author's Jewish background by using more Aramaic constructions than the other Gospels. It is, nonetheless, quite intelligible Koine Greek; the ordinary man in the street should have found no difficulty with it.

Its sentences are uniformly uncomplicated. The proportion of simple and compound sentences to those that are complex is unusually large, a characteristic which the KJV preserves. Its sentences are made like the speech of the less educated man, upon whom the niceties of logically subordinated ideas are largely wasted. As students of historical syntax know, all hypotaxis follows upon original parataxis—subordination of ideas is a later development of expression than co-ordination. The writer of Mark evidently wished to communicate with readers who, however intelligent and sensible, had not the cultural responses of the more highly educated and literate.

The style of Mark has led to the presumption that the writer himself was like the book: intelligent but not literary. Occasionally, however, sentences are used which indicate a far higher degree of craftsmanship than its usual level of expression. An untrained writer could hardly have worked out the involutions of Mark 1:2–4 or 13:28. Either the author was a competent stylist writing down to the level of his audience, or he was aided by such a writer.

A further indication of the intended audience is the rare inclusion of citations from the Old Testament and the frequent explanation of Jewish customs. In the opening quotation the author conflates quotations from two prophets, Isaiah and Malachi, with a hint of Exodus. In the better manuscripts these are ascribed to Isaiah alone, a freedom which would pass unnoticed among Gentiles. The preponderance of action over teaching in Mark would be attractive to readers with little education. In fine, though external evidence is lacking, internal evidence points to an intended audience of Gentiles on this cultural level.

In the selection and organization of material Mark shows the work of a skilled rhetorician. He not only had sized up his audience's interests, but he also knew how to gratify them. Organization, Aristotle and later critics insist, is perhaps the final technique to be mastered by a writer. Mark's organization appears to have had the aid of a trained collaborator.

The rapid sequence of events demands the reader's attention while the brevity of most episodes adapts them to men whose span of attention is probably short. Speedy transitions are nineteen times introduced by the adverb *straightway*. Jesus appears without introduction on the scene and immediately swings into whirlwind campaigns in two districts of Galilee. The shift of scene to Judea occupies a single chapter; Luke makes it a leisurely progress of nine chapters. In Jerusalem within a little more than one week, Jesus combats bitterly hostile Jewish groups, is arrested and crucified, dies and is buried. Although the account of the Resurrection has been lost (16:9–20 was added later), one can readily supply it. Passage of time is utterly ignored; the action as reported could have taken place within a few months.

In arranging his material Mark employed many devices still used in popular literature. After introducing John the Baptist with a few arresting details, the author casually mentions his imprisonment with no hint of the reason for it. Five chapters later, the reader's suspense is allayed by the moving report of John's execution. The account of Jesus' raising Jairus' daughter skillfully combines doubt with delay calculated to rouse suspense. Jesus goes to heal a dying child. Can he heal one so critically ill? While one ponders, he heals a woman of a chronic disease. This delay of ten verses reassures yet tantalizes the reader. Then, he learns that the child has died. While the professional mourners ridicule him, he, nonetheless, persists and restores her to life. Suspense is employed here with more success than anywhere else in the Gospels except in John's account of the resurrection of Lazarus.

Jesus' success in Galilee is obliquely yet clearly measured by the accumulated forces resisting him. In chapter 2, scribes—professional expounders of the Law and the Prophets—are engaged in a witch hunt against him in which they are quickly joined by the local Pharisees. They complain that he disregards the proprieties in associating with undesirable persons. In chapter 5 the local opposition is reinforced by "scribes which came down from Jerusalem" to strengthen the relatively lax religious life of the Galileans. In the interim, local Pharisees have become so disturbed as to accept support from the local Herodians, a political group with whom they normally felt little if any sympathy—strange bedfellows indeed.

By chapter 7, additional scribes have arrived from Jerusalem to help stem the course of Jesus' success. Finally, after Jesus' arrival in Jerusalem, even the Sadducees, who have no love for the Pharisees, join in the attack. A movement able to unite against it Pharisees, scribes, Herodians, and Sadducees must have attained great momentum. The author, however, cleverly lets events speak for him and makes no assertions on his own authority.

A remarkable use of Gentile feeling of the time occurs in chapter 15. The combined Jewish forces could not convince the Roman procurator that Jesus was a malefactor. His decision to crucify Jesus is an act of expediency: the tumultuous Jewish crowds at the Passover could be kept from riot only by his acceding to their request. The responsibility for Jesus' crucifixion is laid upon the carefully fomented mob action of the Jews. The Roman official, with whom Mark's readers would naturally sympathize against the insurgent Palestinian Jews, takes no affirmative part. Any feeling that Pilate showed up badly in this situation would be lodged in him personally. It was known in the Roman world that Pilate had later been impeached and removed from his office for peculation and ill-advised acts in office. As in all four Gospels, no charges are leveled against the Roman government itself.

Less obvious to readers of the KJV is Mark's delay in explicitly asserting the deity of Jesus. In this version the phrase "son of God" (Mark 1:1) is added to the words "of Jesus Christ"; it so appears in Vaticanus and some other manuscripts. In Sinaiticus, however, it does not stand in the text, but was written in by another hand. It is an open question textually whether the insertion was made to emend a scribal error of omission or was piously inserted by a reader who felt that explicit assertion of Jesus' deity should be made here. Modern editions of the Greek text—Westcott and Hort and the prestigious Eberhard Nestle—omit the ascription of deity; the most recent *Greek New Testament* edited by Kurt Aland, Bruce M. Metzger, and others (1968) includes it with grave doubt of its authenticity. The RSV and the NEB include it but note that it lacks full manuscript support.

Literary and rhetorical evidence, as well as the beliefs among Mark's readers, uphold the Greek editors in omitting the phrase which ascribes deity to Christ at the beginning of Mark. If it is omitted, the strategy in Mark is clearly seen as it develops throughout the Gospel: to let the evidence speak for itself without any preceding unsupported claims. When a propagandist does not make bald assertions, his opponents find less in his words to contradict or resist.

The author of Mark was no doubt actuated here by more than a single motive. Besides the reasoning just mentioned, he probably wished to present Jesus as a person with whom they could readily empathize. Of at least equal weight in his mind was surely his awareness that to have stressed the status of Jesus as son of God by a human mother would have confused his image for his Gentile readers and might even have alienated some of them. Greek mythology and legend recorded many such beings, referred to as demigods or heroes. From ancient times families had claimed descent from a divine progenitor as a sort of social cachet. Such claims had long given skeptics ironic amusement. Five centuries earlier, a character in Euripides's *Ion* had caustically dismissed Ion's claim of Apollo as his father: many a girl tries to excuse the consequence of her indiscretion by asserting divine paternity for her bastard. It had become customary also to call the offspring of temple prostitutes "children of the goddess." In such a state of affairs, the divine paternity of Jesus had to be introduced only after careful preparation. It was best to let the reader himself deduce it from the evidence; as his own conclusion, he would hardly deride it.

In Mark, then, Jesus' deity is first introduced by his opponents, the scribes. When he says to the paralytic (2:5), "thy sins be forgiven thee" they make the scandalized yet correct rejoinder, "Who can forgive sins but God only?" In referring to himself as "the Son of man," Jesus again uses a term unobjectionable to non-Christian ears but well established in Christian usage as referring to his deity. To have asserted his deity at that early time would have branded Jesus as a blasphemer and led to his premature execution by incensed Jews. For Gentile readers the idea has been inserted, but it is left to lie fallow for the time.

In chapter 5 the maniac on the eastern shore of the lake addresses Jesus as "thou Son of the most high God." The insane were universally believed to be inhabited by a god or a demon; in either case, by one with more than human knowledge. Both then and in the immediately ensuing episode of the resurrection of Jairus' daughter, the implicit presence of superhuman power at work is clearly indicated, but no claim to deity for Jesus is stated. In chapter 8, Peter's response to Jesus' question, "Thou art the Christ," is again equivocal; to Jewish ears and to many Gentiles it meant simply that he was the Messiah; when Mark was written, it had become to Christians a name for Him as God. Gentile readers of Mark, though not closely acquainted with Judaism, would have gleaned from their interest in the current or recent Jewish war some knowledge of its most noticeable tenets. Even the transfiguration and setting of Jesus with Moses and Elijah in chapter 9 does not assert Jesus' deity. It does however establish him as at least equal with the most revered Jewish religious figures.

In chapter 8, Jesus gives the first overt hint of his deity in his declaration (v. 31) that he will be crucified and then resurrected—a declaration repeated in chapter 9 (v. 9) following the transfiguration. In neither case does this assertion seem to have made much immediate impression upon the disciples, nor does Mark give it prominence. The resurrection itself is the first explicit intimation in Mark that Jesus is indeed divine. Although the loss of the original ending of Mark leaves unknown the author's final expression, the tenor of the passage is unmistakable; like the conclusion later appended to Mark, it must have harmonized with those of the later Gospels.

Popular methods of Bible study account for the failure of readers to note Mark's strategy here. Jesus' career is usually presented as a composite of Gospel accounts. When one enters into detailed study of a single Gospel, his memory of the others hinders his picturing it in isolation. When its structure is seen, readers gain new insights into the writer's intent.

It has been asserted that Mark presents an earlier stage in Christianity, before the cult of Jesus as God had developed. Undercutting such a notion are letters of Paul, which were in circulation and which explicitly declared Him to be divine. The Church would not have accepted as canonical a Gospel which failed to conform to its basic belief. When one sees Mark in the light of its readers' preconceived notions, the writer's strategy becomes apparent. One suspects that early Christian scholars understood his tactics.

Many of the first readers of Mark undoubtedly were acquainted with his characteristic traits of expression. Any trained Hellenistic rhetorician who may have aided him or written for him would surely have taken pains to imitate his style. Such a practice was associated with the orator Lysias, a contemporary of Socrates. His art of *ēthopoiia* (literally, "character portrayal") enabled him to create speeches for clients which copied their expression to the life. Cicero's rhetorical essays mention him a score of times, and the *Rhetorica ad Herennium* and Quintilian's teaching kept his memory alive in the first Christian century. If any rhetorician aided Mark, he would have used this art to attract Mark's readers.

Mark presents Jesus as quite different from the Jewish leaders in both his own day and in Mark's. Such a differentiation was especially advisable in the sixth and seventh decades of the century. The Roman war with the Jews which was concluded in A.D. 70 was a frustrating, expensive, four-year series of campaigns culminating in the siege of the almost impregnable Jerusalem. Roman legions were not suited to the guerrilla warfare to which Palestine lent itself. Casualties were heavy on both sides. Like all wars it was expensive, and the readers of Mark were among the taxpayers who had helped to foot the bill. The Jewish nation was naturally extremely unpopular with Gentiles on this account, an enmity which extended to Palestinian Jews individually. Mark presents Jesus as a Jew who had opposed the very faction of Judaism which had, intentionally or not, contributed most heavily to the fury of the hostilities; and this faction had caused him to be executed. He had also opposed the arrogant isolationist racism of the Jews and had reached out to all men. His message of hope, service, and brotherhood touched a responsive chord in them. The Gospel sets this movement in a light that would have appealed most to its audience.

The propagandist naturally does not make a parade of his purpose, and he employs the arts of persuasion as the tastes of his audience dictate. Educated, cultured readers tend to feel confidence in the writer who obviously knows how to write artistically. Those less cultured tend to be suspicious of what they cannot appreciate. Since they do not recognize artistic work for its art, such effort is largely wasted upon them even if it does not alienate them. Mark would have been less effective as propaganda if it had been written with all the readily identifiable devices of rhetorical skill. The readers of Luke and John, as we shall see, were accustomed to skillfully composed discourse, expected it, and would have been deterred from reading a work whose author did not display rhetorical skills.

As one would then expect, Mark uses fewer of the rhetorical devices than do Luke and John; and such devices as are occasionally employed in it are those which for the most part are practiced by unlettered men. These could be used without arousing suspicion in the readers. The treatise *Rhetorica ad Herennium* lists forty-five figures of speech, of which only ten occur in Mark, and nineteen figures of thought, of which four or five are found in the Gospel. Those used added a force and vigor to which readers might reasonably be expected to respond.

A few instances of the rhetorical devices in Mark will illustrate the point. The most frequently used device is the rhetorical question or question and answer. On Jesus' return to Nazareth (6:1–5) his fellow townsmen's reaction to his teaching is stated as a rhetorical question, "Is not this the carpenter, the son of Mary, the brother of James, and Joses, and of Juda, and Simon?" This belittling "we knew him when . . ." is far more effective than a statement. The well-known reference to the needle's eye (10:25) is a hyperbole. A striking metaphor is Jesus' likening of Pharisaic teaching to yeast at work in dough (8:15). Generalized statement which is perhaps a proverb occurs in the episode in Nazareth mentioned above: "A prophet is not without honour, but in his own country, and among his own kin, and in his own house." As Longinus advised, Mark follows here the practice of combining figures: generalized statement is reinforced by the accumulated, poignant, narrowing focus of this dishonoring reception. In antiquity generalized statement was recognized as proof or supporting evidence to a degree hard for us to appreciate. Allegory is represented by parables and by the apocalyptic thirteenth chapter.

Among other effectively used figures, one notes the carefully stated antithesis of John the Baptist's "I indeed have baptized with water: but he shall baptize you with the Holy Ghost" (1:8;—a form reminding one of antithetic parallelism in Hebrew poetry). Analogy is drawn (4:1–31) between the spread of the Gospel and the sowing of seed. Such familiar parallels keep the topic alive by their causing readers to recall other parallel details. The possibilities in vivid description are seen in the feeding of the five thousand (6:39–44): the crowd sits on the *green* grass in "companies" (the Greek word is *symposia*, people eating and drinking together) "in ranks, by hundreds, and by fifties" (military overtones).

Jesus employs an outstanding paradox in "Whosoever will save his life shall lose it; but whosoever shall lose his life for my sake and the gospel's, the same shall save it" (*will* and *shall* here imply volition, not mere futurity). The peculiar effect of a paradox is to generate first shock and then confidence in the reader: shock, because his immediate response is that the statement is nonsense; confidence, because the reader who has hastily taken the meaning incorrectly will be hesitant to doubt the writer's subsequent statements. Although most of the rhetorical figures occur in quotations of Jesus' words, the writer will share the reader's respect, if only for his having incorporated them strategically in his work.

The value in combined figures, Longinus implies (chapter 20 and *passim*), is that they overcome the resistance of the reader aroused by the feeling that his emotions are being manipulated; we sometimes characterize this feeling as "sales resistance." To shift the figure, the reader is like a boxer who guards against the author's left only to be hit by his right. Such a device may be exerted quite without the reader's awareness of it; it is none the less effective for that. Additional examples of combined figures are the union of accumulation or sequential bits of evidence with a rhetorical question (6:3–4), and of apostrophe (direct address but not to a person) with rhetorical question (9:19).

For all the author's skillfully used figures, the fact remains that arrangement of carefully selected material is his most effective weapon. This arrangement, to be sure, does not follow strictly any established rhetorical pattern. His governing purpose is to persuade a specific class of persons, and his end is to produce what Longinus termed *ekstasis* (not ecstasy as we use the term to denote a merely emotional response, but a literal moving of his readers from one mental position to another). Academic acceptance of Christianity is not enough. As I. A. Richards stated the case in modern terms, the end of persuasion is action or at least readiness for action—a conclusion quite in accord also with Aristotle's teaching (*Science and Poetry*, chapter 2). In each Gospel the writer presents selected matter in an arrangement carefully calculated so that these two components will convert hearers into Christians.

Selective skill of a Gospel writer will show not only in his inclusions but also in his omissions. Consider as an instance the "final examination" administered by Jesus to his disciples at Caesarea Philippi (Mark 8:27–38). To Jesus' second question, "Whom say ye that I am?" Mark reports Peter's response simply as "Thou art the Christ" (i.e., literally, the Messiah). In Matthew's account (16:13–28) Peter's answer is extended, "Thou art the Christ, the son of the living God." The ascription of deity to Jesus overtly did not suit the purpose of Mark at this juncture, as we have seen; Matthew's largely Jewish readers would have no such reason to be misled by it, and Matthew's purpose required it. Jesus' added words about the keys and about binding and loosing (16:19) could have been misconstrued into politically subversive connotations which Mark wished to avoid. The propagandist, if he measures up to Quintilian's requirements for the orator—that he be a good man skilled at speaking, will not falsify or invent evidence; he need not, however, tell the whole truth, provided that he does not by his omissions distort the truth.

The question may fairly be raised, in view of his careful omission of possibly provocative matter, why does the author in this same passage use the term *Christ*, the Greek equivalent for *Messiah*? Why does he repeatedly use the phrase "the kingdom of God" in his Gospel? To the Roman citizen both terms carried subversive connotations; he was surely fed up with the notion of Jewish insurrection. To both questions part of the answer doubtless is that he could hardly have done otherwise. By this time *Christ* had probably become associated specifically with Jesus and in relation to him was generally used by non-Christians as a mere proper name, as it occurs slightly later in the works of Pliny the Younger and Tacitus. At the time Mark was written, too, it seemed unlikely that any rabble-rouser for long to come could stir up insurrection in Palestine.

As for the phrase "the kingdom of God," Mark could hardly have avoided using it for other reasons. For one thing, Jesus had himself used it as an unavoidable term in view of Jewish preoccupation with the concept. Christians were using it, as Paul's letters attest. In Luke, which also is propaganda for Gentiles, and Mark it was preferred to Matthew's "Kingdom of Heaven." Perhaps the writer of Mark felt that it carried more obviously religious connotations than the other term, and would therefore be less suspect. A Jewish insurrectionist might well claim to be establishing a kingdom of heaven when he had in mind an earthly kingdom; he would simply be proclaiming a jihad or its Jewish equivalent. Although there is actually little difference in the two phrases, the "kingdom of God" would be slightly less political, at least to Gentile ears. Jesus could hardly escape using one or the other phrase.

Other omissions are apparently made on account of the readers' interests. Being of the less educated classes, they would prefer action to teaching. Comparison with Matthew, which is heavily in debt to Mark, demonstrates this principle at work. In Mark (3:13–14) we are told: "And he goeth up into a mountain, and calleth unto him whom he would: and they came unto him. And he ordained twelve . . . ." Between these two verses Matthew inserts the so-called Sermon on the Mount, nearly three chapters of instruction. He omits most of John the Baptist's preaching from chapter 1 as well as the verbal duel between Jesus and Satan reported in chapter 4 of Matthew. The two last-mentioned accounts may have been abbreviated partly because they would require extensive glossing for a Gentile audience. With only a superficial acquaintance with Judaism, however, an educated Gentile would find the Sermon on the Mount intelligible and appealing. The chief reason for omission of such matter seems more probably to be that Mark's audience would be less interested in it than in short reports of Jesus' actions and words that men whose span of attention was brief would enjoy reading.

Such sayings of Jesus as are included are calculated to please the audience aimed at in Mark. Encapsulated knowledge in proverbs, adages, and such utterances constituted much of their mental stock in trade. Mark's parables, too, especially those reported near the beginning of the Gospel, are brief, simple, and, to us at least, obvious; yet in private Jesus had to explain their meaning to his disciples. At this early stage of his work, Mark pictures him as relying heavily upon such parables in his teaching. It is sometimes unwise to state novel principles baldly; men need to approach them indirectly. Men always enjoy a good story, and in antiquity the parabolic story was particularly popular. The form is very old; an instance of its use by the prophet Nathan in charging David with murder comes from ten centuries earlier (2 Sam. 12:1–4).

After giving the disciples the clue to his first-reported parables' meaning, Jesus abandoned this practice, preferring instead simply to let them and other hearers interpret for themselves: "He that hath ears to hear, let him hear!" The parables required some attentive thought but were not overly difficult to solve; and the success of the interpreter would gratify him and make him wish to hear more. Incidentally, one should note the simplicity of Mark's parables when contrasted with those reported in Luke alone; here is further indication of the cultural levels of Mark's readers as contrasted with Luke's.

The everyday experiences which constitute the vehicle of Mark's parables are paralleled by homely details in other parts of his account. We hear the professional mourners wailing in the house of Jairus. His daughter immediately after her resurrection had to be fed like any normal hungry adolescent. The five thousand were fed from somebody's lunch of five buns and two fish. Jesus, a good Jew, showed no regret at the loss of the Gadarene swine. Jesus' most vociferous supporter, Peter, under pressure after Jesus' arrest, cursed and swore and denied any knowledge of him. Human interest details like these are especially attractive to people in the lower walks of life.

Mark's audience presumably read little—perhaps they had the book read to them. He anticipated this situation by including startling as well as homely events that would recall the ideas connected with them. Jesus' deity is first suggested in the comment following the lowering of a paralytic through a hole torn in the wattle-and-daub roof of the house in which Jesus was teaching. Although such a roof could be quickly and cheaply mended, such a liberty taken with property would not readily be forgotten. Later, Jesus' seeming denial of his immediate family (3:31–35) shocks the hearers until its paradoxical meaning is recognized. The drama of John the Baptist's death, pointed up by Salome's sensual dance, shows in sharp relief the notorious weakness of the local kinglet. The Syro-Phoenician woman's pert response to Jesus' expression of standard Jewish arrogance towards Gentiles—an answer which delights Jesus—hints at his interest in people outside the Jewish pale. Jesus' preference for children or childlike people in his kingdom ties the kind of faith he demands to man's dearest image. The striking refusal of the rich young ruler to abandon his wealth in order to follow Jesus strongly appeals to the unmoneyed men of Mark's audience. By thus presenting vignettes that vividly show Jesus and his teaching, Mark succeeds in introducing much of Jesus' message without resorting to didactic passages.

The miracles reported in Mark touch the everyday problems of man: disease and the weather. Such inexplicable deeds indicated not a suspension of the known laws of nature—a concept unknown among Jews and all but a few educated Gentiles. The traditions of the Jews held that Jahweh intervenes personally in the world's affairs and directs whatever happens according to his will. From the *Iliad* on down, the concept of a god changing the natural course of events had been bred into Hellenistic traditions. The person performing the miracle was not necessarily superhuman. It was Jesus' forgiveness of the paralytic's sins, and not his healing the man, that seemed to be a blasphemous assertion of his deity and scandalized the scribes.

Jesus healed the sick because he "had compassion on them"; to do so was also sound strategy. Christian evangelistic work in medically backward countries has always been a potent means of approaching and interesting men. Jesus' healings were both physical and mental—though his hearers and Mark's readers did not clearly distinguish the two sorts. The physical diseases mentioned as cured by Jesus were those that have always been widespread. Insanity was believed to be the effect of demonic possession, and Jesus made no attempt to counter this belief. To disagree with the common man's prevailing ideas on religion and medicine is to stir up heated argument. Jesus met sufficient opposition on the religious front, which was his primary concern, without arousing opposition on other fronts.

As in all four Gospels, dramatic conflict in Mark centers on the Pharisaic opposition to Jesus. When other inimical forces enter the scene, they are ancillary to the Pharisees. This focus upon the Pharisees was not only in accord with the facts, it was also timely for Mark. The Pharisees' extreme separatism had for decades singled them out in Gentile eyes as the most unpopular sect of Jews. In the Hellenistic world one of the principal attitudes was a breaking down of racial and national barriers and an emphasis upon human brotherhood. Mark skillfully presented the Pharisees, whom his readers already disliked, as a force adverse to Jesus.

In Mark, Jesus' spiritual, constructive teaching appears in sharp relief against the arid legalism of Pharisaic teaching and practice. It was the Pharisaic spelling out of ways to obey the Law, as Matthew shows, that constituted Jesus' special target. Mark's audience presumably had little detailed knowledge of such matters, and he wisely does not go into detail except in the matter of Sabbath observance, which many of them had no doubt noticed in their Jewish neighbors.

The attack on this slavish observance of the Sabbath rules is continuous in Mark. In chapter 1, Jesus heals a man in the synagogue on the Sabbath and follows this with other healings. There is no indication that any of those healed at this time required emergency help, which would have been permissible by Jewish regulation. It seems inescapable that Jesus here deliberately attacks the reduction of religious faith to religious observance. (It is only fair to add that these rules had been promulgated with no such intent, but as aids to devotion; they had produced an effect which had not been designed.) On another occasion (Mark 2:23–27) his disciples were ridiculously charged with reaping and winnowing grain on the Sabbath when they had casually plucked heads of wheat, rubbed off the awn, and eaten the grain. Jesus' retort, "The sabbath was made for man, and not man for the sabbath," shows their arid formalism in a way quite intelligible to an intelligent Gentile: a religious observance should be beneficial, not burdensome, to the celebrant.

On still another occasion (3:1–6), a man with a withered hand was apparently planted in the synagogue to tempt Jesus again to break the Sabbath law. This time, Jesus angrily turned the tables on his opponents by peremptorily demanding: "Is it lawful to do good on the sabbath days, or to do evil? to save life, or to kill?" When they evidently were at a loss how to counter this frontal attack, he healed the man. This open flouting of their law they could not tolerate; to break *a* law was to break *the* Law in Jewish thinking. Such action endangered their entire system and they angrily set in motion plans to get rid of him.

Later attacks upon him also concerned his cavalier attitude towards their concept of the Jewish law. One group charged him with driving out the demons of disease by the power of Satan. He quickly showed up the absurdity of such a charge: if He were doing this, it would mark the downfall of Satan by making him destroy his own forces. Another group from Jerusalem charged Him and his disciples with failing to wash their hands before eating (Mark adds a gloss for his Gentile readers to explain the Pharisaic obsession with ritual rather than with cleanliness in washing). Jesus answered this charge with a vigorous denunciation of their substituting directions about how to act for those about how to feel in religious observance. The Pharisees were so concerned with ritualistic detail that they had laid aside the commands of God.

Following this defense, Jesus charges the Pharisees with far more serious lawbreaking. Their code makes it possible for a man to escape responsibility for his aged parents' support. He might claim that his property was dedicated to God, and so escape any legal responsibility for their expenses—a flagrant abuse of the law governing gifts to God. While the Gentile reader might not understand the details of such chicanery, he would be horrified at this escape from what he also believed to be a moral duty.

After this attack upon his opponents, Jesus evidently found it expedient to withdraw for a while from Galilee to let their fury diminish. As later statements indicate, he also needed time to round out the training of his twelve disciples to carry on his work after his crucifixion and ascension. For this purpose he needed to escape the thronging crowds of his friends as well as his enemies. In his attempt to escape attention he was not wholly successful. Apparently he did finish the major part of his program for the twelve as his testing of them about his identity and the ensuing Transfiguration indicates. He then returned by a circuitous route to the land about the lake of Galilee, but, finding the hostility still rampant, he took his followers to Jerusalem.

The journey to Jerusalem followed the route commonly taken. To avoid passing through Samaria, which Jews seldom did except under pressure of circumstances, he led them to the east bank of the Jordan and through friendly regions to Jericho. From there a steep but passable road led up to Jerusalem. Mark used this trip to put together six episodes, employing the device of a journey, as Chaucer did centuries later, as a string upon which to put stories together. This device is used by all three Synoptics, Luke using it for one-third of his entire account.

Although it is not made prominent, there is a common theme running through all six episodes. Mark reports first the attempt by sniping Pharisees to embroil Jesus in what was at the time a hotly debated matter among Hebrew scholars, the rules governing divorce. If he were to support the right to divorce a wife, he would contradict the statement of Adam in Genesis 2 that man and wife become one flesh and so cannot thereafter be severed. A negative reply would contradict the statement in Deuteronomy 24:1–4 as well as the practice indicated by Isaiah and Jeremiah. Refusing to let himself be impaled on the horns of this dilemma, Jesus in private with his disciples came out in support of Genesis as his previous response to the Pharisees had indicated. This response pointed sharply at the obstinacy and recalcitrance which had characterized the Hebrews throughout their history. He indicated that the provision in Deuteronomy was the best compromise that could be effected with such stubborn people.

This reminder of Pharisaic, arrogant "hardness of heart" sets the tone for the rest of the journey. Jesus' acceptance of children and setting up a most unpharisaic childlikeness as the pattern for citizens of his kingdom is a sharp antithesis to the previous event. The wealthy law-abiding man who put his wealth above what Jesus demanded of a man gives Jesus an opportunity to dilate upon the problems caused by earthly possessions. When Peter self-importantly calls Jesus' attention to the disciples' having given up all to follow him (actually they possessed little to give up), Jesus rebukes him: although they have done well and will be rewarded, they have no special claim above other men. And he tries, once more unsuccessfully, to remind them that he goes to Jerusalem to be executed, not to be crowned. Matthew (19:27) spells out what Mark merely implies: he adds to Peter's self-satisfied statement the words "what shall we have therefore?"

But pride, the basic deadly sin according to Christian theology, will not easily down. In spite of the rebuff Peter received, James and John next try to get for themselves the highest positions in the kingdom and claim to be fully able to bear all the hardships of such offices. Jesus' response, that they will receive the hardships but cannot be promised the preferment, may seem hardly fair. Although his irritation was surely justifiable, his answer was probably the best way to shock them back into line with what he had been trying to impress upon them. Whether it worked, is not stated. The others, still under the spell of the earthly kingdom, angrily charge James and John with having stolen a march on them; but Jesus, realizing their bemusement, calls them together. He tells them that they should not think in terms of Gentile kingdoms, for in his kingdom "Whosoever of you will be the chiefest, shall be servant of all," as he himself was.

The story of the blind man Bartimaeus fitly closes this chain of events. All he asks of Jesus is his sight, and he is confident in Jesus' power to restore it. His regaining his sight metaphorically places him above the disciples who in spite of all their training could not "see" what Jesus was trying to do.

At this juncture, it is hard for the reader of Mark not to feel that Jesus has failed. It is ironic that Peter, who had hailed him as Messiah and Son of God, and the others who had listened to him should in effect be telling him what he should do. And whatever his plan may be, he has a pitifully inadequate following, it seems evident, to achieve it. Only at the crucifixion do his fortunes appear lower. And Jesus' actions in the following week do not greatly lift the hopes of one who follows Mark's account as a unit by itself.

The name "Passion Week," which has become attached to the period beginning with Jesus' arrival in Jerusalem and concluding with the crucifixion, perhaps requires some explanation. To modern readers *passion* signifies intense, violent, overmastering emotion with a minimum of reason. The Latinate English of the KJV, however, clarifies the use of *passion* in its rendering of Acts 1:3, in which Jesus "shewed himself alive after his passion." *Passion*, as they knew, was a noun made on the root of the Latin *passus*, whose meaning is preserved in our adjective *passive*. Jesus was, it is true, vigorously active both physically and mentally during this week, and emotions did run high on both sides. The significant fact, however, is the manner in which Jesus passively let himself be crucified although, as he declared, he could have escaped if he had willed it so.

Jesus' program during Passion Week was anything but passive. Two major events in it were carefully programmed by him: his triumphal entry and the Last Supper. His entry on the ass's colt was carefully staged to conform to the prophecy in Zechariah (9:9) of the king's coming to Jerusalem. Mark, like Matthew and Luke, follows here what was a well-established account, for their reports of events in Passion Week, as has been mentioned, closely agree. The staging was designed for its effect on the Jewish audience. How much of the symbolism Mark's readers would comprehend is questionable, but they would, no doubt, grasp the tenor of the event. Jesus' entry on an ass instead of a horse would indicate his peaceful intent; warriors and earthly kings rode horses. They would see in this support of Jesus' repeated assertions of the nonsubversive character of his kingdom. After his entry Jesus observed the corrupt secular business carried on in the Temple and then left to pass the night in suburban Bethany. Here occurs one of the few minor variants in Gospel accounts of Passion Week.

According to tradition, these events occurred on a Sunday. On Monday, Mark writes, Jesus revisited the Temple and disrupted the businesses conducted there. Some explanation is due here of these businesses. The chief priest, in particular the sons of Annas, the high priest who controlled Temple affairs, had gotten into their hands the market for sacrificial animals and the exchange of other currencies into the Temple coinage which had to be used in buying the sacrificial animals. Jesus' charge that they had made the Temple a den of thieves implies that they had profiteered on the rate of exchange. Their moving the financial business into the Temple Jesus regarded as profanation of its function. It is probable that the Temple officials also conducted legitimate banking affairs, but this aspect of the situation does not enter into Jesus' action. His action here naturally brought on him the violent onslaught of the two following days of argument. The priests' possible fears that the volatile crowd at Passover might turn upon the authorities may well have contributed to their fury.

A curious episode frames Jesus' attack on the abusers of the Temple. En route to the city, Jesus saw a fig tree in leaf and looked for figs on it, though figs do not ripen in the spring. Finding none, he apostrophized the tree, "No man eat fruit of thee hereafter for ever." Upon his return with his disciples, they found the tree dried up from the roots. Framing the Temple episode as it does, this report presumably refers symbolically to the picture it surrounds. It is a bitter condemnation of Jewish religious condition. Expositors who have too often failed to consider its context have assigned strained interpretations to the episode, even declaring it to be an interpolation into the Gospel. Its significance to one who reads the Gospel as a literary work appears to be sensibly explained by its position in the account.

When Jesus entered the city on this morning, the Temple authorities challenged his right to interfere in their business activities. By his response they hoped to entrap him. If he should assert divine authority, they could charge him with blasphemy. If not, they could have him arrested as a mere seditious person. Jesus offered them a bargain: you tell me the source of John the Baptist's power and I will tell you mine. His offer cloaked a more dangerous dilemma for them. If they admitted John's divine support, Jesus could ask why they had not obeyed John. If they denied it, John's great reputation as a prophet would arouse the crowds against them.

Following this impasse, Jesus took the offensive. He reworked a well-known parable (Isa. 5:1–7) which attacked Israel's shameful ingratitude for God's mercies. Jesus, however, shifted its target to the chief priests and their supporters. (Mark's readers possibly shifted the target back to the Jewish nation.) In this verbal sparring, it is evident that Jesus was not so much enunciating his own teachings as demonstrating his opponents' hypocrisy. In their fury these leaders would have arrested him on the spot if the volatile crowd's obvious preference for Jesus had not deterred them.

But the excitable Passover crowd could quickly be moved in new directions. Realizing this, both Pharisees and Sadducees undertook to discredit Jesus through forcing him to take a stand on a question involving patriotic feeling: ought one to pay the Roman tribute or not? Mark's readers would be as concerned as the Jewish crowd at Jesus' reply. An affirmative reply might please Mark's readers, but it would surely infuriate the Jewish crowd; a negative reply would please the crowd, but it would irritate not only Mark's readers but also the Roman authorities of Jesus' day, who could hardly have ignored it. The questioners may have already been preparing the way for Roman execution of Jesus. Jesus always refused to give a serious answer to an insincere question. Again he adroitly evaded the trap by telling them to face the situation and make their own decision. (Jesus' statement, "Render to Caesar the things that are Caesar's," has often been lifted from its context and has suffered an adventurous existence in later times.)

The next trap was laid by Sadducees, to whom the Temple markets belonged. It was apparently one of their favorite conundrums to propound to theological opponents who believed in a life after death. (To point up the trickery of the question, Mark tells his readers that the Sadducees deny any future life.) The situation posed refers to the ancient Jewish custom of levirate marriage (Deut. 25:5–10), through which the male line of each family could be preserved. (Such a custom is implicit in the story of Ruth except that Boaz actually marries her.) The woman described by the Sadducees had been the wife of seven brothers; whose wife would she be at the resurrection? One can imagine the enjoyment of a Sadducee watching a Pharisee wrestling with the problem.

Jesus almost savagely retorts to his tormentors that they do not really know the Scriptures. Their conundrum was pointless: as rabbinical teaching showed, the future life does not include marriage or the begetting of children. The actuality of the future life, he added in attacking their denial of it, is proved in Exodus 3:6, which Mark quotes from the Septuagint in abbreviated form. Jesus' argument is this: Since the living God is God of the living (Mark 12:27) and the God of those ancient worthies Abraham, Isaac, and Jacob, then they also must now be living though they died fifteen centuries ago (12:26). Jesus uses here rabbinical reasoning to confute the scholars themselves.

At this juncture a scribe in the audience, impressed by Jesus' reasoning, asks him the question that was probably in the back of Mark's readers' minds, and which, incidentally, was hotly debated in rabbinic schools: which is the basic, most important commandment? Jesus, replying seriously to a serious inquiry, quotes Deuteronomy 6:4–5, part of the Shema, the essential creed of Judaism: there is one God, who must be loved with absolute devotion. To this he adds Leviticus 19:18, "Thou shalt love thy neighbor as thyself"—an addition quite in harmony with Gentile thinking. Here ends the contest of wits, with Jesus the undisputed winner.

Jesus, however, has not finished his attack. How, he inquires, do the scribes call the Messiah the son of David? David in Psalm 110 (all the psalms were then ascribed to David) said that Jahweh had told David's lord to sit at his right hand until Jahweh should have brought the world under this lord's control. This "lord" was presumably the coming Messiah who, according to accepted Jewish belief, was to be of David's line. Since the son is subject to his father, how can David's son be also David's lord? This can be true only if David's son is not merely his son—in other words, he must be more than human.

While such an involved argument may not greatly impress modern readers, it is dangerous to assume that it did not impress Mark's readers. His details thus far have been so skillfully arranged to impress his readers that it would be inconceivable for him to blunder at the climax of an important episode of his account. If one can assume, as seems probable, some previous knowledge of Judaism and Christianity in Mark's readers, then the tradition that the Messiah or Jesus was of Davidic descent was presumably known to them.

Another body of material that makes little appeal to the twentieth-century reader is the eschatological account in chapter 13. The concern with the values of Christianity for the present life tends to overshadow concern for the life to come. The first-century Christian's expectation of an imminent end to the present existence no doubt gave him immediate concern in such matters. Perhaps also the lot of the bulk of mankind, less pleasant in many respects than that now, directed his mind to another life, as the hopes of Negro slaves were formerly directed to a life after the conclusion of their sufferings. The three Synoptic writers all made telling use of this material.

The passage is naturally and easily introduced. Fresh from rural Galilee, the disciples were awed by the Temple. Some of the stones they exclaimed at were forty feet long, twelve feet high, and eighteen feet wide. The Temple was a triumph of engineering as well as a marvelous work of art. Jesus' response was startling. Yes, it is a marvelous structure, but it will soon be razed to the ground.

The vividly described suffering in the ensuing pictures has been cited as a strong argument that Mark was written after the war with Rome had ended. Taken by itself, it is not a proof of this. Several other Jewish cities had been taken by storm before Jerusalem was besieged. The assertion that the Temple will fall is evidence that this catastrophe had already occurred. Anyone conversant with the course of Jewish events, however, could have seen such destruction as highly probable. This Gospel used earlier sources, and it cannot in itself be cited for support of dating which may well have been in these sources.

Whatever the immediate situation in Mark's day, it is improbable that the writer invented these sayings. If Jesus had not at some time expressed similar sentiments, witnesses to his life still living could and, no doubt, would have challenged the passage. Those who deny the probability of a reasonably accurate report of Jesus' words are unduly captious in the face of evidence of the retentive verbal memory of nonreaders, especially when no valid reason appears for doubting the validity of Mark's account.

A startling problem is raised by Jesus' admission that he himself did not know "the day and the hour" when the catastrophe should take place. Mark's account surely did not invent this statement. Paul's letters indicate, however, that early Christians had an answer to this problem (cf. Phil. 2:7–8, 2 Cor. 13:4). Reduced to simple terms, the explanation runs approximately as follows: God is infinite, man finite. Therefore, when God in the person of the Son entered into a human body, infinity could not be fully housed in that body. Accordingly, to use Paul's metaphor, Jesus "emptied himself" of some part of his deity while he was also man. Complete omniscience appears by this theory to have been one divine attribute of which Jesus temporarily deprived himself.

The writer includes Jesus' warning against jumping to the conclusion that such catastrophes inevitably presage destruction of the present world. Although they do precede such destruction, no one can tell whether the end will follow any specific occurrence of such disaster. Since no man can know when the end will actually come, everyone should be alert and prepared constantly for its coming. Failure to consider this warning and overstimulated imagination have since then all too frequently combined to produce many mistaken eschatological declarations.

Mark's account rapidly hastens to its crisis. The movement of the Jewish authorities to rid themselves of Jesus has been imminent since the second chapter. It now receives its final impetus from Judas Iscariot, one of the twelve. For undisclosed reasons Judas offers to betray Jesus to the Jewish leaders at the first opportunity.

Like his preparations for his entry on Palm Sunday, Jesus prearranged the Last Supper. While they were eating the Passover, Mark reports, Jesus instituted the symbolic breaking of bread and drinking of wine characteristic of the Lord's Supper, or Eucharist. By this account Jesus' last Passover became also the first celebration of this feast. For Gentile Christians in Mark's day this observance had wholly superseded the Jewish feast. As he and his disciples were eating, Jesus announced that one of them would betray him to the authorities, but he did not point out the traitor. Judas, nonetheless, realized that his intended treachery was known to Jesus. He probably remained with the group after the supper until he discovered its destination and then left to summon those who would arrest Jesus.

Mark here follows the ordering of events given by Paul in 1 Corinthians which had probably become accepted among Gentile Christians. Although Mark omits details which the other Gospels include, such omission does not necessarily indicate that the author was ignorant of them. It would have served little purpose for him to include, for example, Jesus' long discourses included in John. (They may well have been organized by the author of John from other discourses by Jesus.) In any case, Mark's readers would hardly have appreciated their significance or even have read them. Luke's cryptic reference to the two swords (22:38), which figured in later debates on the powers of church and state, would have stirred in Mark's readers latent fear of subversive activities by the Church as charged by its opponents.

For Mark's purpose, the salient points are the announcement of impending betrayal, the disciples' unfounded self-assurance that they would stand by Jesus, the institution of the Lord's Supper, the scene at Gethsemane, the betrayal and arrest, the inept defense by one of the disciples, and Jesus' surrender to the mob sent to take him. Mark's most notable addition to the account of the arrest (14:51–52) tells of a youth apparently wrapped in a sheet who had followed

Jesus. When he was also seized, the boy simply slipped out of the sheet and escaped naked. It is plausibly assumed that Mark himself was the boy.

Mark apparently abbreviates the account of Jesus' hearing before the Jewish religious leaders. After Jesus' refusal to reply with a single word to the contradictory charges that had been made against him, the high priest in desperation asked a two-part question: Are you the Messiah, and do you claim to be the Son of God? The Messiah in Jewish eyes was not divine and the claim to be the Messiah was not blasphemous, but an affirmative answer to the second query could be so construed. A Gentile reader aware of the Jews' monotheistic beliefs would understand the implications of such an answer. Jesus, perhaps seeing no reason to prolong the farcical hearing, answered that he was both, and he added an echo of Daniel 7:13 which left his claim in no doubt. In furious reaction the priests and council charged him with blasphemy.

The referral of Jesus' case to Pilate was caused by the chief priests' desire to have Jesus executed as expeditiously as possible. Although there is some doubt, many scholars assert that the death penalty could have been exacted by Romans alone. Jesus' death at Roman hands would brand him as a malefactor and imply that he had been an insurrectionist. Moreover, Roman execution was prompt as well as discreditable, and the imminence of the Sabbath, which the execution would be defiling, also added to their haste. The mob which had thronged to hear Jesus was now, on the morning after the Passover, emotionally exhausted and unlikely to rouse to vigorous action; but if the execution were delayed until after the Sabbath, it would have recovered its vigor. A *fait accompli* alone could prevent violent disturbance.

The appearance reported before Pilate is given only in its bare outline. His question, "Art thou the King of the Jews?" indicates either that charges by the chief priests have been omitted or that Pilate had previous knowledge of the accused. Jesus' reply, "Thou sayest it," is equivalent to a simple yes in Greek. The Jewish leaders shouted in rage at his assertion; but when Pilate gave Jesus a chance to reply to their charges and abuse, he surprised Pilate by keeping silent. Pilate, who was no fool, saw no danger to Rome from any claims Jesus might make, and he probably wished to avoid any action that might enrage any segment of the Jews at Passover time. Diplomatically, he tried compromise by offering to release Jesus as the customary clemency offered at the feast, but the priests urged the crowd to demand instead a highwayman named Barabbas. Such a demand not only forestalled Pilate's merciful intent, but it also posed a problem for him. Rome prided herself on her control over the highways and was merciless to brigands. Pilate was fairly caught; the Jews had the right to choose the prisoner to be released. He began to weaken, to temporize. What should he do with Jesus? The people shouted, "Crucify him." Pilate pointed out that no capital charge had been proved against him, but he finally yielded to their insistent demand. No doubt he chose to execute one man in order to avoid an incipient riot.

Mark omits any reference to the pressures which the Jews could exert upon Pilate. Pilate had raided the Temple treasury, an act in contravention of Roman practice for which he could have been impeached and probably removed from office by the strict Roman procedure with provincial rulers. The influential Jews had craftily preferred to hold it as a threat over his head to keep him in line with their wishes. Mark's audience would not have liked to hear of a Roman official thus subservient to Jews, and introduction of the details would have distracted from the effect desired in the account.

One should compare this situation with a parallel in the life of Paul. On his final visit to Jerusalem, Paul was accused by a mob of having violated the Temple; and the mob dragged him out of the sacred precincts preparatory to lynching him. The Roman guard at the castle of Antonia rescued him and let him defend himself. When the mob still demanded his death, the Romans rescued him because he was a Roman citizen. Ultimately he was spirited out of the city to save his life.

Jesus had no such shield. Pilate indeed did what he safely could for him, but, after all, he was just another Jew. Undoubtedly Pilate shared the widespread belief enunciated by Caiaphas in John: It is better to have one man die than to imperil a whole nation. Pilate's decision was in line with his duty; Mark brings no charge against him.

The execution was one of those wild mob scenes only too familiar today. To vent his irritation at being forced to do the Jews' bidding, and perhaps to give some semblance of legality to the execution, Pilate had an inscription calling Jesus ironically "The King of the Jews" affixed to the cross. The prisoner was left by the executioners to the mercy of the mob; even the Jewish authorities joined in baiting him.

The crucifixion, however, did not proceed precisely according to pattern. For one thing, Jesus died in six or seven hours, not lingering for days as usually happened. Crucified persons died ordinarily from exposure, exhaustion, and gradual suffocation. The position of the body, which required the sagging abdominal organs to be lifted with every spasmodic breath, made the weakened victim finally unable to draw breath.

Mark reports also a symbolic darkness that shrouded the end of Jesus' suffering, and adds that the veil that normally hid the inner holy place in the Temple was torn from top to bottom. This detail obviously symbolized to a Christian apologist among Gentiles that Jesus' death ended all separation between God and man. His Gentile audience might also see in it the end to Jewish claims of separation from the rest of mankind. (Since gospel is not biography, the author conceivably felt free to add symbolic details.)

Somewhere along the line of Christian scribes a curious minor error crept in. Actuated probably by the same zeal which made a copyist insert "Son of God" into Mark 1:1, another had the centurion in charge at Jesus' execution say, "Truly this man was the Son of God" (15:39). The earliest Greek manuscripts contain no definite article here. What the centurion declared—all he was in a position to think—was that the crucified man was "a son of a god," no ordinary man. Since Latin has no articles, the Vulgate offered no evidence either way. The translators followed the inferior Greek text at their disposal.

An otherwise unknown man named Joseph, a member of the village council of Arimathaea and a follower of Jesus, risked the danger of guilt by association by asking Pilate for Jesus' body. He wished to give it temporary burial in order to avoid breaking the taboo against allowing a body to hang overnight. Pilate was naturally surprised that Jesus was already dead. When assured that this was so, he readily gave his permission. He was no doubt relieved that a dangerous situation had been avoided. Forced to act in haste by the imminent sunset that ushered in the Sabbath, Jesus' followers omitted the customary preparations for burial. They simply wrapped the body in a linen cloth and laid it temporarily in a nearby rock tomb, the mouth of which they covered with a heavy stone.

From near sunset on Friday until near dawn on Sunday, Jesus' body lay in the tomb—for three days, but not for the full seventy-two hours. The three women who went out to complete the preparation of the corpse for burial probably arrived about daybreak. En route they worried about moving the stone that blocked the tomb, but they saw from a distance that it had already been moved. Entering, they saw a young man clad in white who told them that Jesus had risen and preceded them into Galilee "as he said unto you" (foretold in 14:28). Although he bade them to inform the disciples, and especially Peter, the women were so flustered that they ran away and told no one.

At this point in chapter 16 (v.8) the extant part of the original Mark ends. Verses 9–20 are entirely omitted from Sinaiticus and Vaticanus, and are included with some question in the other major manuscripts. It is probable that the last page of the original copy had become lost before the year A.D. 300 and that an attempt was made to round it out from the evidence of the other Gospels. The existence of an alternative ending in later manuscripts is further evidence that these twelve verses are spurious. The translators of the KJV, following the generally accepted text which was also in the Vulgate and unaware that there was any problem here, naturally raised no question about the words they translated.

What these twelve verses contain can be found scattered in the other three Gospels and in the Acts, often in more detail. They lack much of the colorful detail usually to be found in Mark and read rather like an epitome of events and sayings. The final verse, in fact, calls attention to the later work of the Church rather than furnishing a rounded conclusion to a Gospel. It is a skillful stroke on the part of the epitomizers, for it implies the continuity of Jesus' work in the labors of his followers; but it states an accomplishment rather than the command given in Matthew and Acts.

In emphasizing the propagandistic formative principle of Mark, one must not assume that every detail in it is necessarily included for the specific audience to whom it was directed. The author was not a stylist bound by the laws of a specific literary genre, but a severely practical man. He may well have been like Herodotus, who admitted that his account "sought additions." It is possible indeed that the work was a development from the propagandistic labors of its author, but these efforts still give it its form. Perhaps the strongest evidence of its nature lies in the careful omission of what might displease its readers or detract from its propagandistic effect. When one adds to the evidence of Mark the fact that each of the other Gospels indicates a similar purpose, the hypothesis of this study is strongly reinforced. The New Testament is made up of books whose form shows that they were composed to spread the gospel as widely and rapidly as possible in the first five books and to nurture the nascent Church in the rest. The fact that they were useful in other ways as well is undisputed; the organizing principle of the Gospels and the Acts is rhetorical.

I would be the last to deny that these books form the basis of Christian doctrine. It is my belief that their writers were actuated by divine inspiration, though I am not prepared to accept categorically any statement about precisely how the divine inspiration worked in the production of these books. Literary study exhausts itself in the attempt to explain what the books are, what they say, and what their authors were attempting to do. Further study lies in the provinces of other disciplines, which, nonetheless, must begin with literary interpretation.

CHAPTER 2

THE GOSPEL ACCORDING TO MATTHEW

The evidence against the disciple Matthew's having written the Gospel that bears his name is overwhelming. First, why would Matthew, an eyewitness and companion of Jesus' career on earth, make such extensive use of Mark, which could not lay claim to having been written by an eyewitness of most of the events it reports? More than one-half of Matthew derives almost verbatim from Mark, and an additional one-fourth from the hypothetical source Q whose provenience is unknown. Since eyewitness reports were given pre-eminence among early Christians, it seems absurd that an eyewitness should have needlessly made use of other men's documents. The unique one-fourth which the disciple might conceivably have contributed himself seems a strangely small part, and this section does not read like an account by an eyewitness.

Second, Matthew the disciple was hardly competent to make an artistic literary work. As a publican or tax collector for the Romans, he would have been cordially detested by Jews, to whom "publicans and sinners" was as much an indivisible epithet as "damyankee" used to be in the southern United States. In all probability he was not of the educated, religious Jewish classes; yet this writer was not only well versed in Jewish law, he was also a literary artist deeply infused with Jewish symbolism.

Third, the disciple Matthew, who in order to secure the position of tax collector must have been of mature years before A.D. 30, would probably not have lived until fifty years later, the approximate time of writing of this Gospel. Admittedly, such evidence is not clear cut and definite; nonetheless, it makes Matthew's having written this Gospel stand on the outmost verge of probability.[1]

Matthew could hardly have been written prior to A.D. 85. One must presume a lapse of some years after Mark's composition for the author of Matthew to have become acquainted with it, digested it, and fitted it into a scheme of his own. As to the place of its writing, the author's evident desire to attract Jewish readers into the Church has led some scholars to assume that it must have been composed for an important Jewish center like Alexandria or Caesarea. But communications in the Roman Empire made it easy to send the document from almost anywhere to anywhere. Jewish readers were many in the more populous parts of the entire empire. The complex artistic structure of Matthew, indicating careful work on the author's part, makes it probable that it was meant for wider use than any single area.

How Matthew's name became associated with this Gospel, it is impossible to state with assurance. An attractive theory comes from Eusebius' *Ecclesiastical History* (III.xxxix.16), in which he cited a second-century writer Papias of Hierapolis on Matthew: "Matthew arranged the sayings [logia] in the Hebrew language [i.e., in Aramaic], and each interpreted these as he was able." Eusebius himself assigned the Gospel to the disciple Matthew, but the reference to the logia carries perhaps a significance lost upon him.

That at least one collection of Jesus' sayings existed prior to the Gospels is generally believed. It is not unlikely that Matthew, a man trained in handling financial accounts, should have competently collected and arranged sayings of Jesus; one sees the work as suited to a man of his temperament. His name may have been transferred from the work he actually did to a work heavily indebted to it. As already noted, the ancient world was more concerned with the content of a book than with its authorship. This theory cannot be substantiated as fact, to be sure, yet it is a clear possibility.

[1] It should be noted that ascriptions of the Gospels to specific authors were made on other than factual evidence. Among other things, local church politics entered into claims of both the author and place of writing each Gospel.

The writer was probably a Jew of the Diaspora intimately acquainted with the Law and the Prophets. He was also a skillful Christian apologist. Like Paul, whose epistles he knew at least in part, he was deeply concerned for his race. Unlike Paul, whose efforts came to be directed primarily toward Gentiles, he apparently turned his attention toward the Jews. The conclusion of Acts strongly implies that by A.D. 60, Paul reluctantly came to the conclusion that Judaism and Christianity must go their separate ways. Four or five years earlier, his letter to the Romans had indicated that the rift between the two movements was too wide to be spanned.

Writing almost a quarter-century later, the author of Matthew may well be making a late, even a final, effort to reconcile the Jews to Christianity. The chances of success seemed to have improved since Paul's day. Of the two sects which had led opposition to Jesus and had continued to oppose his followers, the Pharisees must have suffered loss of confidence among the Diaspora for their having mingled, however unwillingly, with the forces which had brought the Jewish nation to ruin. The Sadducees had been so wrapped up in the affairs of the Temple that its destruction in A.D. 70 destroyed them also as a force. With these two forces gravely weakened or destroyed, the author of Matthew may have felt the time to be opportune to propagandize the badly shaken Jews of the Diaspora.

The structure of Matthew supports the hypothesis that it was directed primarily to Jewish readers. Although the writer appropriated 90 per cent of Mark, he also made use of the Q source and interspersed materials designated as *M*. His additions would have been best understood and appreciated only by readers steeped as Jews were in heritage and tradition. Half of the introduction, chapters 1 and 2, is given over to a genealogy. Before reaching the conclusion, chapters 26–28, he also makes a great deal of Jesus' reverence for the Law and the Prophets. One key idea in Matthew is expressed in the Sermon on the Mount, "Think not that I am come to destroy the law, or the prophets: I am not come to destroy, but to fulfill" (5:17). Twelve times the author points out that Jesus did or said something "that the Scriptures might be fulfilled." A telling symbolic feature of its organization is its division into five principal sections (3:1–7:28; 7:28–10:42; 11:1–13:53; 13:54–18:35; 19:1–25:46) to correspond with the five books of the Law. No careful Jewish reader could overlook this concern with the Law or fail to be moved by it. It would mean less to most Gentiles.

Something must be here said about Jewish concepts of the Law. The word *law* conveys to most people of the Western world the concept of a code of regulations, a concept stemming largely from the codified Roman law that has played so great a part in Western life. To the Jew, as the late William Barclay pointed out in his commentary on Matthew (pp. 123–24), the word could convey three different meanings. It could refer simply to the Ten Commandments. It could refer, as perhaps it most commonly did, to the first five books of the Bible, the Torah or Pentateuch. The phrase "the Law and the Prophets" also meant to them the whole of the Scriptures in so far as they had been canonized in Jesus' day, and possibly the Writings as well, though these books were not officially canonized until A.D. 90. Finally, it could also refer to the oral or scribal law.

As readers are well aware, the Old Testament contains in the Pentateuch extensive passages which lay out in detail the conduct of man toward man and of man toward God. Many of the regulations here laid down applied to earlier, more primitive life. Contrasted with the insights of the prophets, they show often less insight into the nature of God. Regulations of lasting import, as in Exodus 20:1–17, did not spell out right thinking and right conduct in detail.

Later Jewish thinkers reasoned that detailed rules for life might be rationally deduced from the general provisions of the Pentateuch. These should replace those now outmoded. Thus arose, perhaps beginning with the years of exile in the sixth century, the professional expounders of the Law known as the scribes. They came to have considerable influence and some jurisdictional powers under the Seleucid domination of Palestine. By the second century B.C. they belonged to the Hasidim, "the pious," men especially loyal to the Law. Many of them had formed themselves into a lay party which became known as Pharisees. The New Testament joining of "scribes and Pharisees" properly indicates their history.

The scribes believed that in the principles of the Pentateuch God had expressed his final word. It remained for them to derive from it regulations that would be as fitting to later times as those of the Pentateuch had been in their day. So they set to work. Life was far more complicated than it had been in primitive times. Directions had to be multiplied, and ultimately thousands were made. Jesus scathingly called them "heavy burdens and grievous to be borne" which by their myriad demands "shut up the kingdom of heaven against men" (Matt. 23:4, 13). Peter eloquently spoke against their being imposed upon Gentile Christians (Acts 15:10).

The scribes sincerely intended to aid the Jew to live as they felt God willed. As sometimes occurs when legalists gain a free hand, they built up a system in which action tended to displace spiritual feeling. The pious author of Psalm 119 wrote, "O how love I thy law!" It was a vital entity that served him as affectionately as he served it. Such affection would be difficult to assume toward the scribal law. Paul had earnestly tried to love it but was brought to despair by his failure.

It was against this oral or scribal law that Jesus, and later Paul, vigorously campaigned.[2] Jesus came, as He said, to fulfill the Law, that is, the provisions of the Old Testament law. In a sense, he did spiritually what the scribes had attempted to do legally; the provisions of the Sermon on the Mount clearly show this. In campaigning against the oral law, he strategically attacked it at a most vulnerable point, the provisions for observing the Sabbath, as all four Gospels testify. Mark and Luke, directed primarily to Gentiles, could be sure that the Sabbath and its observance was a universally known Jewish custom. Matthew's primarily Jewish readers among the Diaspora probably felt the severity of these Sabbath regulations and may well have already relaxed their strictest provisions. John uses them as the climactic force at the end of his composite dialectic between Jesus and the Pharisees (7–9).

The development of scribal Sabbath observance illustrates how

[2] The name oral Torah was applied to these regulations because they were taught by word of mouth. It was not until the third century B.C. that a written codification was made.

the scribes worked. In Exodus 20:8–11, where the general provision is stated, the emphasis lies upon the proscription of "any work" by man or beast during its observance. *Work* is not defined here, and the legalists had a field day in spelling out what the word specifically signified. They debated, for instance, whether a woman might lawfully lift her child on the Sabbath. They pronounced it Sabbath breaking to write two letters of the alphabet on that day, but the law was refined until it permitted a man to write on or with anything that left no permanent mark. One might heal on the Sabbath to preserve life, but the remedy must be postponed until the next day if the patient could survive without it.

In attacking the Sabbath regulations, Jesus not only struck at a weak point in the scribal code, he also reduced it to an absurdity in the eyes of all but the most stubborn legalists. The scribes and Pharisees immediately tried to remove him. To them law was a unit, and they realized how effective his attack at this salient would become if not averted.

This clarification of the term *law* must be carefully kept in mind. The Gospel writers for various reasons felt such explanation to be unnecessary. Those who wrote to Gentiles, no doubt, were content to show up to ridicule a system which made religion into mere ritual conduct; to give detailed discussion of the matter would serve no useful purpose. Matthew is addressed to readers who, for the most part, were already aware of the implied distinctions.

At the risk of possibly oversimplifying the situation, one may say that Jesus upheld the Pentateuch against the oral Torah. He did, however, observe several of its interpretations of the Mosaic code. In the so-called Sermon on the Mount, he repeatedly rejected the scribal interpretations to proclaim his "fulfilled" statement of the Mosaic Torah. He attacked "the tradition of the elders"—that is, the oral Torah—about ritual washing before meals and showed how Pharisaical evasion of provisions in the law made them escape heavy burdens which they had placed on other men's shoulders. His fulfillment of the Law was to give it a deeper and wider significance; as Paul declared in a flash of insight (Rom. 13:10), love is the fulfilling of the Law. In Galatians (3:24) Paul had metaphorically described the Law as the attendant to lead men safely to Jesus and his fulfilled law, which in spirit and intent agreed with the older law.

It is obvious that Matthew presumes an audience familiar with and reverential to Jewish law. This is not to say that the book champions Jewish Christianity against Paul's advocacy of the Gentile church. It repeatedly shows the author's sympathy with Paul's thinking and shows no support of the earlier Jerusalem church which practiced a Christianity zealous for the Jewish law (Acts 21:20). As propaganda, Matthew presents a picture that would appeal to Jews; the author repeatedly stresses points that Mark's or Luke's Gentile readers would not appreciate. Addressed to Jewish readers, his account demonstrates clearly the relation of the new faith to Judaism. At the same time, it categorically denies to the Jews their position as God's chosen people.

Probably by intent of the author, Matthew turned out to be useful to the early Church for other purposes than propaganda. It was organized to serve as a manual of instruction: materials of kindred nature were put together so as to be found with relative ease of reference.[3] In Matthew it was relatively easy to locate materials relating to conduct (our chapters 5–7), a collection of miracles (8-9), and a group of parables (13). A second valuable feature for instruction is its extensive reporting of Jesus' teaching. Theologians have stated that if they could have only one of the Gospels, they would wish it to be Matthew. It serves well as a "communicants' handbook" for neophytes as well as a reference book for students of the faith on more advanced stages. Possibly for this reason among others, when collections of the New Testament books began to be made into a single volume, Matthew commonly was placed foremost.

Its basic organizing principle, however, is for purposes of propaganda. To its Jewish readers, made aware of symbolic approaches to the Scriptures by both orthodox and heterodox expositors, the five major sections would clearly symbolize the five books of the Torah. Jesus' statement that he came to fulfill the Law would be reinforced by this form. The end of each of the five sections is

[3] Until the invention of printing, which standardized the amount of printed matter per page in an edition, indices and tables of contents could not be made.

indicated by the stereotyped words, "And when Jesus had ended these sayings . . . ."

Jesus is pictured as delivering his longest discourse on conduct, like Jahweh, on a mountain. That this location was deliberately chosen to point up the parallel, Luke's presentation makes apparent. In it something less than half of this material is spoken by Jesus on a plain; the rest is delivered in other settings throughout the Gospel. Neither writer was bound by the terms of propaganda to adhere strictly to the facts; each could arrange his materials to suit his purpose. Jewish teaching methods, of which James is an example, touched briefly on different subjects as Jesus did here. In Luke, written for a cultured Gentile audience, a different method is followed.

Matthew's beginning his book with an abridged genealogy of Jesus also points to Jewish readers. Gentiles would find no need for it, but Jewish readers needed evidence that as Messiah, Jesus was in the Davidic line of descent. This fact Matthew indicates both literally and symbolically. Not only does David figure in the lineage, but in verse 17 the author also points out that the names fall into three lists of fourteen generations each. Hebrews of the first century A.D. used letters of the alphabet as numerals. Since they wrote only the consonants, *David* was written as DVD. The numerical values of these letters amounted to 4+6+4, or 14. Cumbrous and oblique though such numerical symbolism appears to the modern reader, it was readily recognizable by the Hebrew.

Still another oblique hint to be found in the genealogy is the inclusion of three women; descent was reckoned by the male line. This notable departure from the norm naturally focused the reader's attention upon the three women. Two ideas are subtly suggested. First, Tamar (Gen. 38) and Bathsheba (2 Sam. 11) were both sinners, meriting death by stoning as adulteresses. Later in Matthew the "righteous" Pharisees censure Jesus for consorting with sinners. If David the national hero was descended from a "sinner," why should the Pharisees consider themselves to be defiled by such association? Second, Ruth was unquestionably a Gentile, a Moabite, a member of a nation that had originated from incestuous union of Lot with one of his daughters (Gen. 19:30–38); also Bathsheba, the wife of Uriah the Hittite, may well have been a Gentile. Again, the writer shows that the Jewish hostility to Gentiles is actually baseless. Thus Matthew early prepares the Jewish reader for a breaking down of his racial separatism, but in a way that will not alienate him.

Matthew consistently assigns the guilt for opposing and finally bringing Jesus to crucifixion to the Pharisees and Sadducees. In so doing, the writer is not only correct, but he also skillfully avoids casting any blame on his readers. He follows here the same path that Paul walked when he told the Jewish synagogue in Pisidian Antioch that "they that dwell at Jerusalem, and their rulers" (Acts 13:27–29) had been responsible for Jesus' rejection—not the Jews as a whole and certainly not those of the Diaspora. These culprits had led the Jewish nation to ruin and to the destruction of their holy Temple; they were discredited in the eyes of Matthew's readers.

The author's strategy appears at the beginning when one contrasts his account of John the Baptist with Luke's. In Luke, John excoriates "the multitude that came forth to be baptized of him as a "generation of vipers" (3:7); in Matthew (3:7–10) we read that this greeting is addressed to "many of the Pharisees and Sadducees come to his baptism"; and their claim to descent from Abraham is dismissed with the contemptuous hyperbole that God can raise up from the stones at their feet "children unto Abraham." Later in the account Matthew skillfully yet accurately diverts the blame from the Jews as a race to place it squarely upon their bigoted leaders.

Another point, here differentiating Matthew from Mark, lies in the space given to the temptation of Jesus: two verses in Mark, eleven in Matthew. Mark's readers probably knew that the Jews believed in the existence of an utterly evil being called *Diabolos* (the slanderer) in the Septuagint, though such a concept was alien to their habit of thought. They may have heard of the temptation and fall of Adam in Genesis. Luke's educated Gentile readers, like the Jews to whom Matthew wrote, would have been interested in the parallel between Adam and Christ; they were given an account parallel to Matthew's. Mark's readers would hardly have grasped the implications of Jesus' temptation; Mark contents himself with the mere mention of it.

The expanded account of the Temptation in Matthew and Luke probably reflects these two writers' acquaintance with the ideas of Paul. During the two decades following Paul's death, his letters were widely circulated and possibly made into collections. The author of Matthew had, no doubt, read at least some of these letters. He shares Paul's concern with the temptation of Jesus as the counterpart of that temptation of our first parents in Eden, when the Devil triumphed; in the later temptation, he failed. Readers would be aware, as Milton was centuries later, of the profound consequences following these symbolic confrontations. Whereas Luke's readers—in Luke, Paul's influence also appears strongly—might view it somewhat academically as Gentiles, Matthew's would see it as a matter also of traditional moment to their faith.

Matthew's quality as a Gospel designed to persuade Jewish readers becomes even more evident in the so-called Sermon on the Mount (5–7). Jewish readers would be peculiarly concerned with the relation of Jesus' words to the Mosaic law, while Gentile readers would not feel deeply involved in this relation. This discourse conforms in structure to the conventional rabbinical form of teaching in which without close logical arrangement or detailed discussion facets of a subject are briefly, tersely presented. Although it does conform to the classical Latin meaning of *sermo,* which in literature is exemplified by the *Sermones* (inaccurately called *Satires*) of Horace, the resemblance is probably coincidental. The readers of Matthew would rather be reminded of the rabbinical pattern familiar to them. The modern concept of a *sermo* or sermon as a formal discourse organized on classical rhetorical principles was well established before the days of Augustine, who, along with some of his predecessors as Christian leaders, was a trained rhetorician. The translators of the KJV and theologians of their day thought in Latin and probably failed to realize that English-speaking Christians might be puzzled by the use here of the term *sermon.*

Matthew's opening the sermon with the Beatitudes skillfully wins the good will of the pious Jew by presenting statements like those familiar to him from the Psalms and the Proverbs. The anaphora of *blessed* fixes in the mind the ideas presented. The injunction to good works (5:13–16) is equally in keeping with Jewish thought. Jewish readers are conciliated by pleasantly recognizing in Jesus' exhortations what they have already been taught.

In verse 17, the tone begins to alter. Jesus expresses full support of the Law and the Prophets, but adds that he has come to give them fuller meaning. This added meaning, it immediately appears, is not in line with scribal and Pharisaic teaching. Since the Pharisees controlled the teaching in the synagogue schools, their concepts of right religious conduct exercised strong influence upon Jewish religion. The word translated *righteousness* mean basically obedience to law. In 5:20, Jesus tells his hearers bluntly that the religious observances taught by the scribes and Pharisees were quite inadequate. To enter the kingdom of heaven, a man must go far beyond the practice, to the spirit which should motivate religious conduct. And it is not the niggling scribal guidelines that Jesus has in mind, but those deeper precepts of the Law and the Prophets, that Jesus insists must be obeyed to the full (5:18–19). Later (23:3) Jesus repeats his injunction: when the scribes and Pharisees teach the law of Moses, listen and obey, but avoid their evasions of the Mosaic law.

For the rest of chapter 5, Jesus details his condemnation of the concept of Law as spelled out by the scribes. It is not only the act, but the motive that leads to it, which constitutes sin. He frankly abandons the authority of "them of old time" to declare "But I say unto you . . . ." This formula occurs ten times in the first half of the sermon. The teachers regularly cited authorities for their statements, using the equivalent of our modern footnotes to this end. The Law came by direction from God; the Prophets regularly stated that the work of God came to them. To the Jewish reader Jesus' assumption of similar authority was either blasphemous or the word of God himself.

Such teaching, coupled with healing on the Sabbath, soon to be reported, quickly brought upon Jesus the wrath of the proponents of regulation. They quickly rallied against this heretic and blasphemer. But the sermon had already added specific details to the charge. Practice of their code by its teachers he declared to be largely ostentation. They prayed and gave to others publicly for praise; one should do such service in secret. Ostentatious fasting is equally the conduct of an actor on the stage; when one fasts, he does not call attention to his conduct. Try to win God's favor, not men's. Confident in His care, one should put his trust in God.

With such admonitions Jesus made the Mosaic law more relevant to daily life than the ritualistic scribes could do. The Mosaic law had spelled out prohibitions, as was probably the best way to control men for centuries after it. Jesus, in the spirit of the prophets (cf. Mic. 6:8), substituted affirmative purpose for Mosaic prohibition. Man should aim at divine perfection, not merely at avoidance of sin.

In his advice about taking thought for one's future, Jesus employed hyperbole. Oriental peoples were familiar with this rhetorical device and would know better than to take it literally. The same device startles the reader as chapter 7 opens: "Judge not, that ye be not judged." This cannot be taken literally. T. S. Eliot declared that criticism is as inevitable as breathing; every choice one makes is in fact a judgment. Verse 2 supplies the principle: A man is judged according to his own habit in judging. Applications follow: Do not condemn a man for minor degrees of blindness—literal or metaphorical—when your own is major. Do not make light of holy or important matters.

Reliance upon God is known by its results. God answers prayer. Arguing from analogical probability, Jesus says: you evil human beings give your children what they need; surely God who is good will do better than you. In this, he adds, lies illustrated the substance of the Law and the Prophets; do for others as you wish them to do for you. What you should try to do, God does perfectly. To do this will not be easy: most men miss the narrow gate that leads to God.

Hyperbole is the emphasizing figure in these admonitions. "Everyone that asketh receiveth" is in effect hyperbolic, in that it does not detail the nature of the asking; so is giving one's son a stone instead of bread, and the minutely small number who achieve eternal life. But hyperbole gives way to sound, even homely advice: the comparison of false prophets—leaders of the strange aberrations which crop up amid Christian growth—to wolves disguised as sheep which, in Milton's words "creep, and intrude, and climb into the fold." It has always been the case that successful careers like that of Jesus attract charlatans who cling to them for their own gain.

Shifting his figure, Jesus bids his listeners to test the tree by its fruit, and to cut down what bears bad fruit. Shift to a third figure introduces the sycophantic, profit-seeking person who with empty adulation addresses him as Lord: fawning supplication will not gain him admission to heaven. The man who listens to Jesus' sayings and follows their guidance is like a firmly founded house built on a rock: storms cannot sway it or topple it. The man who listens without obedience will topple under pressure like a house built on sand.

Matthew concludes this collection of sayings with the comment of Mark (1:22) that the people who had been listening with the twelve were astonished (in Greek, "knocked out") by his teaching: it was authoritative, not based on another's authority. To the Jew reading Matthew this statement reveals far more than readers of Mark could realize.

Readers trained in the customary principles of English composition may not readily detect the organizational principle governing this collection of Jesus' sayings. The theme—the God-fearing man's belief and conduct—is amply evident, but the sections do not follow the logical or natural sequence we are accustomed to use. The connection is associative rather than logical, somewhat after the manner in which Emerson threaded his paragraphs made up of gnomic utterances to form an essay. The Jewish readers whom the writer had in mind were inheritors of a long rabbinical tradition of discourse in such associational patterns. It appears again in the Epistle of James, which is also addressed to the Diaspora. As the Church became Hellenized, such writing fell into abeyance as writers trained in Western composition took the lead. The Church, with its practice of delivering homilies upon verses or passages taken out of context, did not seek for connexity in the Sermon on the Mount.

The strategy of placing this discourse near the beginning of Matthew is superb. It clearly supports Jesus' claim to fulfill the Law and the Prophets and separates him sharply from the formalistic Pharisees and Sadducees. In Mark, addressed to less-educated Gentiles, such an introduction to Jesus' teaching would have proved far less effective. Only readers trained in Jewish law and tradition could have derived from it insight into Christian fulfillment of Judaism.

Matthew closes the sermon with a categorical statement of Jesus' authoritative teaching. The writer must now support the right of Jesus to take such drastic steps, for, however closely they might harmonize with much of Jewish thought in the late first century, their basis—Jesus' assertions—departs radically from Jewish religious and legal habit. No ordinary man could claim such authority. His power must be demonstrated. It is by nine miracles performed by Jesus, seven of which are reported in detail. A tree is known by its fruit, Jesus had said.

Events that run counter to observed patterns of nature or life were perhaps more effective evidence of extraordinary power in the first century A.D. than they are today. We realize how far the unknown transcends the known and, in some sense, expect the unexpected. The rudimentary science of that era, largely mythology, contained little mystery and, as William Cullen Bryant remarked, professed to contain all the answers about the world. Consequently, interruption of what myth or experience set forth was far more startling and arresting then than now.

Although learned men were questioning the truth in their myths, the mass of men, Hebrew as well as Gentile, still accepted them as final answers about man and nature. To the Jew a miracle was even more astounding than to a Gentile. His over-all myth or manner of accounting for the world and events was that Jahweh directed everything that happened. If, therefore, anyone should alter what was accepted as Jahweh's normal way of conducting affairs, he must be Jahweh himself or his agent.

The nine recounted miracles (Matthew 8–9) countered several beliefs about Jahweh's established course. Leprosy, universally known to be incurable, was healed by Jesus. He even had the leper submit to the customary physical examination prescribed by Jewish law, to prove the genuineness of this healing. Elisha had by divine power healed the leper Naaman (2 Kings 5)—a memorable parallel that established Jesus as Jahweh's agent. The healing of the centurion's servant without Jesus' even being near him broke with another long-established belief that a healer had to touch the body of the person to be healed—again an indication of special power. Moreover, it was a Roman who had realized the power resident in Jesus, not a Jew; a renewal of the hint in the genealogy that a Jewish line of descent did not separate Jew from Gentile racially. Jesus declared the centurion's faith to be greater than any he had found among Jews. The third miracle falls into the more normal pattern of healing through contact, but the number of healings mentioned with it give it distinction.

One class of miracles was concerned with disease; a second class indicated control over the forces of nature. When a sudden storm on the lake threatened to sink the boat in which Jesus and his disciples were crossing, he was so exhausted that he would have slept through it if his terrified disciples had not called upon him to save them. In calming the waves with a word, he made it clear that he had power over the forces of nature. The disciples' rhetorical question, "What manner of man is this, that even the winds and the sea obey him?" telegraphs the answer that he must be more than man.

Like Mark, Matthew builds slowly before categorically declaring Jesus' deity. In Mark a premature disclosure would have confused the issue for his readers; in Matthew the delay gives the Jewish reader time to accustom himself to the concept of a deity who is not only one "person." A propagandist must make his thesis as palatable as he can before asking his readers to swallow it.

As the ancients viewed the fifth miracle, it belongs to a slightly different class. An insane man, they believed, was not ill physically. Bodily illness was caused by some demon, but insanity was caused by a demon which had gotten control, "possession," of his mind rather than of his body. The account naturally accepts contemporary beliefs. The demons inhabiting the maniacs' minds, recognizing who Jesus really was, knew that he could exorcise them and begged for another dwelling. Here a note of comedy enters the report. Jesus permitted these demons to enter a herd of swine, which then rushed madly downhill into the lake and were drowned. The mere collocation of swine with Jews who abominated them gives a humorous tone to the episode, and so adds variety to the series. The sixth miracle, reported in Mark with more detail, presents Jesus as forgiving a paralytic man's sins and substantiating his right to do so by then healing him. His implicit assertion of deity is reinforced by the evidence of his preceding miracles.

In the resurrection of the ruler's daughter (9:18–26), to which Mark devotes more space, the assertion of Jesus' deity reaches the highest stage short of categorical statement. It caps the evidence of the previously reported miracles. Accumulating evidence without specific statement allows the reader to reach the conclusion himself. Assertion of it could open the way for adverse argument.

The next miracle iterates the point of the first, that the person to be healed must participate in the healing. The leper had to take action; the two blind men must believe in Jesus' power to heal them. In the final miracle (9:32–33) the dumb man could not verbally express his faith, but Jesus apparently recognized its presence in him.

The catalog of miracles concludes on a somber note. To the unorganized masses who declared, "It was never so seen in Israel," the legalistic Pharisees smoothly retorted, "He casteth out demons through the prince of devils"—hardly a logical response, as Mark (3:22–26) points out. In Matthew, Jesus' reduction of this reply to an absurdity is temporarily postponed for later use.

Matthew expands Mark's brief report on the sending out of the twelve with warnings about how they should expect to be received. For the first time in the New Testament they are called "apostles" (10:2) instead of the customary "disciples." Matthew's emphasis on their being sent this time only to Jewish villages, which is not mentioned in Mark, is especially appealing to his Jewish readers. They are reminded that Jesus was himself a Jew who wished to serve his own people. He gave them the first opportunity to enter his kingdom, an idea frequently appearing in Paul's epistles. The message is as Jewish as the preaching of John the Baptist. Matthew's readers were surely aware that in their day the Church was predominantly Gentile; they perhaps needed to be told that Jesus sent his envoys to Jews first.

The sayings of Jesus which are assembled in Matthew for instruction of the apostles were equally applicable to the Christian situation in his own day. They realistically assess the state of affairs in Palestine in Jesus' day as well as Christian fortunes at the time of writing. The envoys are to enter houses only when invited, in towns that are hospitable to them. They are symbolically to shake the dust off their sandals as they leave places which do not welcome them; the fate of such does not bear thinking on. The envoys themselves will be "as sheep in the midst of wolves"; they must expect persecution on account of their message, which paradoxically will have lethal results even as it heals. It will set members of families against each other—"a man's foes shall be they of his own household." Jesus came to bring not peace but a sword, which might be viewed rather as a scalpel: its function is to bring mercy and healing, and it corrects what is evil already; it does not cause evil. The emissaries may even be killed, but "he that loseth his life for my sake shall find it." These sayings superficially present a bleak picture, not unlike what many Jews anticipated would attend the Messiah's coming, and the victory promised is unlike that won by any earthly conqueror.

Insertion of this uncompromising discourse at this point marks the clear separation of Christianity from Judaism. Previous chapters contained teachings that were, on the whole, acceptable to an open-minded Jew. He might feel that he could accept them without abandoning his Jewish faith, for the attacks made upon the Pharisees would strike responsive chords in him. In chapter 10, however, the cleavage between the two is unmistakable. Here it is pointed out that opposition to the new faith will come from Jew as well as from Gentile. Jews of the Diaspora could live on fairly peaceable terms with Gentile neighbors; Christian and non-Christian, in spite of Christian attempts to get along with the status quo, could not do so. The man who embraces Christianity is "taking up his cross" in the sure expectation of persecution and possible violent death as a malefactor. In plain terms this discourse separates the men from the boys. Having done what he could to conciliate Jews, the author evidently feels constrained to show the somber prospects. Such a statement, in common fairness to his readers, could hardly have been delayed longer.

After the grim picture of chapter 10, the account is resumed with episodes calculated to restore the appeal that Jesus' personality and program would have for the readers. The author accomplishes this skillfully with two collections of material: first (chapter 11), with a report of Jesus' mighty works and what they demonstrate, and second (chapters 12–15), with an account of several of Jesus' encounters with the arrogant, unpopular Pharisees.

In the first, Jesus upbraids those Jews who had heard John's preparatory evangelism and his own ministry with its reinforcement of healing and miracle. The notoriously wicked Phoenician cities Tyre and Sidon will fare better than they in the day of judgment because the Phoenicians would have listened to him had they had opportunity. Capernaum, his Galilean headquarters, will have its stubborn pride brought down to Hades, worse than even Sodom with all its unnatural vices. The "wise and prudent" cannot receive him; only those with childlike trust will do so; and to those who accept him, he promises rest of spirit.

This excoriation leads naturally into the discomfiture of the Pharisees which follows. The prayer of Jesus which concludes chapter 11, through Jesus' reference to himself as the Son of God the Father, explicitly asserts his deity which so far had been implicit. To Matthew's readers, shaken by this assertion, the defeats of the Pharisees here reported indicate unmistakably that their rigid codification of the Law is indefensible. If their obsession with the Law is proved erroneous, perhaps the person who has upset their position may be correct in his assertion that he is the Son of God. The concept here advanced by Jesus unsettles the Jews' central religious distinction from the surrounding polytheism when it is first stated, but if the Pharisees who control Jewish education can be worsted, even so upsetting an idea may at least receive consideration by a thoughtful Jew.

Like all the other Gospel writers, the author of Matthew opens his attack at the weakest point of the oral Torah, the Sabbath laws. He first reports a ludicrous detail of it. Jesus' disciples, walking on a Sabbath morning through a grainfield, had casually plucked heads of grain, rubbed them between their palms to strip off the awn, and eaten the kernel. The unbridled legalism of the scribes had classed the plucking of the grain as reaping and the rubbing off of the awn as winnowing, labors forbidden on the Sabbath. The alert Pharisees instantly charged the disciples with this infraction, for which they held Jesus as their teacher to be responsible. Jesus reminded them sharply that David without blame ate the sacrificial bread from the altar when he was starving—a far more flagrant act by their code. He reminded them that on every Sabbath officiating priests blamelessly profane the Sabbath law by offering sacrifice. Then in harmony with his claim to deity, he added that if these two cases carried no blame, the disciples were surely not guilty: they were acting with the consent of One greater than the Temple. To clinch his case, he quoted from Hosea (6:6), a prophet with deep insights, "I will have mercy, and not sacrifice." The Law, like the Sabbath, was made for man.

When Jesus shortly after this entered a synagogue, he found there a man with a withered hand who had quite possibly been planted there to test him further. The Pharisees asked him if it was lawful to heal on the Sabbath. The case was well chosen, for there was no urgent need to heal the man on that day. Jesus responded with another question: If you may lawfully pull an animal out of the mud on the Sabbath, why may you not help a man hampered by a crippling disease? Having posed here the sort of quibbling question in which the scribes themselves delighted, he healed the man. Through these encounters Jesus rendered the niggling Sabbath regulations of the scribes absurd. Realizing their vulnerability but clinging to their system, the Pharisees immediately began to scheme his destruction.

To escape their plots, Jesus withdrew from that area on a tour of teaching and healing. He tried unsuccessfully to persuade the crowds to keep silent about his whereabouts. This attempt Matthew sees as a fulfillment of Isaiah 42:1–3. The relevance of this passage is not wholly clear to modern readers, but often New Testament citations from the Old are, by our standards, not closely applicable. Obliquely, the citation makes two significant points. First, it ties Jesus into the line of Old Testament prophecy of a servant of God who was to come. In so doing, it relates Jesus to Jewish messianic hopes. Although this servant is by no means depicted as militant, he will, with God's spirit on him, succeed in his task. Second, Isaiah emphasized this servant's mission to the Gentiles. He will be their judge, and they will trust him. Coming after Jesus' tirade against Jewish refusal to accept him (Matt. 11:16–24), this acceptance of the servant by the Gentiles—which Matthew's readers knew had taken place—was bitter medicine. As fulfillment of prophecy, it could hardly be refuted.

On a second occasion when Jesus healed a deaf and dumb man, Matthew included the Pharisees' comment that he had "cast out devils . . . by Beelzebub the prince of the devils" (12:22–28). Jesus quickly pointed out their absurdity. A house divided against itself, he said, cannot stand. (The parallel with recent Jewish history is ironically pointed up by Matthew's quotation. Jewish defeat by the Romans had been materially aided by their factional strife. They could feel keenly the truth of Jesus' generalization.) To think of Satan as casting out Satan is ridiculous.

Incidentally, He added, if I do this by Satan's power, who empowers your Pharisaic exorcists to do so? Ask them. If, however, I act by God's power, then the kingdom of God is come through me. Either stand on my side or oppose me. There is no middle ground; a neutral stand is opposition to me. Your refusal to admit that I act through the spirit of God is the unforgivable sin against the Holy Ghost.

Following Jesus' severe charges against them, some of the scribes and Pharisees persisted in asking him for some sign to substantiate his claims. Quite understandably, Jesus angrily called them an evil and adulterous generation—adulterous in the Old Testament metaphorical sense of being unfaithful to God. The only sign, he added cryptically, for them was the allegory of Jonah, who was three days in the belly of the whale. Beyond stating that it typified his being three days and three nights in the heart of the earth, he did not explain. Developing the analogy with Jonah, he added that the people of wicked Nineveh had listened to Jonah, as the Queen of Sheba had listened to Solomon's wisdom; the Pharisees, however, were listening to one greater than Jonah or Solomon, but they would not heed him.

Beginning with the quotation from Isaiah and running throughout this encounter is the undertone of the Jews' losing their birthright, much as Paul had written in Romans. The Messiah will be accepted by the Gentiles; the people of Nineveh and the Queen of Sheba had been open minded; but the recalcitrance of Pharisaic leaders would bring—in Matthew's day had already brought—the nation to ruin. Discomfited Jews of the late first century would thus have been led to consider favorably the universal brotherhood offered by Christians.

Chapter 13 is a collection of parables which show what the kingdom of heaven offers men. To those borrowed from Mark, Matthew adds five more. The new parable concerning sowing of seed relates the scattering of weeds sown by an enemy in the master's newly planted field. The weeds must be allowed to grow until the harvest, when they will be separated from the grain and burned. It is a comment on the question How can a good God permit evil to exist? The tremendous power of the kingdom is in the next parable likened to that of yeast working silently but irresistibly.

Three more parables further define this kingdom. "Treasure hid in a field" was less rare then than now, for banking was not available to ordinary men. Matthew's readers, no doubt, knew of instances in which such a deposit, lost through its owner's sudden death, had been found by another. The dealer in jewels who risked all his assets in one supreme venture was another not unknown character. Finally, the nets with their miscellaneous catch of fish, like the parable of the tares, was everyday experience to people whose meat was often fish from the sea.

These parables subtly offered the Jewish reader, still mourning the shattered Jewish nation, a new, powerful, yet peaceful and life-giving substitute. As an appendix, Jesus' rejection in Nazareth rounds out the account of the ruinous stubbornness of the Jews that was to ruin the nation. Like Paul in Pisidian Antioch (Acts 13:27), Matthew plays upon the difference between the Jews of Palestine and the Diaspora. The former were responsible for Jesus' rejection, not the latter, who constituted probably the greater part of Matthew's readers.

Matthew's account of John the Baptist's death, which parallels Mark's, brings in that bumbling sot Herod Antipas. The story is here used partly to picture the inept and tyrannical rule over the Palestinian Jews. In so doing it turns the readers' favor farther toward the new kingdom of heaven. It shows further the loving care with which Jesus watched over his followers.

Several of Jesus' disciples had previously followed John, and all were downcast at his arbitrary execution. Jesus took them for recuperation from the shock to an unpopulated district across the lake, but his attempt to escape the crowds was unsuccessful. The account of the miraculous feeding of the five thousand Matthew takes from Mark. He adds to the account of Jesus' coming to the disciples across the water the revealing detail of Peter's rash request to come to Jesus on the water and of Peter's failure to do so through lack of faith. Such a concatenation of events—healings, multiplication of food, and now a spectacular demonstration of special power in Jesus that an apostle lacked—restored his disciples' confidence in him and produced their categorical assertion: "Of a truth thou art the Son of God"—a conviction which the author desires his readers to echo.

Although these astounding events must have become known to the scribes and Pharisees, they made no impression on their stubbornly fixed minds. They renewed the contest by introducing additional legal and ritual trivia, showing themselves even more clearly as small minded in contrast with the vital campaign and teaching of Jesus. This time they charged the disciples with failure to wash in the ritually prescribed manner before meals as "the tradition of the elders" prescribed. Understandably exasperated, Jesus countered with their morally greater infraction in avoiding the duty of supporting their parents by the device of corban. He charged them with empty worship without any love of God, following the man-made oral Torah instead of the Mosaic commandments.

To make his position more widely known, he called the crowd to hear his words on the right religious attitudes: what enters into a man cannot defile him, but what proceeds out of his mouth can do so. The disciples warned Jesus that he had mortally offended the Pharisees, but he contemptuously dismissed such opponents. As blind leaders of the blind, they were leading the people off the right path, but they would soon be replaced and destroyed.

Jesus did, however, avoid Pharisaic attack by making a journey to the extreme northwest boundary of Galilee. There Matthew reports from Mark the episode of Jesus' conversation with the Levantine woman. After their exasperation with the Pharisees, the readers could be expected to read with pleasure of Jesus' acceptance of a Gentile as far removed from Pharisaism as could be imagined. Another impression is here made upon them of the closer association with Gentiles which they would practice in the Church.

Upon his return to Galilee, Jesus miraculously fed more than four thousand people. This report may conceivably be a doublet: that is, a slightly varied account of the earlier miraculous feeding, possibly handed down in a different account. Since they are reported so close together, the author of Matthew may have thought of them as two miracles. He may, however, have been following the occasional practice of Old Testament writers, who would report variant accounts of the same event. (The two accounts of the duel with Goliath are an instance.) Lacking footnotes, they could not relegate one variant to the lower position.

In chapter 16 the Pharisees are for the first time reinforced by their enemies the Sadducees. They ask for some sign from Jesus that will display his power. Jesus sarcastically responds that they can read weather signs but not the signs of the times—another deeply significant reference to the coming national catastrophe. This episode apparently serves chiefly to introduce Jesus' analogy of Pharisaic teaching to yeast. It contrasts ironically with Jesus' earlier use of the image as a symbol of the kingdom of heaven. The flaw in the reasoning of the Pharisees is at first barely perceptible. Their treatment of the Law as a code or ritual had gradually, like yeast, supplanted the motivating love of God which had originally inspired it. To Matthew the disciples' finally grasping this point was of considerable importance: it indicated a long forward stride in their education.

For their "final examination" Jesus takes his disciples up onto a spur of Mount Hermon. It is on a mountain, as when Jesus delivered his sermon, that through Peter they declare their belief in Jesus as Messiah and "the Son of the living God." Jesus' response to Peter contains statements omitted by Mark (Matt. 16:18–19). Mark's Gentile readers might in the light of contemporary Jewish militancy have misconstrued these added statements as subversive. Matthew's Jewish readers knew that any danger of Jewish uprising had been effectually removed by the fall of Jerusalem. Jesus' words, which would not then be misinterpreted, pointed to spiritual matters in which his readers might be supposed to have developed some interest.

Jesus' response has had momentous interpretations. The medieval church signified by the crossed keys on the pope's crest that as Peter's successor he had full authority on earth and in heaven. Since the Reformation, Protestants have challenged this claim. Jesus, they say, was actually punning on the Greek name Petros and the Greek word for rock (*petra*). "You are Petros and on this *petra* I will build my Church." Such punning was acceptable practice in both Greek and Hellenistic speech. The Vulgate was able to preserve this pun, English translations cannot. As New Testament epistles amply demonstrate, belief in Jesus' deity as Son of God was the basic doctrine of the infant Church. Protestant apologists declare that the *petra* which is the foundation of the Church is not Peter but Peter's statement as spokesman for the twelve. The binding and loosing, it is added, which are here entrusted to Peter (16:19) are shortly thereafter powers given to the twelve (18:18): the Greek verb in the latter passage is in the plural form. Lasting ecclesiastical quarrels, which have in some cases caused wars, have been instigated by the dual interpretation of these words.

The concept of Jesus as God entailed such revolutionary thought in his Jewish readers that Matthew introduced it gradually, in the hope also of impressing it upon them by iterated implication. The transfiguration which occurred a week later was peculiarly suited to convince Jewish readers of Jesus' claim to be fulfilling the Law and the Prophets. It presented—again on a mountain—Jesus conversing with Moses and Elijah, the personifications of the sacred books. The event was a mystical experience for Peter, James, and John. Such experience was not alien to Jewish or Gentile thought; both traditions reported divine epiphanies. These were not miraculous occurrences, but simply extensions of experience beyond the level of everyday awareness. The voice heard by the three disciples as the vision faded gave divine sanction to Peter's declaration. Symbolically, the speaker remained invisible, as to Moses on Mount Sinai. Readers would inevitably transfer the divine direction to listen to him to themselves.

Immediately after Peter's declaration of faith in Jesus, Jesus tried without success to impress upon the twelve his imminent death in Jerusalem. After the disciples who had not witnessed the transfiguration had failed to heal an afflicted man, Jesus renewed his attempt to convince them that he must die. This was apparently all they could grasp of his words, and they were naturally depressed. Occupied with the notion of an earthly Messiah, they ignored his promise of his resurrection.

Mention of a Messiah always carried with it the concept of an insurrection against Rome, a subject hardly to be calmly considered by a Jew after the fearful fate of Jerusalem. To avoid such a connotation, the author of Matthew inserts here an arresting story of Jesus paying his tax to Rome. As Son of God, it implies, Jesus did not have to pay tribute; he did so to avoid offending the authorities. However one regards the near-magical account, it is clearly aimed at denying any subversive intent in him.

Still worrying the idea of Jesus' earthly kingdom, the disciples, thinking probably of personal advancement, asked Jesus who would be the greatest man in it. He effectively squelched their ambitions and at the same time reiterated the nonpolitical character of his kingdom by setting before them a small child and declaring that unless they became childlike (obviously not childish) in humble trust in him, they could not even become citizens in it. Proceeding associatively in true rabbinic fashion, the author records next Jesus' warning that whoever in any way led astray a childlike citizen of his kingdom was a traitor to him. Childlike innocence, Matthew earlier showed, must not be accompanied by childlike inexperience. In counseling his disciples for their field trip (10:16), Jesus had warned them that though they went forth "as sheep in the midst of wolves," they must be paradoxically "as wise as serpents, and harmless as doves." To take an analogy as completely parallel is misleading.

Chapters 18–19 are organized around the unifying image of the child. From care for children, Jesus shifts to conduct among brothers in the Christian family. How should one deport himself toward a brother who has injured him? As Paul also advised, he should settle the disagreement out of court, and as a last resort appeal to the Church[4] for arbitration. If this attempt fails also, he is to avoid that brother thenceforth.

Peter's restless attention fixed on the idea of forgiveness in the preceding admonition. Should a man forgive an offender more than seven times (18:21)? Jesus' response is that forgiveness should not be calculated but infinite. But the offender must genuinely repent, as the following parable shows. A king found his steward short in his accounts by the astronomical amount of ten thousand talents. When the steward showed willingness to make a restitution far beyond his powers, the king forgave him the debt. Immediately thereafter the steward threw into jail a man who owed him a trifling sum. At this the king rebuked his unjust steward, rescinded his pardon, and permanently removed him from favor.

With this parable Matthew concluded the action in Galilee. The action in chapters 19–20 took place en route to Jerusalem. The theme of chapter 18 continued to occupy his report nonetheless. After twelve verses which substantially repeat Mark on divorce, he clinched the effect of the discourse centering on the child image. When Jesus' disciples attempted to prevent mothers from bringing their children to him for his blessing, he sternly reproved them: "Of

[4] *Ekklesia*, the word translated as "church," (18:17), represented at times the word for "synagogue," according to Lowther Clarke.

such is the kingdom of heaven." Such a sudden reversion to the writer's previous image adds to the considerable force of the image itself.

Like Mark, Matthew employs the literary device of the journey to string together a number of episodes. With some addition it follows Mark's account. The major addition (19:1–12) relates to divorce. After Jesus' strict interpretation of this law, his disciples despairingly comment that it is better not to marry at all. Jesus replies substantially as Paul wrote in 1 Corinthians 7, that some men are better married, while others are better single. Again Peter blurts out a comment that they have abandoned everything to follow him. To this self-righteous remark Jesus responds with ironic overtones that at his enthronement they will sit on twelve thrones to judge the twelve tribes. But he adds a cryptic warning (19:30): "But many that are first shall be last; and the last shall be first." Their complacency is unwarranted.

Matthew's longest personal contribution to these episodes is a parable designed to indicate the terms of admission into the kingdom of heaven. He tells how a landowner hired men to work in his grape harvest: some at dawn, others at various times during the day, and the final laborers when little time remained to work. All received the same wage. Those who had worked longer naturally objected to the disproportionate pay, but the employer reminded them that he had stated no specific wage to any and that he had the right to do as he thought best with his own money. However modern labor unions may look at such a rate of pay, to argue this point is to think anachronistically as well as to miss the story's application. The all-wise God has the right to reward effort for him according to his wisdom and generosity: his ways are above our ways as Isaiah (55:8–9) had declared. Following Peter's pompous claim for the disciples, the tenor of the parable is unmistakable. Jesus did not, however, overcome their obsession, as the next episode of James's and John's mother indicates.

Matthew incorporates nearly all that Mark reports of Passion Week, but with extensive additions; some events are more closely tied to Jewish custom or prophecy, and some variation occurs in the order of events. Matthew, for example, has Jesus cleanse the Temple on Palm Sunday instead of the day after. The chief priests and scribes, "sore displeased," feebly object, "Do you hear what the crowd says?" Jesus responds with the statement (Psalms 8:2) that God had perfected the praise from the mouths of nursing babes.

For the remainder of Matthew, it will generally be sufficient to indicate additions to Mark's report.

After the exchange of questions designed to best the opponent (Matthew 21:23–28, Mark 11:27–33), Matthew inserts a pungent parable unmistakably aimed at Jesus' enemies. A man told his sons to work in his vineyard. One refused, but later obeyed; the other agreed to work but did not. The two are specimens recognizable to all who know boys. The former represents to Matthew's readers the converted Gentiles or, perhaps, themselves. The latter obviously points to the regularly disobedient Jews who had constantly broken the covenants with God. Jesus' opponents are forced grudgingly to admit that the first boy was more obedient than the second. Jesus then forcibly drives in his point: even tax gatherers and prostitutes will enter the kingdom of heaven before them. The first two believed John the Baptist's preaching and repented; the others did not.

There follows the second parable of the vineyard and the citation of Psalms 118:22–23—the parable from Mark, the reference to the Psalm added by Matthew (21:42). Jesus obviously points to himself as the rejected stone which has been made the cornerstone of the kingdom. By the action of this stone, he adds, the kingdom of God shall be taken from them and given to "a nation bringing forth the fruits thereof": Judaism as the Jewish leaders know it will be disinherited and disfranchised. Jews of the Diaspora could hardly deny the accuracy of Jesus' condemnation of Judaism, while they could see themselves, along with Christian Gentiles, as being offered citizenship in this kingdom.

For all their fury, Jesus' opponents dared not brave the enthusiastic Passover crowd to arrest him openly, and Matthew continues to press his attack by parables. A king invited many guests to his son's wedding feast. When he sent them word that the feast was ready, they would not come. He sent other messengers to them, but some ignored the couriers while others assaulted and even killed them. In justifiable anger he destroyed these insulting persons. To replace them as guests, he sent his messengers to the crossroads to invite passers-by to the feast. A large crowd assembled. One guest came without the proper wedding garb and offered no excuse for this slight. He was accordingly expelled. The parable restates the rejection of people like the scribes and Pharisees. It further warns those whom these self-righteous Jews had scorned: if you are to be citizens of the new kingdom, you must act worthy of it.

Matthew reports a greatly expanded condemnation of these scribes and Pharisees (23:1–39). They "sit in Moses' seat"—probably a reference to the seat occupied by the teacher in the synagogue, who was thought of as Moses' spokesman when speaking thus *ex cathedra*. One should do as they say, but not as they do. They prescribe in their oral Torah heavy burdens for the faithful—this is in addition to the truly Mosaic law—but do not obey their own rules except when they wish to be "seen of men." They wear wide fringes on their robes and elaborate amulets. They love prominent seats at dinners and in synagogues, and delight in being reverentially greeted as rabbi. *You*, Jesus commands his followers, are to avoid any such claims to authority or knowledge, for the greatest among you shall be your servant. Jesus thereupon enters into a denunciation of the scribes and Pharisees in true Oriental detail and charges them with responsibility for all the woes to come upon Jerusalem.

The total effect of Matthew's additions to Mark in this confrontation is to make more evident to his Jewish readers the errors in Jewish leadership that had brought the nation to destruction.

The eschatology of chapter 24 fits naturally here. The disciples as they leave the Temple following this encounter point with amazement to the magnificent structure. On the whole, with slight modifications the account here parallels Mark. One interesting addition of interest to Jewish readers is the comparison of the Parousia (the coming of Jesus to rule) to the times of Noah. Then, too, men lived forgetful of all but earthly pleasures until the moment the flood came and carried them all away.

At the end of chapter 24 and throughout chapter 25, Matthew's account adds in parables to the statement of Mark about being ready for the end. Two undeveloped parables picture the householder who is always on guard because he cannot know when a thief may dig through the clay wall of his house, and the faithful steward who keeps alert and watchful over his master's interests because he does not know when the master will come to check on his work.

These are followed by two carefully elaborated parables of the ten virgins and the talents. Both vividly portray aspects of life familiar to the ancient world: the wedding feast, whose customs were basically similar for Jew and Gentile, and the custom of staking one's servants to invest for one's own gain. The stories are too familiar and too clear in application to need extensive comment. It is, perhaps, needless to point out that while the word *talent* means today a gift in a man that makes him competent in some way, in New Testament times it represented a large sum of money, usually standardized as a weight of silver valued at approximately one thousand dollars. Its purchasing power in antiquity, when a few pennies could buy a day's labor, was from twenty to forty times its power today. The master gave each servant a generous amount of capital to invest. Each of the first two realized 100 per cent profit on his capital. The third, cowardly and distrusting his master, simply kept safely what had been given him, with no attempt to invest it.

The Parousia and its final judgment of men is pictured in another parable, a judgment scene familiar to both Jewish and Gentile beliefs. All nations will be assembled before Jesus' throne, where he will separate men according to their merits into two parts, as a shepherd separates sheep from goats. The sheep on his right hand are invited into inheritance in his kingdom because they had befriended him in his need. When they cannot remember having done him any such kindness, he responds that what they have done for any of his needy brethren they have done for him. When the goats, condemned for failure to befriend him, brazenly ask when they had ever failed to do so, they are told that their failure to serve his brethren in need is failure to serve him. This group goes into eternal punishment, the former into life eternal.

Such parables sharply point out to Matthew's Jewish readers the necessity of joining with Gentile Christians in the new Church. Jews, it is clear, have no special place in the kingdom. Their course has abandoned the way outlined by God for the Jews, as Paul also had said, while Christianity fulfilled the Law and the Prophets. The recent tragedy of the Jewish nation supported Matthew's claim; his propaganda was difficult to resist.

The fivefold division of Matthew's work concludes with the end of chapter 25. Although what follows is, in a sense, epilogue, it supports what has already been written. His last three chapters report Passion Week and the Resurrection, with the concluding charge to his followers to evangelize the world. Much of it is material preserved only in Matthew. Several passages report material found in Mark or Luke, or in both. In several of these the expression or detail differs sufficiently to render difficult a decision about whether Matthew presents a modified version of Mark or follows another source.

Among the details in which Matthew differs from Mark, what Matthew records appears to be directed toward a predominantly Jewish group. The role of Judas in the betrayal of Jesus and his remorse are spelled out in greater detail than in Mark: he is specifically named and the sum of money paid him is recorded. The collusion of the Jewish authorities and their responsibility for the crucifixion are expressly emphasized so as to place the blame on them and not on the Jewish people. Their pressure upon Pilate to execute Jesus against his will, which Matthew enlarges by noting that Pilate's wife also interceded for Jesus, goes far to remove from Pilate all blame beyond that of weakness—another detail pleasing to the Diaspora, which, as a rule, was favorable to Roman rule. These Jews wanted no more Jewish revolts, and Jesus' rebuke of the disciple who awkwardly tried to defend him with a sword reminds them of the peaceful submission to authority preached by the Church. These events would interest Mark's readers, and he mentions them briefly; the added details in Matthew peculiarly affect its Jewish reader.

In the astonishing events attendant upon Jesus' death, Matthew quite possibly resorts to symbols rather than to reports of actual occurrences. His readers, Jewish or Gentile, would see no attempt to falsify the record by including them and quite possibly received them in the spirit in which they were included. The tearing of the veil that concealed the holy of holies in the Temple would suggest to them the Christian doctrine that through Jesus' sacrifice man gained direct access to God the Father. The earthquake and rending of rocks with the attendant opening of tombs were not incredible in the Palestine area. The resurrection of "many bodies of the saints" at Jesus' resurrection points to Paul's account of those dead Christians who will be raised at the Parousia to accompany Jesus (1 Thess. 4:16, 2 Cor. 15:20–23). As in several other passages of Matthew, the author's agreement with Paul is noticeable in these marvelous symbols, and Paul's teaching was probably familiar to the Jewish audience of Matthew.

Matthew's desire to influence a Jewish audience made one further account necessary. When the tomb in which Jesus had been temporarily placed was found to be empty, the Jewish leaders claimed that the disciples had removed his body secretly. They promised to defend the Roman guards stationed there from Pilate's punishment if they would tell people that they had slept on their post. The fact that the authorities could persuade the guards thus to risk their lives is an indication of the degree to which Pilate was under their thumbs and further clears Roman authority as a whole of culpability in the entire matter. Pilate had long been discredited and was a convenient scapegoat for Roman action in Judea. The author of Matthew had to counter this propaganda of the Jewish authorities. The other Gospel writers, to influence other readers, used other supporting evidence that the resurrection actually occurred.

With the discovery of the empty tomb by the three women, and the announcement to them by the messenger in the tomb, Mark's account abruptly ends; his conclusion is lost. Matthew, unlike Mark, says that the women did report the message to the disciples. Such differences in minor detail are not surprising. The stupendous event would overshadow memory of small matters, and traditions of these could hardly have coincided. The differences between the details reported by Matthew and Luke clearly indicate the number of events that were remembered and recorded, and apocryphal records add still more.

According to Matthew, Jesus met the women as they were hurrying to the disciples and told them to direct his "brethren" to meet him in Galilee. There for the fourth time he talked with them on a mountain. This symbolic detail places his final words on the level of the Sermon on the Mount, Peter's declaration of his deity, and the Transfiguration. His command to teach and baptize all nations is thus a final proof to the Jews of the breakdown of division between Jew and Gentile.

His words also introduce the concept of the Trinity. Since Matthew did not treat the Holy Spirit to the degree that John did later, it can be assumed that his readers had some knowledge of the concept through previous acquaintance with Christian doctrine as originally spread by the teaching and experience of Paul. Finally, Jesus promised them his companionship in their labors "even unto the end of the world."

With these words of Jesus, the author of Matthew closed his Gospel. It is true that his Gospel became speedily a handbook for Christian instruction in the Church. Here, however, our concern is with its formal structure, which appears undeniably to be designed for propaganda.

CHAPTER 3

THE GOSPEL ACCORDING TO LUKE

There is little reason to doubt that Luke was composed in its present form by Paul's traveling companion whose name it bears. It is also highly probable that he wrote it at about the same time that Matthew was composed. Both writers rely heavily on Mark and *Q*, but each uses also a body of quite independent material. Where Matthew and Mark report the same episode, Luke uniformly follows Mark's wording instead of Matthew's. Luke in particular was industrious in collecting and collating source materials. It is difficult to believe that he would have made no use of Matthew's rendering, had he seen it. Since this Gospel levies consistently on Mark, one must assume sufficient time after Mark's writing for Luke to have received and evaluated it. Scholars accordingly set the date of Luke as contemporary with that of Matthew, a decade or so later than Mark.

The date may also be inferred from the hints the Gospel contains of the Roman attitude toward the Church when it was being composed. In both his Gospel and the Acts, Luke indicates that Jesus and Paul were acceptable to Roman authority. At Jesus' trial Pilate stated emphatically, "I find no fault in this man" (23:4). Paul was a Roman citizen who had no trouble with Gallio, the proconsul of Achaia, had favorably impressed both Judean procurators under whom he had been imprisoned, and had been approved by a Jewish ruler, Agrippa. Luke evidently desired to impress on his readers that Christianity's two leaders were upstanding. This concern would surely have been in the mind of an apologist and propagandist during the reign of Domitian (A.D. 81–96), when Christians were subjected to vicious persecution and informers against them were rewarded with shares of their property.

The ascription of this Gospel to Luke the physician is supported unanimously by early tradition. When a tradition is advanced that served the special interests of no known group and bears strong evidence of being correct, there is a strong presumption of its genuineness. Whoever wrote Luke also wrote Acts, as will later be demonstrated. Since Paul's traveling companion Luke almost certainly wrote Acts, Luke must with equal certainty have written the Gospel.

Various attempts have been made to pin down Luke's identity. Was he a Jew or a Gentile? In Colossians 4, Paul listed Luke with Demas, who is Greek at least in name, apart from a number of his current companions who were "of the circumcision." In this concluding informal chapter, however, Paul was simply appending to the body of his letter the names of companions who wished to send greetings to the church of Colossae. He could have added the names as companions asked him to send their greetings, with Luke and Demas making their request later than the rest. Somewhat stronger evidence that he was a Gentile lies in his fluent, idiomatic use of Greek; the first sentences of Luke and Acts remind one of the style of Thucydides. At the same time, traces of Aramaic usage appear in his writing, which point to his possible Jewish origin. A cultured Jew of the Diaspora, as Philo demonstrates, could become a highly competent Greek stylist. There is little in the evidence to show whether Luke was "of the circumcision" or not.

His superior literary Greek style may be plausibly explained by the highly literate, cultured audience he had in view. This audience may also account for the Greek medical terms in Luke. A knowledge of them may be compared with that displayed today in the vocabulary of educated men, although the use of them in the Gospel was taken at one time to indicate that Luke was a physician—a surmise which Acts makes plausible. Since the days of Aristotle it has been a stylistic principle that logical subordination of ideas is the last quality to be mastered by a speaker; it indicates the matured, rational thinker. One who can read such writing with enjoyment and appreciation of its finesse must likewise have matured in scholarship and culture. He notes the differing values of principal and variously subordinated ideas, the eight differing classes of adverbial clauses, the relative clarity and emphasis of the subordinate clause and the participial phrase, and the nice selection among nearly synonymous words. The less cultured reader will detect nothing of the care exercised in such composition and its involutions will probably bore him.

Take as instances of this difference the opening sentences of Mark and Luke. Mark's is actually a topic, not a full sentence, though the KJV attempts to tie it into verse 2 as part of a sentence. Omitting the final phrase as a gloss, it contains five words in Greek, eight in English. Luke's first sentence contains forty-two words in Greek, eighty-one in English. In Greek it is composed of one principal clause, one relative clause, three adverbial clauses, and three participial phrases—a complex structure like that frequently used as the opening of a work in classical Greek prose. For Mark to have begun with such a sentence would have been a tactical error as grave as for a modern political candidate to address his audience in Johnsonese English.

Luke's style, then, points to his appeal to readers of the middle and upper class, cultured, educated Hellenistic world. Writing some thirty years earlier, Paul (1 Cor. 1:26–28) had declared that the Christian message was effective chiefly among the lower, less educated classes. Evangelism of such classes no doubt still constituted the Church's major work. The death of most of the eyewitnesses to Jesus' work, and, no doubt, by the eighties of many of their converts, made of prime importance the provision of leaders to take their place.

Paul, whom Luke staunchly supported and deeply revered, had been a highly educated Jew who knew how to approach and influence Gentiles; such Jews were rare. Anti-Semitism, always present in the Mediterranean world, had been exacerbated by the Jewish war of the preceding decades. Luke saw that the Church had become largely a Gentile movement, and he apparently foresaw its future expansion as chiefly European. To lead such an Occidental movement, men trained in Hellenistic culture from Gentile stock obviously were preferable to Jews and were probably more readily available. Luke accordingly wrote to interest and convert such men to Christianity partly in order to provide a source of future leadership for a Western church. As will quickly be shown, the organization of Luke conduces to this end.

Luke's undoubted historical interests have misled many into viewing him as an historian. It has been suggested, for instance, that Luke is a history of the new movement under the personal leadership of Jesus on earth, and that Acts continues this history under the guidance of the Holy Spirit. Although he does employ these unifying principles in his two books, he is engaged, like the other Gospel writers, in propaganda. He shows, it is true, a historian's interest in sources and dates, but he does not write history. He can shift the order of events from that in the other Gospels as seems to advance his purpose, and he probably combines or changes some details in Paul's career. Greece and Rome produced competent historians whom Luke could have used as models had he been so inclined. The assumption that he is writing propaganda can alone justify his manipulation of data, which in a historian would be inexcusable.

In Luke's day a popular form of the prose essay among cultured Hellenists was of the nature of an "open letter" addressed to some personage but intended for public perusal. It partook also of the essay dedicated to some prominent person. The name *Theophilus* ("dear to God" or "lover of God") is accompanied by an honorific address used for Roman officials. The work then is probably dedicated or addressed to some official whose name is concealed under the complimentary address to protect him from persecution as a Christian. The honorific title would ensure for Luke's work the prestige of connection with and possible approval by an important official.

Two-fifths of Luke's total material is from Mark, one-fifth from Q. The remainder is his own addition, identified by textual critics as *L*. In his opening sentence he declares that he has carefully evaluated many accounts of Christian fact and faith. He claims "more perfect understanding"—literally, long acquaintance with—"all things from the very first." These sources have attempted to "set forth in order" what they report, a strong implication that he refers to written accounts here—though he no doubt knew oral reports as well. By quoting almost one-half of Mark, he gives that Gospel his accolade of trustworthiness. His not using all of Mark cannot be taken as doubt of the unquoted part; he either found it not pertinent to his purpose or preferred another tradition at times. His quoting extensively from Q attests to the quality of at least that part of Matthew which comes from this source.

In 1924, Canon B. H. Streeter advanced in his *The Four Gospels* the hypothesis that Luke the author had prepared an earlier, unpublished account, before he had read Mark. This Streeter designates "Proto-Luke." Like *Urmarkus*, it was unmentioned in antiquity. This hypothesis was suggested to Streeter by contrasting the manners of Matthew and Luke in quoting Mark. Matthew throughout his work combines his two sources so symmetrically that he must obviously have had both available to him from the start. In Luke, Marcan material appears irregularly in passages of widely varying length, as if Luke had inserted them into a previously written account. By reading consecutively passages from Luke not in Mark—except for some passages otherwise accounted for—Streeter found what appeared to him to be a fairly coherent account composed of Q and Luke's individual material. This, he theorized, is Proto-Luke. Whether it includes all of the hypothetical first edition, one can find no grounds to speculate. Although some of the matters in Proto-Luke are reported also in Mark, their details vary sufficiently to have caused Streeter to believe that they stem from another tradition used by Luke.

Proto-Luke has better attestation critically than had Wolf's earlier *Urmarkus*. From long immersion in the New Testament, the insights of a devout and devoted scholar like Streeter attain at times to the level of intuitions which supplement his rational scholarship where data are unavailable. While such intuitions are not infallible, they deserve serious attention by other scholars. One must admit that Streeter developed a tenable hypothesis.

As Streeter reconstructed the situation, Luke occupied himself during the two years (c. A.D. 57–59) while Paul was imprisoned in Caesarea by gathering materials about Jesus and the early years after the Ascension. Caesarea had already become an important Christian center, as Christians from Jerusalem found safer living in the seaport. There is no indication that Luke had previously visited Palestine, and he was, no doubt, eager to talk with eyewitnesses of the beginnings of the Church. Among his informants was probably Philip the deacon, then living in Caesarea (Acts 21:8–10), who could introduce him to still earlier surviving leaders. At some unascertained date, but before he had seen Mark, Luke put together these materials into a connected account.

After he had done this, Luke read a copy of Mark and realized that he could improve his work by incorporating parts of the earlier Gospel. If he had become acquainted with Mark before he had made his first draft, Streeter reasoned, he would probably have combined the two books more artistically. Under the circumstances Luke simply added here and there passages from Mark of greatly varying length to complement what he had already written, and probably during the eighties he published the combined work. One may add that such use of other men's written work without acknowledgment was quite proper in antiquity.

Several New Testament scholars now feel that Streeter's hypothesis is unsatisfactory. Emphasis today is put upon oral tradition rather than upon consideration of hypothetical documents such as Q. This more recent concern has made its proponents discard almost entirely the theory of documentary sources; it tacitly ignores the probable use by Gospel writers of both kinds of material. The literary student, however, cannot discard Streeter's theory. Although it obviously cannot be established as factual, it admirably accounts for the apparently haphazard appearance of Marcan passages in Luke. In an area for which factual data are far from plentiful, it presents a workable explanation for the method of Luke's citation from Mark.

Streeter did not include in Proto-Luke chapters 1 and 2 of the published Gospel. According to his theory, after Luke made his first draft he may have come upon additional accounts which considerably developed his Gospel. Whatever his immediate source was, the intimate details about the annunciation to Mary must have come ultimately from her. Her kinship with Elisabeth, the mother of

John the Baptist, makes her the most likely reporter also of her visit to Elisabeth and the probable source of the account of the annunciation of John to Zacharias. The narrative serves brilliantly to introduce readers to the birth of Jesus.

The details of the annunciation to Zacharias are accurate. For two weekly periods annually and at special feasts, Zacharias had to perform priestly functions about the Temple to which he was assigned by lot. On this occasion he had won the coveted right to offer incense at evening prayer in the Temple. After the censing he was to pronounce a benediction on the worshipers. While he was offering incense before the holy of holies, an angel announced to him that his wife and he would have a son who would act "in the spirit and power of Elias," the greatest of the Jewish prophets. Gabriel, the divine messenger, asserted that John would "make ready a people prepared for the Lord," an ambiguous pronouncement which Luke's readers, unlike the Jews, could interpret as inclusive of themselves.

Zacharias was so overcome by the appearance and message that he was struck dumb from the shock, much as Paul at the vision of Jesus was struck blind. Part of his shock, like that of Abraham upon receiving a similar message, was caused by his knowledge that his wife was of advanced years and unlikely to bear a child; she had previously borne none. One need not read into this passage any intent of Luke to report a miraculous course of events. Zacharias had undergone a mystical experience, which, though on a higher than ordinary level of events, was not considered miraculous. As for Elisabeth, women aged early in the Near East; life expectancy was probably less than thirty years. An apparently sterile woman might be still of childbearing age though "well stricken in years" by the life expectancy of the time. The firm believer in miracles need not call miraculous what is explicable on other grounds.

Some six months earlier, another annunciation had come to a virgin living in Nazareth who was betrothed to a man named Joseph. This time, Gabriel announced a miraculous birth: Mary would bear a son without a human father. He should be named Jesus, and God would give him the throne of his ancestor David to rule forever as "Son of the Highest." Mary, though naturally astonished, accepted without complaint the possibly equivocal position in which she might be placed. Presumably, though it is not mentioned in Luke, Joseph accepted the situation much as Matthew records, and Jesus became the legal son of Joseph.

Luke records also a visit of Mary to Elisabeth when the latter was in her fifth month of pregnancy. When Mary spoke to her, Elisabeth's child, apparently for the first time, moved in her womb. Elisabeth, inspired by the Holy Spirit, interpreted this movement to indicate that Mary was bearing her "Lord." This homely bit of detail incorporated a common belief of that time, that unborn infants could respond to the presence of deity.

Luke skillfully uses the accounts of these two births for propaganda, as intimations of what he wishes to teach. These intimations are cast in the form of poems uttered by three of the agents. Many scholars believe that he used in the poems parts of early Christian hymns. Although these pronouncements follow Jewish poetic practice, Luke's Hellenistic readers, of whom many must have been previously attracted to the new faith, would have been fully able to appreciate their form, symbolism, and especially their content. In fact, their content implies more than the average Jew could envision for the whole world.

Mary's words (the Magnificat) describe the golden age which the Messiah was expected to bring. The wealthy and proud would be reduced to the common level of all. The monopolies of wealth and property which had plagued Jew and Gentile for centuries would be broken, and all would have whatever they needed. Here at the outset Luke presents a social gospel acceptable on a worldwide scale.

Zacharias' words upon recovering from his aphasia (the Benedictus) are an essentially messianic hymn evidently presenting the outlook of the Jewish branch of the Christian church. As Luke's Hellenistic readers interpreted it, the hymn carries also overtones of Virgil's so-called messianic ecologue, in which a Roman rule like the millennium was foretold. They would be especially moved by the prophecy of John's mission of salvation brought to "them that sit in darkness"—an ironically ambiguous phrase which was a standard Jewish reference to Gentiles but which here could refer to the Jews themselves. Although first-century Jews wished to spread their faith among Gentiles, the Benedictus points to an extension far beyond the ritually hedged Judaism that Luke's readers had encountered. In thus using two hymns from early Christianity before it became ecumenical, Luke skillfully implies that from its inception the Church has contained the seeds of a message for all men.

So far, Luke's account has dwelt on a level of events approaching the sublime. From this elevation he transports his readers abruptly to the lowly circumstances attending Jesus' birth. Hellenistic readers would not miss the artistry of such shock tactics; in the fifth book of the *Odyssey*, Homer had employed a similar technique. Following four books in which Odysseus is built up as well-nigh invincible, he is presented as weeping salt tears into the brine because a woman will not let him go home to Ithaca. After a prophetic account of Jesus' coming greatness which mingles mystical experience, prophecy, supernatural messengers, and hymns full of religious hope, Jesus is born in a stable because no better place can be found by his father. Shock, however, as also in the *Odyssey*, must not degenerate into disenchantment: Angelic choristers announce to humble shepherds the birth of the child who shall bring joy to all people.[1] Readers at once feel assured that this humble infant has divine support, as the coming of Hermes brought to Odysseus the support of father Zeus. Since the Hellenistic world was almost as well versed in Homer as the Hebrew world was in the Old Testament, its awareness of the parallel here is not overdrawn.

At the presentation of Jesus in the Temple, Luke seizes the opportunity through inserting a third Christian hymn to emphasize the worldwide application of Christianity. Divine revelation sent Simeon to the Temple as Jesus was brought in and revealed to him what Jesus would do for "all the people," as the better manuscripts record the passage. Again we note the ambiguous application of *people*; here, however, in the *Nunc dimittis*, the statement is made explicit. Jesus is the "salvation, which thou hast prepared before the face of all people [in Greek the word is pointedly plural, *peoples*]; a

[1] The Greek word *laos* (2:10) ambiguously can refer to a nation or to mankind in general.

light to lighten the Gentiles, and the glory of thy people Israel" (2:30–32).

It is perhaps pushing the parallel with the *Odyssey* too far to note that fulfillment of divine promise is in both accounts delayed. With the exception of a single episode in Jesus' life when he was twelve—an early hint that he is more than ordinary man—he lived quietly for almost thirty years in Nazareth with his parents. In the *Odyssey* the interposition of a long narrative told by Odysseus postpones the fulfillment. The devices are different, the effects alike.

Luke alone among New Testament writers took pains to date events. His concern with dates was probably reinforced by his readers' habituation to their use in Roman documents and inscriptions on public works. The Julian calendar, of which our Gregorian calendar is a modification, had been devised by Julius Caesar more than a century earlier, but like the Gregorian it was slow to win general acceptance. Dating was still effected by a cumbrous multiplying of imperial and local data. Luke used this latter method. In chapter 3 (vv. 1–2) the items are listed in usual epigraphic order. Tiberius became Caesar in August of A.D. 14. The fifteenth year of his principate by Roman reckoning began in August of A.D. 28. Pilate was appointed procurator of Judea in A.D. 26. Herod Antipas became tetrarch of Galilee about 4 B.C. and ruled until the year A.D. 39. Dates for Philip's rule are not extant. According to Luke's dating by the reign of Tiberius, Jesus probably began his active ministry in the latter half of the year 28. His data were probably collected some thirty years later, and men's memories for dates are notoriously uncertain.

Luke's previous dating of Jesus' birth also poses problems. The earliest recorded imperial census occurred in A.D. 20, but it was not probably the first. Since the censuses were conducted at fourteen-year intervals, one should have taken place in 8 B.C. Roman tax collecting, which accompanied the census, was a cumbrous affair at best, and in Palestine one cannot doubt that Jews were especially slow in paying this detested poll tax. Three or four years may have elapsed before the individual taxpayer finally paid.

Luke's informants may have suffered a slight confusion of memory. Cyrenius or Quirinius was governor in A.D. 6. This term of office may have become confused with another office in Syria that began in 10 B.C. He could then have possibly been in some office at the time of the presumable tax of 8 B.C. The historian Josephus (*Jewish War* II.viii.1, VII. viii.1) referred to an enrollment and tax in A.D. 6 or 7, probably the tax mentioned in Acts 5:37. Judea was reckoned as part of Syria. In Luke 1:5 it is implied that Jesus was born while or shortly after Herod the Great was king; he died in 4 B.C.

Luke, one must remember, was dealing with events as much as seven decades old by any reckoning. It is not surprising that his informants made errors. Without going into full details about this dating, Luke thought of Jesus' birth as having occurred about 2 B.C., give or take a year or two. His reference to "the days of Herod" (1:15) may be taken as an approximation; Herod left his imprint on his kingdom for years after his death.

It is probably Luke's concern to emphasize Jesus' universality that caused him to trace Jesus' genealogy not merely to Abraham, as the Jewish-aimed propaganda in Matthew does, but to Adam "which was the son of God." A Gentile reader of the Septuagint would not share the obsession with "our father, Abraham" which held the scribes and Pharisees of Jesus' day. It is perhaps for the same reason that he traced the line back to Adam rather than from him; his order makes the universal parent more prominent in the climactic position. Luke minimized all tendency to equate Christianity with the racially restricted religion from which it was developed. He was not anti-Semitic; at the same time, he wisely avoided arousing that feeling in his Hellenistic readers.

What sort of man was Luke's Hellenistic reader? It is time to draw his profile. It has already been indicated that he was of the educated, intelligent, middle- or upper-class Gentiles. As a man interested in ideas and philosophical systems, he had a fair acquaintance with Judaism and its principal tenets. Although he could not accept its cramping restrictions, he recognized the lofty thought in the Septuagint, in which he had read extensively. In the latter half of the first century, Judaism had become a fashionable religion among many Gentile women. On account of their abhorrence of physical mutilation involved in circumcision, few men followed the women to Judaism; but their interest would further stimulate the men's curiosity about Judaism.

Second, he was not usually an active anti-Semite. It was rather the case that the Jew disliked him—a feeling that varied with the Pharisaic influence upon the Jew's training. One seldom feels affection for those who look down upon him. The recent costly and bloody Jewish war had no doubt aggravated whatever latent anti-Semitism existed in the Hellenist. Third, and arising out of the Jew's scornful rejection of the belief among many Hellenists that all men were brothers, he found great difficulty in approaching the Jew. Socially, the Jew would reject him; ideologically, the Jew would repel him.

Finally, though interested in the philosophies implicit in the current religions, the Hellenist was not usually attracted to them. Like the English deists two or three centuries ago, he was inclined to discount heavily any belief in supernatural intervention in the world. Gods might or might not exist. If they did, they were careless of mankind; hence, prayer to and worship of them were largely wasted effort. As a matter of patriotic form—possibly also for insurance in the remote contingency that gods might be actively interested in man—he participated in the ritual observances of the state religion. Julius Caesar, a religious skeptic, had regularly presided as *pontifex maximus* ("chief priest") at the public religious sacrifices. In the growing practice of deifying the Caesars, which was strongly developed in the Near East, he saw a cynical attempt to adopt a custom that already existed in the Orient.

For a philosophy, the Hellenist followed the Epicurean or Stoic principles as a rule, unless he held to an eclectic mixture of such beliefs. These all viewed the world materialistically and taught that death brought personal annihilation. Such spiritual needs as the Hellenists knew were often satisfied by resort to one or other of the many mystery cults, which claimed to restore a sense of spiritual adequacy and to cleanse one from a sense of sin. Some of them—perhaps many of those who were interested in the Septuagint—had become acquainted with Philo's elaborate blend of Old Testament account with Platonic philosophy.

The members of Luke's proposed audience, then, would not easily respond to a supernatural religion. He had to lure them into the faith by degrees, putting forward what they would respond to favorably while audaciously inserting ideas to which they would at first object. His readers could accept his first two chapters in spite of their repeated bits of supernatural action as symbolic rather than literal statement; to this interpretation they were accustomed. Luke had couched them in superb expression, with three eloquent hymns interspersed. The readers appreciated his level of style and found in these hymns ideas which they approved, which made them feel included in the world picture presented. Thus, even before he entered upon his concentrated propaganda, Luke had prepared his readers to look with favor upon a movement which had had such universal principles from its inception.

Luke's procedure in persuading his hardheaded readers emerges clearly in chapters 6 through 8, as the arrangement of details clearly shows. Attentive reading of these chapters reveals the skillful yet simple design. Luke's readers possibly interpreted the supernatural events in chapters 1 and 2 symbolically; so understood, they would cause no difficulty in acceptance. Now he must win the Hellenists over into belief that the divine Jesus did actually intervene in human affairs. This belief required them to abandon the accepted position that the gods, if they do exist, take no personal interest in men or in their affairs. They would, on the whole, approve the scattered reports of Jesus in earlier chapters.

Beginning with chapter 6, Luke obliquely approaches his goal. In fifty-nine verses (6:1–7:10) he builds up a picture of Jesus designed to establish him firmly in their good opinion. Jesus first refutes the Pharisees' charge of his disciples' Sabbath breaking by citing an obviously more reprehensible act of David's in eating consecrated food, which he had done with priestly approval—a story known to many of Luke's readers from the Septuagint. Jesus adds that he is Lord of the Sabbath. Next, he mounted a frontal attack on the Sabbath laws by first reducing them to an absurdity and then flouting them by healing a man on the Sabbath. In brief space Jesus has routed the Pharisees and established himself as a healer—surely no ordinary man. The Pharisees being among the most disliked Jews among Gentiles, their discomfiture would gratify Luke's readers.

Luke introduces from Q twenty-nine of the verses which in Matthew constitute the Sermon on the Mount. In them Jesus counsels conduct towards other men quite in harmony with Hellenistic social ideals. It would have been unwise to report such a long account as that found in Matthew. Many of its contrasts with Jewish law would have failed to interest them.

The Pharisaic teachers have decidedly had the worst of it. Luke now quickly reverses the coin by commending the Gentiles. The confidence of the centurion who realized that Jesus was no ordinary faith healer with a charismatic touch went far beyond, as Jesus testifies, anything he had found in Israel. Luke has by this time built up a heavy credit for Jesus with his readers.

Immediately after this episode Luke first ventured to insert material (7:11–17) with which his readers would take issue. It is a carefully calculated risk. The raising of the widow's son in an obscure village, they would say, is the sort of apocryphal tale that clings to any great healer. No names are given, they would note; the story can clearly be dismissed as fictitious. For all this, they have become interested in the appealing figure of Jesus and continue to read.

To rebuild Jesus in their favor, Luke recalls dramatically to their minds Jesus' extraordinary deeds. Instead of arguing or reminding them, he pictures envoys from John the Baptist—an arresting figure, too—inquiring whether Jesus is really the Messiah whom John had foretold. Jesus had been engaged in healing, restoring sight, and curing the insane. He simply told them to report to John what they had seen him doing. In his ensuing panegyric of John, Jesus reproaches the Pharisees and scribes with not knowing what they want. They had called John an insane recluse for his abstemious life. They now called Jesus a glutton, a drunkard, and an associate of bad company. His picture of their childish disagreeableness would delight Luke's readers.

Jesus follows his excoriation of the Pharisees with a pungent vignette. One of them had invited Jesus to dinner but had snubbed him by offering him none of the amenities customarily given to guests. As Jesus was quietly dining, a prostitute who slipped in washed his feet with her tears, dried them with her hair, and rubbed them with an expensive ointment. The shocked Pharisee decided that Jesus could not be a prophet or he would have recognized the woman as an untouchable prostitute. Jesus then in a brief parable elicited from the Pharisee the admission that a man should be more grateful for freedom from a large debt than from a small one. Jesus thereupon, pointedly ignoring Simon, says to the woman, "*Thy* sins are forgiven." Luke covertly enters also an idea which he is aiming at in his propaganda by reporting the Pharisees' question, "Who is this that forgiveth sins also?" Intelligent readers by this time have grasped the conclusion toward which Luke is tending.

Luke continues to depict Jesus favorably through his parables, pithy sayings, and proclamation of human brotherhood. He thus keeps his readers' minds on edge and undecided. While claims have been made or intimated for Jesus which they are unready to accept, he is shown to be one whom they are irresistibly drawn to admire. Luke takes pains here to build up their good will because he will need it in the ensuing episode.

The raising of the widow's son at Nain was an episode which his readers felt free to ignore as a folktale. The resurrection of Jairus' daughter cannot be so readily confuted. In place of an anonymous widow he presents a prominent citizen who occupied a position of some eminence in a flourishing Galilean city. The account can be checked for its truth as that about the widow's son could not. Luke had previously left a loophole for his readers' skepticism; now he closes it. His line of development begins to take shape; the mention of a resurrection at Nain is followed by the incontrovertible evidence in the case of Jairus' daughter. The final stage will be Jesus' own resurrection.

To maintain his hold on his audience, in chapter 9, Luke resumes the building of his structure supporting the claims of Jesus in his readers' eyes. Like Matthew, he builds on Mark's description of the trip undertaken by the twelve, but he significantly omits Matthew's restriction of it to Jews only. He clearly wishes to focus attention on the ecumenical scope of the Church. When the twelve return, Jesus takes them away for a rest. When a crowd of followers overtakes them, he teaches, heals, and miraculously feeds them. Later he calms a storm. Jesus has now been presented as healing the sick, curing the insane, miraculously multiplying food, raising the dead, and controlling the elements of the weather.

Luke cannot afford to report to Hellenists as Matthew had done to Jewish readers Jesus' comments on Peter's statement of the twelve's belief in him as Messiah and Son of God. Like Mark, Luke wrote for an audience who had had their fill of Jewish insurrectionists. He records simply that Peter called Jesus the anointed one of God (*Christos*), and follows that with Jesus' injunction that the disciples tell no one of this. Luke emphasizes further the peaceful mission of Jesus by including not only Jesus' prophecy that the Jewish authorities will disown and kill him—though he does insert Jesus' declaration that he would rise on the third day. He adds the adverb *daily* to give added point to Jesus' requirement that a man take up his cross and follow him. Luke went to extremes to show Jesus as no subversive traditional Messiah, even to omitting Peter's spirited remonstrance with Jesus' declaration of his approaching execution.

No such risk of offending his readers limits Luke's account of the transfiguration. Excepting his addition of the explanation that Moses and Elijah were talking with Jesus about his coming death in Jerusalem—an addition to focus meaning upon this paradoxical event, as it would seem to his readers—Luke follows closely Mark's account. He also describes the slow-witted state of the three disciples upon awakening from heavy sleep, a genre detail such as Luke enjoyed in his accounts. In addition to their acquaintance with mystical experiences from reading the Septuagint, Luke's readers would be aware of the mystical level from records and experiences in their own world. They would readily interpret the symbolism that placed Jesus squarely in the Old Testament tradition, which Luke had already carefully shown to be broadened by Jesus to be for all races.

It has been necessary to report Luke's practice of propaganda in detail to make it readily apparent. He could not hope to convince his readers through argument, as John later could do; they would deny his premises and skillfully object to each point as he presented it, thus preventing any cumulative effect. He must by indirections find direction out. He must painstakingly build up Jesus as an appealing figure to whom they feel sympathetic. Having accomplished this, he can covertly insert matters alien to their habit of belief without destroying their feeling for his protagonist. Through repetition of this process, he hopes gradually to erode their resistance to the concept of a deity who intervenes in man's affairs yet far transcends their notions of deity.

The final episodes in Galilee present Jesus as emphasizing the childlike nature of his followers and the breadth of his cause. When John reports that he has tried to silence a healer not of their group who was curing insane persons in Jesus' name, Jesus forbids him: "He that is not against us is for us." The episode tantalizes twentieth-century readers with the suggestion of other followers of Jesus besides the twelve; to Luke's readers it emphasized how far Jesus stood from Pharisaic separatism.

Luke greatly expands the account connected with Jesus' last journey to Jerusalem. Mark had reported it in a single chapter; Matthew gave it two; Luke allocates to it nearly one-third of his entire account. This long passage (9:51–18:14) has been called "the travel document." It purports to tell what Jesus said and did on his journey; it is entirely from Luke's own material (*L*), and according to Streeter is the largest single surviving block of Proto-Luke. In any case, from the literary point of view it is a device used by Matthew and Mark, an example of the journey used as a string on which to collect varied items not otherwise unified.

Luke sets the tone for his collection by declaring at the start that Jesus "stedfastly set his face to go to Jerusalem." In Greek the idea is more vigorously expressed: Jesus "braced himself," "propped his face in that direction," as it were. Desiring to interest his readers in this god-man, Luke here emphasizes almost painfully the strength of Jesus' will in voluntarily facing what must happen to him in Jerusalem. Readers are to keep in mind the pressures on him until the resurrection. At the last chance for him to evade his fate, in Gethsemane (22:24), Jesus' sweat was "as it were great drops of blood falling down to the ground." The extreme tension underlying this journey and the ensuing Passion Week added depth to the readers' concern, whether they were convinced of Jesus' deity or not. They would surely read on with absorption, which it was Luke's concern to generate in them.

By accident or design, in his travel document Luke ignores geography. Like the other Synoptic writers, he obviously pictures Jesus as following the circuitous route that bypassed Samaria by following a course east of the Jordan River as far south as Jericho, where he crossed the river in order to climb the steep, rugged mountain trail to Jerusalem. In some fifteen miles as the crow flies, considerably farther by the trail, the path climbs more than three thousand feet through the wilderness of Judea. Once committed to this route, for more than one hundred miles there was no feasible crossroad to the route through Samaria, and surely no conceivable reason for cutting across country. Nonetheless, Luke near the start (9:52) reports Jesus as passing through a Samaritan village and later (17:11) as passing "through the midst of Samaria and Galilee." Yet in a later passage (18:35) he passes through Jericho, which was on the circuitous route. It may well be that Luke was using accounts of two trips to Jerusalem, on one of which Jesus did cross Samaria as John reported later (4:1–46). If so, he simply conflated two accounts into one, ignoring the geographical inconsistency. Whatever the case was, he was surely actuated here by literary, not factual, purposes, as was Chaucer in his *Canterbury Tales*.

Luke's purpose in shaping this section was probably threefold. Although his account indicates that Jesus was more than human in nature as in power, he has not yet affirmed that he was the divine Son of God. Luke's mind, unlike his traveling companion Paul's, did not lean toward theological reasoning, yet he could hardly have shared Paul's evangelistic career without sharing also his beliefs. Paul did not tolerate lukewarm adherents. As we have shown in discussing Mark, any Gentile audience would have taken in stride the concept of a son of a god; it would have simply classified him along with many members of its pantheon. Mark's audience might have accepted him as such a being. Luke's would probably have regarded the claim as ridiculous, a throwback to earlier superstitions. Luke must clearly differentiate Jesus from this category. He must at the same time establish his peaceful, nonsubversive mission and keep interest in him fresh and enthralling.

The travel document serves all three of these purposes. Among the ideas stressed in it, the following are especially noteworthy. First, Jesus came to save life, not to destroy it. James and John, still laboring under their previous conception of Jesus as Elijah reincarnated, wish him to call down fire from heaven upon an inhospitable Samaritan village. Jesus sternly rebukes them. He sends out seventy workers to spread his message, heal the sick, and prepare men for his arrival en route. Here Luke inserts the directions which he had omitted from his account of the earlier mission of the twelve, with which Matthew had reported them. Whereas Matthew's report restricted the emissaries to Jewish villages, Luke's report of seventy emissaries —supposedly there were seventy nations in the world—symbolizes the worldwide scope of Jesus' message. Luke adds to the account Jesus' joyful reception of their success: "I beheld Satan as lightning fall from heaven." He symbolized their power over evil, as Luke's readers would see their successful healing, by their immunity from poison or other harm (10:17–20).

Proper attitudes are inculcated: toward God in the anecdote of Mary and Martha (10:38–42), toward God and man in the parable of the Pharisee and the tax collector at prayer in the Temple (18:10–14). Finally, relations between man and God are presented in three famous parables: the lost sheep, the lost coin, and the more complex parable of the prodigal son.

To allay any suspicions of subversion while presenting Jesus' future program to his readers, Luke utilizes Jesus' analogies of the kingdom of God to mustard seed and yeast: both spread quietly and imperceptibly, the one into a large plant, the other into the entire mass of dough, without any tumult or turmoil. The parable of the great supper likewise indicates that those who enter this kingdom are in no position to break the peace. A Jewish reader with all the hedges built about him by his scribal law could hardly have grasped implications in these parables which the more widely versed Hellenistic mind would readily grasp and appreciate.

Luke uses some of the parables from Q to illustrate Jesus' basic principles. Those which he alone reports are far better suited to the cultured Gentile than to the Jew. Whether he simply selected for his audience more complex parables used by Jesus or edited some which he had told, it is not possible to say. Since Jesus' hearers were nearly always Jews, the latter alternative is perhaps the more probable. To have invented parables as told by Jesus would have seemed not quite proper. It would have exposed him to later danger, as he must have realized, that some reader might realize that he had invented a parable instead of reporting it, and thus asperse the trustworthiness of his account. His promise (1:4) to tell Theophilus "the certainty of those things, wherein thou hast been instructed," no doubt, had particular reference to Christian principles. Luke might, however, have felt that he would imperil his purpose if he used nontraditional materials to support his principles, even if such practice was considered proper.

Those parables which come from Luke's account alone include artistic, well-rounded stories. Their plots, as Aristotle had required, have beginning, middle, and end. Unlike John, who could interrupt a brilliant report like his account of Nicodemus' visit to Jesus with meditation upon its meaning and forget his conclusion, Luke was consciously engaged by the charm of his story. In accord with contemporary Hellenistic interest in allegorical interpretation of literature, Luke's parables convey more than a single emphasis, and sometimes tantalize the readers with multiple suggestions.

Although Luke's parable of the great supper bears a general likeness to one reported by Matthew (22:2–14; cf. Luke 14:16–24), it evidently came from another source. Jesus used parabolic themes in various ways. Luke sets up his parable in the setting well known in everyday life, in which one expects to be entertained in turn by his guests. Why not rather invite those from whom you can expect nothing in return? This is the sign of true goodness, which will receive its reward "in the resurrection of the just." Someone interjects a pious comment on the blessedness of the man who should eat in the kingdom of God. Ignoring this pious platitude with a distaste which Luke's readers would share, Jesus embarks upon a brilliantly ironic parable in which the duplicity of the invited guests is neatly indicated. Each pretext is obviously lame. One must inspect land he has purchased *after* buying it. Another—an answer to a horse dealer's prayer—must go at once to inspect five yoke of oxen he has already bought. A third has just married and cannot come—a situation quite uncharacteristic of newlyweds. Justifiably angry, the host orders his servants to bring beggars and other sweepings of the streets. When there is still room, he sends a servant into the surrounding country and brings pressure on tramps who may be collected there to come to his dinner. If any of those previously invited should decide to come after all, they are to be excluded. The application of the parable to the Pharisees is obvious: the common folk whom they habitually consigned to hell will be accepted by God. The vividness of ironic detail here is characteristic of Luke's telling a story.

Upon a succeeding occasion the Pharisees' supercilious segregating themselves from "sinners" who did not comply with all their ritual requirements makes them the butt of the triplet of parables concerned with God's anxiety for what the Pharisees considered lost to salvation. Luke arranges them on an ascending scale, two drawn from homely incidents and the third less common perhaps but still within the knowledge of most men. The first describes a shepherd who at the end of the day misses one of his one hundred sheep. Without waiting to bring the rest into the fold, he at once searches for the lost sheep until he finds it. The second tells of a woman who has lost one of the ten silver coins of her dowry; she lights a candle and sweeps her entire house until she finds it. Each closes with the refrain that the joy of these two is like the joy in heaven at recovery of one who has been lost to God. The second time this is told, the statement that this joy is greater than for those who did not need repentance is omitted, but it is not forgotten.

These stories proceed from one in a hundred through one in ten to the climactic of one in two. This third parable has more intricate ramifications. The younger son of a wealthy landowner demands his share of the patrimony before it is due him, and receives it. Converting it into cash, he goes into a strange land and squanders it "with riotous living." When he is penniless and a famine strikes that land, he is reduced to tending swine for a living—as degrading a task as a Jew could perform. Coming to his senses, he decides to go home and see if his father will give him a job; he could expect nothing more. As soon as he comes in sight, his father recognizes him, ignores his plea for work, and restores him to favor. So far, the situation parallels that of the preceding parables. Luke, however, skillfully adds a sequel to his story which gives it a direction hinted at in the first appearance of the refrain. The "good boy" who has stayed at home and worked becomes incensed that the prodigal should be restored to favor: it is his property that is being lavished on his vagabond brother. When his father tries to remonstrate with him, he—like the Pharisee in the Temple—catalogs all that he has done. He has worked himself to the bone without ever being given any celebration for his steady service. The father concedes that the older son has worked steadily and can lay claim to the property, but he says "we"—a polite avoiding of *you*—are in duty bound to rejoice at your brother's return.

To call this the parable of the prodigal son is to miss Luke's artistry. A good writer would not leave his principal character at the climactic point of his story to bring in someone from the background. It is surely the story of the two brothers; possibly the second is finally the protagonist. Told as it is in response to Pharisaic complaints, it can hardly be meant otherwise; read in context, such a conclusion is inescapable. Read by Hellenists one-half century after Jesus' day, when the Church had become predominantly Gentile, its application, with the Jew as the older brother and the Gentile as the younger who was "returning" to the fulfillment of Judaism in Christianity, is unavoidable.

Another parable, that of the unjust steward, appears deliberately intended to puzzle its readers. Addressed to the disciples, it may have been designed to keep their self-assurance in check. Such problems serve to tantalize those to whom they are posed and thus to keep them thinking on the subject which a teacher wishes to occupy their minds. Placed immediately following the parable of the prodigal son, it invites the reader to associate the two.

This parable is bitterly ironic. A rich man, finding that his steward has been mismanaging his affairs, demands a reckoning before firing him. The steward tries to curry favor with his employers' debtors by sharply reducing the amounts of their indebtedness. The employer realizes the agent's cleverness and commends it for its building him a refuge from future want. Luke editorializes by using money as the symbol of the service it enables one to perform. Help other men in need, and they will help you. Serve God, and he will at death receive you into eternal life. The morality of the steward's action is not condoned; it is not the question here.

Luke enjoys reporting parables that are clearly designed as "teasers"—problems which cling to one's mind because they cannot be wholly settled. Loose ends are left. The prodigal's repentance was praiseworthy, his spendthrift ways were not. The older brother's jealous avarice, the contrary extreme in handling money, is likewise condemned; yet he has some degree of right on his side. Similar irony pervades the later parable of the unjust judge (18:1–8), in which an unscrupulous judge settles fairly a widow's claim only to rid himself of her importunity. The analogies to God in these parables are almost paradoxical, but highly effective. Irony was a potent weapon in the Hellenistic arsenal of persuasion.

In the parable of the rich man and Lazarus (16:19–31), proper handling of money continues to be the theme. A rich man enjoyed the good things of life on earth, while a beggar named Lazarus at his gate was neglected. Lazarus died and angels carried him to Abraham's bosom. The rich man also died and was buried. An eloquent silence briefly hints at his fate. "And in hell" he saw Lazarus cherished by Abraham while he was in torment. When he called to Abraham to send Lazarus to him with water, Abraham told him that justice was now balancing the account. The rich man had not stooped to help Lazarus. Now Lazarus was set off from his sufferings by a great gulf. Showing at last some thought for others, the rich man begged that Lazarus be sent back to warn his brothers against sharing his fate. Abraham replied that they had the Law and the Prophets to guide them. The rich man asserted that they would not listen to these. Abraham then closed the story by saying that if they ignored the Law and the Prophets they would not listen even to one who returned from death. The Jewish leaders were failing to employ the spiritual wealth available to them.

The climax of Jesus' attack on the self-righteous Pharisees comes when they are finally condemned in the parable of the Pharisee and the publican (18:9–14). The ostentatiously pious Pharisee was a type undoubtedly known to Luke's readers, and they could not have escaped awareness of the tax collector. The Pharisee, according to the pattern of the scribal law, presents his accounting of his conduct to God while standing up front in the Temple where he will be noticed. Luke implies ironically that his prayer is recited to himself rather than to God—he thanks God that he is so pious, not for any gift of God. Like so much of the formal notion of the conduct of life, the prominent part of his accounting states what he is not: an extortioner, unjust, or contemptible like the tax collector. On the positive side, he fasts twice weekly and tithes all his property; in these respects he claims additional merit for exceeding the standard requirements. Any reference to his religious feeling is conspicuously absent. Meanwhile, the tax collector is so burdened by his shortcomings that he stands far from the conspicuously righteous Pharisee without venturing to lift his eyes in prayer to God, beats his breast, and prays for forgiveness of his sins. Jesus pungently comments that the tax collector's contrition justified him rather than the Pharisee's accounting of deeds alone. People who think too highly of themselves, he adds, will be brought low, while the humble will be exalted. This principle is immediately reinforced by Jesus' declaration that a childlike attitude is the best passport into his kingdom.

The condemnation of Jewish religious leaders, specifically the chief priests and Pharisees, that pervades these parables mordantly satirizes their religious attitude and conduct. Since Pharisaism was the leading Jewish opposition to Christianity in Luke's day, his pro-Gentile attitude further strengthens his dislike of this sect. From the Hellenistic view, separatism was the most glaring fault of Pharisaic

Judaism. Against this fault Luke unlimbers his heaviest guns, from the parable of the good Samaritan near the beginning of the travel document to that of the Pharisee and the publican near its close.

Luke would probably have agreed with modern opponents of the well-made plot which leaves no loose ends to the action. Cultured readers like Luke's prefer to have something left for them to work out. Such mental fight holds their interest more firmly than full explanation. Against the possibility that some readers might be inept at interpreting parables, he had already included (8:9–15) from Mark Jesus' analysis of his parable of the sower. Hellenists were familiar with the parabolic form and would enjoy the nuances of plot and expression that Luke delighted to insert.

A prominent specimen of such teasers is the episode of Martha's impatience with her sister Mary for listening to Jesus instead of helping her to prepare dinner (10:38–42). After politely complimenting Martha on her labors, Jesus gently suggests that she might better seize the opportunity to learn from him while he is still here. (From that day to this the story has needled homemakers; it roused Rudyard Kipling to retort to it in behalf of the engineers in "The Sons of Martha.")

Three other such stories may be noted. A man as fussy as Martha asks to delay his following Jesus until he shall have buried his father. (His father is not necessarily dead, but may be aged and unlikely to live long.) To him Jesus replies far more harshly than to Martha, bidding him to let the dead bury their dead and to follow him now. To another who would bid farewell to his relatives before following him, Jesus sententiously replied that once a man wishes to follow him there can be no looking back to other concerns. Jesus' hyperboles raise the question, which every man must answer for himself, how to be a Christian leader amid his other responsibilities. Following these two, Luke records Jesus' response to his host, a Pharisee who was shocked at his not having ritually washed his hands before dinner, that it was more important to wash the inside of the cup. In this brilliant metaphor Jesus reduced to absurdity the Pharisaic preoccupation with ritual at the expense of inner conviction.

The fourth episode concerns an unreasoning act of Pilate in slaughtering several Galileans while they were sacrificing at the Temple (13:1–4). He may have suspected them of plotting against the government; similar acts of Pilate performed without regard of consequences are recorded by Josephus. Jesus' informants may have been tempting him to some seditious utterance by which to make him liable to Roman punishment. Jesus, whatever their intent, uses it much as Jeremiah (whose methods he frequently borrowed) employed current events—to introduce a moral or religious principle. Do they suppose that these Galileans were greater sinners than all other Galileans, because they suffered such a bloody fate? He then caps it with the instance of eighteen men who had died when a tower collapsed: were they greater sinners than all others in Jerusalem? The Hellenistic world, along with the Hebraic, was concerned with the possible consequences of wrongdoing and with retribution for it. Men who persist in sin, Jesus declares, will all perish; but death by murder or accident is no criterion of sin.

In addition to these telling episodes and parables, Luke included in Jesus' words another form of instruction effective throughout the ancient world: the sententious utterance. Greek and Roman literature made constant use of the generalized statement of truth or experience, as Greek speeches and dramas testify. Theognis in Greece and Publilius Syrus in Rome collected proverbs often closely resembling those of the ancient Hebrew. Before our more meticulous scientific thinking came to the fore, such generalized statements often served as proof in court and were used to conclude a debate or argument. Jesus' sayings fall often into such a category; in some instances he may have been quoting current proverbs.

Whether it originated in Proto-Luke or not, this long travel document is our best evidence of the literary style and method of Luke; here we see him at work on matter that Matthew and Mark did not see fit to include. However much he enriched his account with Mark and Q, the travel document, supported by his shorter additions to the record of Jesus, points unmistakably to his peculiar purpose and to the audience which he had in view. Considered in the structure of the Gospel as we now have it, the function of this third of his work shows clearly. He had spent the first nine chapters in building up the person of Jesus and overcoming basic prejudices of his readers. In the travel document, he tried by incessant attacks of Jesus upon the Jewish modes of thought and action embodied in Pharisaic teaching to sharply differentiate Jesus from these now discredited ideas which had brought the Jews to ruin and made them a dangerous and, what was peculiarly close to Hellenistic life, expensive enemy to defeat. Jesus is pictured, in effect, as on the Roman side and not on that of the Jewish nation. Early in this section the sharp severance of Jesus from his people had been emotionally expressed (13:33–35): "O Jerusalem, Jerusalem, which killest the prophets, and stonest them that are sent unto thee; how often would I have gathered thy children together, as a hen doth gather her brood under her wings, and ye would not! Behold, your house is left unto you desolate." These prophetic words, now fulfilled, show that the Jewish authorities themselves would have no part in him.

As Jesus, on the last leg of his journey, was passing through Jericho, two episodes reminded his readers of Jesus' concern for the outcast. The first (18:35–43), taken slightly altered in wording from Mark, tells of a blind man whose sight Jesus restored on account of his faith in him. The second (19:1–10), Luke's addition, reports how a short tax collector named Zacchaeus, as the *New England Primer* has it, "climbed a tree His Lord to see." Jesus shocked the crowd by inviting himself to dinner with this Jewish outcast—a signal mark of honor. At dinner Zacchaeus, deeply moved by Jesus' conversation, offered to make restitution for any wrongs he had done according to the provisions of both Jewish and Roman law against fraud. By declaring that Zacchaeus had found salvation, Jesus pointedly reminded his hearers that though he was a tax gatherer he was not to be excluded from his rights: "he also is a son of Abraham." Luke probably meant that according to Paul's argument in Romans he was doubly Abraham's son: not only was he racially a Jew, he became also Abraham's spiritual son as a believer in Jesus. Such a reminder that all men were embraced in Jesus' plan could not fail to please Luke's readers.

Luke's readers would severely try during Passion Week all the good will toward Jesus that Luke had mustered. They must have been convinced, if they had continued to read, that his protagonist was an extraordinary being. They were now in the state, Luke hoped, that was later to be described by Coleridge as exercising "the willing suspension of disbelief for a season" which he demanded of all readers of imaginative literature. Luke, to be sure, wished to carry his readers beyond this state to acceptance of the situation; he was narrating true, not fictitious, events. The supreme stunning miracle of Jesus' own resurrection was soon to be presented; and although Luke had prepared his readers for it by two previous reports of resurrections through Jesus' power, an even more incredible occurrence remained to be presented. Luke had performed a remarkable literary feat in presenting his material to cultured but skeptical readers; he now must face the supreme test of his entire Gospel.

For his account of events in Passion Week leading to the Last Supper, Luke employed almost nothing that can be separated from Mark. He omitted some Marcan details: the episode of the barren fig tree, the discussion about which is the greatest commandment and he both added to and subtracted from the items in Mark's eschatology. He possibly borrowed from other sources, or even developed of his own accord, a few details not in Mark. At the triumphal entry (Luke 19:39–44) he added that when the Pharisees, incensed at the acclaim he received, told Jesus to make the crowds be quiet, Jesus replied in characteristic Old Testament hyperbole that if the crowd should become silent, the stones would cry out. Then as he gained a clearer view of the city, Jesus broke into tears at the thought of what Jerusalem might have been if it had known "the things that belong unto peace" and what it would become in consequence of its obstinate course of action. Such additions and omissions clearly make the account better adapted to the concerns of Luke's readers

A like dependence upon Mark continues through the narrative of the Last Supper and the events leading up to Jesus' arrest. Possibly to heighten the readers' suspense, Luke did not specifically name Judas as the traitor who had sold out to the chief priests; this he emphasized by mention of the disciples' nervous uncertainty about the traitor's identity. He apparently followed a slightly different account in his mentioning the bickering of the disciples during the dinner about who should have precedence in the kingdom of God. He also built up slightly Peter's self-confident claim that he would follow Jesus even to death, and Jesus' deflating reply.

Another addition is perhaps more noteworthy (22:35–38). Jesus reminds them that on a precious mission he had directed them to take no provisions. Now, however, he admonishes them, they must take with them what money they have and be prepared to face enemies, sword in hand. Like Paul after him, who habitually spoke metaphorically of the armor of the Christian, Jesus surely spoke metaphorically of swords to indicate the circumstances of their future careers. The history of the early Church shows clearly that they soon realized the metaphorical sense in which Jesus spoke.

Later Christians unfortunately were less perceptive. Fifteen centuries and more later they were still strenuously arguing the symbolic significance of the disciples' two swords, and using their own to support their theories. Luke's penchant for genre pictures, no doubt, led him to see the ironic humor in these fishermen with swords and to feel that Jesus saw it, too. Eleven verses later, when one of them swings his sword at a guard and succeeds only in cutting off his ear, the latent irony still persists.

To stress the hearing of Jesus before the Sanhedrin, Luke added details that place the onus of this travesty of justice squarely upon the shoulders of the Jewish authorities. He also handled Pilate sympathetically. With his intimate knowledge of Paul's imprisonments, Luke undoubtedly understood that Pilate was unwilling to foment a riot when patriotic feeling among Jews was at fever heat. To him Jesus, though obviously innocent of the charges brought against him, was not a Roman citizen and, therefore, was expendable. Luke doubtless felt that Pilate's venality and weakness laid him open to Jewish pressure. To say this was not to condemn Roman power as being unjust, for Pilate's subsequent disgrace relieved Rome of the major responsibility.

Luke inserted one detail which placed Pilate in a slightly better light. Herod Antipas, tetrarch of Galilee, was in the city for the

Passover. When Pilate discovered that Jesus was a Galilean, he tried to escape from responsibility by sending Jesus to him for trial. Herod was under less pressure in Jerusalem than Pilate and could have stood against the pressure of the Sanhedrin if he had wished. Herod, evidently drunk as usual, tried unsuccessfully to get Jesus to show off his powers for Herod's entertainment. Irritated at Jesus' refusal, Herod dressed him in a parody of royal garb and returned him to Pilate. With all his weakness, Pilate had endeavored to treat Jesus fairly. Luke made no mention of Pilate's soldiers dressing Him in mock regal robes as Mark had recorded.

Luke added several details to the account of the crucifixion. As Jesus was carrying his cross along the Via Dolorosa, a crowd of lamenting people accompanied him. Jesus bade them to mourn rather for themselves and their children for the evil days to come upon them. This was, Luke's readers would feel, a prophecy of the fate recently suffered by the city. He added also the contrasting attitudes of the two malefactors crucified with Jesus, one abusing him, the other realizing his fate as deserved and asking Jesus to remember him. Even at this extremity of torture, Luke noted, Jesus forgave his sins and promised him entry into his kingdom.

These two episodes show Jesus' overriding interest in his fellow men even at the height of his suffering. Jesus had even prayed God to forgive his executioners: they did not know what a crime they were committing. Luke included also Jesus' last words, a prayer to God to receive him, as he died. His rounding out the picture with these details pictured to his readers one who never ceased from love of men and trust in God.

All three synoptic Gospels tally closely in their accounts of the interment. Luke follows Mark's account, in fact, to the point where Mark breaks off, the sole notable difference being that "two men in dazzling apparel" instead of "a young man . . . arrayed in a white robe" speak to the women at the tomb. Luke reports ensuing events more dramatically than Matthew. Peter at the announcement of the women started running to the tomb, inspected the neatly folded garments in it, and went off completely puzzled; the other disciples thought the report to be nonsense and did nothing. Peter's impetuous character persisted, but Luke was rehabilitating him in preparation for the leading part he was to play in Acts.

The first reappearance of Jesus after his resurrection that Luke records—it is colorlessly mentioned in the summary appended to Mark (16:12-13)—brilliantly answers the perplexed mind of Peter as well as Luke's readers. A disciple named Cleopas and another were walking on the road to Emmaus, a village seven or eight miles from Jerusalem, and naturally were discussing the report that He had risen. They were so absorbed in their news that when Jesus fell in with them as a casual traveler, they failed to recognize him. He skillfully drew out of them a statement of their perplexity: Jesus had been a mighty man, a good man, who they had hoped would be the long-expected Messiah; but the Jewish authorities had worked upon Pilate to have him executed. They had heard reports of his resurrection, but were quite at a loss to know what to believe. Their mental perturbation probably represents the confused state of mind of most of Jesus' followers. Thereupon, Jesus, still unrecognized, explained to them that everything done to Jesus, and in fact his whole career, had been the fulfillment of the Law and the Prophets. In Emmaus, Jesus accepted their invitation to dine and spend the night with them. When he performed the familiar act of breaking the bread, they recognized him, whereupon he vanished.

In their excitement they immediately rushed back to Jerusalem to inform the other disciples. Apparently Peter had in the interim seen Jesus, for they confirmed his account by their own experience. While they were reporting, Jesus suddenly reappeared among them. He calmed their fear of his being a ghost and proved his corporeality by bidding them to touch him and by eating food. The wounds inflicted at the crucifixion proved him to be no impostor. He then restated that in his life on earth he fulfilled what had been foretold in the Law and the Prophets, as well as in the Psalms, concerning him. From its start at Jerusalem, he told them, his message of repentance and remission of sins was to be preached to all nations. They were to testify as witnesses of all that had happened and been taught.

Luke's Gospel concludes with no further detail; he reserved his

Dalmatia
Illyricum
Adriatic Sea
Moe
Rome
Three Taverns
Appii Forum
Puteoli
Naples
Italy
Macedonia
Philippi
Thessalonica
Beroea
Achaia
Nicopolis
Rhegium
Sicily
Syracuse
Corinth
Cenchreae
Malta
The Eastern Mediterranean World
in
New Testament Times
Cyrene
Libya
0
100
200
300
Miles

Black Sea
Thracia
Byzantium
Bithynia et Pontus
Galatia
Regnum
Polemonis
Adramyttium
Asia
Pergamum
Thyatira
Sardis
Smyrna
Philadelphia
Antioch
Hierapolis
Laodicea
Colossae
Iconium
Cappadocia
Antiochi
Lystra
Derbe
Miletus
Regnum
Tarsus
Cilicia
Lycia
Perga
Attalia
Cos
Cnidus
Rhodes
Patara
Myra
Seleucia
Antioch
Salamis
Syria
Cyprus
Paphos
Sea
Sidon
Damascus
Tyre
Phoenicia
Ptolemais
Palestine
Joppa
Jerusalem
Gaza
Alexandria
Egypt
Arabia

account for a brief summary at the beginning of Acts. He tied his Gospel to its sequel by Jesus' command to the disciples to remain in Jerusalem, "until ye be endued with power from on high"—the power of the Holy Spirit which is the moving force behind the apostles in Acts. He then led them out to Bethany, and while he pronounced a blessing on them He left them and was carried up into the sky. The disciples obediently returned to Jerusalem joyful after their being in the depths of despair and awaited what was to happen.

In his final report of the tremendous drama, Luke followed the Greek stylistic principle that ornaments of style should never be employed at high stages of action: they stand on their own feet; ornament detracts from the action. Since he contemplated a sequel to his account, a rounded conclusion was superfluous. The disciples' strained but joyful expectancy carried the reader eagerly into Acts.

How successful Luke's propaganda was in achieving its purpose to bring competent Hellenistic leaders into the Church, it is impossible to measure. Such leaders did, however, appear. At the risk of indulging in the *post hoc, ergo propter hoc* fallacy, and in the absence of any report of other causes, it seems reasonable to assume that his work achieved its purpose. Admittedly, he wrote for an audience so difficult to persuade that Paul had some twenty years earlier almost despaired of convincing it. It is difficult to imagine propaganda that more skillfully handles the problem of convincing the educated, upper-class Hellenist.

CHAPTER 4

THE ACTS OF THE APOSTLES

Ancient books were in many cases not given titles by their authors. Those subsequently added by others were sometimes not well chosen. The title given to Acts is particularly misleading. It treats chiefly actions of two original disciples, Peter and John—with John usually a silent partner—and of Paul, who claimed the position of apostle. A more truly descriptive title would be "The Acts of Peter and Paul." Other unnamed apostles participated at the beginning and, no doubt, in the Council of Jerusalem; and Stephen and Philip the deacons play brief but important roles. For the major branches of Christianity which were to become the Roman Catholic and Greek Orthodox churches, Peter and Paul stood pre-eminent.

No one doubts that the same author composed Luke and Acts. They amount to two volumes of a single work. The prologue to Luke probably refers to both, with the brief prologue to Acts little more than a summary of that to the Gospel. The clause translated in the KJV as "those things which are most surely believed among us" (Luke 1:1) is more accurately "the things which have been accomplished among us"—that is, from the start in Bethlehem to the arrival of Paul in Rome, which symbolizes the worldwide scope of Christianity.

The abrupt conclusion of Acts formerly led some scholars to speculate that Luke had in mind a third volume. This view is extremely unlikely. Clearly, Luke saw his project as an account of the Church, first under the leadership of Jesus on earth and followed by its subsequent progress under the present but disembodied guidance of the Holy Spirit. What possible third leader can be suggested for a third volume? Far more probably, the abrupt ending of Acts is a skillful symbolic touch of the author. The lack of a rounded conclusion suggests to the attentive reader the continuing state of the Church—a device used for a similar purpose by John Steinbeck at the end of *The Grapes of Wrath*.

Like the synoptic Gospels, Acts is a document in propaganda. Although Luke clearly had strong historical interests, his book is not a history of the movement. When one keeps in mind this concept, discrepancies between Luke's account and Paul's biographical data furnished in Galatians (to name but one point hotly debated among scholars) will cause him far less concern. As a propagandist Luke was free to foreshorten or combine incidents as suited his purpose. Paul, in warding off attacks by opponents, must have realized that his data given in Galatians would be scrutinized for errors. His data are more likely to be factually accurate than Luke's propaganda. While an honest propagandist will consistently tell the truth, he need not be minutely factual in his report.

Viewed as propaganda and as continuing Luke's Gospel, the Acts is skillfully designed to parallel the form of that Gospel. Each book spans somewhat more than thirty years. Luke covers the period from approximately 4–2 B.C. to about A.D. 29. Acts starts at the latter date and recounts events up to about A.D. 60; but it almost gratuitously adds two years at the end (28:30), a supplement which brings its span of years closely parallel to that of Luke. The themes, as already mentioned, are also parallel. The Holy Spirit, the "power from on high" which Jesus had promised to his disciples (Luke 24:49), is again promised in Acts (1:4–5), comes on Pentecost (2:2–4), and is repeatedly mentioned throughout the book as directing the action.

The books are also structurally parallel. Just as Luke falls into three major segments—events in Galilee, the travel document, and events in Jerusalem—so Luke orders Acts in three stages. These stages are intimated by Jesus' last reported words (1:8): "Ye shall be witnesses unto me both in Jerusalem, and in all Judea, and in Samaria, and unto the uttermost parts of the earth."[1] The first stage is reported in chapters 2–8, concluding with Stephen's tactless speech and violent death. The second, while introducing Paul, focuses on Philip the deacon and Peter and on operations in Samaria, in Judea, and in the Gaza Strip. The third part occupies the remainder of Acts. These three parts are not separate: Luke provides connecting links while shifting his scenery.

Three motives at least underlay the writing of Acts. First, as propaganda it was designed to keep the record straight and to spread as rapidly as possible the knowledge of the Christian message and movement. As Paul's traveling companion for more than a decade, Luke must have shared Paul's expectation of an imminent end of the world. Jesus' command to preach repentance and remission of sins among all nations (Luke 24:47) combined with expectancy of Jesus' immediate second coming to make their task urgent. It is the same driving force that actuated the writing of the synoptic Gospels.

Second, it had an equally immediate purpose in defending the Church from the charge that it was a subversive movement. Although details are not available, Christian writers long believed that this charge was sponsored by inimical Jewish leaders whose influence at Rome prior to A.D. 70 had been powerful. For whatever reason, the blame for the great fire at Rome during Nero's principate was charged to the Christians. To escape persecution, Christians went underground and became a secret society in Rome. Roman authority, no doubt rightly in many instances, looked upon secret organizations as subversive; in escaping persecution the Christians faced a dilemma by protecting themselves. Luke had to reassure his cultured Hellenistic audience, who for the most part found Roman rule congenial, that Christianity had no subversive intent. Paul, a Roman citizen who respected Roman government, was an admirable protagonist for Luke's purpose.

Finally, Luke had to defend Paul's record against hostile parties within the Church itself. Those who had attacked him during his lifetime had still to be answered after his death. Although he prided himself on his Jewish race and loved the Jewish faith, Paul had de-

[1] The punctuation in the KJV hints that its translators failed to see this tripartite division; the NEB and Today's English Version of the New Testament show awareness of it.

veloped into the principal champion of Gentile Christianity. Entrance of Gentiles into the Church depended heavily on the decision whether they had to submit to the Jewish rite of circumcision. Such a requirement might well stop any further expression of interest.

The Jewish wing of the Church viewed Christianity as a sort of reformed Judaism. It welcomed Gentiles as did other Jews, but insisted that they become ritually Jewish through circumcision. Paul—and Peter, though perhaps less consistently—refused to load such a burden upon Gentile converts. With the support of Peter and James, Paul succeeded at the Council of Jerusalem in A.D. 49 in lifting this requirement from Gentiles. Nearly a decade later, however, the mother congregation in Jerusalem, as James told Paul (Luke 21:20), was "zealous of the law" and believed that Paul had not enforced it among any Jewish converts he had made. The influence of this group was formidable, and it appears, on the whole, to have been more than dissatisfied with Paul's discarding of ritual law as a Christian requirement. It was against remnants of this wing that Luke had to defend Paul's position.

In reading Acts one should distinguish four categories of people who figure in it. First, there are those Jews who did not accept Jesus' message or deity, whose leaders included active enemies of the Church. A second group accepted Jesus' deity and teachings but still considered itself to be Jewish. These are the "Judaizers" or Christians who felt themselves to be still Jews in religion. Among the Gentiles are two corresponding groups: the great majority still unconverted to Christianity and the Christian Gentiles. The unconverted Gentiles are in some cases unfriendly to the new movement, in others uninterested.

Only rarely is it possible to fix specifically the dates of events in Acts. Since Luke was not writing history, he was under no obligation to record dates or even to observe accurate chronological order of events. Some dating is, however, possible. Jesus' crucifixion and resurrection took place at the Passover season, most probably in A.D. 29. Pentecost—our Whitsunday—was seven weeks after the resurrection, some ten days following the ascension. There is no attempt in Acts to date events—perhaps Luke's sources were not clear about them. Herod's death (12:20–23), we know from Josephus, occurred in A.D. 44. The Council of Jerusalem (Acts 15) probably met in A.D. 49. Gallio (18:12–16) became proconsul of Achaia in 52. Festus (25:1) became procurator of Judea approximately in the year A.D. 60. Using these dates as points of reckoning, one can construct a working order of events as Luke reported them.

ACTION IN JERUSALEM (1–8:3)

From the mass of material available to him, Luke selected accounts that fall roughly under seven heads; they present a picture of the new "Way" as a tremendously dynamic power badly in need of a governor—a service successfully provided by the conversion and leadership of Saul of Tarsus. Luke presents his account without overt criticism of the early leadership, but in the light of what followed under Paul's leadership, his judgment of these first years of activity is clear.

His first subject compares the disciples before and after their receiving the Holy Spirit. After his resurrection Jesus spent forty days with the disciples "speaking to them of the things pertaining to the kingdom of God." Their continuing denseness, however, concludes Jesus' teaching on a pessimistic note boding ill for the success of their teaching: "Lord, wilt thou at this time restore again the kingdom to Israel?" Understandably near exasperation that they are still held by Jewish traditional ideas, Jesus curtly informs them that such matters are none of their business; but he adds a hopeful note in the promise of the power proceeding from the Holy Spirit which they should receive. Then, Luke simply records, Jesus rose into the sky until a cloud hid him. As the disciple-apostles gaze after him, two men in white robes remind them that he will return just as he had gone.

After their return to Jerusalem, the little group of about 120 men and several women quietly waits for what will transpire—all but Peter. That restless man, whose attention continually roved from subject to subject, conceives the idea of replacing Judas so as to have the symbolic number twelve in the disciples' inner group. The group acts on his suggestion and chooses a man named Matthias. Peter's nervous motion is perhaps evaluated in the fact that, as Luke notes, "he [Matthias] was numbered with the eleven apostles." There is no indication that Peter's action bore any significant fruit; Luke may have been playing down Peter's leadership in this bare report.

Luke next recorded the coming of the Holy Spirit on Pentecost. The arrival coincided with Shavuot, the Jewish Feast of Weeks commemorating the revealing of the Law on Sinai; it was also the wheat festival. The celebration was a holiday from work; crowds thronged the Temple and public places, not only crowds of dwellers in Jerusalem but also of pilgrims from other lands. The followers of Jesus, already tense with expectation of they knew not what, were further aroused by the Jewish scriptural lessons for the day: the stirring account of the giving of the Law (Exod. 19), the mystical vision in Ezekiel 1, the visions of Jahweh's coming in Habakkuk 3 and Psalm 29, and the praise of Jahweh for having restored his people in Psalm 68. They were at a high pitch of excitement.

Under such emotional stress, men find difficulty in reporting what has happened, especially when it was a mystical experience for which words are seldom adequate. Luke, moreover, got his information some four decades later at second hand. As he recorded the event, those gathered heard a sound *like* a "rushing mighty wind" and saw "cloven tongues *like as* of fire" settling upon each of them; and they spoke "in other tongues." Their overcharged emotions burst forth in an ecstatic utterance, only partly intelligible.

Such expression was recognizable by Hebrews as a characteristic of some Hebrew prophecy. It was not unknown in paganism, as a concomitant, for example, of messages delivered by the Pythia, the priestess who delivered the oracles at Delphi, and by the Sibyl at Cumae. This "speaking in tongues," as it was called, persisted in the early Church, sometimes to the embarrassment of thoughtful leaders like Paul, although he also possessed this gift (1 Cor. 14:1–28). (This phenomenon still occurs from time to time; it is an established part in the worship of some Christian sects; and several Christian denominations who do not practice it, nonetheless, seriously investigate it.)

The crowd who heard it were for the most part astounded by what they were hearing—Luke says that they literally "stood outside of themselves" emotionally. To attempt to rationalize such an event, even if more details about it were available, would be risky; yet some matters may be noted. First, the crowd included Jews or adherents to Judaism from all over the Near East. All understood Aramaic, the language also spoken by the apostles, no doubt with varying local peculiarities somewhat as Yiddish is spoken today. The Galilean dialect of the apostles also had noticeable peculiarities. In their excitement they possibly associated the non-sense sounds intermingled in the apostles' speech with words which they knew and, by a sort of tied image, made sense out of it. The charge of skeptics in the crowd that the apostles were drunk and babbling indicates that they were uttering nonsense sounds along with intelligible words. It is also possible that the shock of their religious experience may have affected their speech. Even the most skeptical of Luke's readers could not deny that some powerful force had taken charge of the apostles—a force, Luke repeatedly notes, that was to seize early converts as well.

Readers who had just finished Luke received a nearly equivalent shock in the change that came over Peter. His final condition stated in the Gospel had been a puzzled inability to comprehend the evidence in the tomb that pointed to Jesus' resurrection. His previous action in Acts had been a nervous motion to round out the number of the twelve by electing a successor to Judas—an act which Luke's readers perhaps knew had proved inconsequential. At Pentecost, within a few weeks of the Resurrection, he showed complete confidence and deeper insight into Jesus' purpose than any other disciple had yet demonstrated. He felt himself to be a prophet of doom to all who would not accept Jesus' teaching and purpose, a later Amos or Hosea. He bluntly charged the Jews with the responsibility for Jesus' crucifixion and declared that God, turning their evil to his own good purpose, had brought Jesus to life and made him Lord as well as Messiah. The speech was copiously interlarded with proof texts from the Old Testament that revealed its author a competent student of the Scriptures. It was so effective that some three thousand people were moved to accept Peter's message. Although the speech no doubt owes much of its learning to Luke who composed it, his readers would still be struck by the change indicated in Peter. His readers' probable awareness of this fact detracted little if at all from the effect produced by this courageous utterance.

Luke, who of course knew Peter, probably followed in this speech the long-established rhetorical practice of *ēthopoiia,* which presented a speech written for another man in his customary personal manner of thinking and speaking. Lysias, its developer, had even reproduced idioms and colloquial expressions of the person whose speech he wrote. Not to have done so might have seemed a defect in his work to Luke's cultured readers, of whom several may also have known Peter or at least known a great deal about him. The speech probably presented also the gist of the primitive Christian message: a declaration of Jesus' life, resurrection, and deity; a warning against neglect of the opportunity offered through him; and an invitation to join the movement. And, as soon appeared, Peter was still essentially the same man in spite of his greatly increased confidence.

Luke stresses the naïveté of the Christians during these first developments in the Church. Without thought that they had still to reckon with an implacable Jewish religious authority, they saw the way as clear before them. In their inexperience of society, they even embarked upon a socialistic organization of the kind that history has since shown to be impractical: they pooled all their resources and made them common property. And without realizing that spiritual leaders are rarely sound administrators, they placed the management of this common fund in the hands of the apostles. The outcome of this experiment, which Luke postpones narrating, was precisely what the intelligent reader would expect.

For these years of the Church before Paul appeared, Luke contents himself with including interesting, revealing, sometimes slightly related episodes—a sampling, so to speak, of what happened. Although the events are reported without comment, the infant movement was given full credit for what it accomplished. Nonetheless, it impresses his readers as floundering for lack of a competent human agent to give it form and direction. Luke never gives Paul the credit for the growth of the Church except as the agent used by the Holy Spirit to accomplish its purpose. It is clearly his conviction that the Spirit would form the Church by choosing the right man through whom it would work. The contrast of these chaotic years with Paul's constructive expansion of the movement constitutes an excellent defense of Paul's program.

Peter's exploits indicate that he was still, for all his support by the Holy Spirit, the same man who had often shown tactlessness as a disciple. As the disciples' spokesman with Jesus, he had upon occasion made remarks which showed flashes of insight. More often he had shown facility at saying whatever popped into his mind. These weaknesses appeared in his dealings with the Jewish authorities, though his former lack of courage had left him. Arrested by the chief priests and Sadducees after his first speech in the Temple, Peter did nothing to lessen their rage when he offered a slight excuse for their killing of Jesus. His admission that the Jews and their rulers had acted through ignorance (3:17), in fact, exacerbated their leaders by its implication that these Galilean fishermen knew the Law and the Prophets as well as they did.

Peter's speech further includes (3:25–26) Paul's much discussed verse from Genesis (22:18), which deprived the Jew of his vaunted favor with God. (This could have been edited into the speech by Luke, who undoubtedly composed the address.) Comparison of Peter's and Stephen's speeches with Paul's similarly organized speech at Pisidian Antioch (13:16–43) reveals how bluntly tactless Peter and his imitator could be in contrast with Paul's skillful play upon the prejudice of his hearers.

Peter's initial successes, Luke implies, lay less in his oratory itself than in its unexpectedness. Jewish authorities had reasonably supposed that with Jesus' crucifixion his ragtag following would break up. Now, amazingly, the bumbling figure of fun that Peter had seemed to them to represent was persuading people that Jesus had come to life again and was actually divine. In spite of the blasphemy which they saw in this claim, they were temporarily stunned and took no action. At Peter and John's second irruption the priests ordered the two to cease their preaching. When the two claimed divine compulsion on them to speak, the authorities merely dismissed them with threats (4:18–21).

Such inaction convinced the Christians that the authorities would not take steps against them, and they were exultant over their supposed victory. Their activities were so successful that soon the apostles were once more arrested. They escaped and reappeared teaching in the Temple. They were re-arrested quietly, so as not to arouse the crowd to riot, and charged before the Sanhedrin. Peter's bluntness once more appeared in his answer (5:30): "The God of our fathers raised up Jesus, whom ye slew and hanged on a tree." This time, he nearly precipitated the death of the twelve by his tactlessness.

Once more Luke tacitly hints at the difference between Peter and Paul in the introduction of Paul's teacher Gamaliel, a learned Pharisee who had been president of the Sanhedrin. Apparently noting the force and sincerity of the apostles, Gamaliel suggested to the Sanhedrin that they let time test the validity of this movement. Twice recently, he reminded them, apparently strong popular movements had come to nothing because they lacked God's support. If God supports a movement, its opponents find themselves to be resisting God; if he does not support it, it will perish. This sane advice was in full accord with Jewish belief that Jahweh manages affairs in the world according to his plan; it was accordingly adopted. The apostles were once more admonished to cease their teaching, beaten to impress the admonition upon them, and released. Rightly seeing in this second reprieve that the authorities were in a quandary, the apostles felt free to continue their evangelism. For the time an uneasy truce existed between them and the Jewish leaders.

Meanwhile the communal experiment of the Christians (4:32–37) was running its predictable course. Many honest men like Barnabas, a Jew from Cyprus, had contributed all their property to the common fund. At least one fraudulent family, however, tried to hold back part of the proceeds of their property while contributing the rest as if it were the entire sum. Having learned of the fraud, Peter summoned the man, Ananias, before the assembled members and accused him so violently of his trickery that Ananias instantly died of the shock. His body was summarily removed and buried. Some three hours later, when his wife Sapphira came in, Peter asked her if the sum they had paid was the price of their property; and she, ignorant of her husband's exposure and death, assented. Peter assailed her so furiously that when he added to his excoriation the news that her husband had died, she also died of the shock. The Christians were in terror at this apparent divine judgment.

To balance this adverse item, Luke later adds an account of one good outgrowth of the communal system; but this, too, arose from an inherent weakness in the organization. Friction arose between the orthodox and the Hellenized Jews in the community. The latter claimed that the widows of their side were being slighted in the distribution of the common fund. Finding this problem a burden they could not assume, the apostles wisely recommended that a separate board of seven men be appointed to handle the fund. Less wisely, the group elected seven men who all bore Greek names, which may indicate that all the board were of the complaining party—a possible instance of over-correction not unknown today. Aside from this tactical error, the move was sound. These seven were called *diakonoi* ("people who perform services for others"), and such boards continue to be a valuable part of religious organizations today. The fact that two of the seven, Philip and Stephen, proved also to be notable preachers has led to a diaconate in some denominations which has the duty of clergy also.

Having mentioned this constructive result of the communal experiment, Luke dismisses it from his account. According to Paul's sketchy outline in his letters of church organization in the fifties, it played no part in the Church; it had evidently disappeared. Under Paul's saner leadership, Luke may have intended to imply, no such impractical program had a place.

Luke's selected episodes from the first stage of the Church rapidly drew to a dramatic close. He notes that a number of the priests were attracted to the movement (6:7), surely a disquieting trend to Jewish authorities. It was, however, the violent tirade of Stephen which ended the truce instigated by Gamaliel's prudent advice. Apparently patterning his methods after Peter's, he went far beyond him in bluntness. Having irritated a group of opponents, he was falsely charged before the Sanhedrin with blasphemy—presumably his claims for Jesus formed the basis for their slander.

In his defense, Stephen evidently assumed that tactics which Peter had previously used effectively would still prove to be so. At any rate, he employed them at far greater length and with even more bitter condemnation of the authorities' obstinate refusal to accept Jesus as Messiah. After his historical résumé, which he concluded with the declaration that God does not dwell in temples made with hands—an affront to the Sadducees, but based on Solomon's dedicatory prayer for the Temple (1 Kings 8:27)—he attacked the entire Sanhedrin with invective such as Peter had never employed. It is hardly surprising that the Sanhedrin were infuriated beyond endurance. They dragged him away and lynched him. A general attack upon Christians followed, many of them fled to outlying parts in Palestine and even farther afield, and the scene was set for the second stage of the movement.

ACTION IN JUDEA AND SAMARIA (8:1–12:23)

Although the apostles remained in Jerusalem, their followers had been scattered. Stephen's aping of Peter had precipitated the apparent disaster. Luke is preparing to discard Peter as protagonist to install Paul in his place. Such a shift in leading agent is artistically dangerous, but here it was unavoidable. He inserts transitional matter, in part of which Peter appears in a minor role, while in the rest Peter's action paves the way for Paul's coming Gentile program. Luke also uses the opportunity to gradually introduce Paul into the action. He employs Paul as part of his interlocking device to keep his book a literary unit.

Luke's report of action in Judea and Samaria is brief, yet it materially advances the action. Two episodes show Philip the deacon working among Samaritans. In one of these Peter plays a prominent part. Two other episodes center on Peter, one of them pivotal to the action: he admits Gentiles into the Church without requiring them to be circumcised. In playing up Paul's services to the Church,

Luke has no intent to belittle Peter. He gives Peter full credit for what he has accomplished yet lets the facts speak for themselves. His travels with Paul have convinced him that the future of the Church lies with the successful projects initiated by Paul.

Among those scattered abroad in the persecution starting from Stephen's intemperate speech was Philip the deacon. Like the others forced out of Jerusalem, he looked upon the event as providing opportunity to speak to new audiences. He perhaps had contacts in Samaria—he subsequently made his home in Caesarea, a port on the northwestern shore of Samaria—and he went to the city called Samaria from Jerusalem. There he taught with considerable success. The power of the Holy Spirit enabled him to perform mental and physical healings.

His work here marked a step away from strictly Jewish evangelizing. Although the Samaritans were religiously a heretical sect dating from the fourth century B.C., they were, according to Jewish history, of mixed descent; as John remarks, "the Jews have no dealings with the Samaritans." John's words understate the situation: there had been long-standing, aggressive hostility between Jew and Samaritan. The welcome given to Christian teaching where Jews from Jerusalem were hated clearly betokens the nascent Gentile acceptance of the apostles, while at the same time it is implicitly critical of the Judaizing Christians who opposed Paul. Philip was, in fact, so successful that he soon needed reinforcements, and the first team of Peter and John came down to assist him. Wherever Peter came, however, he took over the leadership.

Among the people attracted by Philip was a magician named Simon, a Samaritan who claimed to be "some great one." Recent scholars see in him one of the early leaders of the Gnostic heresy which for many decades troubled the Church. Simon became a famous charlatan and leader of a cult in subsequent years. Luke's readers were possibly acquainted with his spectacular career in Rome and elsewhere throughout the empire. As a thorn in the side of the Church, he offered here a good target for attack by Luke.

Simon Magus (*magus*, a Latinized form of the Greek *magos*, "a magician") was doubtless attracted by Philip's healings, but he apparently believed Philip's message as well as he could understand it and was baptized. He noticed that when Peter and John laid their hands on Samaritan converts, the converts underwent the striking experience of receiving the Holy Spirit with manifestations presumably akin to those which had occurred at Pentecost. Simon's professional feelings were aroused as he watched; this effect could be used in his business. Like magicians today, he offered to buy this illusion, as it seemed to him, from the apostles; it is unlikely that he had any sacrilegious intent. Peter, horrified, repulsed him so violently that Simon in a panic asked the apostles to intercede with God for him. Peter's unthinking response further demonstrated that he lacked the tact to spread Christianity among people of cultures alien to his.

Philip's second exploit, this time without Peter, occurred in what we now call the Gaza Strip, on the caravan route to Africa. He fell in with an Ethiopian, the treasurer of the queen of that country, a Jewish proselyte returning to Ethiopia from a pilgrimage to Jerusalem. Philip heard him reading aloud the passage in Isaiah (53:7–8) which describes the suffering servant as "brought as a lamb to the slaughter." At the traveler's request Philip explained it to him as a prophecy fulfilled by Jesus. This, the earliest recorded application of the passage to Jesus' suffering, represents what from an early date became standard practice in Christian interpretation of prophecy. The Ethiopian was convinced, and when they passed a body of water, he asked Philip to baptize him. Here Luke presents an even greater departure from the concept of the new faith as merely Jewish in scope. The Samaritans, though heretics, had some claim to Jewish descent; the Ethiopian, though a Jew in faith, was not so in race. The tie with the Jews hung here by a slender thread. Moreover, these two episodes in which Philip initiated the action serve to divert briefly the readers' attention from Peter.

The critical break from Judaism came surprisingly through Peter who otherwise had not distinguished himself as champion of Gentiles. Cornelius, a Roman and a centurion, was stationed in Caesarea. He was an adherent of Judaism who had not actually become a proselyte. In a mystical experience as he was praying, he was instructed to invite someone named Simon Peter to tell him what he ought to do. Like Saul of Tarsus, Cornelius apparently was dissatisfied with his religious experience. Peter at the time was living in Joppa, some thirty miles south of Caesarea. As Cornelius' messengers were approaching Joppa, Peter likewise had a mystical experience while at prayer on the housetop. He saw a sheet let down from heaven with various animals in it that were taboo to Jewish diet, and a voice invited him to kill and eat some of the animals. Peter had strained the proprieties in living with a tanner, whose trade made him ritually unclean; but he recoiled in horror from the thought of breaking a dietary taboo. The vision was presented to him three times—Peter required iteration to drive home a point—with the brusque admonition, "What God hath cleansed, that call thou not common."

The arrival of Cornelius' emissaries at this juncture convinced Peter—unlike Jonah at Joppa (Jon. 1:3)—that he should accede to the centurion's request. At Caesarea he found in Cornelius' house a considerable gathering. After frankly reminding them that in entering a Gentile's house he was breaking a Jewish taboo, he added that God had shown him that such a restriction was contrary to His will. Upon learning from Cornelius of his vision, Peter declared that God accepts in every nation those who revere and obey Him. He attested as an eyewitness to what they had heard about Jesus, asserted the genuineness of his resurrection and position as judge of the living and the dead, and supported his message from the Prophets, with whom they as adherents to Judaism were acquainted. While Peter was speaking, the manifestations of the Holy Spirit appeared, including the speaking with tongues as at Pentecost. Peter's Jewish companions were amazed at the Gentiles' receiving this gift. Peter, deeply stirred by the phenomenon, demanded that his companions show a valid reason why he should not baptize these Gentiles. Thereupon they were baptized.

Such a radical departure from their preconceived notions upset the "apostles and brethren that were at Jerusalem," and upon Peter's return they called him to account for his action. Luke repeats Peter's speech instead of summarizing it. The duplication indicates how significant Peter's action had been. Avoiding the main issue, however, the leaders proceeded obliquely by charging him with entering a Gentile's house and eating with Gentiles. Brushing aside all subterfuge, Peter reported that God had given these Gentiles the same gift which they had themselves received. He concluded with a rhetorical question which demanded acceptance of his action: "What was I, that I could withstand God?" Accepting the unavoidable, the Christian leaders praised God for his act. Their comment, however, indicated more surprise than conviction: "then hath God also to the Gentiles granted repentance unto life." The subsequent report in Acts indicates that they—or at least those who remained in Jerusalem—failed to accept the principle obviously indicated in Peter's experience.

Luke uses this episode as telling support for Paul's later program. With his customary tact he omits mention of Peter's later reservations about eating with Gentiles (Gal. 2:11–17), for which Paul bluntly upbraided him. In defending Paul's mission Luke did not wish to tear down the position of Peter in the Church as a great and good leader; and many years later Peter turned the tide toward Paul in the Council of Jerusalem. The evidence he included was enough: Peter and the leaders in Jerusalem had themselves accepted as divinely ordained the very conversion of Gentiles to which those in Jerusalem stood later opposed. It is particularly significant that Peter did not here require that the new converts be circumcised.

This second section concludes with a persecution of the Church in Jerusalem under Herod Agrippa I, whom Claudius had made king of Judea in A.D. 41. Presumably instigated by Jewish authorities, Herod executed James the brother of John and arrested Peter. The night before Peter's trial and execution, the "angel of the Lord" helped him to escape—not necessarily a supernatural agent. Luke's account reads here like the successful working of a well-laid plot to gain his release. Upon escaping, Peter went to Mark's home—a center of Christian activity—and knocked, but found difficulty in gaining entry because those within thought he was a ghost. After persuading them and telling them to inform their leader, James the brother of Jesus, he left the city and went to Caesarea. Herod executed the guard.

Shortly thereafter, Herod made a public appearance in full regalia before a crowd who hailed him as divine, an honor occasionally accorded to Oriental rulers during their lifetime. Quickly after this blasphemy, as both Jew and Christian saw it, he died suddenly, "eaten of worms," as the Jewish formula for such divine judgment described it symbolically. This death occurred in A.D. 44. At about this time, then, as this date enables us to fix it, the second section of Acts comes to an end, and the stage is now ready for Paul's entry as protagonist.

In this transitional section Luke achieves by means of selected episodes a rounding off of Peter's early leadership. He was not inimical to Peter and obviously felt him to be a man thoroughly devoted to the Christian cause. Luke showed through what Peter had done since the coming of the Holy Spirit that the former hotheaded disciple was still not the kind of human leader that the movement needed. At the same time, he credited Peter with the cracking of the shell around early Christianity that seemed likely to restrict it to Jewish milieus. Whatever misgivings Peter may have had, he was obedient to the clear direction of the Holy Spirit. The introduction of two episodes in which Philip led the action, one of them skillfully attached to Peter as well, prepares the reader for the complete shift of leadership to Paul.

Luke has also broken ground for Paul's taking the center of the stage by relating the beginnings of his meteoric career and then tantalizingly removing him from the action for a time. Perhaps with symbolic intent he sent Peter from the opening scene in Jerusalem to Caesarea. The expression implies that Peter went to Caesarea and stayed there. The only later appearance of Peter in Acts presents him as supporting Paul.

TO THE UTTERMOST PART OF THE EARTH (12:24–28:31)

With Peter removed from the stage, Paul is free to play the leading role. His spectacular introduction in the previous section serves to link these two parts. He first appeared as Saul, a young man holding the cloaks of those who stoned Stephen. During the ensuing persecution he "made havock of the Church" as an agent of the Sanhedrin. He raided the homes of Christians and imprisoned them. Unsatisfied with his scope here, he got authorization from the high priest to arrest Christians in Damascus. The Sanhedrin had no jurisdiction in that city, some 125 miles distant, but the authority of the high priest would stir Jews in that city to give Paul aid.

Information about Paul's previous life comes from his letters rather than from Acts. Many of Luke's readers, no doubt, had some acquaintance with these letters, which began to circulate widely not long after his death; Luke may depend on their previous knowledge from the letters to fill in the picture. Intelligent readers would fill in the gap in Acts with some accuracy. Here is a young Jew high in the confidence of the Sanhedrin and violently hostile to the Christian heresy. After vigorously persecuting the Church, he all at once turns about-face and becomes its equally vigorous proponent. Ultimately he became the leader of the Church better known to most of them than any other. However terrific the shock at the pivotal point of his life, the readers would realize that strong emotional and mental disturbance must have preceded it. More detailed treatment of Paul's psychological and religious problems will be presented in connection with his letters.

Paul's mystical experience near Damascus was shattering. Like other such experiences, it was not only beyond the power of human vocabulary to adequately report, it also occurred under emotional stress which made difficult accurate recollection of its details. Luke's three reports of it in Acts quite probably represent three slightly varying traditions. Paul, no stranger to mystical experience, fell to the ground from the shock. He recognized the presence of a superior being—he declared in a letter that he had beheld Jesus just as had the other apostles—and heard a voice demanding, "Why persecutest thou me?" Although the question implied clearly the speaker's identity, he understandably stammered, "Who are you, my lord?" Luke deliberately uses an ambiguity here: the word *lord (kyrie)* could refer either to Jesus or to any superior person. Jesus named himself and commented that Paul was like a balky mule kicking at the goad —a hint of Paul's spiritual turmoil. When Paul asked what he should do, Jesus told him to go into Damascus and wait for guidance. Upon opening his eyes he saw nothing, and for several days he remained blind. During these three days he observed a complete fast. When sight was restored to him, something like scales fell from his eyes. His blindness, as Luke the physician realized, was not organic but psychosomatic, induced by a cause like that which may bring amnesia or aphasia.

During his fast Paul had evidently had time to think through his religious condition. When he appeared in public upon his regaining his sight, he immediately began to preach the Christian message in Damascus. This complete reversal in such a prominent apologist of Judaism naturally stunned his auditors at first, then aroused to fury the Jews he had come to lead against the Christians. As in later circumstances, Paul showed a strange lack of understanding about how others would probably react to his work, and assumed that they would accept him without question. When opposition became murderous, his friends had to get him out of the city by lowering him at night from the city wall to avoid the patrols of Jews determined to assassinate him.

Returning to Jerusalem, he exhibited the same blindness to the reception others might give him. He went directly to the Christians, naïvely expecting them to receive him without question. Naturally, they suspected that he was trying to infiltrate their group in order to make further arrests. Barnabas, who came from the same general region as Paul, vouched for him and told the apostles of his conversion.

Luke notes in particular how Paul confuted the "Grecians," that is, the Jews of the Dispersion living in Jerusalem, and roused their anger to such a pitch that they plotted to kill him. The irony of the apostle to the Gentiles getting into trouble with the Jews who were accustomed to live among Gentiles would not escape Luke's readers. Even these comparatively liberal Jews were fanatically opposed to the new movement—a state of affairs which would clarify the separateness of the new faith from Judaism to these readers long before the Christians themselves had come to realize it.

As in Damascus, Paul had to leave the city to save his life. The Christians got him safely to Caesarea, where he sailed to his home in Tarsus. "Then," Luke remarks—possibly with ironic intent—"had the churches rest" throughout Palestine. Paul's entry had been turbulent. He disappeared from the account for perhaps five or six years. Presumably he stayed in Tarsus. Whatever he did there is not mentioned; but when he returned to the stage, he worked for perhaps three years in Antioch without apparently stirring up violent trouble. He was never a peaceable evangelist; not without provocation his opponents charged him with turning the world upside down. In his subsequent adventures, however, he generally governed his activities so as to turn the excitement he caused to the advantage of his purpose.

When Paul re-entered the stage, the center of Christian activity had shifted from Jerusalem to Antioch, the principal city on the northeastern coast of the Mediterranean and the funnel through which poured commerce and travel between the Roman world and the Middle and Far East. Its situation offered a hint to Paul and other Christians about the most rapid method of disseminating their faith which Paul later used to great advantage. The first Christians had not come to Antioch with any such plan in mind, but chiefly to find refuge following the persecutions in Jerusalem. It had a large Jewish population and probably offered them opportunity for work to support themselves among people of their own race. Among those from Jerusalem who came to Antioch were Jewish natives of nearby Cyprus, who found Antioch probably a better refuge for employment than the comparatively rural island.

These Christians told their message to the Jews of the Diaspora with great success. As previously in Samaria, the home church sent them reinforcements, choosing Barnabas naturally because he had contacts in the region. After looking over the situation, Barnabas decided to bring Paul into the active center in Antioch. Accordingly, he visited Paul in Tarsus, some 160 miles to the northwest, and brought him back. Soon Barnabas and Paul formed a team that within a year had converted great numbers to the new faith.

Until developments in Antioch, the followers of Jesus had no specific name as a movement. Possibly they referred to themselves as "the Way," taking the term from Jesus' use of the metaphor as reported in John (14:6). In Antioch they first were named, possibly nicknamed, Christians. The term possibly carried an opprobrium like the modern expression "Christer" which enemies of Christianity sometimes derisively apply to its members. Before the end of the first century, the name *Christian* had become the name accepted by the followers of Christ, and the stigma at first attached to the name had largely disappeared.

Until Jerusalem was destroyed in A.D. 70, it was considered the home base of the Church. In Luke's account, the center of action was Antioch. Paul dutifully reported to the leaders at Jerusalem after each of his journeys, but he speedily returned to Antioch as a more congenial home. Within the first decade of his activities, a deputation from Antioch could face the leaders in Jerusalem on a fairly equal footing and wrest from it a compromise by which Antioch gained what it had demanded. The church in Antioch was apparently the more prosperous of the two, for it contributed to the support of the mother church when famine threatened its survival. In this community in Antioch, Barnabas and Paul had risen within some three years to prominence.

The Antioch church prospered until by about A.D. 47 it was ready to undertake new projects. The dynamic driving force, the Holy Spirit, led the church to dispatch Barnabas and Paul to spread the Christian message abroad in obedience to Jesus' final word. Without any apparent fixed itinerary, they added Mark, Barnabas' nephew, to their party and set out. They first sailed to the island of Cyprus, perhaps because it was Barnabas' home, and traversed the island from east to west. By the time they left Cyprus, the description of the party had significantly shifted from "Barnabas and Saul" to "Paul and his party," and regularly thereafter to "Paul and Barnabas." Saul's Jewish name was abandoned in favor of his Gentile name Paul, a foreshadowing of the imminent shift in emphasis of the Christian program in Luke's eyes.

Their next goal was Pisidian Antioch. This small city had been established by the Seleucid kings of Antioch in Syria as a military outpost of their empire. Quite possibly among its citizens were relatives of people related to or known to some of the Christians who had sent out the deputation, and for this reason they gravitated to it. Pisidia was a rough, frontier region which throughout history had been imperfectly controlled by more civilized empires. Mark apparently became frightened at the prospect and left to return to Jerusalem. His desertion, and Paul's subsequent refusal to allow him a second chance, was the immediate cause of the breaking up of this effective team of workers.

In Pisidian Antioch, Paul's coming shift from Jewish to Gentile evangelism was clearly foreshadowed. On the Sabbath, Paul as a distinguished visitor was invited to address the synagogue. Luke seized the opportunity offered by Paul's address to point up sharply the difference between his rhetoric and Peter's. He cast Paul's speech in the same mold as that employed by Peter and Stephen: a recounting of the great events so dear to Jewish memory from which the speaker could deviate at will to introduce his own message. Paul carried his catalog as far as David, whom popular belief held to be the ancestor of the Messiah, and then introduced Jesus as that Messiah. Peter had at this point tactlessly condemned his audience for having had Jesus crucified. Paul, correctly but far more tactfully, blamed this sin on "they that dwell at Jerusalem, and their rulers." In view of the enmity existing between Palestinian Jews and those of the Diaspora, his statement almost implied: "That's the sort of thing they would do!" He then reported Jesus' resurrection with Old Testament support of it and called upon them to accept the forgiveness of sins brought by Jesus.

Paul's conciliatory approach won him the interest of many Jews and Gentile proselytes, so that the next Sabbath, at the Gentiles request, he addressed "almost the whole city." The Jews themselves were angered at his success with Gentiles, which far exceeded theirs and broke up the assembly with charges against Paul's words. Their effrontery stirred Paul and Barnabas to declare that the Jews by God's will were to first hear their message, but their refusal to listen now was the cause of the apostles' turning to the Gentiles. The Gentiles listened eagerly, but the Jewish leaders—possibly the hard Pharisaic core—instigated such a persecution that the two men were forced to leave. This same Jewish influence broke up their efforts at Iconium and Lystra. At Lystra, Paul was stoned and left for dead, but he was able to get up and walk away. The pattern of Jewish opposition was to be repeated in the years following wherever Paul went (2 Cor. 11:23–27).

One episode at Lystra affords a hint of the appearance of Paul and Barnabas. Paul effected the healing of a lame man. The villagers immediately assumed that the two were gods in human form. Ovid (*Metamorphoses* viii. 620–724) reports the legend that Jupiter and Mercury had visited an aged couple Baucis and Philemon in that same region. The simple villagers believed that they were receiving gods, too, and readily identified Barnabas as Jupiter and Paul as Mercury. Sculptors have preserved the ancient likenesses of these gods. Jupiter was depicted as a venerable, impressive, full-figured man with a flowing beard, while Mercury was shown as a nervous, wiry, nimble fellow who never stood still for an instant. These two men, then, are at least typed for modern readers if not individually portrayed.

In the light of the ensuing journeys, one must look upon this first expedition as a kind of "shakedown cruise." Throughout the tour of some 1,400 miles, they visited no large city or center of commerce or government. Pisidia as a whole was as remote from the stream of Hellenistic life and culture as could well have been found. In order to spread their message rapidly throughout the world, some other procedure had to be devised. At the same time, the inexperienced mission faced fewer and less complicated problems than large cities offered. They got a hearing and made converts who formed churches, and these successes gave Paul and Barnabas confidence and practice for the more difficult problems that lay ahead. Most significant of all their conclusions was the realization that while Jews were likely to turn away from the new movement, Gentiles would listen and accept their ideas much more readily.

Shortly after Paul and Barnabas returned to Syrian Antioch, repercussions of their work were felt in Jerusalem. The leaders there approved of bringing Gentiles into the Church, but only if the male converts underwent the Jewish rite of circumcision. To the men in Jerusalem, Christianity was an advanced Judaism. It speedily became known that Paul and Barnabas had not required their converts to submit to this rite.

Paul had conferred with Peter (Gal. 1:18) at length some three years after his conversion. He surely learned from Peter about his baptism of Cornelius without requiring him to be circumcised. His acquaintance with Gentile prejudices would have made him eagerly grasp at this precedent to avoid what would for many Gentiles be an insurmountable barrier to their conversion. And his logical mind, already dissatisfied with the effects of Jewish law, would in any case dispose him to dispense with such an overwhelming requirement when he saw its uselessness for the faith.

Before the Church in Jerusalem had taken action, a self-appointed deputation of right-wing Jewish Christians came to Antioch and asserted that a Christian had to be circumcised to attain salvation. Supposing them to speak for the mother church, the Antioch church argued vigorously with them. It was finally decided to send a deputation to Jerusalem led by Paul and Barnabas to settle the dispute officially.

In Jerusalem the overwhelming majority of Christians were Jews; circumcision constituted no problem there. In the Hellenistic world it would be a barrier to men's joining the new faith. Circumcision (delightfully defined by a former coed member of my class as the irretractable badge of Judaism) was objectionable to Hellenists because many of them opposed any physical mutilation as well as because it subjected a man to anti-Semitic prejudice. Since men exercised nude in their gymnasia, it could not be concealed. If the Church had required circumcision, the new faith would have spread but slowly among Gentiles and might never have become a world religion. No doubt many of the men attracted to Judaism were of a mind to listen to Paul because his teaching contained much of what had already attracted them without this objectionable requirement.

Readers of Galatians 2 are sometimes disturbed by the different details about this meeting in Jerusalem reported by Luke and by Paul. Luke as a propagandist was under no obligation to report precisely the events that occurred. Paul, writing an apologia for his claim to apostleship and his program, had to anticipate rigid scrutiny of his account by unfriendly readers. No doubt he felt constrained to make a factual report. It is also probable that the council held first a session of the leaders with the deputation and later a public hearing, and that each writer made use of such events as suited his purpose. Luke's account impresses one as drawn from the public meeting, while Paul's relates to an agreement arrived at in an official group.

Although the leaders had earlier accepted Peter's conduct in the case of Cornelius, the religious and social taboo for Jewish Christians was clearly not erased by this decision. It seemed unlikely that either Jerusalem or Antioch would yield an inch in its position. At this impasse it was Peter in his final appearance in Acts who rose magnificently to the occasion. In an emotional speech he reminded them that the Holy Spirit by its customary sign had approved his baptizing Gentiles without circumcision. In so doing, God had clearly indicated the identity of "us and them" (15:9), but had proclaimed faith to be the only requirement. Taking advantage of Peter's speech, Paul and Barnabas immediately recounted in detail their successes in the Gentile mission. After a brief interval James, as spokesman for the apostles, reminded them that Amos (9:11–12 in the Septuagint) had prophesied that Gentiles also would "seek after the Lord," a prophecy now clearly coming true. He pronounced for the conference that Gentiles should have no difficult barrier imposed on their conversion. By way of compromise James proposed that the Gentiles give up all relation with idolatry, observe the Jewish moral code, and accept the Jewish dietary law. The decision was clearly a victory for Antioch. The first two of these requirements were already part of Paul's teaching. The third, whether attempted or not, within five years was proclaimed by Paul to be unimportant. This so-called Council of Jerusalem made practicable the coming European expansion of the Church.

Shortly after their return to Antioch, Paul suggested to Barnabas that they revisit the churches they had founded in Asia Minor. Barnabas stipulated that they give Mark a second chance, but Paul obstinately demurred. As a result, they parted company, Barnabas with Mark going to Cyprus and Paul with Silas, a Roman citizen from the Jerusalem church, going to Asia Minor. Barnabas, though Luke tactfully omits mention of it, had also weakened from his stand that Gentile Christians and Jewish Christians were all one body (Gal. 2:13). With this separation Barnabas leaves the account in Acts.

Luke's skillful shift of protagonists from Peter to Paul merits careful scrutiny. From the religious point of view, indeed, Acts has a single protagonist throughout in the Holy Spirit. As propaganda for a largely non-Jewish, Hellenistic body of readers, the account needed something else: human agents, who would naturally be more acceptable on literary grounds. Luke's Hellenistic readers would, no doubt, realize with Aristotle that unity of protagonist does not of itself create unity of action; Aristotle would probably have agreed that a shift from one leading agent to another constitutes a danger to a unified effect. To avoid this weakness in the course of events, Luke skillfully interweaves the actions of his two protagonists Peter and Paul until, with the aid of an interlude involving Philip the deacon, the reader is smoothly transported over the rough spot in the course of events. Although Luke as a good artist does not make it obvious, his handling of the problem may readily be discerned. Its stages are as follows:

1. Barnabas is mentioned for no other apparent reason than to bring his name before the reader (4:36–37).

2. The sensible advice of Paul's teacher Gamaliel, on how to handle the situation between Jewish authority and the new movement is stressed (5:34–39).

3. Paul is mentioned for the first time, passively sharing in the lynching of Stephen (7:58–8:1).

4. Paul's vigorous police-work against the new movement, para

doxically, by acquainting him with it, opens the way for his career (8:3).

5. Paul is converted and makes his initial appearance as a Christian apologist (9:1–30).

6. Peter first admits Gentiles to the Church without requiring circumcision (twice reported for emphasis, 10:1–11:18).

7. Christian work in Antioch spreads to Hellenized Jews (11:19–21).

8. Barnabas, after bringing Paul from Tarsus to Antioch, forms with him a team which takes a leading position among the Antioch Christians (11:22–30).

9. "Barnabas and Saul" sent to Cyprus (13:1–8).

10. "Saul (who also is called Paul)" heads the team as they leave Cyprus (13:9).

11. Paul is spokesman for the two henceforth, with two exceptions in which both are reported as speaking (13:16–14:26).

12. Paul and Barnabas part company; from now on Paul holds the stage (15:36–40).

In this carefully extended series Peter has entries and exits and is briefly replaced by Stephen and Philip. Peter's exit lines let him leave the stage, to alter a phrase of T. S. Eliot's, with a bang, not a whimper. Luke felt no enmity toward Peter. Although tactfully indicating Peter's inadequacies as leader, Luke never explicitly stated them to be so. He let the events speak for both Peter and Paul.

Paul's original plan to revisit the churches of Asia Minor expanded into a journey of more than two years and some 2,800 miles. It was a ground-breaking tour that in some respects may be considered his most productive journey. Concerning his revisiting his churches, one significant event must be noted.

Probably at Derbe, Paul met a young convert named Timothy, whose mother was Jewish and father Greek. Before permitting Timothy to join his party, Paul required him to be circumcised. As son of a Gentile father, he had not been rated as a Jew, but Paul counted him Jewish. There was no inconsistency in Paul's decision. To him Timothy was a son of Abraham, and Acts nowhere indicates that Paul felt that a Jewish Christian should be uncircumcised. He possibly wished also to forestall the charge later leveled at him (21:21) that he taught Jews not to circumcise their children. Timothy became one of Paul's principal aides.

Paul's itinerary as he struck out into new country was not according to any preconceived plan. As Luke later viewed it, he was under guidance by the Spirit. He followed a generally northwestward course across the Anatolian plateau until he reached the Troad, the region of ancient Troy more than a millennium earlier, along the Dardanelles.

Here Luke reveals, perhaps more clearly than elsewhere in Acts, that he was writing for Hellenists brought up in the classical tradition. To these readers, the Troad possessed deep cultural and historical associations. Luke would have ignored these at his peril; his readers' attention would wander if he omitted them, and their interests would deepen as he indicated them. All serve as background, sometimes ironically humorous, for Paul's next move.

Four centuries earlier, Alexander had paused here in reverence to his fancied ancestor Achilles, before setting out to conquer the East. Alexander had made possible the Hellenistic culture and paved the way linguistically for the new faith. By a ludicrous contrast a small band of Jews were now reversing Alexander's course to set in train what Luke believes to be a more significant force than Hellenism. Twelve centuries earlier, Achaeans from Europe had humbled the Asiatic Trojans who had balked their power. Now from the East comes a force more significant by far than the culture descending from Homer. Still earlier, legend reported, the Argonauts had sailed the Dardanelles to bring back to Europe the fabled Golden Fleece. Paul and his band were bringing across the Dardanelles to Europe something yet more precious. The paradox of Paul's band as conquerors comparable to these was by his day, Luke believes, being proved fact.

These are not the only parallels which Luke skillfully suggests. In the Spirit's prohibiting Paul from following his own projected courses, Luke's readers would see a parallel with the *daimon* or guardian spirit of Socrates, which always warned him from a wrong course of action. Unlike Socrates' guide, however, Paul's guiding

Spirit in a dream showed him his proper course. Incidentally, Plato reports in the *Crito* (XLIV) that Socrates shortly before his execution saw in a dream a woman who said to him "O Socrates, 'the third day hence to fertile Phthia shalt thou go.'" Phthia was in Macedonia, where Paul was to go.

Such a ludicrously heroic juxtaposition of Paul's venture with a number of classical memories could not fail to interest Luke's readers. The martyrdom of Socrates for holding to the truth was here set beside the steadfast course of Jesus to Jerusalem (Luke 9:51) as well as beside the heroic deaths some twenty years earlier of Christians in the Coliseum. Writing in the ninth decade of the first Christian century, Luke could see Christianity well established as an Occidental religion, which he foresaw would in time conquer Europe.

Luke followed the practice of classical writers in reporting this dramatically important event without rhetorical fanfare. Classical authors felt that impressive action needed no ornament, only report. The critical event, like the supporting members of a building, was left simple, while ornament was added to parts less subject to stress.

Luke first interjects himself clearly into his account at Troas, from which place "we endeavoured to go into Macedonia" (16:10). From here on he several times inserts what seem to be passages from his journal. It is true that Greek stylists felt free to shift their accounts in person or by shifting from direct to indirect discourse and back again. These were considered devices to break up any possible monotony in the account. If this were his intent, however, it is strange that he did not earlier resort to this device. It seems more likely that here he thus indicates his first participation as starting in Paul's travels.

Following their divine guidance, Paul and his party made their first European visit, to Philippi, a Roman military colony. The location would once more recall to Luke's readers a crucial event when at Philippi a century earlier Mark Antony and Octavius (later called Augustus) had by their victory over Brutus and Cassius ushered in the Roman imperial power. That battle had done much to establish Rome as a world power; would Christianity follow a parallel spiritual course?

It was in Macedonia that Paul hit upon a new strategy that greatly speeded up the dissemination of Christianity. Some seventy-five miles westward along the Via Egnatia, he came to the city of Thessalonica. This city funneled commerce and travel between the Mediterranean areas and the Balkan region as far north as the Danube River. Since commerce and travel were conducted necessarily in more leisurely fashion than today, travelers frequently spent some time in centers like Thessalonica. Here they collected news and miscellaneous information which they transmitted to other lands. The Christian message could be readily grasped; a man did not need to be a theologian to master its principles. Thessalonica was, in fact, a smaller Antioch. It is a matter of some surprise that the advantages in teaching at such a center had not been realized earlier. There the efforts of traveling evangelists were multiplied many fold and spread to places they would not visit.

In Thessalonica, Paul's fortunes followed what was rapidly becoming a stereotyped pattern. His feelings dictated that he preach "to the Jew first, and also to the Greek" (Rom. 1:16). Some slight success among Jews was overshadowed by wide acceptance by Gentiles. Hostile Jewish leaders, irritated that he superseded ritual and the Law with faith and jealous that he treated Gentiles equally with Jews, stirred up a riot among the roughnecks of the city. The local converts sent Paul secretly to a small city some sixty miles away named Berea. Here the Jewish community studiously considered Paul's message, but Paul's enemies from Thessalonica stirred up opposition once more. Paul pretended to leave by sea but proceeded afoot to Athens.

Athens was no longer commercially significant; it was the second important university city after Alexandria. Paul visited presumably as a tourist. He reacted to its crowd of statues as a well-trained Jew would naturally do. To the Hellenists statues were works of art; to Paul, mindful of the Second Commandment, they were sin. Many of the statues represented deities which were potential objects of worship. As he engaged in customary debates with people he met in the Agora, the omnipresent statues moved him to public action; and when the Athenians invited him to address them, it was these images that led directly into his theme. His words had attracted Stoics and Epicureans as well as the crowd.

Once more Luke presents his readers with a startling, ironic parallel. The slope of a hill called Areopagus where Paul spoke was the traditional site of the Athenian town meetings. Here Themistocles had stiffened Athenian backs to resist Xerxes. Here Pericles had delivered his masterly funeral oration over Athenian dead in the war with Sparta. Here also Socrates had courageously upheld legal procedure when acting as chairman of the town meeting. Now an insignificant-appearing Jew is to deliver a message which, though not honored here, was, in Luke's estimation, likely to supersede in importance all that had ever occurred at Areopagus.

Luke, who had not accompanied Paul to Athens (at least, he reported it without useing *we*) probably wrote the speech from what Paul subsequently reported to him. The organization of it is probably Paul's; it belongs rather to Hellenistic rhetoric than to Jewish. The speaker started with a local allusion couched in an ambiguity. The word translated "too superstitious" (17:22) can also mean "very god-fearing," and his listeners would enjoy the doubt whether he was complimenting them or not. He had noticed a statue "to an unknown god"—the KJV incorrectly inserts a definite article. This God, he announced, he would now introduce to them. His depiction of a creator-god was directed at the Stoics, as his quotation (17:28) clearly attests. It is taken from the hymn to the sun by the Stoic philosopher Cleanthes, who in the third century B.C. had succeeded Zeno as teacher in Athens. This God, Paul continued, is God of all mankind. He needs no statue and is to be worshiped in no temple; he is everywhere. He has overlooked until now the evil that men have done, but now calls upon all to mend their ways.

So far, Paul had been on safe ground; his hearers could echo his words. Now he must risk their disapproval by declaring that this God had set up a Judge of mankind whom he had raised from death. Paul's tactics here, designed to conciliate his hearers before stating truths hard for them to accept, parallel those that Luke had employed in his Gospel. Here they failed. The philosophers present of both schools repudiated the idea of life after death; their atomic theories of the universe ran counter to it. Many of the hearers ridiculed his speech. Others politely brushed him off with the stock response in such cases, "We will hear thee again of this matter."

Although he made some converts in Athens, Paul did not establish a church there. A few years later (1 Cor. 1:23) he wrote pessimistically about the likelihood of converting men to whom resurrection was "foolishness": "not many wise men after the flesh . . . are called" into the faith. Luke was more hopeful for them when he wrote Luke and Acts some thirty years later.

At Corinth, some fifty miles westward, Paul's urban program again hit its stride. Corinth was situated near what was probably the busiest point of transit in the Mediterranean world. Since unfavorable winds constantly rendered difficult the rounding of the southern tip of the Peloponnesus, travel and commerce were regularly routed across the Isthmus of Corinth. Safety and quicker travel counterbalanced the expense of transshipping cargo. The *Odyssey* relates how Odysseus, endeavoring to round the Peloponnesus en route to Ithaca, had been blown across the sea southward to Africa. Here Paul enjoyed his longest visit but one and probably his greatest success.

Paul arrived in Corinth late in A.D. 50 or early in 51. The date can be fixed with some certainty. Claudius had expelled Jews from Rome by an edict in A.D. 49, and Aquila and Priscilla had recently come from Rome to Corinth when Paul arrived. Gallio (18:12) was proconsul for Achaia in either A.D. 51–52 or 52–53. Paul's visit began between these two events. Paul remained in Corinth at least one and one-half years, perhaps longer, and Luke implies that much of his time there had elapsed before he was brought before Gallio.

Corinth gave him a large transient population to address as well as local listeners. It also presented a specially difficult problem, as might be expected. Like sailors' cities before and since, it was a center for immoral activities. In Greek the verb *korinthiazesthai* denoted extreme sexual depravity. Christianity with its insistence upon the body as the temple of the Holy Spirit (1 Cor. 6:19 and elsewhere) had a difficult problem here. Difficult also was the multiplication of religions and cults brought here by travelers with their pretentious rituals which were attractive to the curiosity of people. The ever present enmity of the Jews showed itself here.

In his rage at the Jewish opposition in Corinth, Paul in the traditional Jewish gesture shook off his robe and the dust of the synagogue and declared, "From henceforth I will go to the Gentiles." Nonetheless, he immediately started to teach in a house "joined hard to the synagogue"; he could not for all his irritation abandon his people. He converted the chief ruler of the synagogue and several others, a feat which doubtless further inflamed his enemies.

Shortly after Gallio had arrived as proconsul, the Jews brought charges before him that Paul was teaching an unlawful religion, by which they probably meant that his teaching went counter to Roman law. Judaism was a religion recognized by Roman law; if Christianity were not truly Jewish, it was an unlicensed religion. To what extent such a charge carried weight outside of Rome, and particularly in cult-ridden Corinth, one cannot tell. Gallio in correct official fashion refused to assume jurisdiction; officials in the provinces were wisely reluctant to interfere in local religious squabbles. He threw the case out of court. This defeat seemingly took away the edge of Jewish opposition in Corinth while Paul was there.

As Paul's letters indicate, the Corinthian churches were anything but placid. Paul wrote at least four letters in an attempt, apparently successful, to settle their disputes. This dissension was, however, a sign of life. For all the worry that his Corinthian converts caused him, they represented one of his most successful evangelizing projects.

Upon his leaving Corinth, Paul could look back upon great progress. He had solidified the technique he henceforth followed, of working principally in commercial centers. Although he did not abandon efforts among Jews, his major successes were scored among Gentiles. His reputation as an evangelist was now firmly established, and his Gentile program bade fair to become the dominant wing of the Church. Luke's cursory mention of Paul's report to the church in Jerusalem (14:22) may indicate something of his increased stature in the movement.

Luke's account of Paul's second journey considers several of Paul's visits along with his shift in program. He now adds variety by making the third journey a report in depth of Paul's successful work in one center, Ephesus. Ephesus was the principal port of entry and exit for Asia Minor. The plateau of Anatolia, like the Balkans, provided for the Mediterranean world grain, lumber, hides, and naval stores. All these had long been in short supply in the Hellenistic world. Through Ephesus those regions in the hinterland of Anatolia which Paul had not previously traversed could be reached by converts traveling inland through Ephesus. Those sailing from the city would swell the numbers converted in Thessalonica and Corinth. In this city Paul spent his longest reported tour of evangelism, perhaps two and one-half years.

Luke indicates the results of Paul's extended stay by briefly reporting two of Paul's experiences and recounting a third in greater detail. The first was a tantalizing contact with followers of John the Baptist, who evidently survived as a group a quarter-century and more after John's death. (Whether they bore any relation to the still extant Mandaeans of Mesopotamia who reverence John, cannot be determined.) They had never heard of the Holy Spirit's coming or even of its existence; but when Paul instructed them, they accepted the Christian faith.

The second episode is possibly included to correct derogatory opinions of Paul's healing powers. More probably, it is included to dissociate Christianity from activities like that of Simon Magus, who was by this time a well-known representative of magical performers. An itinerant family of Jewish exorcists visiting Ephesus claimed the power to drive out evil spirits by stronger spirits under their control. Having heard Paul in the name of Jesus heal sick people, they added to their armory the name of "Jesus, whom Paul preacheth." (The Paris Magical manuscript attests to such non-Christian use of Jesus' name. One non-Jewish exorcism even reads, "I adjure thee by Jesus the God of the Hebrews!") Unfortunately for them, they evidently used this formula on a man who knew about Paul. Flying into a rage at their opportunism, he beat them severely. The upshot of this event was that many magicians in Ephesus burned their books of spells and abandoned their pursuit.

The third episode reports a far more significant result of the Christian teaching upon business. A fairly accurate measure of a social or religious force is derived from the opposition it arouses. Luke uses this episode to that end. The temple of Ishtar or Astarte, "Diana of the Ephesians," was one of the seven wonders of the ancient world. It was a leading attraction in the city and caused enormous pecuniary activities among both natives and tourists. Ishtar the moon-goddess was naturally associated with female fecundity, unlike the spiteful old-maid huntress Diana of classical mythology. Surviving amulets of Ishtar show her with multiple breasts, and rams and goats were associated with her as symbols of masculine virility. The rites celebrated in her worship were of unbridled sensuality. Women wore her amulets to ensure fertility.

The Ephesian silversmiths carried on extensive trade in these silver amulets as an important part of their occupation. The fact that they were disturbed even to rioting against the Christian movement indicates the effect on Ephesus of Paul's teaching. The new religion steadfastly combated sensual vices and was evidently sharply reducing the trade in these amulets. It was bad for business.

Their riot followed the universal pattern: "Some therefore cried one thing, and some another: for the assembly was confused; and the more part knew not wherefore they were come together" (19:32). After they had exhausted themselves, the Asiarch or town clerk warned the mob that Rome punished riotous cities by placing them under military restrictions. At this hint they quickly dispersed. Paul, with less wisdom than courage, wished to speak to the mob, but was sensibly restrained by his friends.

It was obvious that Paul's usefulness in Ephesus had ended. After bidding farewell to his followers, he sailed off to visit his churches around the Aegean Sea. At Corinth he settled for a three-months visit. Events now caused him to alter his plans radically and to return to Jerusalem.

While he was in Corinth, he was in all probability making preparations to travel westward to Rome. Luke omits details of the situation which Paul faced; we are obliged to supply what we can from his letter to the Romans written at this time. Luke indicates only that hostile Jews forced Paul to change his itinerary en route to Syria. The facts, which were not edifying for the Church, he passes over.

The situation was apparently somewhat as follows. At the request of the Jerusalem church, Paul had for some years supervised a collection of money among his churches for the aid of the mother church. This collection had now been completed. Paul wrote in Romans (15:26–27) that he would come to them after he had taken this collection to Jerusalem. This letter expresses repeatedly his eagerness to visit Rome and its tone strongly implies extreme disappointment that his visit must be deferred. It is hardly too much to assume that something more than delivery of a gift to Jerusalem drove him to go there.

His purpose in going to the mother church appears to be indicated by the tone and subject of Galatians, written some three years earlier, in the argument which looms large in Romans, and by his reception at Jerusalem. It goes back also to the compromise effected at the Council of Jerusalem. Such a compromise hardly ever satisfies all those concerned. Galatians implies unmistakably that some Jewish Christians had undercut Paul's work in these churches by continuing to insist upon circumcision and observance of the Jewish law as requisite to Christian membership. If at these churches, presumably the same tactics were pursued at others. It is extremely probable that Paul went to Jerusalem because he felt that the time had come for a showdown. The donation which he brought would help to give him a favorable welcome, a strategic advantage from which to launch his complaint.

He set out for Jerusalem with gloomy forebodings. At the start he had to foil a Jewish plot to kill him en route. He told the Ephesian elders who met him at Miletus that he would never again see them. At Tyre he was warned against going to Jerusalem. At Caesarea, after warnings from a prophet named Agabus, his companions tried to deter him from going further. The auspices, as Hellenistic readers would feel, were unfavorable.

The Christians at Jerusalem were friendly. The day following his arrival, Paul reported to James and all the elders "what things God had wrought among the Gentiles by his ministry." The atmosphere reminds the reader of Peter's reception by the same officials after he had baptized Cornelius: they praised God and then got down to other business. Before Paul could enter his complaint, they countered with a charge that he had taught his Jewish converts to ignore circumcision and other Jewish customs. Paul's having required Timothy to be circumcised (16:3) Luke considers sufficient evidence against this charge. Paul's position with respect to Jewish Christians on such matters is not defined in the Acts; it seems likely that he had not fully made up his mind.

Pressing their advantage—Luke's report is here supplemented by other evidence and speculation—the elders proposed that Paul defend himself by undertaking an unmistakably Jewish rite. He should undertake to pay the expenses of four men who should shave their heads and perform the ritual in the Temple prescribed for fulfillment of the Nazarite vow (Num. 6:13–20). Paul's assent indicates that he still regarded himself as within the Jewish fold.

For nearly a week the program proceeded without a hitch. Then Jews from Asia Minor who were in the Temple recognized Paul with these beardless men and immediately mobbed him. Among the proscriptions observed by a Jew was the prohibition of any trimming of his hair or beard (Lev. 19:27). Hellenistic styles prescribed that a man be either clean shaven or wear a closely trimmed beard. Since Paul and his companions had only a few-days growth of hair and beard, these hostile Jews jumped to the conclusion that Paul had unlawfully introduced Gentiles into the Temple beyond the Court of the Gentiles. The offender in such a case was summarily lynched without trial outside the sacred precinct; and Paul's enemies eagerly acted to rid themselves of their archopponent while defending the sanctity of the Temple.

Paul's Roman citizenship here saved his life. The captain of the

Roman guard in the nearby Castle of Antonia had evidently been alert to capture an Egyptian Jew who as a spurious Messiah had tried to start an insurrection and on the supposition that he was at the center of this uproar, Paul was rescued from the mob and hustled into the castle. There he identified himself in Greek to the captain, declared his citizenship of Tarsus, and asked permission to address the mob.

Permission being granted, Paul stood on the castle steps and finally got a hearing. Speaking in Aramaic, he identified himself as a Jew from Tarsus, who had been taught by their revered rabbi Gamaliel. He had prosecuted Christians vigorously as an agent of the high priest. Through mystical visions, Jesus had told him what he must do. When a respected Jew of Damascus as God's agent had restored his sight, he had brought God's command: "The God of our fathers"—a standard Jewish reference to God—"hath chosen thee, that thou shouldest know his will . . ." (22:14). Back in Jerusalem, while he was, in good Jewish fashion, praying in the Temple, he fell into a trance in which he received divine orders to leave Jerusalem as an emissary of Jesus to the Gentiles.

Paul had presented his case in a form calculated to get Jewish hearing if not Jewish sympathy, until he mentioned his mission to the Gentiles. No doubt the mob was restive at his mention of Jesus, but at least it listened; when the hated Gentiles entered the account, Paul lost all control of them. They responded so violently that the captain, probably ignorant of Aramaic, thought him to be some rabble-rouser if not the Egyptian Jew he had been seeking, took him into the castle, and ordered that he be beaten to make him tell the truth. Paul demanded by what right he could scourge a Roman citizen condemned of no crime. Paul, it turned out, had been born into citizenship, whereas the captain had "bought" his, that is, obtained it through bribery. Claudius's wife Messalina had made such purchases notorious. Having thus established a degree of superiority over the captain, Paul received better treatment under protective custody.

With Paul's arrival in Jerusalem, Luke's account shifts from one of travel to one of intrigue. For the ensuing two years, the Jewish leaders were plotting to kill Paul, a Roman governor was trying to bribe him for his release, and Paul repeatedly had to outmaneuver the priests. Luke ran no risk of boring his readers through sameness of situation. A number of episodes illustrate the course of events.

The day after the riot, the captain held a hearing to investigate Jewish accusations of Paul. Facing the chief priests and the Sanhedrin, Paul proclaimed that his conscience was clear before God. The infuriated high priest ordered him to be struck on the mouth for blasphemy and disrespect. For this Paul hotly cursed him in Jewish fashion. When rebuked for cursing the high priest, Paul bitterly retorted that he had not recognized in such a man the leader of his people.

Deciding that this hearing was a waste of time, Paul cleverly broke it up by declaring that he was on trial for his belief in resurrection of the dead. Such a statement won him the support of the Pharisees on the court, who immediately echoed Gamaliel's earlier warning that to condemn him might be to oppose God (5:38–39). Seeing that the court had dissolved into a riot, the captain in disgust broke up the meeting. Upon the captain's learning of a plot to assassinate Paul, he sent Paul secretly with an armed escort to Caesarea, and in a report turned the case over to Felix the procurator. Paul cheerfully accepted the change of scene. He had learned in a mystical vision that he would escape these dangers and go to Rome as he had wished.

Felix was the brother of a freedman named Pallas who had been a favorite of the Emperor Claudius. Tacitus, who wrote of Pallas, characterized him as exercising the functions of a ruler with the lustful disposition of a slave (*Annals* XII.iv; *Histories* V.ix). Felix, now that his brother was dead and his influence at court diminished, found it generally advisable to follow Jewish preferences. Shortly after Paul's arrival, the Sanhedrin brought charges before Felix, using a Greek advocate. Paul quickly showed that as a prisoner in Jesusalem he could not have taken part in any disturbance such as the charges mentioned. He also demanded that the plaintiffs at his arrest in the Temple be presented to press the charges.

Felix, who had married a member of the Herodian family, doubtless knew something about Judaism. He also had in mind the principle of Roman government to avoid interference in local religious affairs. Paul's Roman citizenship hindered Felix' surrendering him to local jurisdiction. He accordingly temporized and for the next two years kept Paul under light guard to please the Jews without ever bringing the case to trial. Occasionally, he listened to Paul's discussion of "justice and self-control and future judgment." Paul so effectively tied his message with Greek philosophical ideas as both to frighten and fascinate Felix. When Felix was finally recalled in disgrace on account of Jewish charges, he tried to placate their resentment by leaving Paul in prison.

Porcius Festus the new procurator appears in Acts as an honest administrator, a down-to-earth fellow, and no fool. In clearing up matters left by Felix, he quickly asked the Jewish authorities for a conference about Paul. When they demanded a hearing for Paul in Jerusalem, Festus, who probably had informed himself about the case, set the hearing in Caesarea. At the hearing Festus asked Paul if he was willing to stand trial in Jerusalem. Paul replied by demanding as a Roman citizen to be tried by the imperial court in Rome. Festus, no doubt glad to be relieved of responsibility in a case which could embroil him with Jewish authorities, assented.

Paul's demand for a change of venue was sound. He could win no fair hearing in Jerusalem and would probably be assassinated. At Rome the case would not come up for several years, by which time the fires would have died down. Most of all, he got free transportation to Rome—some 2,200 miles as it turned out to be. After two years in prison, he was, no doubt, out of funds in spite of help from friends. He would be under house-arrest in Rome, but he was now used to that.

An interesting interlude occurred before he sailed from Caesarea. Herod Agrippa, king of various parts of Palestine, paid Festus a state visit. He was the son of the Herod mentioned in Acts 12 as first persecutor of the Church. Among his powers were supervision of the Temple treasury, which served also as a bank, and appointment of the high priest. To entertain him and to transfer to him some of the responsibility for Paul's case, Festus had Paul speak before Agrippa.

Paul's address before Agrippa is perhaps his best rhetorical effort reported in Acts. Since Luke was in Caesarea at that time and could have heard it, Luke's report may well closely record Paul's speech. Paul's compliments on Agrippa's knowledge of the Scriptures and Jewish affairs were sincere; Agrippa would surely have informed himself in this sensitive area of his responsibilities. As a local ruler, he could not have put aside jurisdiction in religious matters. Paul handled his material expertly. Omitting his early biography as already well known, he stressed his Pharisaic rearing as leading to his teaching about resurrection. He stated his services as prosecutor of Christians. Then he recounted his stunning mystical experience which brought his conversion and divine direction to serve as Jesus' emissary to the Gentiles. In obedience to his heavenly vision he had spent his life ever since. His entire teaching accorded with what the Law and the Prophets had foretold; Jesus' suffering fulfilled their message. Agrippa, he concluded, as a believer in the Prophets would realize the factual accuracy of his claims.

The practical Festus, quite lost among unfamiliar ideas, bluntly interrupted: Paul's learning had unhinged his mind—he was mad. Agrippa, however, was greatly impressed, almost convinced by Paul's address. Paul, he assured Festus, might have justly been set at liberty if he had not appealed his case. Paul's masterly speech and Agrippa's approval would greatly enhance Paul's image among Luke's Hellenistic readers, many of them versed in the niceties of dialectic and oratory. This final speech, while only approximating traditional rhetorical organization, nonetheless presented Paul as one whose mental habit agreed with theirs.

For his final section of Acts, Luke returns to adventure after two years and more of intrigue. He shifts his scene to the sea and reports a voyage and shipwreck, an eternally enthralling action for male readers. He flatters his readers by "telegraphing" the outcome of the voyage through his repeated reminders that the voyage began late in the season for sailing. From late in October until some time in March, travel by sea was suspended on account of the violent winds and storms during these months.

Paul was embarked on a sailing vessel which, as was customary, hugged the shore or went from island to island; at night it either cast anchor or was drawn up on a beach. Like most ships of the day, it followed no fixed schedule but went where weather and ladings dictated. Stopping at Sidon, it followed the mainland; the wind favored its turning westward along Asia Minor. At Myra the party transferred to a ship bound for Rome. From this point wind and weather were against them. With difficulty they reached a port called Fair Havens on the southern shore of Crete. So much time lost after leaving Myra brought them into the period when sailing was normally suspended, and Paul advised the sailors to winter in Fair Havens. For obvious reasons the crew was unwilling to winter in a small village, and they persuaded the officer in charge of Paul to continue their course to another harbor to the west in Crete called Phoenix or Phenice. Since the wind had become deceptively mild, he fell in with their demand.

Suddenly, as they were sailing, a violent northeaster struck and drove the ship far from its projected course toward the mainland. For more than six hundred miles they were driven westward out of sight of land. So violent were the blasts that struck the stern of the clinker-built craft that the pressure against the bow caused the danger of the planks spreading and sinking the ship. The sailors atempted to counteract the fore-and-aft pressure by looping heavy cables around the hull. Later, they lightened ship by casting overboard their cargo and even the ship's tackle. The ship floated, but out of control.

After two weeks of buffeting from the winds, Paul encouraged his companions by reporting a vision from his God. He told them that they must be shipwrecked but with no loss of life. When one night the swells of the sea indicated shallower water, they cast the lead and found five fathoms. Casting anchor, they waited for dawn. Daylight revealed an inlet in a small island with a smooth bank for beaching their ship. As they tried to enter, a tide rip threw them onto a sandbar, where the ship broke up. Those who could swim got ashore without difficulty, the rest floated in on planks from the ship. All of them—276 men—were saved.

On this island—Malta, south of Sicily—they were well received by the inhabitants. As Paul was gathering wood for a fire, a snake warmed by the heat bit his hand. Malta has no poisonous snakes, but the unreasoning horror of them made the inhabitants expect him to die of the venom. When he did not, "they changed their minds, and said that he was a god," as Luke ironically reports. When sailing was resumed about March, the party found shipping which took them to Pozzuoli on the Bay of Naples, from which they followed the Appian Way to Rome. After a stormy passage of some 2,200 miles, Paul had arrived.

Paul's arrival in Rome was symbolic to Luke that his work was triumphant. From Rome's Golden Milestone in the Forum all roads radiated; the Church could spread everywhere. Rome was central to earthly government and power; Paul had brought his message to a point from which it too would become supreme.

One final episode had to be added. A day or two after his arrival, Paul summoned the Jewish leaders in Rome to hear him. Discovering, as he had expected, that no shipping had yet arrived from Palestine, he seized the opportunity to present his case before the opposition could interfere. A few days later, at a convocation, many Jews listened to his message. He spent a day explaining the relation of Jesus to the Law and the Prophets and urged them to accept his teaching. Some believed, most did not. Convinced finally that Judaism and the new faith must follow separate ways, Paul dismissed them with a stinging application of Isaiah 6:9–10 to the situation. They shut their minds against God's message. Therefore, God was sending it to the Gentiles, "and they will hear it."

Paul's final decision that severed Christianity from Judaism in his mind is perhaps as climactic a point as his arrival in Rome. Luke had arrived at two crucial points in his story at the same time. His seemingly abrupt conclusion is actually a logical place for him to stop. Christianity was still expanding, and any rounded conclusion would have been inappropriate.

CHAPTER 5

THE FOURTH GOSPEL

In contrast with the Fourth Gospel, the other three seem to present a common view of Christ. Their differences then seem to diminish, however basic they actually are. Only some 9 per cent of the material used in the synoptic Gospels appears in John, which also reports extensively of Jesus' activities in and around Jerusalem. Its literary form also bears little relation to those of Matthew, Mark, and Luke.

Like the synoptic Gospels, John is propaganda. It is directed at readers sharply delineated in the author's mind. As in the Synoptics, one must determine through internal evidence the composition of the audience. External evidence shows that such an audience existed as a significant part of the society in which the Church developed. Having such an audience and a discourse fitted to it, one may reasonably assume close relation between the two in the forming of the book.

Nearly unanimous scholarly opinion dates John as the last written of the four Gospels. Tradition and scholarship agree in assigning it to the period between A.D. 90 and 110. This agreement does not extend to identification of its author. Tradition assigned it to John the apostle, the son of Zebedee. In the last century Marcus Dods argued from external evidence that this apostle could have written it as late as the end of the first century. If, as tradition held, John was a youth when he followed Jesus, he would have been some eighty-five years old by A.D. 100—an advanced age but by no means unknown in ancient times. Finding passages in John in writers of about A.D. 115, Dods deduced that it must have been written long enough before that date to have gained circulation and authority to be quoted in support of any position. He failed, however, to consider the possibility that the passages in question could have come from the logia or some other earlier source; and he did not consider the superb literary art of this Gospel.

The skillful artistry of the fourth Gospel is almost certainly the work of a writer well grounded in Greek philosophy and Hellenistic rhetoric. John was a Galilean fisherman, associated in Acts as a silent partner with Peter. Such a connection would have probably directed his evangelism toward Jews primarily for many years, at least until after the Council of Jerusalem at midcentury. Until middle age he cannot be shown to have needed much skill in addressing Hellenists. Such a man could hardly have made himself a master of current philosophies and of the most highly developed Hellenistic art, rhetoric.

Notwithstanding this evidence, the work clearly stands related in some way to John the apostle. John is never named in it—a surprising omission in view of his membership in the élite inner circle of disciples. Three times the author employs an awkward circumlocution in mentioning one disciple; he is "the disciple whom Jesus loved" (13:23, 19:26, 21:20). The strongest indication that the epithet refers to John appears in chapter 21. On the shore of Galilee were Peter, Thomas, Nathanael, the sons of Zebedee—one of whom was John—and two unnamed others. Peter asked Jesus about the fate of this beloved disciple. There is no reason to suppose he referred to Philip and Nathanael, and surely not to the two anonymous men present. By elimination, James and John are left. James, too, is a minor figure though sharing in the inner circle of disciples. His later career was cut short by Herod in A.D. 44. John, the single man left, was Peter's intimate companion according to Acts, and he would naturally be solicitous about John.

Verse 24 must also be considered: "This is the disciple which testifieth of these things, and wrote these things." This statement seems at first glance to certify John's authorship. "These things" (*tauta*) is, however, a reference to something not clearly defined: it could refer to the Gospel, or to the source from which the author drew his information. In view of the literary excellence of John, a skilled Hellenist author may be assumed and the reference made to his source. The cumbersome epithet then would have appeared in the source, and preserved. (However one may decide this question, he may feel free to refer to the book as John.)

The synoptic writers, Matthew's author especially, show interest in conciliating Jewish readers. In varying degrees they took pains to differentiate between the common people who had "heard Jesus gladly" (Mark 12:37) and the immovable sectarian Pharisee and Sadducee opponents of Christ. In John, while the Pharisees are the focus of opposition to him, his opponents are often referred to simply as "the Jews." (A highly educated Jewess in one of my classes read the Synoptics with enjoyment, but charged John with anti-Semitism. It is not surprising that she should have come to such a conclusion.)

Before the fall of Jerusalem in A.D. 70 to Titus, most of the Christians had apparently read the signs correctly and had left the city. Many of them were Judaizing Christians (Acts 21:20). The shattering blow dealt to those of Jewish faith was shared almost equally by these Judaizers. When John was written, about a quarter-century after this catastrophe, they seem to have no longer been a force in the Church. The author of John wrote to an audience overwhelmingly Gentile, and was under no compulsion to distinguish among Jewish attitudes toward Jesus as his predecessors had done. Possibly the anti-Semitism of the ancient world had entered the Church with its Gentile members. Without condoning this prejudice, the author could reckon it as reinforcing the effect of Jesus' part in the debates which he reported.

Both form and content of John indicate that its propaganda was directed at readers influenced by current philosophical Hellenistic movements. Of these, two were especially influential: the movement represented by Philo of Alexandria and the incipient stages of Gnosticism. Both were rapidly spreading ways of thought. The Church had to reckon with them not only in its propaganda to nonmembers, but also inside its own ranks. Among adult converts were those who brought with them acquaintance with such beliefs and attitudes. These would impress other church members more intimately than the unconverted could do. From both sides came ideas that militated against basic Christian doctrine.

Philo, the leading Jewish philosopher of the first century, was a wealthy and politically important Alexandrian Jew who died about A.D. 50. He was a devoutly religious man who regarded the Septuagint as verbally inspired. Hellenistic philosophies also deeply interested him as well as the classical Greek philosophers. In his view, philosophy and the Scriptures fully harmonized. To combine philosophical reasoning with Hebrew revelation, he composed voluminous comments and exegeses on the Septuagint. The vogue of allegorical interpretation received vigorous impetus through his work. Ideas probably deriving from him entered into the later Neoplatonism, so that for about four or five centuries Philo and his influence were to be a thorn in the flesh of the Church. Here, without entering into the complex ramifications of Philo's thought, only such matters need be considered as were affecting Christianity at the time when John was written.

The doctrine of Philo which most gravely affected the early Church was that of the Logos. This Logos, an emanation from God, was the agent through whom God created the world. In Greek, *logos* means both the spoken or written word and what the word signifies—the "twofold Logos" of Cardinal Newman. Philo declared that in Genesis 1 the recurrent words "and God said" pointed to the activity of the Logos. (*Legō*, to say, is the verbal form of the noun *logos*). The reason of God, but not God in person, worked at the Creation. This Logos, though emanating from God, was not himself divine. The author of John (1:1–3), while agreeing that the Logos created the world, declares that "the Word was God," and "all things were made by Him." He adds (1:14) that this Logos was at one time in the world in corporeal form. Such a union was repugnant to Philo's belief. He felt that this Logos was a continuous governing principle of nature in the world. The Christian believer in the Incarnation could not here agree with Philo.

Perhaps a more serious contender with Christian doctrine was Gnostic theorizing. Whether Gnosticism had yet developed its system or not, scholars disagree. Its incipient stages, at any rate, appeared in the period when Paul was writing as dangerous to orthodoxy. The origins of Gnosticism were diverse and are still under investigation, and like Emerson's transcendentalism it was a highly individualized kind of speculation.

Two major Gnostic positions were of prime concern to the Church when John was written. First, as their name indicates, its advocates claimed a special, personal *gnōsis* or knowledge which took precedence over the Church's teaching. The Gnostic would respond to a Christian doctrine, "Oh, but it has been revealed to me that . . . ." He would then advance a possibly quite heterodox doctrine as superior to Christian teaching. To a young organization with its own message to proclaim, such dissidents constituted a deadly peril. Since this position caters to man's innate self-assurance, the movement readily found followers within the Church itself.

The second Gnostic tenet, a dualistic concept of the universe, would undermine basic Christian doctrine. Drawn presumably from preceding ideas like Persian dualism, this concept set up an opposition between light and good on the one hand and darkness and evil on the other. Spirit was good, the material world evil. The Gnostics thus stood in complete disagreement with the Christian doctrine that man and God were united in Jesus. God as spirit would be defiled if he touched matter. Since God is good, such contact can never take place. Somewhat like Philo in this respect, the Gnostics held that God in creating the universe had employed a Logos, an agent on a level between the divine and the human.

Religious movements tend to reproduce by fission, and Gnosticism followed the pattern in this. Some Gnostics within the Church held that Jesus never had a human body but only seemed to have one. Others held that the deity in Jesus somehow escaped taint by being dissociated from his body. A third group believed him to have been man prior to his resurrection but a disembodied phantom thereafter. These Gnostics who allow for a duality in Jesus came to be called Docetists, a name deriving from the verb *dokein,* "to seem or appear to be." These Gnostic heresies within the Church struck heavily at the basic Christian principles, the Incarnation and the Atonement.

The fourth Gospel steadily contradicts these assertions of Gnosticism. In the author's mind it may be that Neoplatonism and Gnosticism were lumped together as a common enemy. He was engaged in a polemic propaganda, not in an inquiry into the nature of philosophical points of view. He was proclaiming a gospel to those within the Church who had become infected with heretical notions. His program is first to establish the dual nature of Christ and then to present the doctrine of the Trinity.

Both content and form of John indicate that the author had such purposes in mind. He aimed his work at men within the Church—and probably to some extent outside it—who had become attracted to dualistic concepts of the world with their effect upon Christianity. The cultural attainments of these men, no doubt, varied considerably, but they were acquainted with dialectical methods of instruction. The classical pattern of such methods is the Socratic dialogues of Plato, which subsequent teachers adapted and applied to their teaching. Along with Greek rhetoric, dialectic had been spread wherever Greek culture had penetrated. With slight modifications necessitated by his subject and by his interlocutors, the author of John cast Jesus' teaching into dialogue.

John's author also employed oratory, which had also been widely spread as Greek culture had permeated the Near East. Although he indicates that dialogue was Jesus' method, he frequently recasts dialogue into continuous speech by omitting the comments or questions of Jesus' interlocutors and by combining several conversations into one discourse. He interpolates hints of the latter at times (cf. materials in chaps. 7 and 8), and in the long discourse at the Last Supper he keeps just enough of the disciples' questions to indicate his technique.

In the dialectic as practiced by Socrates, Plato shows that the interlocutors are, for the most part, open minded to ideas not their own. Here there is a genuine search after clearer knowledge. In John this is not the case. The opponents of Jesus are anything but disinterested, and neither is he. The opposition has no desire to learn from the dialogue, but intends to discredit and even to kill him—a situation which occurs with Socrates only in the dialogue at his trial. Such a hidebound insistence on their position in the Jewish leaders, and Jesus' oracularly authoritative declaration of his nature, inevitably require alteration of the traditional pattern of dialectic. The author of John, nonetheless, employs Greek dialectic and rhetoric as well as can be done in the circumstances.

John's omissions are also in keeping with the sort of reader posited above. It is hard to believe that he was not acquainted with some at least of the other three Gospels. Even if he were not, he would have known much of the sources from which they were drawn. He omits the simpler parables dear to the less lettered man as well as the artistically developed parables found in Luke. The few miracles reported are used as "signs" for demonstration or proof to support the claims of Jesus. John's readers were accustomed to the give-and-take of dialectic and the address, and the author gives them their familiar forms of discourse.

The nature of John's message made necessary emphasis on Jesus' use of symbols, which in fact replace the synoptic writers' parables. Ideas presented here range in many instances far beyond the normal level of human experience expressed in everyday terms. One cannot merely state the paradoxically dual nature of Jesus and the concept of the Triune God. Neither can one rationally explain them. To clarify them, the author had to employ symbols of far greater depth than the synoptic writers had done. They resemble parables in that they too are drawn from familiar experience. Even the father-son symbol of the relation of Jesus to God is drawn from human relationship—a not wholly adequate symbol in this case, yet the best available.

The audience for whom John was written was accustomed to symbol and allegory in the works of Philo and the teaching of the Gnostics. It is significant that John's ever present symbol of light and darkness, which pervades the book, echoes the dualistic habit of their thought.

The spiritual significance of John, which almost two millennia of theological study have been unable to plumb, lies outside the purpose of this study. If the reader discovers what the author was trying to do, and how he set about doing it, he will be better prepared to enter upon other investigation of John's *message*.

THE PROLOGUE

The first eighteen verses of John, which some scholars plausibly consider to have been made out of an earlier Aramaic Christian hymn, constitute the prologue. They express an earnest, eloquent attempt to conciliate heretical readers—as well as to fortify the orthodox—by employing expressions familiar to them and accepting their beliefs as far as is possible. These beliefs the author expands or modifies to bring them into line with orthodoxy. This introduction may be paraphrased with parenthetical comment to show partial agreement with heretical assertions:

> The Logos has existed from the beginning (as you say) face to face with God; but this Logos was divine.[1] He was the agent in creating everything (as you say); but the life transmitted to men by him was in him exactly as it is in God. This life was the light of men, the Logos himself. This light keeps shining amid the darkness of evil, and the darkness has not overcome it.
>
> This light was announced by a man named John, who was sent to testify to it but was not himself that light. The true light did exist, that shines upon every man who comes into the world. This light was at one time in the world which He had made, but the world did not know him as that light. He came to his own possession, the world, but his own people did not accept him. But he gave to those who did accept him the capability of becoming God's spiritual children—those believing on his name—who were begotten not through any human passion but by God.
>
> This Logos did become a human body and lived among us, and we saw his radiance, a radiance he received as the Father's only Son, full of grace and truth. (John testified of him and prophe-

[1] The connective *kai,* translated "and" in the KJV, may carry the force of "and yet" or "but."

> sied about him: "This is the one of whom I spoke: 'The one who is coming after me ranks above me, because He existed before me.'") And from his fullness we all received, grace upon grace.
>
> The Law was given through Moses; this divine gift, the truth, came into being with Jesus Christ. No man has ever seen God. An only begotten God who is in the bosom of the Father has made him known.

Throughout this paraphrase echoes of Gnostic belief may be identified; more may be detected as our currently limited knowledge of Gnosticism expands. The author shows that he thinks in the Jewish tradition. His initial phrase, "in the beginning," reproduces verbatim the initial phrase of Genesis in the Septuagint. The author wishes to place his message in a context which makes Jesus the completion of what Matthew (5:17) designated the fulfillment of the Law and the Prophets. For the benefit of his heretical readers, he emphasizes the fact that this creating agent is also God, who once dwelt in and had contact with a material body and the material world.

Besides his intent to disprove heretical ideas, the author wishes to develop the doctrine of a Triune God. If he can convince his readers that two can be mystically one, that the Father can be also the Son, his problem is nearly solved. If he can lead them to accept this belief, the addition of a third element into this Unity can be accepted with far less difficulty. Accordingly, in the first half of his Gospel the author intersperses anti-Gnostic propaganda into repeated statements pointing to and asserting the duality of God. He must win acceptance of his readers to the idea that God can reside in a human body before the duality he presents can be accepted. When later he introduces the concept of the Holy Spirit, he makes no argument for it. This concept of the Holy Spirit had already been established in Christianity, but needed iteration under Gnostic pressure.

DIALOGUES WITH JEWISH AUTHORITARIANS

Jesus' encounter with Nicodemus (3:1–21) is a sample of Jesus' clash with a prominent member of the Sanhedrin. Nicodemus, *the* teacher of Israel according to the manuscripts, possibly represents other members of the Sanhedrin, unless "we know" (v. 2) is pompous self-assertion. He patronizingly compliments this backwoods teacher by calling him "rabbi" and admitting that he clearly has some divine support. Recognizing the man's self-assurance and attacking the literalism of contemporary Jewish thought, Jesus presents him with an ambiguity which taken literally is patently absurd: "Ye must be born again." *Anōthen* means either "again" or "from above." Here it is properly translated as Nicodemus's answer shows his understanding of it. His dignity wounded at what he takes to be a nonsensical remark, Nicodemus tartly shows it to be impossible.

After hinting at his meaning by saying that baptism and spiritual rebirth are prerequisite to entering the kingdom of God, Jesus rocks Nicodemus with a second ambiguity. This time it concerns the word *pneuma*, properly translated in verse 5 as "spirit." It also means "wind" or "current of air." (Since breathing is the most obvious indication of life, the transfer of meaning was inevitable.) Nicodemus no doubt knows the two meanings of *pneuma*. When Jesus in verse 8 said, "The wind bloweth where it listeth . . . ; so is every one that is born of the Spirit," his literalist tendency a second time made him confused. Like the interlocutor in a Socratic dialogue, he is reduced to hopeless uncertainty: "How can these things be?" Jesus ironically inquires how *the* teacher in Israel can be ignorant of such matters. We, he adds, speak from knowledge and yet you, who lack it, refuse to listen to us. If you cannot understand what you take literally, how can you understand matters on the heavenly plane?

One cannot tell precisely where the author ceases to report this conversation and begins his own comment. Verses 14–21 would hardly have been addressed to Nicodemus, but are more probably from the author himself. They possibly represent words of Jesus uttered upon some other occasion. John, unlike Luke, is willing to abandon an account which he has brilliantly reported in order to comment on it. His literary skill is perhaps superior to his literary appreciation.

The significance attached in John to the spiritual blindness of the Jewish leaders cannot be overemphasized. In fact, the contrast between darkness and light in the introduction leads directly to them. Before the episode of Nicodemus, it had appeared in the literalism of the Jews when Jesus cleansed the Temple (3:13–22), an episode which in John is placed at the beginning of his career. To their angry demand that Jesus show a "sign" to establish his authority for such an action, he replied, "Destroy this temple, and in three days I will raise it up." In true Oriental passion for gesture, he had, no doubt, pointed to himself as he spoke, but they had missed the ambiguity created by his gesture. As Paul wrote (2 Cor. 3:6): "God, . . . hath made us able ministers of the new testament [i.e., covenant with man]; not of the letter, but of the spirit: for the letter killeth, but the spirit giveth life."

Nicodemus was a highly educated, orthodox, upper-class Jew. To show that literalism was not confined to such people, the author next demonstrates its presence at the opposite end of the socio-religious ladder, in Jesus' encounter with the Samaritan woman (4:3–30). For once Jesus and his disciples had returned to Galilee by the shorter route across Samaria. At evening they stopped to pass the night near a Samaritan village. As Jesus was waiting alone by the village well while his disciples had gone to buy food, a woman from the village came out to draw her evening water from the deep well. Jesus asked her for a drink. She asks in surprise why a Jew would accept a drink from a Samaritan. Jesus replies once more ambiguously that he could give her "living water." The phrase refers to fresh water, but he means the "water of Life." She retorts that he cannot draw water from the well without a rope, unless he is greater than "our father Jacob" who had dug it. Jesus replies that the water which he provides will slake thirst forever. The literal-minded woman sees it as a welcome relief from a daily chore.

Abandoning this approach as hopeless, Jesus tells her to bring her husband. She replies with some embarrassment that she has no husband. Jesus agrees: like the wife of Bath, she has had five husbands, and she is now living with a man out of wedlock. Disturbed by such uncanny knowledge, she tries another gambit: we have for centuries worshiped on Mount Gerizim, but you Jews say we should worship at Jerusalem. Declining to accept the bait, Jesus declares that from now on men may worship anywhere. God is spirit (*pneuma* again), and men should worship him spiritually. Such matters are beyond the woman's mind, which flits restlessly from topic to topic. She replies hazily that when the Messiah comes he will tell men "all things." I, said Jesus, am the Messiah.

The return of the disciples breaks up the conversation. Rushing into the village, the woman shouts that Jesus had told her everything she ever did; he must be the Messiah. Her garbled exaggeration is the measure of her mind. When the villagers go out to meet him, Jesus starts a two-day visit in their village. Such an episode, showing that a dense literalism pervaded even the lowest, barely Jewish mind, shows how widespread and deadly this point of view was.

Although John is no more concerned with order of events than the other Gospel writers, a confusion arising after chapter 4 is not of his making, but caused by later error. Chapter 4 concludes with Jesus' arrival in Galilee. Chapter 5 has him returning to Jerusalem and in violent debate there. Chapter 6, without returning him to Galilee, reports events in Galilee. Chapter 7 shows him as returning to Jerusalem from Galilee. If one transposes chapters 5 and 6, the order of events is better preserved. Such an error is probably caused by a copyist's losing his place after a break in his work, resuming it at a later page than where he had left off, and then after subsequent interruption inserting, unconscious of error, the part he had omitted. Such errors are not unknown in manuscripts. It might also have been caused through an error in assembling pages. This discussion will follow the emended order.

One can only speculate about why the author of John abandoned the plan of the synoptic Gospels which report only one visit of Jesus to Jerusalem and placed Jesus in Jerusalem on three successive Passovers. As a propagandist, he was, of course, at liberty to do so. He may have concluded that events centering in Jerusalem were a more appropriate setting for the beginnings of the Church. Jerusalem had been the home base of the Church for several decades before it fell, and it was there that it could be symbolically shown as confronting Judaism at its center. Scattered brief reports of Jesus' activities in

Judea appear also in the synoptic Gospels. There was evidently a tradition of events there on which the author of John could draw.

The author arranged several of Jesus' arguments with his opponents into two major dialogues. Reversing the order of the earlier episodes, he presented first a dialogue with ordinary Galileans and next a dialogue in Jerusalem in which Pharisees are his principal interlocutors. The first confrontation conforms more closely to the tradition of dialectic than the second. Feelings run much hotter in the second, so that vituperation frequently takes the place of debate. Even in the first dialogue, however, there is a departure from the pattern. Jesus appears by its end to have been using it for an ulterior motive beyond the attempt to seek out the truth. It is, of course, possible that dialectic was in John's day used as the author here used it.

The first dialogue (chap. 6) stems from Jesus' miraculous feeding of five thousand Galileans in an uninhabited area on the shore of the lake. His disciples and he left the place separately by night in order to return to his headquarters at Capernaum. Next morning the crowd returned to Capernaum in search of him. When they had found him they naturally inquired when he had returned. Partly to discourage their intent to make him leader of an insurrection, Jesus from the start deliberately antagonized the crowd.

Jesus accuses them of seeking him for another free meal. Instead of this, they should labor for food that "endureth unto everlasting life" which he can give them. Somewhat better informed than the Samaritan woman but still confused, they ask him to give them this food. Like her reaction to "living water," they are swayed by food in the literal sense rather than by the symbolical overtones which they vaguely discern. How do we work for it? Jesus responds that they must believe his words as God's emissary. They demand that he prove this claim. He replies that he is that bread of life that has come to them from heaven. God his Father has sent him to receive all who will receive them and to give them eternal life.

Stunned by Jesus' assertion of his divine parentage, the crowd recalls that they know his parentage; how can he make such a claim? He replies that he is indeed the bread of life. Referring to their unspoken memory of manna as bread from heaven, he reminds them that manna did not give eternal life as he does. Manna, which they associated with Moses, symbolizes the superiority of Jesus' message to the Law. John's readers would see this even if the excited mob did not. As their fathers ate manna, Jesus continues, they must metaphorically eat him. Their characteristic literalism governing them, they ask in horror if he wants them to be cannibals. John's readers would interpret Jesus' words in the light of the Eucharist; Jesus is trying to make the crowd think beyond the literal sense, as faith in Him demands. In this attempt he fails with most of the crowd.

Jesus' tactics throughout this dialogue are obviously designed to shock his hearers into a new pattern of thinking. It was imperative, too, that he rid his movement of any subversive atmosphere. In a sense, he was also "separating the men from the boys," as the episode added about the disciples' response shows. Some of his followers are swayed by doubt and leave him; they are not equal to the demand upon them. Depressed at their defection, Jesus asks the twelve, "Will ye also go away?" Peter, for once responding rightly, asks bluntly, "To whom shall we go? Thou hast the words of eternal life." In spite of his knowledge that Judas would later betray him, Jesus is heartened by Peter's rough but effective reply.

A far more elaborately worked out dialogue between Jesus and more highly trained opponents is presented in chapters 5, 7–9. On this visit to Jerusalem, possibly at Pentecost, seven weeks after the Passover, he heals a crippled man on the Sabbath at the pool Bethesda. He not only heals the man, he also bids him to carry the stretcher he had been brought on to the pool. Jesus' opponents first see the man carrying the bed and rebuke him as a lawbreaker. Later, when they learn that Jesus had healed the man and told him to carry the bed, they try to kill Jesus, ostensibly as a lawbreaker, but actually because he blasphemously made himself equal with God. John's readers, to whom Jewish Sabbath regulations had long seemed ridiculous, would see a comic tinge in the situation, a tinge which the author preserves throughout the dialogue.

Jesus defends himself with the simple statement that his Father and he keep working continuously. This idea Philo had stressed; it would appeal to John's readers. To Jesus' enemies, he now stands convicted as both Sabbath breaker and blasphemer. Jesus, however, is more concerned with indicating his unique status than with defending himself. The Son does what the Father does, knows what the Father does. Like the Father, the Son gives life—a foreshadowing of Lazarus' resurrection, but even more a reference to his giving eternal life. The Father has entrusted to the Son the judging of men. In failing to honor the Son, they dishonor the Father also. The man who accepts Jesus' message will escape his condemnation and "is passed from death into life."

As in the preceding dialogue, Jesus is anything but conciliatory. Here, as in Galilee, his hearers must be shocked out of their complacent literalism and self-assured legalism. His attitude is not anti-Semitic, but it is opposed to the blinders that hinder the Jews from clearer sight. With such people conciliation is ineffectual.

The extended statement (5:17–47) indicates by its shifts of topics that the author has recast question and answer here into continuous discourse. Its substance centers in Jesus' support for his claims. He has two witnesses, John the Baptist and the Father, on his side; yet his opponents prefer unsupported testimony. If they truly loved God, they would accept his witness. Moses also accuses them. Moses in the Law points to Jesus; if they don't believe Jesus, they don't believe Moses. Blind literalism and low-level interpretation trouble all with whom Jesus speaks. Throughout this Gospel this is the continuous defect in his hearers.

Such devastating charges forced Jesus to leave Judea to escape assassination. He remained in Galilee for some months—perhaps from June to September. He timed his return to Jerusalem toward the conclusion of the week-long feast, in order to capitalize upon the tension roused by his absence. People were still excited about his charges at the previous confrontation. This interval does not actually affect the continuity of the debate which John has put together. It resumes where the previous part had left off.

Jesus' hearers, obsessed by the authoritative lore of the scribes and Pharisees, wonder how a man without such training is so effective in speech. Jesus replies as he had earlier that his teaching is God's who had sent him. Resuming also the argument on Sabbath breaking, he asks why he cannot heal on the Sabbath if the Sabbath regulations permit mutilation on the Sabbath. A son was circumcised on the eighth day whether it fell on the Sabbath or not. His appeal to right judgment (7:24) would delight John's Hellenistic readers.

Some of the Jewish hearers at this debate were surprised that Jesus spoke with impunity. Do his opponents have some secret knowledge that he really is the Messiah? Others deny that the Messiah could come from Galilee. Jesus, admitting that he was from Galilee, says that he actually has come from God: "I know God; you do not." The infuriated crowd try unsuccessfully to lynch him. Great numbers who are present cannot believe that any Messiah could perform more miracles than Jesus has done. The authorities seize the opportunity to have Jesus arrested. The crowd is getting out of hand.

Jesus presses his attack. I shall soon go, he says, to him who sent me, for "where I am, thither ye cannot come."[2] The Jews wonder angrily whether he means to desert them for the Gentiles—a consummation which the readers of John would see as fulfilled because the Jews had deserted Christ.

On the last, climactic day of the feast, Jesus takes advantage of the ritual to repeat the water symbolism which he had used so effectively with the Samaritan woman. Each day had witnessed a procession to the pool of Siloam, where the officiating priest filled a golden pitcher, which he solemnly carried to the Temple and poured on the altar in thanks to God for the physical blessings. On the final day the procession marched seven times around the altar before the water was poured. It is probably at this high point in the rite that Jesus calls out, "If any man thirst, let him come to Me, and drink." Whoever believes in him will himself become a source of living water. His meaning, as the author interpolates, is that

[2] The translators were apparently affected by their belief that Jesus had ascended into heaven in 7:34. The verb form which they translated "am" may also mean "go."

such a man will receive the power of the Holy Spirit after Jesus' ascension.

The crowd, deeply moved at this dramatic outburst, divides into his supporters, who are convinced that he is either the Messiah or the great prophet who is expected, and his opponents, who declare that the Messiah must come from Bethlehem and be of Davidic descent, not a mere Galilean. At this point the police sent to arrest him return to the authorities empty handed. When asked why they had not brought him, they reply, "Never man spoke like this man." The priests and Pharisees loftily reply, "Have any of *us* believed Him?" The crowd he sways are going to hell anyhow because they do not observe the Law as we do.

Their peroration is marred by Nicodemus' asking whether they would condemn a man without a hearing. Furious at his having spoiled their effect, they sneeringly ask whether Nicodemus, too, is a Galilean. They clinch their case by citing an aphorism, which was then considered a valid proof: "Out of Galilee ariseth no prophet." They decide, nonetheless, against an arrest while feeling was running so high. The immediate confrontation ends in a stalemate, with Jesus enjoying some advantage in that the authorities have not dared to arrest him.

It is generally agreed—and two of the best manuscripts support the contention—that the episode of Jesus and the adulteress which follows does not belong here in John (8:3–11). One late manuscript inserted it following Luke 21:38 as properly following the Sadducees' attempt to entangle Jesus in a question about levirate marriage—an arrangement hardly acceptable. The passage is quite in harmony with Jesus' practice, but its origin cannot be traced.

The debate resumes at 8:12 under unspecified circumstances. Jesus reiterates the light-darkness dichotomy so impressively employed in the introduction. His followers, he declares, shall not walk in darkness. The Pharisees immediately take exception to the implied slur upon their enlightenment and repeat their charge that Jesus' assertion of power is unsupported by witnesses. To this Jesus retorts that the Father is his witness. When they sarcastically reply that his father is not present, he bitterly replies that they know neither him nor his Father. "If ye had known Me, ye should have known my Father also." Enraged at this seeming blasphemy, they still deem it impolitic to lay hands upon him.

Throughout this dialogue the interlocutors operate on two far separate levels: the Jews, on the literal, material level; Jesus, being from another world, on the spiritual. Jesus iterates his statement, "Whither I go, ye cannot come" (8:21). This time the Jews suspect in bewilderment that he plans to kill himself. In desperation they ask again, "Who *are* you?" Jesus impatiently replies that he is whom he had been claiming to be from the beginning, the spokesman of his Father.

With these words Jesus has begun to impress a part of his hearers. These new adherents he admonishes to hold fast to their belief: "Ye shall know the truth, and the truth shall make you free" (8:32). They are precariously balanced between their new acceptance and their traditional position, and the implication that they are not already free tilts their balance against Jesus. They are Abraham's children and were never enslaved. On their factual level, their statement was untenable, but racial pride never let them admit this. On the spiritual level, Jesus patiently explains to these neophytes that men who are slaves to sin can be disposed of as their master wills, whereas a son is a member of his father's household. Jesus adds that as the Son of God he can free them from bondage to sin and restore them to sonship in his Father's household, if they know the truth. His underlying idea, that only the wise man is free, was a Stoic proverb known to John's readers as well as acceptable to Jewish readers of Proverbs.

Reverting to their obsession with Abraham, Jesus adds: I know that you are descended from Abraham, but you have not inherited his trait of obedience to the word that came to him from God. You are more like your real father. Angered, they demand whether he means they are bastards, not Abraham's sons. Jesus retorts that they show the traits of their actual father the devil, who was a liar and murderer from the beginning.

Too angry to think of a reply, they resort to vituperation. He is a Samaritan, and crazy as well. Jesus replies that a man who holds fast to his teaching will never die. The God-fearing Abraham and the Prophets are dead, they exclaim. Are you greater than they? Who are you anyway? My Father, Jesus answers, whom you believe to be your God, honors me. "Your father Abraham rejoiced to see my day: and he saw it, and was glad." How can you have seen Abraham? they jeeringly ask. Jesus replies pregnantly, "Before Abraham was, I am" (8:58). He thus declares himself to be the Logos, as John's readers will interpret the response. In fury at Jesus' calm declaration, his recent followers tear up paving stones of the Temple court to lynch him. Once more he escapes their fury.

This conversation departs radically from the pattern of Greek dialectic, in which interlocutors seek to discover the truth. John shows by this contrast that Jewish opposition to Jesus was not rational but emotional, unreasoning, and biased. The attitude of Gamaliel (Acts 5:34–40) to the new faith sharply points up their fault. Jewish leaders were blind, unable to investigate truth. Although these scenes are powerfully dramatic, the intransigence of the Jews made the true purpose of dialectic unattainable.

The ensuing episode of the man born blind (chap. 9) would, in the eyes of John's readers, serve as the concluding myth of a Platonic dialogue. This episode serves the purpose of illustrating Jesus' statements with an incident. (A myth is not necessarily a fanciful tale, but is often historical or biographical.)

As Jesus is passing by—John implies that it was after he had escaped the mob in the Temple—He sees a man who has been blind from his birth. Brushing aside with a brusque negative his disciples' speculation about the origin of the man's blindness, Jesus rubs damp clay on his eyes and bids him to go to the pool of Siloam and wash off the clay. Expectantly obeying Jesus' direction, the man returns seeing. Jesus has gone on his way in the interim. The man says that someone named Jesus told him what to do.

The neighbors excitedly bring the man before the Pharisees. These, still shaken by Jesus' rough handling in the debate, now find themselves faced with a *fait accompli*. Once more it is the Sabbath, a fact which ties together the two healings which frame the entire dialogue. The Pharisees' initial response repeats that of the Jews at the pool of Bethesda: "This man is not of God, because he keepeth not the Sabbath day"—hardly an approach to the main problem before them. Violent disagreement arises when the more logical members of the group assert that a sinner cannot perform miracles of healing, while the blind man declares him to be a prophet.

To escape their awkward quandary, the literalist Pharisees call in the blind man's parents. They are terrified because a rule has been established that anyone who calls Jesus the Messiah shall be expelled from the synagogue—a punishment tantamount to medieval excommunication from the church. He was born blind, they admit, but they deny all knowledge of his healing: "He is of age; ask him." Baffled again, the inquisitors recall the beggar and tell him to thank God for his restored sight; Jesus' part in it was coincidental, for he is a sinner. After obstinately holding to his story under repeated examination, his patience wears thin: Why should I tell you over and over? Do you also want to be his disciples? In true Oriental fashion, they revile him: You are his disciple; he is a nobody from nobody knows where. God spoke through Moses; this man has no credentials.

Comedy now reaches its climax. The blind, uneducated beggar instructs the Pharisees in elements of theology. If a man has such power, he tells them, surely you should know where it comes from. My restored sight is an unparalleled event which could be performed only through divine agency. Everyone knows that.

In chapter 10 there appears to be a second though minor dislocation of passages. Verses 19–21, which recur to the episode of the blind man, more naturally follow chapter 9, while verses 1–18 seem more suitable when inserted between verses 25 and 26.

The major part of chapter 10 is connected with Jesus' visit to the Temple some three months later, in the winter, perhaps during Hanukkah. The Jews come to him with a demand for a plain answer whether he is the Messiah. He declares that his works speak for him. They will not believe him because they are not sheep of his fold. His sheep hear his voice, follow him, and receive eternal life. His Father has given them to him: "I and my Father are one."

When they prepare to stone him for this blasphemy, he demands which of his good works that prove his claims is the reason for their stoning him. They reply that he deserves stoning for his blasphemy in claiming to be God.

Jesus' response (34–36) becomes intelligible when one discovers that he was following the Jewish rabbinical interpretation of Psalm 82:6. This psalm, which attacks unjust judges, was given wider reference, at least for this verse, to influential wrongdoers. In the psalm, this verse seems to be an ironic comment on exaggerated claims to self-importance; and a similar irony may be noted in Jesus' use of it. If God calls such men gods, why may I not also call myself the Son of God? My claim is substantiated by my deeds. Having been foiled by Jesus in their attack, they once more resort to violence; but he again escapes. This time he leaves Jerusalem to stay across the Jordan, where John the Baptist had begun to announce him.

This return to John's scene of action symbolizes that Jesus' first stage of activity as reported in John has come full circle. He has unsuccessfully endeavored to convince the Jews, and especially their leaders, to accept his claim to be the Son of God. The author reports no later similar attempts in detail. John the Baptist has been equally unsuccessful with the Pharisees. The author has presented to the Jews the dual nature of Christ as both human and divine. In so doing he has contradicted the Gnostic denial that such a duality is possible. He has also tried to present through the father-son analogy the seeming paradox that these two are actually one. When in subsequent pages he presents the concept of a divine Trinity, he evidently feels that a man who has accepted the concept of a two-in-one God will find no problem in accepting the Trinity. From this point onward, the nature of the fourth Gospel changes noticeably, the watershed being the dramatically reported resurrection of Lazarus.

Since the family of Lazarus are already known to his readers through the story of Martha's petulant request that Jesus ask Mary to help her prepare dinner (Luke 10:38–42), it is unnecessary for them to be reintroduced in John. (Other accounts of them, now lost, may also have been circulating.) While Jesus is teaching some three-days distance from Bethany across the Jordan, Lazarus falls ill, and his sisters send word of this illness to Jesus. Upon receiving the message Jesus remarks that this sickness is not "unto death, but . . . that the Son of God might be glorified thereby"—a cryptic, ambiguous, apparently unconcerned comment in spite of its implication that some importance attaches to the illness.

After two days Jesus leads the disciples back into Judea. Overriding their fears for him, he again replies that he goes to awaken Lazarus from sleep. When the disciples reply that Lazarus' illness must have lost its hold if he can sleep, they imply that the journey is unnecessary. Jesus then explains that Lazarus is dead, but that his going will strengthen their faith. They accompany him expecting the worst.

Some two days later, as Jesus approaches the village, the author with consummate skill employs suspense to heighten the impact of the coming sign. Jesus stops and sends word of his arrival. Martha, the first to learn of it, slips away and goes to him. She expresses implicit faith in his healing power but has no inkling that he can now help. When Jesus ambiguously says that Lazarus will rise again, she assumes that he refers to the future resurrection of the dead. Jesus cryptically says, "*I* am the resurrection and the life," and adds that the believer in him shall never die. She is confused by his words, but declares her belief in him as the Messiah and the Son of God.

Returning home, she whispers to Mary that Jesus has come and wishes to see her. Less successful than Martha in eluding the mourners in the house, Mary is followed by them. She repeats Martha's mild reproach to Jesus for his absence. Deeply moved, Jesus is taken to the tomb. Over Martha's practical protest, the tomb is opened. After a brief devotional prayer to God, Jesus cries out, "Lazarus, come forth!" Bound in cerements though it was, the body came forth alive.

Although most who were present were convinced of Jesus' power through the undeniable miracle, some quickly reported it to the Pharisees. The Sanhedrin immediately convened to consider the situation. No one denied what had happened. Nonetheless, it was the consensus that action must be taken to stop Jesus. Their reasoning is in three stages, of which the second is so obvious to them that they do not even express it. If he is not halted, all men will believe him; like other Messiahs, he will start an abortive insurrection; and the Romans will place Judea under martial law which will abrogate the Sanhedrin's authority. Their fixation on the factual level is nowhere more evident in John.

Caiaphas, the current high priest, broke into their worried bumbling. Why not face the issue squarely? It is expedient *for us*—good manuscripts read "for you"—to get rid of one man if the nation may be saved by his death. The author ironically comments that Caiaphas unintentionally utters an implied prophecy: Jesus' death was for the good of the Jews and in fact for all mankind. Caiaphas' rough, direct facing the issue met their approval, and they took steps to have Jesus killed.

A little later, the author of John attempts to account for the invincible ignorance of the Jews by citing Isaiah (53:1 and 6:10). The recalcitrant Jews appear to the author (12:37–41) to be instruments of God's plan as well as culprits. Ironically, they occupy the same position with reference to the Christians that the prophets had assigned to the Gentile nations around the earlier Jewish kingdoms.

The resurrection of Lazarus not long before Jesus' death and resurrection serves a purpose analogous to the healing of the woman inserted in synoptic accounts of the resurrection of Jairus' daughter. It prepares the readers to trust more securely in the far greater miracle to come. It also arouses the Jews to all-absorbing interest in Jesus. Will he come to the Passover? The Sanhedrin's intention to get rid of him was known among too many to be kept secret.

Six days before the Passover, John reports, Jesus slips quietly into the house of Lazarus in Bethany, which was to be his base for the ensuing struggle. Here occurs a variant of an event reported in the synoptic account. During dinner Mary pours an expensive ointment over Jesus' feet and dries them with her hair as a sign of gratitude. Judas violently protests that the money which the ointment would bring would have been a gift to help the poor. The author comments that Judas, who served as treasurer for the party, actually wishes to get his hands on the money for himself; he was a thief.

The author seems here to suggest the final irritation that was to incite Judas to betray Jesus.

John's account of the triumphal entry is briefer than those in the synoptic Gospels. The author introduces three new details. The crowd, he says, is motivated to see Jesus partly by the recent resurrection of Lazarus, which was everywhere talked about. He adds also the chagrin of the Pharisees who had unsuccessfully tried to kill him along with Lazarus before they should leave Bethany. The third new episode in his account reports that some of the Greek converts to Judaism in the crowd ask Philip to introduce them to Jesus.

Without reporting this meeting, the author seizes the event to introduce Jesus' final public words before his arrest. His words fit the immediate occasion in their climactic statement, "I, if I be lifted up from the earth, will draw all men unto me" (12:32)—Gentiles as well as Jews. "To lift up" is the colloquial expression for crucifixion, as the author reminds his readers. In this brief final speech, which, in fact, reads as if put together by the author from various sayings of Jesus, his message is successfully condensed. To believe me is to believe him who sent me. To see me is to see him who sent me. I am here as a light to keep believers from stumbling in the dark. What I say is not mine alone, it is the Father's word as well. This is the epitome of Jesus' message.

DIALOGUE AT THE LAST SUPPER

The synoptic writers write of the Last Supper as eaten on the occasion of the Passover, as a replacement or fulfillment instituted by Jesus immediately following the traditional feast. In John it is reported as taking place on the previous evening. Some scholars feel that the author of John, and presumably Paul also, have permitted doctrinal symbolism to override the more factual synoptic dating. One must bear in mind, however, that none of the Gospel writers were concerned with strict biographical accuracy, and none of them can be taken as factually specifying the date.

Like the earlier occasions on which Jesus has been pictured as talking to an audience, the author indicates conversation while at times turning it into continuous discourse. Here the acrimonious note of the earlier confrontations with hostile Jews is totally absent. Jesus is speaking in circumstances fraught with deep feeling to his most intimate friends. One may doubt that John preserves anything like the actual conversation. What he reports is admirably compounded from Jesus' preserved words to fit the occasion. He indicates the importance of the occasion and the words he attaches to it by devoting one-fifth of his entire Gospel to this single episode.

John's account sets at the start the keynote of service. Jesus dramatically assumes the role of the slave who was in great houses chained to the door as welcomer and protector. Jesus performs the service welcome to travelers afoot on dusty roads of washing his disciples' feet. In the hierarchy of posts in a household, the doorkeeper stood lowest. Jesus' target on this occasion is, no doubt, the wrangling of his disciples over preferment in his kingdom, to which all the Gospels testify. You should wash one another's feet as I wash yours, he says.

Since the ritual of the Lord's Supper or Eucharist was well established by the time the author wrote, he omits an account of it. He devotes himself rather to a few illustrative anecdotes and especially to the long spiritual discourse.

Back in Galilee, Jesus had asserted that one of the twelve was a devil (6:70–71). Now, he declares that one of them will betray him (13:21). As the shocked disciples sit silently at a loss, Peter once more rushes headlong into the breach. He whispers to the "disciple whom Jesus loved" that he should ask Jesus who is guilty. Jesus, without naming the man, replies that it is the man to whom he will give a piece of bread dipped in gravy—an Oriental token of esteem. Judas, unmoved by Jesus' generous gesture, immediately leaves to tell the authorities where Jesus may later be arrested.

Without grasping the significance of Judas' departure, the remaining eleven tensely feel an approaching crisis. Jesus' next words, that he will shortly leave them, do not relieve the tension. Without him, Jesus adds, they are to become unified in love "as I have loved you," as proof of their discipleship. Peter demands to know why he cannot accompany Jesus. He declares that he would gladly die for Him. Jesus tries to check his cocksureness by declaring that Peter will deny three times before cockcrow that he had ever known Him. Peter, apparently shocked into silence, briefly subsides.

Putting his encouragement into simple terms, Jesus speaks to calm their sorrow. I am going away to prepare a place for you in my Father's spacious house. I shall come again to take you to live there with me. You know the way to it. The hard-headed realist, Thomas, impatiently asks, "How can we know the way if we do not know where you are going?" Patiently continuing his metaphor, Jesus replies, "I am the way [i.e., the road], the truth, and the life; no man cometh to the Father, but by Me." When Philip asks Jesus to show him the Father, Jesus replies that whoever has truly seen him has seen the Father, as Jesus' acts and words furnish convincing proof. Under the Holy Spirit's guidance, they will perform more extensive works than he has done.

Excepting one or two interjected remarks by the disciples, the author here virtually abandons dialogue to report continuous discourse by Jesus. He has, however, so well established the pattern of dialogue that the sense of such intimate conversation persists.

Not until now does the author emphasize the concept of the Holy Spirit. It is not new. Paul had referred to it, it figured constantly in Acts, and John had already mentioned it. The Spirit, Jesus now tells them, will comfort them in his absence and always be with them. As already stated, the author does not need to persuade readers of a third person in God. If they have accepted the belief that God can be two yet one, a third element offers little or no problem. Realizing the incapability of the disciples to grasp what he has been telling them, Jesus adds that when the Holy Spirit comes they will better realize the complete union of Jesus with the Father and of themselves with Jesus.

The remainder of the discourse (chaps. 15–17) is represented as taking place while they walk to the Garden of Gethsemane. As Plato's *Phaedrus* shows, the traditional pattern of dialogue to which this discourse partly conforms made use of such shifts of scene during the action.

Jesus' symbol of the vine (15:1–8) is one of the better-developed symbols in John. Others, such as analogies to light, the road, and the shepherd, are self-explanatory; this is somewhat more complex. Hebrew tradition represented Israel by the vine. Jesus' assertion that he is the true vine chimes with his previous assertion (8:33–59) that the Jews are not true sons of Abraham. Before John was written, Paul had worked out the charge in Romans. Identification of the Father with the husbandman ties the symbol to the allegory in Isaiah 5. The practice of cutting off suckers and dead wood and pruning branches to make the vine more productive would be familiar throughout the Mediterranean world.

A somber picture is next presented. They must be ready to die for him as he is about to die for them. They will be hated as his friends in the same way that he has been hated. They will undergo persecution at the hands of men whose invincible ignorance renders them unable to understand his message. The Spirit as comforter will enable them to endure expulsion from the synagogue, a suffering like death to a Jew. As for me, he adds, I came into the world from the Father; having done what I was sent to do, I now return to the Father. The disciples, bemused yet grasping something of his summation, assert full confidence in him as the Son of God. Their self-confidence, Jesus sadly replies, will soon desert them as they abandon him in his hour of trial. His example, however, will help them to endure their future suffering in the assurance that he has overcome the earthly powers of evil.

This second scene concludes with Jesus' prayer consecrating his disciples to their work (chap. 17). He prays for divine support in his imminent testing. He prays for all mankind, and especially for his disciples, that they may be steadfast in faith and service, that, to borrow the words of 2 Peter, they may "grow in grace, and in the knowledge of our Lord and Saviour Jesus Christ" (3:18).

THE FORTUNATE CATASTROPHE

From the spiritual height of Jesus' discourse, the action drops steeply to the catastrophe. Mark's skillful preparation for it (14:32–42) is omitted; such details would be anticlimactic to the moving account just finished. When the arresting band—mindful perhaps of their companions' declaration, "Never man spake like this man"—hesitate to take him, Peter, impulsive but ineffectual, draws a sword and slices off a man's ear. Jesus sharply rebukes Peter for trying to interfere with the divine plan. Jesus is bound and taken before Annas, the high priest's father-in-law. Caiaphas was a vigorous leader but was subject to the autocratic head of the family.

Most of the following account differs but slightly from that of the synoptic writers and need not be recounted. The part played by Pilate, however, deserves attention. It is daybreak when the chief priests, having held their hearings, bring Jesus before Pilate. In accord with Roman practice, he tries to escape handling the case. Failing in this, he asks Jesus ironically, "Art thou the King of the Jews?" Jesus responds by asking whether he brings the charge of his own volition, to which Pilate asks scornfully, "Am I a Jew?" Somewhat hazily, he admits that the charge comes from the Jewish authorities and the Jewish nation. Jesus, perhaps wryly recalling Peter's inept swordsmanship, replied that if he were a king his servants would fight. His kingdom is not earthly. Out of his depth, Pilate persists on the only level he understands: "Art thou a king then?" Jesus answers that his entire earthly career has been directed to such a fulfillment; all who know the truth will listen to him. Pilate testily dismisses the ethical level with the question, "What is truth?"

Concluding that Jesus is either a madman or a harmless fanatic, Pilate honestly tries to work out a compromise with the determined Jewish leaders. Why not release this fellow as the customary Roman gesture of good will at the Passover? It would save an innocent life and save face for the authorities. The authorities, however, demand the execution of Jesus and the release of a robber named Barabbas. The latter is a *lēistēs,* a highway robber. Roman law, always sensitive to commercial advantage, vigorously protected its arteries of travel. To release him would place Pilate in a dangerous position if it was reported in Rome. The demand constituted a vicious attack on Pilate for temporizing about Jesus. After further futile efforts Pilate yields and orders Jesus' execution.

After the soldiers have beaten and ridiculed Jesus, Pilate presents him again to the Jews, hoping apparently to satisfy their thirst for Jesus' downfall. Look, he says in effect, my soldiers have beaten and disgraced him; but I really find no just cause to execute him. They respond, Crucify him as a rebel against Rome. In exasperation he shouts, You take him and crucify him—which of course they cannot do. They next play on Pilate's superstitions: By our law he should die for blasphemously calling himself the Son of God. Pilate, in some apprehension that he may become embroiled with the Jewish God, demands on pain of death that Jesus tell him about his origin. Jesus calmly responds that Pilate can do only what God lets him do. He then eases the Roman's mind by declaring that his accusers are more to blame than Pilate. Thereupon Pilate tries feverishly to save him.

The Jewish authorities then play their trump card. It would be treason for Pilate to free any man who set himself up as a king—Caesar appointed such local rulers. The influential Jewish lobby at Rome could ruin Pilate with such a charge. In his defeat Pilate, nonetheless, shrewdly salvages an important advantage. He dramatically points to Jesus and sarcastically shouts, "Behold your King!" As they scream for Jesus' crucifixion, he asks insinuatingly, "Shall I crucify your King?" To this they frantically respond, "We have no king but Caesar." Pilate has outmaneuvered them at the height of their chief patriotic feast and has led them to make an unprecedented pledge of loyalty to Caesar. It will sound well in his dispatches to Rome, for the Jews were among the most stubbornly opposed to foreign rule of any Roman subjects.

Pilate is, however, deeply irritated that the Jews have forced him to bend to their will. He vents his pique by having a sign placed on the cross above Jesus' head: Jesus of Nazareth, the King of the Jews. The author ironically implies that Pilate unwittingly states a truth. When the Jews violently protest at the sign, Pilate turns them away with the brusque "What I have written, I have written."

Details relating to the Crucifixion are apparently chosen for their interest or their symbolic meaning. Readers will be interested to know that Jesus' mother will be cared for by John. The fact will also add prestige to the account associated with his name. Other passages show Jesus as fulfilling Old Testament prophecies about the Messiah, which would interest readers imbued with Philo's allegorical interpretation.

The finishing off of the two malefactors is quite in keeping with the facts. Crucified men sometimes lingered for days before death supervened. In their exhausted condition the shock of breaking their legs would kill them. The author certifies that Jesus had died before this: his blood had separated into serum and corpuscles, which occurs only after death.

The hasty temporary burial of Jesus was required by the imminence of the Sabbath. Jewish law (Deut. 21:22–23) provided that no body should be allowed to hang on the Sabbath, and the prohibition was extended to crucified bodies. Since no kind of work could be performed on the Sabbath (Exod. 31:14–15), which was reckoned from sundown to sundown, the customary preparation of the body for burial had to be curtailed.

The last two chapters of John stress evidence of Jesus' dual nature after the resurrection. This clearly is designed to confute the school of Docetists who declared that Jesus was only a phantom after the resurrection. With the synoptic Gospels already in circulation—the author knew undoubtedly one or more of these—he could omit much that they had already reported and concentrate on his anti-Gnostic argument.

Ten disciples, while hiding from the Jewish authorities, see and converse with Jesus. He shows the wounds in his body, commissions them as apostles, and prays that they receive the Holy Spirit. Thomas, a practical, down-to-earth disciple, was absent. He demands tactile evidence for himself before he will believe. A week later, Jesus reappears. After offering to let Thomas touch the wounds, Jesus mildly rebukes him for demanding material proofs: "Blessed are they that have not seen, and yet have believed"—an encouraging word to John's readers to stand fast in the faith.

Milton had seen the failure of Adam and Eve to be a paradoxically fortunate fall for man. In the same way, the crucifixion and death of Jesus proved to be a fortunate catastrophe for mankind.

THE EPILOGUE

The Fourth Gospel in all probability concluded with chapter 20. Its final two verses read like a reminder of the author's purpose and round off the account. Chapter 21 is an epilogue. Its authorship cannot be determined. Whoever wrote it knew intimately the purposes and content of this Gospel, for he undertook to settle two problems that must have been thought of: the rehabilitation of Peter, and the identity of "the disciple whom Jesus loved." He also corroborated the anti-Docetic argument by presenting Jesus as having a physical body that can build a fire and prepare food.

After the turmoil of Passover in Jerusalem, the epilogue presents a peaceful rural scene. Back in Galilee, Peter restlessly announces that he is going fishing, and six other disciples accompany him. All night long they cast their nets in vain. At daybreak someone on the shore calls to ask whether they have caught anything. When they say no, he bids them to cast the net on the right side of the boat; and the shoal of fish they caught almost broke the net. From the shore the different angle of vision could show the surface of the water roughened by the feeding fish, while the men in the boat were unable to see it. The "disciple whom Jesus loved" now recognizes Jesus and tells Peter. The latter impetuously leaps overboard and makes his way to the shore. The others come with the boat, drawing the net full of fish.

The 153 fish may be symbolical; it was believed that there were that number of species of fish, which represent all mankind. The author of the epilogue may be thinking of two sayings of Jesus recorded in Matthew. At the call of Andrew and Peter (Matt. 4:19) Jesus had invited them to become "fishers of men," and one of Jesus' parables (Matt. 13: 47–48) pictured the kingdom of heaven as a net containing all kinds of fish.

Jesus already has fish broiling over a fire and loaves of bread for their breakfast. The disciples being tongue-tied at this sudden appearance of Jesus, breakfast is eaten in silence. Then comes Peter's rehabilitation. Jesus literally makes Peter eat his words by having him declare his love for Him three times for each denial he had made that he ever knew Him. By the time John was written, Peter had long been known as a tested and able Christian leader. The writer may have wished to remove any stigma attached to his moment of weakness by showing how Jesus forgave and took him back to feed his sheep.

Peter is still the tactless man with a short span of attention. Forgetting his recent emotional experience of rehabilitation, and mindful of the somber picture Jesus had drawn of his death, Peter notices John and abruptly asks, "What about him?" (This question literally translates the Greek words.) Jesus forcibly reminds Peter to mind his own business. Peter leaves the scene on an ironically humorous note quite fitting his nature.

Jesus' response to Peter's question furnishes another ironic note. Jesus told Peter, "If I will that he tarry till I come, what is that to thee?" As has frequently occurred ever since, people mistook a conditional clause for a declarative statement. The story went around that John was to live until the Parousia, the second coming of Jesus. At the time this was nothing remarkable, but as the decades passed without Jesus' return, John's survival began to assume miraculous proportions. Later yet, he became, like the Wandering Jew, a legend of survival until the end of the world. Since the author concludes with this episode, it must have seemed to him of major importance. If the epilogue was not by the author of John, it could have been written well into the second century.

Verse 24, the certification of the epilogue and presumably of the Gospel to which it became attached, was made by some official group of the Church. It asserts that John the disciple of Jesus wrote these matters, while at the same time respecting his desire not to be named. As has already been shown, the vague reference of "these matters" (a neuter plural pronoun in Greek) may refer to the materials on which the author of John drew in composing his work. It is extremely unlikely that John the fisherman could ever have composed a work of such literary art and subtlety of thought.

CHAPTER 6

THE LETTERS OF PAUL

PAUL OF TARSUS

Paul of Tarsus is, after Jesus, the most prominent agent in the New Testament. Through his letters his complex character is clearly indicated. The ten letters now ascribed to him deserve special detailed study, for they show him as he appeared to himself. The Acts adds items about him as seen through the eyes of a devoted companion. Paul's explanations and defenses of his teaching and conduct were delivered not only to hostile Jews and unbelieving Hellenists but also to leaders of his own faith who disagreed with him. This opposition obliged him to write extensively about himself.

Paul's writing reveals his personality especially to competent literary observers. Such an interpreter was Adolf Deissmann, whose *Paul: A Study in Social and Religious History* is perhaps as much a psychological study as well. Deissmann possessed qualifications for literary interpretation that the brothers Schlegel and Heinrich Heine in the early nineteenth century considered basic for such endeavor. These qualifications are such as to enable the interpreter to enter into a writer's personality and intelligently follow his processes and experiences as he writes. Heine called this reproductive criticism. Their successor August Boeckh declared that this intuitive insight on the part of a trained scholar who has immersed himself in his author's works is the *sine qua non* of literary interpretation. The late Joel E. Spingarn was a more recent advocate of such a method, which was notably illustrated by John Livingston Lowes in *The Road to Xanadu.*

Paul's letters reveal him at the height of his activity. So far as he could understand himself, he honestly and frankly reported his beliefs and emotions. He was obliged also to report his actions; and since he could anticipate that his data would be checked by opponents as well as friends, he had to accurately recount his doings. As for the data in Acts, Deissmann and other scholars have tended to doubt its accuracy, and have denigrated Acts in consequence. Acts, it is argued in this study, is a document in propaganda rather than a factual history. It can, therefore, take liberties with factual data in order to effect its purposes provided that it does not pervert the evidence. Where Paul's account and the Acts disagree, Paul's account may reasonably be considered closer to the actual event. Since Luke did not presume in Acts to analyze Paul's mental and emotional processes, one has to rely upon Paul's letters to show them.

Paul's family were Jews of the tribe of Benjamin living in Tarsus, the principal city of Cilicia. His Jewish name was Saul; he used his name Paul as a Roman citizen when he began his work outside of Jewish society. Tarsus, no doubt, contributed much to his conditioning as a worker among Gentiles. It was a prosperous commercial city at the northwest corner of the Mediterranean near the Cilician Gates, the mountain pass in the Taurus range which afforded the sole entry into Anatolia. More than four centuries earlier, Xenophon had found it to be a prosperous city in a fertile delta, as he wrote in the *Anabasis*. Less than a century earlier, at Tarsus, Cleopatra had "pursed up" Antony's heart and set in train events which were to establish the Augustan Roman Empire.

In Paul's day Tarsus' principal commercial product was *cilicium*, a fabric used extensively for tents. It was natural that Paul should learn tentmaking and repairing as his trade. The city also boasted a university, which Strabo reported in his *Geography* was attended chiefly by local students, but it had produced eminent philosophers and philologists. In this city Paul was born perhaps a decade or so after the birth of Jesus.

Of his family little is known. A sister's son in Jerusalem (Acts 23:16) had been instrumental in saving Paul from assassination on his last visit. The Jewish community in Tarsus was considerable, and his father's Roman citizenship presumably gave him a degree of prestige among the Jews. The boy attended the school connected with the synagogue, which in that time was customarily controlled by the Pharisees.

Paul's declaration to King Agrippa (Acts 26:5) that he had lived an extremely strict life as a Pharisee need not apply to his childhood and youth. Among the Jews of the Dispersion, strict enforcement of Pharisaic law was almost impossible, especially upon an inquiring young mind like Paul's. Although he would not have studied at the university, he was undoubtedly exposed to Hellenistic thinking. It was perhaps here that he picked up some acquaintance with Greek literature—how extensive or systematic it was, one cannot tell. He would have learned the Greek ways of public speaking and debate from the rhetoricians declaiming in the city square. In the synagogue, moreover, he came to know the Septuagint, which he habitually cited in his letters. As he later wrote, he could be a Hellenist among the Gentiles and a Jew among Jews (1 Cor. 9:20).

His Jewish training drilled him in the Jewish law, both oral and unwritten Torah, whose commands were to be obeyed without question. His Gentile influences, Deissmann plausibly suggests, made him rebel at such an attitude. He disobeyed the Law—at what age and in what detail he did not state—and so became a sinner. The wages of such lawbreaking was spiritual death. Possibly in adolescent despair over his condemned state, he turned to extreme Pharisaic pietism, observing the precepts of the Law to their minutest detail.

Such fanatical concern may have been part of his motivation in going to Jerusalem to study the Law at its fountainhead. There he came under the instruction of Rabbin Gamaliel, a leader in a more moderate wing of Pharisaism. One wonders whether his family may have hoped that Gamaliel would bring him to the more moderate views found in the Diaspora. He remained a fanatic. He could claim (Phil. 3:6) to be "touching the righteousness which is in the Law, blameless." In bitter self-condemnation he could write that he had prided himself on his knowledge of the Law and on his ability to teach it. He had "the form of knowledge and of the truth in the Law" (Rom. 2:20).

Before long he began to be deeply dissatisfied. His inquiring mind, actuated by his earlier Hellenistic contacts, was opposed to tacit acceptance of principles. His conscience by its stirrings indicated to him the inadequacy of external piety to combat inner depravity (Rom. 2:21–23). The Jewish pride in circumcision was a mere reliance upon a physical mutilation. He could not have overlooked Jeremiah's plea (4:4) six centuries earlier that the Jews circumcise their hearts, not merely their bodies. This rite, to a man who truly understood the law, was only a symbol, valueless in itself.

Throughout the events reported in Acts, however, pride in his race kept Paul outwardly a Jew. Despite his attacks on Jewish concepts of their Law, he despised the Jew who tried—by an operation or otherwise—to conceal his circumcision in order to "cross over" into the ranks of Gentiles. He required young Timothy, whose mother was a Jew, to be circumcised. Two decades after he had become the advocate for Gentile Christians, he thought it proper for him to undergo Jewish purificatory rites and worship in the Temple. Repeatedly he proudly referred to himself as a Jew, an Israelite, of the tribe of Abraham by descent as well as by faith. He reckoned time by Jewish feasts. He could not jump off his Jewish shadow, nor did he wish to do so.

His Judaism had from the start been colored by his reading the Septuagint rather than the Hebrew Scriptures. The Hebrew text, however extensively the earlier accounts in them had been edited by later scholars, still bore unmistakable traces of the long span of time represented in them. A reader could sense that some pronouncements in them represent earlier stages of insight than others. Such a sense was less noticeable in translation. The same Spirit spoke throughout. An earlier insight was set beside a later with no hint of which was the more profound. Like readers of English translations, the Septuagint presented without comment Jehu's bloodbath in exterminating Ahab's family and the priests of Baal (2 Kings 9:22, 10:30). It also presented Hosea's bitter condemnation of Jehu's murders (1:4) a few years later as deadly sin. A careful reader of the Hebrew text might notice such a contradiction more readily than the reader of a translation. To Paul the Septuagint was authoritative. He shared to some degree Philo's literal acceptance of it. He cited passages from it to clinch arguments with the formula "It is written"—a formula applied in Hellenistic business to the fixed terms of a contract.

For all their literal acceptance of the Scriptures, Philo and other exegetes were engaging in allegorical interpretation to an extent far beyond their Hebrew or Hellenistic forebears. Paul did not need contemporary scholarship to start him on the allegorical path. He found it in earlier Jewish practice: in Joseph's and Daniel's interpretation of cryptic dreams, and in the parable told to Nathan by David (2 Sam. 12:1–13)—to cite a few instances—he had a precedent. Rabbinical scholarship also practiced it. Contemporary Hellenistic Jewish methods, nonetheless, must have impressed him. Allegorical interpretation, then, offered an avenue of escape from acceptance of the Law as binding and efficacious.

Paul's letters are, on the whole, informal communications treating current problems in the churches. They have, however, been assiduously mined for doctrine and dogma. Paul did indeed lay the groundwork of much Christian theology, but his intent in writing was not theological. Although he was a logical thinker, he was too impatient a letter writer to expound a system on paper. He belongs rather, as Evelyn Underhill has shown (*Mysticism*, 178–79), to the company of mystics, of which this author considers him a typical case. He shows in his letters the characteristic abrupt shifts between joy and sorrow. His dramatic conversion to Christianity is also true to type.

However they may have been altered by his new beliefs, Paul's fanatical tendencies persisted after his conversion. He found difficulty in seeing from another's point of view. He could not realize, for instance, that the change in him, so apparent to himself, would not be equally evident to others. He could not foresee or comprehend the skepticism with which the Christians in Jerusalem received him upon his return, however natural their reaction was. Such impetuous assurance in his own conduct was to continue throughout his career. He would not give Mark a second chance. He bluntly called Peter to account for hesitating to offend Judaizing Christians (Gal. 2:11–14). Each time he was rebuffed in a synagogue, he angrily turned to Gentile audiences, only to go first to the synagogue in the next city he visited. The abrupt shifts of subject and anacolutha in his letters are, no doubt, the effects partly of his impetuosity and "one-track" vision.

Romans testifies that Paul could brilliantly develop a coherent argument. He could more than hold his own in debate, as Acts frequently shows. He was, however, a mystic at bottom. His forte lay in persuasion incorporating flashes of intuitive insight, specimens of which profusely adorn his letters.

Such a man made firm friends; inevitably, he also made violent enemies. One may doubt whether his friendships could have stood the strain of his constant presence. How well he could have served as pastor of a congregation is open to doubt. He was a superb itinerant evangelist who, except in cities with large floating populations, seldom worked long in one place. As for hostile reactions, he described his fortunes tersely (2 Cor. 11:24–26): five times he had been beaten with the statutory "forty stripes save one. Thrice was I beaten with rods, once was I stoned . . . in perils by mine own countrymen, in perils by the heathen." Even among Christians he met vigorous opposition, not only from Judaizers who resented his treatment of the Law, but also from among his own converts.

During a considerable part of his career, Paul suffered a "thorn in the flesh" (2 Cor. 12:7), a nagging chronic debility. Its nature is nowhere clearly stated. He believed that it had been inflicted on him to keep him from undue pride. It may have been in part a consequence of his physical hardships as they affected his highly sensitive nature. Whatever it was, his ailment required medical attention. Once, at least, it came to a crisis that required careful nursing. It seems reasonable to assume that Luke joined his party to care for him. His persistence under such a burden testifies to the energy and devotion to his cause that actuated him.

Some theologians have charged that Paul shifted the gospel founded by Jesus into a new channel which they label "Pauline." Such a charge would have scandalized him. He declared that he taught only "Jesus Christ, and Him crucified" as the core of his apostolic message. Inevitably he modified the shapeless early Christian sect by adapting it to Hellenistic mores; but he never altered the essence of what Jesus had taught. As followers of a great teacher have always done, he developed his message on the basis of Jesus' simple yet earth-shaking principles.

Paul was uniquely equipped by character and prepared by experience to develop the Church for the Western world. He had been acquainted with the faith first as its enemy and had gained a clearer perspective of it than many of his contemporaries. By the time he wrote the first of his surviving letters, he had been actively teaching for nearly two decades. His mystical insights brought a deepening knowledge of the new faith as the years passed. This combination of nature, experience, insight, teaching, and thought enabled him to write letters of unique value to solve difficulties.

Benedetto Croce has shown that a man may arrive at reasoned conclusions which he thenceforth treats as axiomatic. He uses them as if they were intuitions. Paul had passed through such a process in accepting Christianity and pondering it. As a rule, he did not reason out systems of belief in his letters. In treating specific problems submitted to him, he proceeded upon his intuitions together with his conclusions-become-axioms to solve these problems. From these letters, then, Paul emerges as a man somewhat like Wordsworth's conception of the poet: as a man who has felt strongly, thought long and deeply, and then has written under the spontaneous overflow of powerful emotions.

As a traveling evangelist, Paul had taught orally, somewhat as he had been taught in Greek and Jewish training. Communication by letter provided new problems to him. Public speaking has been aptly defined as conversing with an audience: the hearers tacitly comment on the speaker's words and stimulate him by their presence. Every speaker for the first time on the radio remembers the handicap of speaking alone in a small room to an invisible audience. With a man like Paul, who spent most of his teaching hours in the give-and-take of conversation, the lack of response while writing must have been doubly restricting. As his letters show, he was more at ease in oral communication than in written. He had to develop his capacity for literary composition.

Paul was, however, frequently obliged by circumstances to advise his converts through letters. Sometimes he was engaged in projects which required his presence. At other times he was imprisoned. Whether free to travel or not, he would have wasted many weeks in travel if he had answered each request with a visit. Although his letters often indicate that he used letters as a stopgap (cf. 1 Cor. 11:34), he had to write many letters, of which only a few survive.

A major problem for Paul lay in the difficulty of adapting oral devices to written expression. Fortunately the Greek language had made provision to alleviate this difficulty. Spoken Greek, like Mediterranean languages generally, was supplemented with copious gestures. It was also a language in which vocal intonation was peculiarly significant. Written Greek attempted to supply these aids by indicating them through otherwise meaningless sounds called particles. New Testament writers either did not know these niceties of classical Greek or, more likely in some cases, felt that their readers could not appreciate them. Oral devices such as change in tempo of delivery, shift in pitch of voice, and rhetorical pause obviously could not be used in written discourse. Paul's letters show him as accustomed to use anacoluthon and aposiopesis, devices more effective in oral than in written delivery. One can detect marked improvement in Paul's written composition during the six years or so spanned by his letters.

For Paul the labor of writing constituted a real difficulty. He evidently dictated his letters, and dictation is itself an art that must be learned. Possibly his toil at tentmaking, with the sewing of heavy fabrics, may have stiffened his fingers so as to make them awkward at writing. His mention of his "big letters"[1] points in this direction.

[1] Galatians 6:11 has "large a letter," but the consensus of modern scholarship would have "big letter."

It is also possible that a visual defect or ailment made it difficult for him to see what he wrote. (One is here reminded of James Thurber's "big letters," made necessary by his near-blindness.) Whatever the cause, Paul did not as a rule write his letters himself.

In one letter (2 Thess. 3:17) he included a specimen of his own script, which is the token in every letter. This is how I write. Evidently forged letters purporting to be by him were circulating. Like some modern trade-marks, he had to certify, "None genuine without this signature." In Philemon 19, a promissory note, he again used his own handwriting.

Such, then, was the man who, more than any other follower of Jesus, left his mark upon the beginnings of the Christian church: a man of brilliant intellect with astonishing versatility at handling men of varied cultures; a mystic with frequent and deep insights; and at the same time a troubled, highly emotional character.

Paul's letters follow the pattern of informal letters preserved in Greek papyri. They usually have five parts: a greeting which includes the signature, a prayer or expression of good wishes; thanksgiving to a deity; the message; and special salutations and greetings in a sort of appendix. Minor variations occur. Paul generally follows this pattern, which readers would expect in a letter. It is a sufficiently flexible pattern to serve for personal notes like Philemon and carefully thought-out communications like Romans.

The order of Paul's letters in the New Testament, though quite defensible for religious purposes, is not the order in which they were composed. Romans, as Paul's most systematically reasoned letter, rightly leads, followed by the Corinthian letters, which are also of prime importance for the doctrine and practice. The shorter letters follow, including three no longer regarded as truly Pauline.

Dating these letters has constituted a problem, since early Christians, little concerned with their chronology, left no indication of it. Internal evidence is helpful but not always decisive concerning date of composition. The dating currently accepted by the greater number of scholars is as follows: 1 Thessalonians, c. A.D. 50; 2 Thessalonians, c. A.D. 52; Galatians, c. A.D. 53–54; 1 Corinthians, c. A.D. 54–55; 2 Corinthians, A.D. 55–56; Romans, A.D. 56–57; Philippians,

Colossians, Philemon, and Ephesians, c. A.D. 58–60. (It is not possible to set the last four in serial order.)

Some justification exists for discussing these letters in their New Testament order, since this study deals with the New Testament. They are, however, separate documents. Taken in their probable order of composition, they show Paul grappling with problems of belief and conduct as they cropped up, as well as developing literary and judicial skill in his handling of them.

To charge Paul with inadequate treatment of issues involved, or to assume a lack of orderly progress in his arguments, is unjust. We have no letters of his correspondents which elicited these replies—most are replies—and consequently must discover the immediate situations that provoked them beyond the meager evidence in these replies. It is somewhat easier to discover the situation in correspondence which he initiated, such as Romans and Philemon.

The fact that his letters were informal, friendly presentations of advice or criticism must also be kept in mind. His informality was far more likely to conciliate his opponents and build up their sense of community with each other and with him than a formal disquisition would do. Carefully organized outlining and progress are alien to the informal letter. Goethe and Henry James both insisted that the author must be allowed to decide what literary form he will employ. Goethe added that his work is to be tested by the degree of success he achieved in what he produced. So far as can be ascertained, Paul's letters were remarkably successful in effecting his purposes; as to their continuous effectiveness, Christian history attests.

The letters to the Thessalonians and those to the Corinthians will be treated in each case together; they form part of one effort. Each of the others will be treated separately. They will be put together into three chronological groups: the first group, A.D. 50–52; the second, A.D. 54–57; and the so-called captivity epistles, A.D. 58–60.

THE LETTERS, GROUP 1

How many letters Paul exchanged, or when his correspondence

began, is not known. The ten letters which survive represent probably twelve. These letters were written to specific groups to settle immediately pressing problems. To understand them, one must investigate each not only from what the letters present but also from various other available sources of information. Histories, books of travel, and geographies composed in the ancient world are helpful. Incidental comments in the creative literature of the first Christian century and archaeological discoveries also convey useful information or hints.

Thessalonica was the bottleneck through which passed commerce between the Mediterranean world and the Balkan hinterland. It stood also on the Egnatian Way, the principal highway between Rome and the East. With all this traffic it was far from an isolated provincial town. As the political capital of the province of Macedonia, it was also alert to public affairs both local and imperial. It was Paul's first visit to a large city on his travels. His work there accordingly set the pattern for much of his later evangelism.

The city had a flourishing Jewish synagogue. It also sheltered religious cults of Orpheus, Dionysus, and a primitive group, the Cabiri—all of them fertility cults with the customary phallic symbols and unbridled sexual practices among their rites.

A year or so after Paul had left Thessalonica, the church there came under fire both from its unconverted Gentile neighbors and from Jews who stirred Gentile mobs to riot. Christian refusal to join in any pagan rites and their strict moral code stimulated pagan enmity. Forged letters purporting to have come from Paul confused the converts. The church itself contained members who, by claiming to prophesy by the Holy Spirit, undermined Paul's teaching. Whether these heterodox speakers can be classed as pre-Gnostic, cannot be determined, but their influence upon the members was much like that of the later Gnostics.

When the Thessalonian church begged Paul to return to re-establish his teaching, he was too deeply involved at Corinth to leave. Instead, he sent Timothy to encourage their steadfastness. Although Timothy brought back good news of their condition, Paul felt that they needed advice upon certain pressing matters that were still disturbing them. He accordingly wrote his first extant letter to compliment them on their progress and to guide them in handling these problems.

Paul reminded the Thessalonian church of his warning that they should expect persecution from both Jew and Gentile for their new beliefs and changed conduct. They should continue to strive for greater attainment in both. They must particularly abstain from the sexual license of the pagan cults—a difficult problem, he undoubtedly realized, for men who had not grown up under the Jewish moral code. He seized with each note of praise the opportunity to insert an epitome of his teaching about God and his Son Jesus, a reminder of their abandoned pre-Christian state, or an exhortation to continuous attainment in the faith. By thus balancing praise against blame, he sent a more palatable message than unmixed censure. He added diplomatically that he did not need to encourage them in brotherly love, in which they showed themselves to be pre-eminent.

In reply to slanders circulating against Silas, Timothy, and himself, Paul declared that, unlike many mendicant teachers who thronged ancient cities, his party had accepted no money or support in return for their services. They had supported themselves by their own labor. Since they received no material reward, some high purpose must have driven them on in the face of toil and persecutions.

Their most pressing problem concerned the Parousia, the return of Jesus to establish his rule on earth. Like many Christians, Paul expected this return to take place soon, and had probably transmitted this expectation to his converts. The messianic concept was familiar to Jews but novel to Gentiles; Paul had evidently given it inadequate clarification. The Thessalonians were confused in particular by the status of those members who had died; would they share in the blessings of the Parousia or not?

Paul directed his argument to this specific question. In baptism all Christians symbolically died and were buried in water. They had risen from the water as new creations. Subsequent death in no way affecting their sharing in the Parousia: the dead would rise to take part in it. Possibly embarrassed that he should have confused them, he reminded them that no man could know the precise time when Jesus should return.

Expectation of an imminent Parousia entailed a second problem. Since the end of the present life would occur soon, some Thessalonians reasoned, it was needless to work or be provident. Paul's vigorous statement on this matter may indicate an uneasy awareness that he may have been partly the cause of it. Only by continuing to work, he declared, could they hope to remain good Christians, sober, alert, in harmony and brotherly love.

The severity of his second letter indicates that his former communication had failed to produce the desired effect. The letter starts and concludes with almost identical words, but is blunt and tersely corrective. Possibly in added awareness that his teaching about the Parousia had been misleading, he added here evidence about it designed to clarify the ideas of the Thessalonians. They must endure present sufferings in the anticipation that Jesus will bring release from them at his coming. There is some indication that other teachers were responsible for the error in having ascribed to Paul teachings not his.

Paul's reply included a Jewish belief which could hardly have been known to his readers; he therefore stated it in general terms. Before the Messiah's supremacy "the man of sin" will rebelliously seek to establish himself as God and demand worship for himself. (This idea was later brilliantly incorporated in the Revelation.) Paul perhaps referred to Jewish opposition or to the nascent emperor worship practiced in neighboring Berea. Since the cult of emperor worship had not yet fully developed, while Jewish opposition was already with them, the latter appears to be somewhat the more likely. Paul warned the Thessalonians not to let this "man of sin" mislead them. If they would hold fast to the faith as taught by him, they would not err. By subjoining a request that they pray for his escape from wicked men in Corinth, he subtly reminded them that he was sharing their dangers.

They must not, he sternly continued, tolerate those who refused to live the orderly life prescribed. Besides the ever present temptation to break away from Christian morality, he referred to a chronic problem in their religious activities. Many members spoke under genuine impulse of the Holy Spirit. Other unstable or perverse persons claimed this inspiration in asserting heterodox beliefs and modes of conduct. They belonged to the lunatic fringe inevitably accompanying new movements. Christians should isolate these people and have no dealings with them. They may by this treatment be shocked into realization of their error. Loafers also are vigorously censured. Good Christians will keep quietly, peaceably busy until the Parousia.

Paul's concluding note warned not to heed letters that were circulating as if written by him. He called attention to his signature in this letter as a warranty of its genuineness. In the future he would thus sign all his letters.

Except in the passages referring to the Parousia, in which he used imaginative Jewish terms, these letters present a uniformly low stylistic level. Figures of speech are rare because Paul wished to present categorically his advice and supplementary teaching. His most notable emotional outburst is a hyperbole couched in simple terms: "Now we live, if ye stand fast in the Lord" (1 Thess. 3:8). He employs frequently the concept of daily life as walking, common in the Old Testament and particularly familiar to his readers from the early designation of Christianity as "the Way." The thrice-used image in the verb *stablish* is forceful: *stērizō* means to "prop up." A moving image for the athletically oriented Hellenist is in Paul's analogy of the course of God's word to the runner in the stadium (2 Thess. 3:1). Paul's hope (2 Thess. 2:2) that they will not be "shaken in mind" uses a verb (*saleuō*) referring to seismic tremors. The local allusion in an area subject to earthquakes carries special force.

According to Paul's later contemporary Longinus (XV), the orator employs figures to produce vividness, in contrast to the poet, who would produce a sudden shock like a bolt of lightning. Paul followed here the rhetorical practice of using images to clarify his readers' vision. Without much ornamentation these letters admirably present his message to people in need of aid.

CHAPTER 7

THE LETTERS OF PAUL, GROUP 2

In this second group of letters are Galatians, 1 and 2 Corinthians, and Romans. Galatians served as a trial run for the later Romans, though written for a different purpose. These four letters express Paul's polemic against opponents within and without the Church and defend major principles of his teaching. They also, especially Galatians, provide much of our biographical data concerning him.

GALATIANS

Paul's generally sympathetic attitude towards the Thessalonians did not continue towards the Galatians. The former were not being led into serious doctrinal error. In his Galatian converts Paul had to combat fatal divergences from his message. To support his case, he had first to defend the authority of his message and of himself as messenger. His censorious attitude is sharply implied by the omission of thanksgiving to God for their healthy religious state which he had used to greet the Thessalonians and would regularly include in subsequent letters. He could not use it.

The Galatians were, as their name implies, related to the Gauls or Celts of western Europe. In the third century B.C. Celtic mercenaries had been hired for a civil war in Bithynia, a large area fronting the Black Sea in Asia Minor. They settled in the central region of Asia Minor south of Bithynia after their military service. An unruly people, they were subjugated in 189 B.C. by the Romans, and in A.D. 25 were incorporated into the province of Galatia. Paul and Barnabas had established churches in its southern part on their first journey, and Paul had revisited them on his second and third trips.

The situation facing the Galatian churches illuminates the Gentile problems discussed by Paul. Although mildly Hellenized, Galatia lay far from sophisticated metropolitan areas and preserved the less-civilized primitive religious cults. The best known of these honored the great mother of the gods, Cybele (appropriately called also Ma), the center of whose cult was at Pessinus in nearby Phrygia. Her worship entailed crudely primitive rites, involving castration, in its orgiastic frenzies. Although in 204 B.C. it had arrived in Rome, no Roman citizen was permitted to share in its mutilation, and it was naturally abhorrent to Greeks. Such emasculation was likewise prohibited by Jewish law.

Traces of primitive Olympian religion lingered also, as Paul and Barnabas had discovered at Lystra (Acts 14:11–13). The Jewish synagogues in the small cities had proselyted with some success among Gentiles, who became a nucleus of Gentile Christian converts. Diverse though they were, these religions all emphasized ritual observance and obedience to religious codes. These influences on his converts combined to produce the results against which Paul stood opposed.

On two previous visits Paul had established cordial relations with his converts. They had nursed him through a crisis in his chronic debility on his first trip. On his second visit he had reported to them the decisions reached in the Council of Jerusalem. He had left them with high expectation of their steadfast faith.

Paul habitually followed the basic formula of Christian *kērygma* ("evangelism"). He later expressed it, "I determined not to know any thing among you, save Jesus Christ, and him crucified" (1 Cor. 2:2). The life, death, and resurrection of Jesus formed the core of his message. From it he drew the belief that Jesus' sacrifice of himself offers escape from the lethal consequences of sin to all who will to accept it and follow Him. By this act of grace (i.e., a gift which one in no way deserves or has earned), one can here and now enter the kingdom of God. Through receiving this gift he sloughs off his former unlovely self and becomes a new person. He no longer need follow any such rituals or codified systems of conduct as Jew and pagan demanded. These are all now done away.

The converts speedily found that it was far more difficult to follow such an unhedged course of conduct than to live by prescription. Under a code one can check his conduct by the several items listed in it, as Benjamin Franklin worked out a system of self-improvement and then checked himself by the thirteen requirements in it. The Christian can never become satisfied in his conduct. Pagans and Jews could be complacent in their attainments; the Christian never can be so. Naturally, converts were tempted to revert to use of such a scale of values without abandoning their new faith. The Christian convert would revert to the Jewish rules as more closely related than paganism to his new faith. Paul set out to prove that such a syncretism was impossible.

Sometime within three years of Paul's departure, visitors from Jerusalem arrived in Galatia who represented dissatisfied Judaizing Christians unwilling to accept the council's relaxation of requirements for Gentiles. The Galatian converts, they said, had made a good start, but to become full-fledged Christians, they must obey the Jewish law. In particular, the male converts must be circumcised. Paul, to be sure, had made no such requirements, but he was not an apostle and his words lacked authority.

Such, in brief, appears to have been the report that reached Paul in Ephesus. To counter the Judaizing demands, he had first to re-establish his authority. Only after doing this would his attack carry much weight.

Paul carried the fight to his opponents even in his salutation. He signs himself "Paul, an apostle"—not so called by men but by Jesus and God the Father. Readers of Acts will recall Paul's vision in the Temple (22:17:21). In it, using the Greek verb from which *apostle* is derived (*exapostelō*), Jesus had sent him to the Gentiles. He had also seen Jesus as had the other apostles, though at a later time. The Council at Jerusalem, he added, realizing his success among "the uncircumcised" (Gal. 2:7), had assigned to him the conversion of the Gentiles on equal status with Peter, who would work among Jews. Such an assignment recognized his status as an apostle.

The Galatians' backsliding would be absurd, Paul bitingly declared, if it was not also dangerous. How could they have so soon abandoned the gospel of Christ for a teaching that bore no such honorific name? They had let themselves be misled by men who wished to pervert the gospel. Anyone who preached any modification of it is utterly damned. His own message came from a divine source. He had "conferred not with flesh and blood" (1:16) in order to receive it.

Paul's apologia in Galatians may be taken as biographically more accurate than Luke's account in Acts. The latter presumably knew about Paul's early career chiefly from what Paul had told him, probably in condensed, disjointed fragments. Moreover, as a propagandist Luke was under no obligation to adhere strictly to such facts as he had learned, but could modify it to serve his purpose. Paul in defending his apostolic claim could anticipate that his accuracy would be carefully checked. He could not afford to leave any opening that might discredit his statements.

Seventeen years after his conversion, Paul stated, he had returned to Jerusalem to report on his first missionary journey and to defend his position on Gentile circumcision. (Acts 15:1–5 sets the scene.) In Jerusalem, Paul wisely presented his case, as it were, *in camera*; he anticipated a saner hearing from the leaders than from the mass of Jewish-oriented Christians in Jerusalem. His hopes were not fulfilled.

Paul's opponents won their way into the executive session of the leaders and bitterly attacked his not requiring circumcision of his converts. Paul's account shows him as deeply moved even several years later. Galatians 2:6–9, a confused aggregate of ninety-five Greek words, which expands farther in English, requires careful sorting of its content to clarify what occurred. At first, evidently, his opponents carried with them some influential leaders. When, however, they saw that their "pillars" James, Peter, and John approved Paul's practice among Gentiles, they also supported it. As

Paul summed up their action, work among Gentiles was entrusted to him.

Paul's position concerning circumcision cost him support. Barnabas had seconded him in Jerusalem, but soon abandoned his party. Even Peter, whom Acts reports as tipping the scales in Paul's favor in an eloquent speech before the council, failed subsequently in Antioch to stand firmly by his expressed principles. Paul reports that he told Peter bluntly to stand up and be counted on one side or the other. If he could thus rebuke even Peter, the Galatians could expect little mercy.

Paul's letter is built on this apologia. He proceeded immediately to condemn the Galatians who had been bewitched by Judaizers to add to Christian belief the Jewish rite of circumcision and adherence to the Law. So far as the Law provides, he declared, he was himself dead in sin. So far as Christ was concerned, he was justified. To paradoxically claim to be justified by Christ and a sinner by the Law would be to blaspheme the name of Christ. In a brilliant paradox he declared that he was daily crucified and died with Christ, yet he lived in the true faith which the indwelling spirit of Christ brings. He reduced to an absurdity the Jewish legalistic way: "if righteousness come by the law, then Christ is dead in vain"—a proposition which every Christian's experience should prove to be contrary to fact.

Paul never suffered fools gladly. The Galatians are senseless (*anoētoi*); they have let men bewitch their minds in disobeying the truth of Jesus' atoning death which Paul had so clearly set before them (3:1). They had received the Holy Spirit without obedience to the Law; why revert to it now?

Paul turned their own arguments against the Judaizers. Abraham, whose children they claim to be, had lived centuries before the Law was promulgated at Sinai. How could he have accepted the Law? By their standards, then, Abraham was unrighteous; but no Jew believed this. Genesis (15:6) declared that Abraham's faith made him acceptable to God. A few verses later (2:4) Paul quoted Habakkuk: "The just shall live by faith." He had both Law and Prophets on his side.

In fact, Paul added in a complicated analogy, if the Law is right, then Jesus by dying became a curse. The Law declares that an executed malefactor's body gives off a deadly miasma if not promptly interred (Deut. 21:23). Christians know, however, that by his execution Christ has bought freedom from sin and eternal death for all who will accept it. In fact, Jesus' death transfers to Gentiles the promises made by God in covenants with Abraham and Moses.

In view of this fact, of what use is the Law? It had been an interim device to keep man from wrongdoing until Jesus should come. It could only ward off evil; it could not give life. It served as a *paidagōgos*.[1] Jewish teachers, recognizing this function, referred to the hedge of the Law. It warded off evil from the spiritually juvenile, or was designed to do so. Paul dryly remarked that it had not kept Jews "shut up unto the faith which should afterwards be revealed" (3:23–24). This argument is presented in greater detail later in Romans.

After further pointing out the Galatians' error in listening to Judaizers, Paul adjured them (5:1) to stand firm in their liberty as Christians. If they feel that they must be circumcised, they no longer accept God's free gift through Jesus. They cannot consistently have the Law *and* the gift. They should prefer Christian liberty. This liberty, however, is not license (here Paul touched upon Gentile, pagan temptations). It is a spirit of love, and those who "walk in the Spirit" love one another. With such love they will feel no attraction from "the works of the flesh," the sensual conduct allowed to pagans.

The Christian is still body as well as spirit, and physical desires can still lead him astray. If a member backslides, he is to be brought back to right conduct. Those who help him shall not feel superior, for they are equally liable to sensuality. In spiritual and material matters a man reaps what he has sown, a good crop or a bad one. He is free to choose. Faith in God helps him to choose wisely.

Paul's irritation at senseless backsliding crops up again at the con-

[1] The KJV lost this brilliant metaphor by translating the word "schoolmaster." The *paidagōgos* was the slave who attended a child en route to and from school to protect him from molesters and kidnappers.

clusion: "From hence let no man trouble me: for I bear in my body the marks of the Lord Jesus" (6:17).[2] He had plenty to do without handling such absurd cases, and had scars as Jesus had had to show for it. They had known better than to be so easily misled. He wished to hear no more of such imbecility.

As Juvenal declared in Rome, "Indignation produces verses." Paul's irritation at the Galatians prompted and validated vigorous figurative expression in prose. His ire led him to use more and more violent figures than in the two earlier letters. He wrote in justifiable anger. His entire Gentile campaign was imperiled by such Judaizing attacks.

The literary devices of Galatians clearly reflect his emotional state. He uses thirteen rhetorical questions, as opposed to one-third as many in the preceding letters to the Thessalonians. Twice he indulges in hyperbole. The remark about the scars on his body (6:17), and his declaration that the Galatians had been willing to pluck out their own eyes to serve him (4:15) are effective overstatements. Such figures, ancient rhetoricians attest, effectively move readers when the emotion of the author prevents their seeming to be exaggerated.

Longinus recommends also the use of figures in combination. The sophisticated reader may be wary enough to resist the force of one while feeling the full force of another. The effect of figures upon the emotions is at least partly subliminal, particularly when the author has deeply stirred his emotions.

Paul was fully aware of this practice. In 2:20 he used together hyperbole, metaphor, and accumulation: "I am crucified with Christ: nevertheless I live; yet not I, but Christ liveth in me: and the life which I now live in the flesh I live by the faith of the Son of God." Paul's crucifixion is hyperbolical and metaphorical. The two men crucified with Christ had died; Paul lived; paradoxically, however, he was not living, for Christ lived in him. The three

[2] Later interpretations of this verse to mean that Paul bore the stigmata, the actual scars on Jesus' body from the nails at his crucifixion, are the result of vivid literalist imagination let loose by failure to realize the force of metaphorical analogy.

verses introducing this message also combine figures, but less startlingly, in order not to anticipate the force of verse 20. Verse 17 combines a rhetorical question with an oath of asseveration which is also a formula to avert evil. At the same time it renders his opponents' position absurd. Verse 18 pictures the absurdity in a man's tearing down what he has been at pains to build—another absurdity. Verse 19 by a near paradox shows a man dying "legally" to enjoy life in Christ.

The metaphor still holds priority among figures as it did in antiquity. Repeated use can rob metaphors of their original effect. The ancient audiences were more vividly sensible of the pictures they convey than modern readers are. Several of Paul's metaphors here are still living.

Paul employed metaphors in Galatians almost from the start. He marveled (1:16) that his converts had been so soon moved or had moved themselves—the verb is either passive or reflexive—from the religious position in which he had set them. The figure is aided by the ambiguous form. In 3:1, combining rhetorical question with metaphor, he demands to know what envious person had bewitched them. Since witchcraft was a sin to Jews, he hints that the Judaizers are not themselves good Jews.

Four verses later, the verb translated "minister" (*epichoregeō*) describes the special service assigned to a well-to-do citizen as a surtax. It subtly reminds the Galatians that Paul had not been performing a service for hire in converting them but something beyond a *quid pro quo*. He did not expect to be supported, as he later hinted was the case with other Christian leaders. In verse 6, Abraham's faith is an entry in the credit column of his spiritual ledger. The brilliant metaphor of the *paidagōgos* has already been mentioned.

Paul treated at length of Christians as former slaves to sin who have been bought by Christ (3:29–4:8). Having been bought, they have been adopted as sons according to the provisions of Roman law. Now they share with Christ in all things. The image of the freed slave's adoption leads the way for the allegory of Sara and Hagar already discussed.

A major point in Paul's attack on the Judaizers dealt with God's approval of Abraham long before the Law had been promulgated at Sinai. One facet of his argument concerned God's promise to Abraham: "In thy seed shall all nations of the earth be blessed" (Gen. 22:18). Paul interpreted the singular *seed* in the Septuagint as referring to Jesus rather than to the descendants of Abraham. Such an argument ignores the obvious collective sense of *seed*. Evidently realizing the weakness of this contention, he omitted it when he wrote Romans.

Paul concluded his demolition of the Judaizers with an insult quite proper by ancient standards but not acceptable to the translators of the KJV and RSV. In 5:12 he hinted at a parallel between these Judaizers and the pagan worshipers of Attis. They were as insistent upon circumcision as their counterparts were upon castration. He wishes that they would castrate themselves (*apokopsontai*). The Jewish wing of the Church would then be spared their presence, because Jewish law (Lev. 21:20–21) forbade anyone with even injured testicles to serve as priest. Such a blast from Paul evidently seemed to the translators likely to scandalize their readers. As Lessing noted, such a response blots out other emotional responses. To Paul's readers it would have conveyed no such disgust.

Galatians served Paul as a preliminary sketch for his logically argued and more detailed letter to the Romans a few years later. The early Church correctly felt that it was itself an important document. In it Paul hit his stride as an apologist for the faith competent to defend it from foes within as well as without. It marks a notable advance in his letter writing.

LETTERS TO THE CHURCH IN CORINTH

The pressing problems in Corinth which required Paul's personal attention when the Thessalonians asked him to come to them required his most skillful handling. The Corinthian Christians were in a turmoil from a number of causes, some inherent in the local situation, others caused by visitors who disagreed with Paul's practices. Disagreement is a sign of vitality—one reason, perhaps, why

Paul liked them so well. It was, however, at the same time a feverish activity which had to be reduced to normality.

Corinth had been described by Horace as *bimaris*, "on two bodies of water." Situated close to the Isthmus of Corinth, it dominated east-west commerce in the Mediterranean. It was a sailor's city where crews and travelers relaxed during the delay caused by the portage of cargoes across the isthmus. This fact made it the mecca of those who prey on the traveler, who cater to his needs, his habits, and his vices. For centuries the Greeks had had a verb *korinthiazesthai*, "to Corinthianize, act like a Corinthian," to describe fornication metaphorically. Strabo a few decades earlier reported that the Corinthian temple to Aphrodite possessed one thousand slaves, prostitutes of both sexes. Private enterprise furnished many more. All sorts of religions and religious cults flourished to serve the preferences of citizens and travelers. It was from people in such an environment that Paul made his converts.

The entire population was, of course, not profligate. It lived, however, in surroundings dangerous to sound morals and sober life, with constant enticement away from the faith. Paul, no doubt, found his first converts, as usual, at the Jewish synagogues, some of them Jews but many from Gentile adherents to Judaism. They knew the Septuagint and lived by the Jewish moral code which Christianity also taught. From this core his influence spread more widely among Corinthians and travelers. The latter carried the new faith wherever they went.

Paul faced here a formidable problem in Jewish opposition, the attractions of pagan living, and the pressure of faiths from which converts had come. Citizens of Corinth were cosmopolitan, aware of trends in religious and secular life, and apparently inclined to be unstable and readily embrace new ideas or variants of old ones. These new Christians reacted to the faith in highly individualistic fashion.

The converts eagerly listened to Paul. Soon, however, they were visited by other leaders who disagreed with parts of his message and methods. Apollos, who came soon after Paul had finished his visit, won Paul's unqualified approval; others did not. Peter came and gained a following. His followers held themselves aloof from Paul's. The ubiquitous Judaizers also made their influence felt. Such divergent leadership brought about hostile sectarian division. Some claimed to follow Paul, others Apollos, and a third sect claimed to directly follow Christ. Even before Paul had left Corinth, one unnamed member in the church was spearheading vigorous opposition to him.

The difficulties within the church of Corinth are not mentioned in Acts. True to his practice elsewhere, Luke did not wash the Church's dirty linen in public. As a propagandist he would have gained nothing by reporting the less attractive parts of his picture. In fact, his report on Paul's year and a half in Corinth is noticeably brief. It focuses on the opposition of the Jews to Paul's gospel. Gallio's rebuff of Jewish rioters (Acts 18:12–16) was stressed for its presentation of Roman refusal to consider Paul subversive.

Among the divergent Corinthian groups were four emancipative movements, each a potential source of danger to the Church. Some interpreted Paul's declaration that faith alone is essential to salvation as implying complete freedom of conduct, though his statements to the contrary were as explicit as those later embodied in James. These Corinthian antinomians engaged in sexual promiscuity in the notorious Corinthian manner. Some Jewish converts, in their eagerness to divorce themselves from Judaism, attempted through an operation to remove the mark left by circumcision, an action which scandalized Paul. It may have been the basis for the charges later made by the Judaizers in Jerusalem against him (Acts 21:21). A third group prohibited far more strenuously than Paul required the eating of food previously sacrificed to idols. A fourth emancipative movement appears to have arisen among Christian women, a sort of "women's liberation" from the restrictions imposed by society as a whole upon women. These factions, and possibly others not mentioned, kept the Corinthian pot furiously on the boil.

Paul's handling of these cases mingled arbitration with authoritative legislation. His decisions were, for the most part, responsive to the specific situation in Corinth rather than directive for the entire Christian church—a fact often overlooked by later readers. Although he regularly gave doctrinal reasons for his position, it cannot be argued that in every instance he was setting up correct procedure for all later Christians. As in the letters written much later to Timothy and Titus, which bear his name but are not by him, some directives are now impracticable.

Paul's decisions on these four problems are, nonetheless, interesting and to be considered on their general merits as well as on their immediate applicability. The claim to be followers of any human leader, Paul summarily dismissed with a horticultural metaphor: "I have planted, Apollos watered; but God gave the increase" (1 Cor. 3:6). Christians are all one in Christ, not divided under his emissaries. The differences in the teaching of Peter, Apollos, the Judaizers, and himself had in them an element of the dispute between Jew and Hellene. Paul curtly retorted that the Greek desire for wisdom had not enabled them to find God, while the Jewish demand for a sign, as in the Pharisees' demand of Jesus, had made them stumble and fall. (Although the Gospels were still unwritten, Paul had available collections of Jesus' experiences and sayings.)

Paul commented that few of the Corinthian converts had belonged to the "wise" (*sophoi*). Why should the worldly "wisdom" of a man like Apollos lead them to assume, as Apollos had not done, that this wisdom was essential to faith in Christ? Christians, he forcefully declared, to survive at all had to constitute a unit. Paul's directive here is practically as well as doctrinally sound. In spite of his recent failure at Athens, Paul was not anti-intellectual: he meant simply that for Christian faith wisdom was not prerequisite.

Antinomians received bitter denunciation. Faith shows itself in action. Christianity was "the Way," the road along which its believers must travel. His response develops into an extended discourse on moral conduct and relations with non-Christians.

Jewish Christians must not be ashamed of their racial heritage; one can imagine Paul's beard bristling at such belittling of his race. They should not try to hide their origin by attempting to pass as Gentiles. Paul's position on religious relations with Judaism was still ambivalent, but he had no patience with Jews who tried to "cross over" into the Gentile ranks.

Restrictions on diet as stated by the Council of Jerusalem some five years previously (Acts 15:29) had included provisions against meat not drained of blood and food offered to idols. Gentile Christians, it seems likely, had not generally been required to obey it. In Corinth the question concerned the propriety of Christians eating food sacrificed to idols. Such food included the choicest cuts of meat, which were subsequently sold for food. Paul admitted that such sacrifice did not taint the food, but added that some Christians felt that it did. As a matter of expediency, he declared that he would not eat it, nor should other Christians, if such action troubled fellow Christians. In such trivial matters it is proper to concede to prejudice.

The proper conduct of women was a problem which Paul wisely handled with great care. To have advocated greater liberty for women than society in general allowed would have laid the Church open to violent attack on the charge that it was subverting the social order. The Church had problems aplenty without adding another that ran counter to ages of practice. Paul, moreover, was a man of his age, sharing its views and prejudices. He made it clear (1. Cor. 7:6, 12, 40) that he was expressing his own opinion and not the command of God; he was, nonetheless, convinced that he was right.

If a man earnestly desires to marry, Paul said, let him do so; marriage is an honorable estate. The wife must realize that the husband is head of the family. He must treat her kindly, but she must obey him. Paul's position is substantially that held by Judaism. In one respect, however, he was more lenient than Ezra had been (Ezra 10). He did not object to marriage between a Christian and a nonbeliever. The believer may be able to lead his spouse into the Church.

Paul's equivocal position regarding marriage is partly accounted for by his belief in the imminent Parousia and the duty of all Christians to spread their message everywhere before Christ's return. A married man must provide for his family and cannot devote all his energy to spreading the gospel. Ever practical, Paul saw no reason to enlarge this contract by bringing more lives into the world.

If any personal motives actuated Paul here, they cannot be discovered. Other passages in the letters clearly indicate that Paul was not the misogynist that some readers consider him.

Other problems handled by Paul in these letters dealt with problems of general concern to the faith. They concerned the celebration of the Lord's Supper, the nature of the resurrection, and the place of glossolalia in the Church.

At Corinth, the sacrament of the Lord's Supper had come down evidently from the level of a sacrament to the level of a disorderly congregational dinner. Banquets held in the pagan cultic worship no doubt contributed to such debasement. At Corinth, in part perhaps due to the influence of the antinomian element, it had become an orgy of overeating and drunkenness. More than this, Christians were eating the feast in separate cliques instead of as one body. Paul severely castigated them on both counts (1 Cor. 11:17–21.)

Subsequently in this letter (11:23–32) Paul set up a procedure for proper observance of the Lord's Supper, on the pattern which Jesus himself had instituted. It should be a simple, unadorned rite far removed from the Corinthian orgy. The celebrant should follow the same symbolic action that Jesus had used; Paul clarifies the symbolism. The participants are all to drink of the wine and thus to ratify the new covenant with Jesus. The Jewish references in the symbolism would be known to many Corinthians through their reading of the Septuagint; and some of the cults imported into Corinth to pander to travelers quite possibly practiced a similar rite using actual blood. The Corinthian Christians could not celebrate Jesus' feast "worthily" (11:28–30) with a surfeit of eating and drinking or dining in separate cliques.

Paul's next problem, though less basic ritually, was a delicate matter with strong emotional involvement. It concerned what is now called glossolalia, "speaking with tongues," uttering generally unintelligible sounds under the real or fancied power of the Holy Spirit. Such a phenomenon had accompanied the arrival of the Spirit at Pentecost (Acts 2:4–13). In the early Church the phenomenon continued. It was accounted a genuine gift granted by the Spirit to certain members. To some members this babbling was intelligible. It could also be imitated in hysterical outbursts without meaning. Paul had himself experienced the power and knew it to be a genuine gift. It was a sensitive area that Paul had to approach with great tact.

Paul opened his comment obliquely by reviewing spiritual gifts in general (chap. 12). The Spirit, he noted, endows Christians with various gifts, which are to be employed for the good of all men. He lists them: expression of wisdom and knowledge; strengthening of the faith; performing extraordinary deeds; arbitration of matters in the Church; administration of Church affairs; and, finally, speaking with tongues and its interpretation. Glossolalia comes last on the list. It stands last also in its service to other men, which was his criterion of order in listing them. A Christian should practice the highest gift which he possessed.

Paul could himself speak with tongues, but he had abandoned doing so for higher services. In so doing, he believed, he best showed in himself the love (*agapē*) of God for man working in himself. This love Paul eloquently praised (1 Cor. 13). Wisdom and prophecy afford only partial knowledge. Along with the other gifts of the Spirit, these will become ineffectual when the Parousia brings perfect knowledge. Our current wisdom and other gifts, including glossolalia, will then be like the reflection in a polished copper or flawed glass mirror. Our knowledge is childish. At the Parousia only faith, hope, and love will survive, "and the greatest of these is love."

At present, Paul continued, the most serviceable gift is prophetic. He thinks of the prophet (*prophētēs*) as one who speaks before an audience, primarily as the deliverer of a message from God. Only intelligible speech is useful then. To use a strange tongue is to make oneself an alien unable to communicate with his hearers. A stranger hearing this might conclude such speech to be a sign of drunkenness (as men had supposed at Pentecost). One should practice glossolalia only in small groups and only with an interpreter present.

Such outbursts can be restrained in public. God is not a god of confusion. "Let all things be done decently [i.e., with propriety] and in good order." Only so can the Church be built up. In lessening the importance of glossolalia, without offending its practitioners, Paul all but put an end to its practice for most later Christian groups. There is no reason to suppose this to have been his intention. He may have realized that even when the gift was genuine the speaker was unconsciously moved by the exhibitionism inherent in human nature. By his recommendation hysterical or fraudulent babblers were robbed of their strongest motive for speaking.

With respect to the Resurrection, Paul had already written briefly in 1 Thessalonians (4:13–5:4). There he had faced a minor problem in regard to it. Here he began with proofs of Jesus' resurrection before treating of the human counterpart (1 Cor. 15). His is the earliest surviving record of that stupendous Resurrection and of events following it. As with glossolalia, he put his theme into proper perspective.

Jesus' death, burial, and resurrection, Paul declared, fulfilled the Old Testament. He had, no doubt, so thoroughly presented details in his preaching that he needed to add no proof texts here. That it had actually occurred, he proceeded, there were too many witnesses to make denial effective. First he cited Peter as a witness known to them, next the apostles, and then more than five hundred who had seen Him after his resurrection. He listed also Jesus' brother James, the prominent leader in Jerusalem (apocryphal accounts of this appearance have survived). All the "apostles" are next mentioned (apparently a larger group than the twelve is meant).

Finally, Paul listed himself. He referred to himself as an abortion (*ektrōma*) of an apostle, who did not appear when the twelve were called by Jesus, but was made equal with them by the grace of God in spite of his untimely birth. The Greek verb apparently need not refer only to premature birth. It has been suggested also that Paul may be referring to his insignificant appearance, or that he may be recalling his preconversion life. The metaphor is ambiguous, startling, and arresting.

How can one deny the testimony of all these witnesses? In view of the actuality of Jesus' resurrection, how can one deny the resurrection of men effected by it? If you deny it, Paul reasoned, you make the other meaningless. Without both, all Christian work is ineffectual, all men are still slaves to sin and spiritually dead, and we who have taught you are liars. Without such hope, we are the most pitiable of men.

The fact is, Jesus *has* risen. History has come full circle from the old Adam, in whom all died, to the new Adam, Jesus, in whom all men regain life. His followers shall rise from death as he did.

Paul shored up his statement with argument drawn from his own experience. Do you suppose, he asked, that I should suffer and risk my life as I constantly do if I were not convinced that I shall live after death? Without such hope, I might as well accept the debased Epicurean maxim: Eat, drink, and be merry, for tomorrow we die. But do not let such maxims mislead you. As Menander wrote, "Evil communications corrupt good manners"; the RSV modernizes it, "Bad company ruins good morals."

Paul then answered specific questions for his readers. How are the dead raised? What kind of body will they have? People were not then sheltered like modern man from the stark facts of dissolution. In his mystically conceived reply, Paul resorted to an agricultural analogy perhaps not wholly accurate in detail yet clearly conveying his idea. (He had grown up in cities and was hazy about the gardener's calling.) A seed dies when planted in the ground in order to produce a new plant. As the seed is to the splendid new plant, so is the physical body to the resurrected body. Paradoxically yet reasonably, the new body is a spiritual body.

This matter, Paul realized, lies in an area beyond human experience. Borrowing a term from the cult practices familiar to his readers, he related to them a "mystery"—a dramatized truth. The mystery served a purpose similar to the "myth" often used by Plato to round out a dialogue, somewhat as the account of the Creation in Genesis served Hebrew thought. A myth is not necessarily a factual account. It states an idea in a picture dramatically conceived. At the trumpet blast Christians, both the dead and the living, will instantaneously undergo a change; they shall put on as a garment an imperishable, immortal nature. There shall be no more death. Knowing this, they can stand immovable, confident in the glorious conclusion of their present hardship and toil in the faith.

From this mystery Paul's first letter hastens to its conclusion. The lowering in importance of glossolalia freed him to emphasize his major theme in teaching: Jesus, his death and resurrection, and his gift of eternal life to his followers. The Lord's Supper has been established as both a commemorative and a forward-looking rite to Christ's return. And the resurrection of the dead with the metamorphosis of Christians into "spiritual" bodies rounds out the message Paul was constantly preaching.

As in earlier letters Paul authenticated the letter by his signature. It was well that he took this precaution. Hardly any of his extant letters contains so much dynamite which could be ruinously detonated by unscrupulous alteration or addition. His work in Corinth, and with it much of his success as teacher and adviser, stood or fell with this letter.

Paul's final surviving letter to the turbulent Corinthians, 2 Corinthians, includes materials written at intervals probably a year or more later than 1 Corinthians. His first letter having evidently not produced the desired effect, he had sent another in which he severely castigated recalcitrant members. After he had sent it, he feared that he had been too severe and had perhaps turned the tide against his cause. His relief and pleasure at news of their submission to his admonitions and orders shows throughout nearly the entire letter, excepting chapters 10–13. The most reasonable theory accounting for this different tone is that they were part of the severe preceding letter, which by accident or design was subsequently combined with his thankful final letter. This letter will be considered as it has been preserved.

Paul composed a tactful salutation. Although careful to restate his apostleship, he addressed his correspondents as "saints," that is, people dedicated to the Christian life and gospel. The term concerns desire and effort more than actual attainment. His faith in them stood unshaken. Their prayers for his safety had contributed heavily to his escape from a deadly though unspecified peril. His opening words are all for conciliation.

The impetuous, volatile Corinthian character still controlled his correspondents. When he had not come to Corinth as he threatened, some of them petulantly complained that he could not be trusted. Instability was apparently characteristic of Corinthian Christians. Forty years later 1 Clement accused them of fickle insubordination. Paul had not come because condemnation of them in their presence would have been more than he could bear. He had been duty bound to show them God's will and beg them to obey it. It was an episode now to be closed. In particular, "if any have caused grief"—*any* is singular but may refer to more than one troublemaker—he is now to be restored to favor in the Church in order to facilitate his entry into the Kingdom. God, not Paul, had triumphed. He was only God's emissary.

Reminder of his function as God's emissary naturally introduced a panegyric of the apostolic office. We are not hucksters of God's word, who brought letters of introduction to deceive—an oblique reference to those who had opposed Paul's teaching. Yourselves are our references and can testify that we impart sincerely what we received from God. Fragile pottery like us, he showed in four antithetical statements, could endure the pressures through its own strength. We are hemmed in on all sides, yet free to act; unable to find a way out, yet never without one; persecuted, yet never abandoned; struck down, yet not destroyed; carrying physically marks of Jesus' dying in order to show his life in us. It brings death to us physically, but spiritually eternal life to you. What we lost through current affliction is slight contrasted with what we gain: "for the things which are seen are temporal, but the things which are not seen are eternal" (2 Cor. 4:18).

Suddenly realizing that his catalog of loving service to them might sound like boasting, he declared that in everything he was the servant of God (2 Cor. 6:4). His catalog seems to have been inspired by what Wordsworth called the "spontaneous overflow of powerful emotions"—poet and rhetorician coincide in such experiences. Wordsworth's prompt completion of his definition—"on the part of a man who has thought long and deeply"—also describes Paul's state.

A phrase used by Petronius to describe Horace's felicitous style—

curiosa felicitas—an oxymoron freely rendered as a carefully wrought impression of verbal good luck, also applies here. Highly finished oratory in ancient times led its hearers often to react skeptically to its polish. A man who had taken such pains had also opportunity to fabricate an ingenious lie. To produce the effect of sincerity, it was often wise to write an apparently impromptu passage for which one might later apologize. Paul's readers in Corinth perhaps never fully realized the artistry in this passage.

Chapter 6, verses 4–7 provide a remarkable example of anaphora; eighteen prepositional phrases introduced by the preposition *in*, strung loosely in asyndeton. (The stylists of the KJV evidently felt the anaphora to be excessive and, after the tenth appearance of *in*, substituted the preposition *by*. Paul, no doubt, intended to hammer home to the volatile Corinthians his service and that of his fellow apostles to God.) This effect he follows (vv. 8–10) with another device which Coleridge was later to label the reconciliation of opposites. Here the opposites are paired in what amounts to an extended oxymoron presented in asyndeton. The value Longinus attached to combined figures is seldom better illustrated.

Paul's overwhelming evidence supporting his denial that he was self-centered paved his way to censuring his readers. The besetting temptation which everywhere faced the Corinthian converts was the sensual practices, evil in themselves, which enticed men to backslide into paganism. He expressed no regret for his previous stern letter because it had brought them again through repentance into harmony with God. He pictured their regeneration by the familiar image of climbing rung by rung a ladder of heightened response (7:11). In Greek the rugged catalog of solitary Greek nouns is unusually effective. See how much carefulness it created in you, but also eagerness to clear yourselves, but also indignation, but also fear, but also longing, but also zeal, but also punishment. The last item referred to the ringleader of the revolt, for whom Paul immediately interceded. "I rejoice," he concluded his comment, "because I have confidence in you in every respect" (7:16).

His elaborate benediction (13:14) is pronounced upon them

"all." His first letter (16:23–24) had omitted "all" from his benediction. In their former recalcitrant state, grace could not come to all of them.

Second Corinthians is narrower in scope than his first letter, but in some respects it is even more revealing of Paul's extroverted nature and literary skill. He sorrowed to have hurt the feelings of these Christians, he rejoiced at their reformation, he tactfully warned and advised them for the future. His letter is the work of a highly competent artist in words. Quintilian's description of the orator as "a good man skilled at speaking" has seldom been better illustrated.

ROMANS

When Paul was writing Romans he was at least temporarily free of the pressures that had hurried his earlier efforts. He had recently left Ephesus following the silversmiths' riot (Acts 19). He was temporarily in Corinth en route, as he had hoped, to Rome and perhaps points even farther west. In Asia Minor, the Balkans, and Greece he had finished his pioneering work in focal cities not previously exposed to his message. For reasons discussed in connection with Acts, he now felt it imperative to return to Jerusalem instead of proceeding to Rome. He did not expect to survive this journey. Feeling that he must present his message to the capital of the empire, he took time while waiting for a ship to work out a carefully organized letter to the church already established in Rome.

From scattered bits of information it is possible to compose a picture of the Roman church. Jews had quite possibly settled in Rome as part of the Diaspora. When Pompey returned to the city in 63 B.C. after his intervention in the Maccabean wars, he brought with him Jewish slaves, the first Jews mentioned in Rome. Many of them won their freedom and established or added to the Jewish community there. The community attracted attention of the Romans partly by its industry, but more by its peculiar religious customs, especially circumcision and Sabbath observance. By the middle of the first century A.D., it was gaining many Gentile adherents. It suffered a brief setback in A.D. 49 when Claudius expelled the

Jews from Rome. According to Suetonius, who wrote several decades later, they were expelled on account of riots headed by someone named Chrestos. Suetonius occasionally garbled his accounts; possibly the riots had been attacks by Jews on the Christian church in the city. This expulsion led to Paul's meeting with Aquila and Priscilla in Corinth. Since this couple had returned to Rome by A.D. 56 or 57, Paul presumably had sympathizers in the Roman church.

The tone of Paul's letter indicates that the Roman church had a strong element who favored the position of the Christians in Jerusalem. Paul could anticipate from former experience that his more receptive readers would come from the Gentile adherents who had found Christianity more congenial. The Judaizing Christians, however, presumably dominated the church. His problem bore some relation to the situation which he had faced in Galatians.

Although Paul's authorship of Romans has not been seriously questioned, some uncertainties about it have plagued scholars. In the third and fourth centuries manuscripts existed without the specific address to the Roman church in 1:7 and 15. On this admittedly slender evidence it has been assumed by some that Romans was a circular letter to several churches. If this were so, the copy originally addressed to Rome happened to be copied when Paul's letters were collected, and it then became the standard text. In such a case, chapter 16 would have to be considered a fragment of another letter accidentally attached here by some copyist. The Chester Beatty papyrus also raises some doubt that chapter 16 belongs here. Without ignoring such indications, most scholars accept the letter with chapter 16 as originally written to the Roman church.

Some four years earlier, Paul had hastily handled the Judaizers' opposition in the letter to the Galatians. It was written under pressure of his Corinthian labors. In it he had argued forcefully for the complete efficacy of faith and against the fatal inconsistency of relapsing into Jewish rites. Now he faced a Judaizing form of Christianity that had apparently been standard from the first. Moreover, Paul's regular procedure was to travel where Christianity had not yet been presented.

Paul spoke accordingly of his projected trip to Rome as a visitor en route to points as far west as Spain. As a visitor he would naturally present to the church in Rome his concept of the faith. The principles enunciated in Galatians make it clear that his concern for the faith constrained him to do so. His friendly tone shows that he realizes his status. There is no expression of authority like that which he had exerted in the Corinthian letters.

As John Knox acutely remarks, Paul appears in his letters as a practical, realistic theologian rather than as a speculative philosopher in the field of religion. Even in Romans, his nearest approach to a theological treatise, the practical note dominates. The gospel, he declared (1:16–17), is the power of God for salvation to every one who has faith, to the Jew first, and also to the Greek. In the gospel, the intrinsic justice of God is revealed to man through faith; he cited Habakkuk 2:4, "The just [man] shall live by his faith." Paul's efforts were directed to the practical end of saving man from the sin which has enslaved him.

The metaphor of enslavement served Paul effectively throughout his writing. God, he believed, made man originally good—in Milton's phrase, "sufficient to have stood, though free to fall." Man, in the person of Adam, deliberately chose to submit to the power of sin—a demonic power who from Adam's fall has dwelt in man. However man may recognize his kinship with God and will to live in accord with him, sin has enslaved man and keeps forcing him to disobey what he knows to be right. Man lacks the means to free himself from this slavery.

Paul carried his analogy to its logical outcome. God by offering Christ, who is both God and sinless man, has provided the means to buy man out of his slavery to sin. He will do this for every man who has faith in Him. Habakkuk (2:4) provided Paul a text to develop: The just man—the man who, though not perfect, desires to be in right relation with God—attains that state through his faith. This categorical statement leaves no room for obedience to the requirements of the Law. In our colloquial phrase, such a man lives by his faith, period. That is the whole of it.

Paul had written Galatians to thwart attempts to govern Gentile converts by Jewish law. He had now to face this problem in wider relations. What is the value in obedience to religious law and ritual as both Jewish and Gentile systems viewed them? In Galatia, the Judaizers had been interlopers into territory pre-empted by Paul; here, the situation was reversed. In Galatia, Paul could argue from a basis he had already established; here, he had to argue from a situation set up by others. Since his audience was living at the hub of Roman law, he could include the concept of law in general as it relates to grace and faith. His readers were familiar with the idea stated by Virgil that Rome's contribution to the world was rule by law, an idea quite acceptable to Paul. Whenever the subject of law came up, Paul's readers would be thinking of Roman law as well as the Jewish law.

According to John Knox, a key concept in Romans is spiritual life. Earthly law directs man's earthly life. The Christian, however, lives also in the nascent new existence which Christ will bring at his coming. Law on earth is protective and punitive, functions which man restored to his primitive harmony with God finds no longer necessary. The Hebrew law-ritual has been replaced by the grace of God, and is now valueless for spiritual life. The Christian's new nature makes him a law-abiding citizen on the earthly plane.

Mindful of his Hebrew heritage that saw God as the director of history, Paul declared that all should, nonetheless, obey their earthly rulers. They have been ordained by God; to resist them is to disobey God. Rulers are not a terror to good works, but to evil (13:1–3). Paul realized the danger that the Christian might fall into antinomian conduct, as seems from other New Testament letter writers to have happened. He is "not to think of himself more highly than he ought to think; but to think soberly" (12:3) on the earthly as on the spiritual plane.

Paul's salutation offers a further parallel to Galatians: as "Paul, a slave of Jesus Christ," he declared again his apostolic office and mission. He apparently anticipated a Judaizing slur on his office in Rome also. His emphasis in the letter, it appears, was on the concept of slavery. This early insertion of the idea effects a nearly subliminal force upon his readers, who would unknowingly record it without realizing that it is a major metaphor of his letter. The image is not resumed until, after a terrifying depiction of the debased condition into which man has let himself fall, the buying of this slave out of bondage is explicitly stated (3:24).

To show the deficiency of the Law as a saving force, Paul cited human experience. In eleven emotionally charged questions and answers (3:1–9) he showed how man realizes his incapacity to live up to the standards to which he knows he should attain. Even without knowing the Law, a man's conscience makes him aware of his state. Paul evidently had in mind also principles such as those enunciated by Stoic philosophers which represent the highest moral awareness attained in the Gentile world. The Jews have not only conscience like other men, but the revelation from God in the Law and the Prophets. Jews are doubly culpable for their disobedience. Paul thus struck a shrewd blow at Judaizing reverence for the Law. Both Jew and Gentile realize their lost state as slaves to evil and wish to return to their primitive goodness. Paul, no doubt, had in mind the state of man in Eden, but he knew also the Gentile longing for a lost Golden Age. Both traditions were known to Paul's readers.

Jewish transgressors naturally fared worse in Paul's thought than did Gentiles. Hearing the Law without obeying its intent confers no benefit. But obedience is more than observance of ritual and regulation. Remembering his own state before his conversion, he satirically pictured the Jewish legalist as "a guide of the blind, a light of them which are in darkness, an instructor of the foolish, a teacher of babes, which hast the *form* of knowledge and of the truth in the law" (2:19–20). The operative word is *form*; like the Pharisee in Luke's parable (Luke 18:10–14), the legalist is unjust in God's sight. In a stunning image Paul declared that such a disobedient Jew is spiritually uncircumcised, while the Gentile who lives rightly by the law is spiritually circumcised (2:25–26).

The Judaizers' pride in lineal descent from Abraham, Paul continued, has nothing to do with obedience to Mosaic law. Moses and the Torah existed centuries after Abraham. Moreover, Abraham's faith was his justification before God (Gen. 15:6). As a final blow to the Judaizers' position, Paul added, God's approval of Abraham was expressed some fourteen years before the rite of circumcision was instituted (Gen. 18:11 ff.). He thus neatly cut the basis of their claims from beneath their feet.

Paul was not yet finished with the Judaizers' claims based on descent from Abraham. He cited Genesis 17:5, in which God changed Abram's name to Abraham as a sign that he would be the father of many nations. (Paul probably had in mind not only Abraham's son Ishmael but also the six sons mentioned in Genesis 25:1–4.) Abraham's "seed" are not Jews alone but all those who have faith in God like Abraham's. Genesis, Paul declared, cannot be interpreted to refer to Hebrews only in speaking of the children of Abraham. Promises of God to Abraham cannot be restricted to Hebrews alone. To sum up, Abraham's faith—without the Law, without circumcision, and without lineal descent from him—is God's pattern for any man who will conform to it. Through faith in God and that alone, then, which leads a man to ask for God's grace, the Christian is purchased out of his slavery to sin. This grace is made available through the sinless suffering of Christ.

Reverting to the concept of law, which recognizes that no penalty can be exacted from a man after his death, Paul drew an analogy between the suffering, death, and resurrection of Christ on the one hand and the symbolic ritual of baptism on the other. In baptism the Christian figuratively dies to sin, is buried in the water as Jesus was buried in the tomb, and rises as a new creature from his watery "tomb." His former master, sin, has no longer control over him after this symbolic death and burial. "He that is dead is free from sin" (6:7).

The KJV through a linguistic error mistranslated the metaphor in 6:5. Two similar Greek words were confused. The translators assumed that the adjective *sumphutoi* derived from the same root as *sumphuteuō*, to plant two varieties of seed together, as farmers used to plant pumpkin seeds in their hills of corn. It derives rather from *sumphuō*, to exist or grow side by side; it is used of bones smoothly articulating in a joint. It is this latter sense, as the RSV shows, that is in Paul's mind: the Christian's articulation with Christ in and following his baptism.

A flippant antinomian might hastily assume that escape from the penalties of death through baptism licensed him to sin again. Paul was horrified at the notion and replied in some detail (6:15–23). Having become God's slaves by purchase—he resumed the metaphor which he had quietly inserted into 1:1—we must now obey God's commands. Our new natures will make us wish to follow God's will and sin no more. We may, to be sure, backslide through the allurement to sin in our still human bodies in spite of our will not to do so. Our will keeps us true to our new master. The man who deliberately runs away from this master in order to sin meets the fate of the fugitive slave, eternal death, just as physical death is the penalty for it on earth.

Feeling the need of further illustration, Paul resorted to a second analogy, the parallel in marriage. This analogy, however, is confusing. Starting with a compliment to his readers—you understand law (7:1)—he introduced the marriage contract. A woman is legally bound to her husband as long as he lives, but after his death she may marry another. At first reading, the passage seems to mean that man is bound to sin until the death of sin, which appears to reverse the terms of the previous illustration. Analogy is an enlightening device; it may also be dangerous to the user. As C. H. Dodd has said of this passage, one should forget what Paul says in order to concentrate on what he means. This meaning has been clarified in his analogy of baptism to death (6:4).

Paul used this analogy partly to shock his Judaizing readers. Formerly man had been under sin. Formerly man had been under the Law. The startled reader would be "needled," as it were, by the implication here that the Law is sin. Upon their discovery that he meant no such equation, their relief would generate a degree of kindliness toward him. The Law, he quickly added, had taught him what sin was; in so doing it was "holy, and just, and good." It could not help him, however, to escape spiritual death. Such escape becomes possible only through the gift of God to those who believe the revelation of him through his Son (8:1). Shock tactics of this sort affect the reader like the paradox. Upon discovering that he has misjudged the writer, the reader is likely to give him a more favorable hearing for a while.

Paul supplemented the effect of his argument here (8:18–39) with what Sir Thomas Browne described as an "altitudo." This elevated emotional outburst, Longinian rhetoric asserted, was designed to produce a sudden emotional shock that would sway readers toward acceptance of his teaching. For such a purpose Longinus prescribed a figure of speech or of thought. With vivid images Paul stated here the glorious future for the believer. The whole creation has been suffering the pangs of childbirth to bring forth the new dispensation (v. 22). Our transition from natural to spiritual men is accomplished with like pangs (v. 23).

Next (vv. 29–30) he combined anaphora with a special form of amplification in which successive elevation is added to successive waves of emphasis. The first member, "Whom he did foreknow, he also did predestinate," is supported by a statement of the purpose in this predestination. Then, in swift succession follow three more rungs of the ladder in anaphora with the first. This powerfully impressive structure gives place to six questions and answers (vv. 31–35) of which the last three begin with the anaphoristic *Who*. Of these six the final two units add a catalog to the question and anaphora. He followed this combination with a pessimistic note citing Psalm 44:22, but countered it with a triumphant note: "We are more than conquerors through him that loved us" (v. 37). "I stand persuaded," he concluded, with combined anaphora and catalog, that nothing can separate us from God's love. What seems an impromptu outburst is actually a carefully compounded altitudo calculated to move the reader in accord with Paul's own genuine emotion.

Such an outburst signals a shift in subject. The next part (chapters 9–11) leads Paul by association to discuss God's purpose for Jew and Gentile. Paul had to remove from his Judaizing readers any misconceptions about his presumed enmity to the Jewish heritage of Christianity. After the preceding emotional passage, passion would be temporarily spent. He could hope to receive rational attention on a hotly debated theme.

Paul began by declaring, in the spirit of Moses after the episode of the golden calf (Exod. 32:32), that he would offer himself as scapegoat provided that the Hebrews, "my kinsmen after the flesh," could thereby be saved. They had received from God preferential treatment in the covenants, the Law, and in knowing God's promises. The patriarchs and the prophets had furnished example and warning. They had been a people set apart by God. Paul was proud to share in such a heritage.

He reminded them, however, that not all Abraham's offspring had been Hebrews (9:6). God had chosen only Isaac's line. Of Isaac's twin sons, only Jacob became progenitor of the chosen people. In like manner, God knows that only part of those who are Jewish by birth shall become part of the true Israel, the Church. However arbitrary this may appear to human judgment, God has the right to dispose of his creation as he wills.

Actually, Paul added, God's selection is not arbitrary; man has always been free to accept or reject God's offer. Israel is still free to choose; God has never in all history finally rejected her as a whole. Paul interjected a paradox: Israel's temporary estrangement from God may well have been a means of bringing Gentiles into the Church. The Christians had to be driven by violence from converting Jews alone (cf. Acts 8). Jews have the same entry into the new universal Israel that Gentiles have (11:10–12). Although not expressly stated, it is evident that Paul allowed no special place for converted Jews, a condition they must accept.

To illustrate his point, Paul drew a parallel with the grafting of trees, which he distorted. The Jewish people are a cultivated olive tree from which branches have been broken. Upon its stock wild olive branches have subsequently been grafted—a startling reversal of the usual practice. Some of the broken-off branches may be later regrafted to the stock. The Christian church is the true stock from Abraham. Not all his descendants have remained attached to this stock. The grafted branches of wild olive are the Gentile converts. And the Jewish branches that have been broken from the stock may be grafted once more to the true stock.

Jewish zeal for God, Paul admitted (10:2), was a sign of life but unintelligently directed. They had tried to pursue righteousness (the participle in 9:31 has conative force), but in choosing the path of ritual obedience, they had lost their way. Works without faith were dead, and much of the Jewish law was outdated as well.

To express his hope for the Jewish people, Paul here resorted to the argument from probability, a device honored among rhetoricians. He had to shift from logic or allegorical interpretation to depend heavily upon speculation. God, he argued, has repeatedly forgiven and restored Israel to his favor. Is it not probable that he will again do so? Such speculation is necessary where one cannot know the facts, but Israel had often in the past wandered from God and returned.

With this final argument, as Gerald Gragg has noted, Paul concluded the theological part of his letter. The last four verses of chapter 11 again use an altitudo to indicate transition. This time it is an apostrophe to the wisdom and knowledge of God. But, as indicated earlier, such a passage is no mere mark of transition. Like the Church's later practice of *didachē* and *kērygma*—instructive and emotionally appealing discourse—Paul tried to make his readers act upon what he had logically presented. He introduced his emotional outburst with a paradox. God has included all men, Jew and Gentile, in unbelief in order to show his mercy for them all. This single insight into God's plan amazed him. If it alone opens such vast prospects, what must be the whole wisdom of God!

Always practical, Paul would not conclude a letter without applying his gospel to man's needs. In view of God's wise planning—he tied his advice fast to his apostrophe—Paul begged men to keep their bodies ready for God's use, to offer their bodies as a sacrifice to God. As sacrifices, these bodies must be living, without blemish, a *logikēn latreian,* the logical and proper offering to Him. They should not try to adjust themselves to life in the world (Paul would have had little patience with recent works on this subject), but they should try to become "metamorphosed," with minds remodeled so as to know the will of God. He cataloged briefly the facets of such a devoted life (12:9–21) which he had previously discussed in writing to the Corinthians. To drive home his brief comments on each facet, he employed parallel structure combined with asyndeton. The imperative forms are in Greek more tersely expressed than in English.

Next (chapter 13) Paul took up the Christian's conduct as a citizen. If not then, a little later, some Christians were bitterly inimical to the Roman state, perhaps partly in consequence of antinomian temptations their new freedom had tempted them to enjoy. Paul had fared well under Rome. His evangelism would have been severely hampered if he had been obliged to cross frontiers, and the highways he traversed were well kept and carefully guarded. His Roman citizenship had already protected him at Philippi and was soon to save his life in Jerusalem.

Paul's support of civil government was firmly based in theory. God rules the world—his Jewish grounding shows here. Accordingly, existing governments rule under divine sanction. To resist them is to resist a power ordained by God. When this rule is abused at the hands of evil, unscrupulous men, one must disobey their bad regulations; but it is designed to punish evildoers. In return for government's services, one owes it taxes to be paid like any just debt. The only account that cannot be paid in full is the debt of love. As Leviticus 19:18 tersely summed up the prohibitions in the Decalogue, "Thou shalt love thy neighbor as thyself." Paul stated it more inclusively, "Love worketh no ill to his neighbor: therefore love is the fulfilling of the law" (13:10).

Paul turned briefly (chapter 14) to a problem which he had discussed in 1 Corinthians: proper conduct with respect to less robust believers. His underlying metaphor pictured an army which loves its enemies. Here he treated the case of the recruit who is in some matters a conscientious objector: he is unable to fully grasp the principles involved in the conflict. How should his stronger comrades-in-arms treat him? First, if he prefers to observe the Jewish Sabbath or to keep the day in any personal way, let him do so. Second, he commented on matters of diet briefly as in 1 Corinthians. One should respect the other's prejudices here also. Motive is all important. If a man observes these trivia in the conviction that he serves the greater glory of God in them, he is not to be condemned for making a mountain out of a theological molehill. The new movement needed above all harmony in its members, not uniformity.

After these tactful hints for correction of faults which he believed to exist in the Roman church, Paul tempered his message by complimenting their many virtues. Since he had not founded that church, he held no position of authority. He stated his need to postpone his visit and repeated his earnest desire to visit them after his pressing trip to Jerusalem. With the brief benediction of 15:33 he seemed to finish his letter, but he added chapter 16 as a postscript.

Feeling perhaps that contentious people might use his argument to divide the church, he warned them against letting anyone break their harmony. He had good reason to fear dissension from his experiences in Corinth and possibly felt some degree of personal responsibility for them. He did not want any repetition in Rome. The remainder of his postscript conveys greetings and good wishes from Paul and his fellow workers to members of the Roman church.

It has been necessary to examine Paul's techniques in some detail in order to show how he handled a difficult problem, of conveying his ideas to a church not established by him. So examined, Romans shows itself to be a masterly effort in propaganda for Paul's gospel. He skillfully presents positions counter to those held by many of his readers while at the same time laboring to keep their good will. A theological treatise it is not, though it more closely approaches that form than do his other surviving letters. Theological studies may be cautiously based on it; but such study lies outside the scope of this work.

CHAPTER 8

THE LETTERS OF PAUL, GROUP 3

PHILIPPIANS

Accompanied by Luke, Silas, and Timothy, Paul went to Europe in A.D. 50. Philippi, the administrative center of Macedonia, was his first stop. Situated on the Egnatian Way, the major artery from Rome to the East, it was in a strategic position for commercial and military affairs. Here in 42 B.C. had been fought the decisive battle which started Augustus on his way to uncontested sovereignty a dozen years later. Augustus had made the city a Roman colony and settled there Roman citizens on the relief rolls and veteran legionaries in retirement. Such colonies were self-governing and their organization was usually modeled on that of Rome itself. Never a large city, Philippi afforded a transitional community between the rural areas of Paul's first journey and the urban centers he was about to enter.

Paul remained in Philippi long enough to establish a church, an energetic group devoted to its founder. He twice revisited it in the course of his travels. Although the precise date of this letter cannot be determined, it was probably written during his Roman imprisonment.

His ostensible purpose in writing was to thank the Philippians for their assistance to him during his imprisonment. Besides sending him money, they had commissioned one of their members named Epaphroditus to assist him in Rome. Soon after his arrival with the money, Ephaphroditus fell seriously ill, and during convalescence he became homesick for Philippi. Paul wrote his letter to certify that Epaphroditus had performed his commission well and was returning because Paul did not require his services.

A mere "thank you" letter would hardly have been incorporated into a collection of Paul's letters designed for reading in other congregations. He did not mention Epaphroditus until halfway through the letter (2:25–30) and delayed his thanks for their gifts until its end (4:14–18). Obviously Paul's love of the Philippians would have made him mention these matters earlier if something else had not taken pre-eminence in his mind.

The Philippian church had a problem that was simple yet potentially destructive of its unified action and spirit. A division had developed among its members, brought about by the rivalry of two influential women in it. Paul approached this problem obliquely as he had done in Corinth in discussing glossolalia. Such animosities, dangerous to any congregation, are especially destructive to small groups like that in Philippi.

As E. F. Scott has shown, three dominant themes appear in this brief letter. The word *joy*, which occurs here more often than in the whole of his other letters, indicates the proper spirit of Christian life which the Philippians exemplify. The second theme lies implicit in his frequent emphasis upon continuity of service to Christ: he iterates "ever," "every," and "always," in 1:3–4 using them twice in a single sentence. Many of his verbs referring to conduct carry the overtone of repeated action which belongs to the present tense in Greek (e.g., 1:18, 27; 2:5, 12; 3:1–2; 4:8).

His third theme is the Parousia, the approaching "day of Christ." Paul appears to have envisioned it, like many other Christians, as due to occur in the not-too-distant future. These three themes converge upon his covert intent in the letter: Replace transitory, trivial concerns with continuous, joyful, concentrated joy in serving Christ in the troubled present and in the life to come. Obliquely but no less clearly, Paul showed the folly in the rivalry for leadership in the church. Instead of forbidding a course of action, he urged a program which would crowd out trivial ambition.

Not until the last chapter (4:2) did Paul name the two women, Syntyche and Euodias, who were evidently principals in the rivalry.

He entrusted to a man named Syzygus the handling of the situation. His name means "yokefellow," as Paul indicated. He urged the two women to "be of the same mind in the Lord," and then took any sting out of the implied censure by calling them his former coworkers "whose names are written in the book of life."

Paul wrote that he was optimistic about his coming trial in a Roman court. The charges which he faced are not fully clear. Preaching Christian doctrine was not yet actionable in the empire. Charges of having disturbed the peace several years before in Jerusalem would not loom large so far from the scene of action. His appeal to the Roman court had been made in the face of charges not established by his opponents in Palestine. As a prisoner since his arrival in Rome, he had been given no opportunity for sedition. He therefore could feel secure about the court's decision; and if tradition is to be trusted, his confidence was justified.

Paul was actually of two minds about the court's decision. Death would free him from the rigors of his life for the past quarter-century and bring fulfillment in existence with Christ. Continued life on earth would give him opportunity to extend his mission to new areas and to be of service to friends like the Philippians. He could see advantages in either case.

So much for Paul's situation; he dismissed it for more congenial matters. For your part, he declared, conduct yourselves publicly and privately in a way worthy of the gospel of Christ. Try to develop a state of mind like that of Jesus (the present tense carries also conative overtones). He, divine by nature, yet lowered himself to become God's servant in a confining body and to die shamefully on the cross. For this abasement God rewarded him by elevation to the highest position—a hint to the ambitious women in Philippi. Paul could now safely state his principal advice.

Chapter 4, verse 4 carries the tone of farewell. *Chairete* ("rejoice"), like *aloha* in Hawaii, means either "hello" or "good-bye." Paul found difficulty in closing this letter; the admonition to fix their minds on constructive ideas had to be reinforced. In verse 8 he summarized his instruction in perhaps his best-known combination of anaphora with asyndeton; *finally* is literally "for the rest."

It forcefully gives Syntyche, Euodias, and anyone else sound advice eloquently expressed to get rid of base ideas and purposes by thinking on higher directions.

In this letter, remote from the doctrinal matters of previous letters, Paul exercised the same careful handling of an apparently picayune squabble. The skillful rhetorician handled this minor yet dangerous situation as seriously as he had treated Old Testament tradition and the promises made to Abraham.

COLOSSIANS

It almost seems at times that one principle guiding the preservation of Paul's letters was the desire to present specimens of his handling of varied problems faced by the infant Church. In Colossians the problem is the parasitic addition to Paul's teaching of cultic elements from the mystery religions and philosophies so prevalent in Phrygia. Upon the faith taught in Colossae by Paul's Ephesian converts, a secret cult had been superimposed. Unable to break its hold, the Christian leaders in Colossae had written to Paul in Rome for help. In response he composed one of his finest literary efforts.

Colossae, a city in southwestern Phrygia about one hundred miles east of Ephesus, had been, according to Herodotus, a large city as early as 481 B.C. It became Hellenized after Alexander's conquests; in Paul's day it was a center of textile manufacture. Neither it nor its neighboring resort city of Laodicea could have escaped the mystery cults of the region. Paul therefore directed that his letter be read in Laodicea also.

Since the cultic teaching at Colossae was revealed only to initiates, it is too little known for detailed reconstruction. Such cults, however, have always fallen into a common general pattern. From knowledge of pagan mysteries in general as well as from hints in Paul's letter, one can gain some knowledge of the Colossian incubus on the church.

The cult went far afield from Paul's simple preaching of "Jesus Christ, and Him crucified." It was a syncretism of the new faith with pagan and Jewish ideas and practices. Belief in Christ, it taught, had to be supplemented with additional teachings and observances. As one progressed through its stages or degrees, he added recognition of "elementals" (*stoicheia*), an astrological concept of spirits of the universe, which were connected with planets and stars that affect man's fate. With them were joined angels drawn from Hebrew belief. Probably the usual cultic purificatory rites of mystery cults were included, and the practice of circumcision may have been borrowed from Judaism. Paul's vocabulary in this letter employs terms borrowed from the standard jargon of such ancient cultic groups.

After a résumé of the Colossians' previous instruction in the faith, Paul emphasized the need of affectionate unity in the congregation. In so doing he struck at the divisive nature of the cult. It parted the church into cultic members and nonmembers, and separated cultists into degrees of presumed attainment. Always practical, Paul attacked vigorously this deleterious social force of the cult.

Paul did not linger on this practical level. He declared the complete sufficiency of Christ as revealer of God and redeemer from sin through belief in Him. Christ is the beloved Son of God, the intermediary in the entire creative plan, and victor over "angelic powers." These powers were apparently supposed beings drawn partly from Oriental astrology, partly from Jewish tradition. They were the "thrones, or dominions, or principalities or powers" (1:16), a demonology pressed into service by Milton in *Paradise Lost*. Jewish sects, as the documents from Qumran indicate, had developed a formidable angelology differing somewhat from the orthodox concepts of angels.

In his attack Paul strategically employed for his own ends the jargon of such cults. He proclaimed as the only genuine "mystery" or hidden truth God's scheme of redemption through Christ, now revealed through Christ's teaching. Christ is both the Messiah and the "Lord." *Kyrios* ("lord") was the cultic title for the being worshiped by the cultists. Christ was both man and God. He was killed but rose from the dead to reign at God's right hand. He is lord over all angels (Paul presumably accepted the Jewish concept of angels). He is head and nourishes the entire body of believers. This metaphor (2:18–19), misunderstood by the KJV, is quite in accord with Greek concepts of the head as focus of all vital powers. The Christian need not undertake any further "degree" of enlightenment through a cult.

Recurring to the divisive and limiting tendencies of the cult, Paul declared that men who have put on the image of Christ live in a state "where there is neither Greek nor Jew, circumcision or uncircumcision, Barbarian, Scythian, bond or free: but Christ is all, and in all" (3:11). Cultic mumbo-jumbo fosters division; the Church, unification. One cannot purify himself as the cultists assert. Christ has already purified him.

Paul added further specific charges against the cultists. His first target was the cult's ascetic code, in which Jewish sectarian—possibly Essene or Zadokite—influence is apparent. In Galatia and Corinth, Paul had found pagan cultic observances lurking in the Christians' background; here, along with Jewish coloring, they had seized the center of the stage. Asceticism does not appear to have been a quality much favored in most pagan cults, but here it is a Jewish tenet indicated in Essene practices. The cult's rule apparently quoted by Paul, "Touch not; taste not; handle not" (2:21), requires a more than Pharisaic strictness.

The leader of the cult aped the ecstatic Hebrew prophet's manner. Senselessly blown up by his sensuous mind, he retailed visions he claimed to have seen. Such exhibitionist rigmarole, Paul declared, was alien to the true Christian life, which is "hid with Christ in God" (3:3)—more cultic jargon adapted to Paul's message. The only *Kyrios* is Christ—a cultic term used twelve times in this brief letter. Acceptance of Christ confers the only degree of salvation.

Cultic rules of conduct may seem to exert a wise discipline on the body; they provide no aid against fleshly indulgence. Men who have truly died to the flesh through the symbolic rite of baptism, and risen thence as Christ's men, strive for those things which are above, where Christ sits at the right hand of God (3:1). Their old life is a corpse. They should let die along with it their bodily motives that had led them to sexual immorality and perversion, evil passion and desire, and that covetousness which is itself idolatry. Paul chides: You Colossians used to walk clad in such vices. Now take them all off and clothe yourselves in compassion, kindness, humility, meekness, and patience. Above all, put on love, which binds all into one harmony. Be thankful to God (thankfulness is twice enjoined within three verses, 3:15–17). Encourage one another, and let all you do be done in the name of the Kyrios Jesus.

Such admonitions form the basis for his words on the family. Wives are to be obedient to their husbands. No equality of the sexes was then possible, and Paul apparently never dreamed of such equality. Husbands are to love their wives (the verb does not stress sensual desire) and to treat them kindly. Children must obey their parents, but fathers must not keep nagging them until they become discouraged. Slaves should serve their masters devotedly as they serve Christ; he will give them full civic rights in his kingdom. Masters, emulating their Master in heaven, should treat their slaves fairly. All should pray constantly to God and give him thanks. Paul's directions take into account the social structure of the times. The Christian must operate within it. Life with non-Christians must be conducted circumspectly. Always be gracious and good humored with them. Choose carefully your approach to each of them. Paul had in mind propagation of the faith: tact and persuasiveness are keynotes in this program.

Here Paul carried out with distinction a difficult rhetorical task. It was no simple problem to intervene, even on invitation to do so, in a church which he had never visited. The problem was complex, for he wished to rid the church of its cultic incubus without alienating the cultists from the Christian faith which he proclaimed. Such cultic practices have always been attractive to men. It is no small problem to show their inherent dangers without alienating those who enjoy them.

PHILEMON

By far the briefest of Paul's letters, Philemon is also the only genuine letter surviving which he addressed to an individual. In style and diction it is characteristically Pauline; and one can hardly conceive why anyone should have forged it. No one has seriously doubted its genuineness.

The situation in Philemon is fairly evident. In prison in Rome, Paul wrote it to Philemon in Colossae. He had converted Philemon to Christianity, probably during his long stay in Ephesus, and friendship had sprung up between them. Philemon was a member of the Colossian church. The letter was brought to Colossae by Onesimus with the letter to the Colossians. Two men named in Philemon, Archippus and Epaphras, are also mentioned in Colossians.

The occasion for the letter is clearly stated. Its bearer, Onesimus, an unruly slave of Philemon, had run away with money or property belonging to his master and had hidden himself among the crowds in Rome. In Rome he had somehow encountered Paul and had himself become a Christian. He had in unspecified ways made himself extremely useful to Paul. Paul, as the Roman law provided, had persuaded Onesimus to return to his master. He wrote this personal note to intercede with Philemon and plead for good treatment for the runaway.

Runaway slaves were usually branded with the letter *F* (for *fugitivus*) and severely punished. They might even be executed, though a slave was too valuable a property to be maimed or killed without strong motivation. As a thief, he was also subject to branding with an *F* of another shape (for *fur*, "thief"). In spite of Philemon's being a Christian, public sentiment against rebellious or runaway slaves might have forced him to severe punitive action. Romans lived in fear of slave uprisings and kept them under harsh restraint.

Paul had had experience of the violent reaction against Christianity when it ran counter to vested interests. In Corinth, its stand against sexual immorality had, no doubt, brought it enemies among those who owned the businesses affected. The silversmiths' riot in Ephesus showed how far reaction could go. Any infringement upon the institution of slavery, real or fancied, would have been far more dangerous. Paul had to proceed carefully in order to avoid arousal of hostility in such a sensitive area. There is little if any reason to suppose that he personally opposed the institution. It was a fact of life and accepted as such by both Jew and Gentile. He thought of the present world as soon to pass away. To dilute the effectiveness of the Christian program by attacking what could not endure for long would in any case endanger the very existence of the Church, and it would have seemed impractical even if he had opposed slavery.

Paul put into this difficult letter his best efforts at tactful persuasion and enlivened it with a sparkling wit which his other letters seldom permitted him to show. To ensure that Philemon might not succumb to the temptation of ignoring his letter, he addressed it also to two other members of the Colossian church as well as to the group which met at Philemon's house. He tactfully complimented Philemon for his faith and love of *all* Christians (Onesimus was a Christian). It would be contrary to Philemon's reputation as a man "abounding in good works" to deny Paul's plea.

Although Paul hinted that his position in the Christian church gave him the right to demand good treatment for Onesimus, he represented himself rather as an old man in prison with a personal request. *Presbytēs*, the word for "old man," may imply either the weakness or authority of age. It is also related to the word for elder in the church. Philemon could not fail to recognize the ambiguities in this word, even if he were not well disposed to Paul.

After this artful preamble Paul came to the point. He asked Philemon to receive Onesimus as a Christian brother—to remit the punishment by law provided. The scapegrace slave had been useful to Paul after his conversion; Paul puns on the relation of his name to *ōnēsis* ("profit") and to *ōnē* ("price")—a subtle reminder that Onesimus was a valuable property not to be roughly handled. In spite of the slave's usefulness, Paul added, he was returning Onesimus to Philemon as honesty required. With Philemon's consent he would like to have the slave's services again. Paul added the already trite comment that Philemon had lost a slave only to win a brother, but he gave it a new turn by adding "in the Lord."

Paul's final appeal was to Philemon's pocketbook. Stopping his amanuensis at this point, Paul wrote in his own hand a promissory note. Whatever loss Philemon had incurred through Onesimus' peculation, Paul would himself repay. He added the semiplayful comment that in making out his bill Philemon should remember his own debt to Paul, who had led him to become a free man in Christ.

Again, in verse 21, Paul added a playful overtone to his serious purpose. Philemon possibly expected some reference to Paul's *paraklēsis,* "urgent plea"; instead, with respect to Philemon himself, Paul substituted *hypakoē,* "*your* obedience." Paul was bringing to bear upon Philemon all the pressure he could tactfully exert, and at the same time he was sweetening the dose with ambiguities, puns, and sly humor. His concluding request that Philemon entertain him as a houseguest when he visited Colossae was highly complimentary. A guest of Paul's stature in the Church would confer an honor on Philemon.

Fifty years later, shortly before his martyrdom, Ignatius wrote to the Ephesians in high praise of their bishop Onesimus. John Knox has suggested that the collection of Paul's letters presumably made in Ephesus late in the first century may well have been supervised by this former slave. If so, Onesimus may have exerted influence to have this note included.

Philemon was badly misinterpreted during the debate in the United States over Negro slavery. Proslavery orators asserted that in not asking Philemon to free Onesimus Paul supported human slavery. In his *Biglow Papers,* James Russell Lowell wittily satirized the charge made by these politicians against those who proclaimed "onscriptur'l views relatin' to Ones'mus." The letter treats of a particular slave, not of slavery.

This letter deserved inclusion in the collection if only for its revelation of Paul's singular talent in handling people and his personal charm. It demonstrates also how a Christian, in Paul's belief, should conduct himself toward other Christians, even his own slaves.

EPHESIANS

Ephesians occupies a position between the generally accepted letters of Paul and the three pastoral Epistles of later date. After centuries of belief in its Pauline authorship, many reputable scholars have become of the opinion that he did not write it. Details of this debate need not be reported here. As it seems to me, the objections to Pauline authorship merit the Scottish verdict of not proven. The urge to discredit tradition in some critics may be counterbalanced by the dogged reliance upon it among others. One argument, however, illustrates an important literary fallacy.

The thinking of those who would discredit Paul as author of Ephesians comes close to the circular fallacy. Ephesians, it is agreed, differs in important respects from Paul's other writings. It is on these differences that much of the refusal to accept Paul as author has been based. On the other hand, all that we know of Paul's literary style comes from his surviving letters. To discard one letter because it is unlike the others is to doctor the evidence. It sets up a standard based on a part only of the available material evidence, while it ignores another part simply because it is different. Unless the ideas presented contradict those expressed in Paul's other letters—and they do not—there appears to be inadequate support for the doubters. The arguments against his having written it cannot be brushed aside; but in this comment the letter will be considered as Paul's.

The title "To the Ephesians" is quite possibly misleading. The earliest surviving copy, the Chester Beatty papyrus from the second century A.D., omits this title. Codex Sinaiticus and Codex Vaticanus have it, but written in another handwriting. For reasons not stated, Marcion, about the middle of the second century, listed a letter "To the Laodiceans" but not one to the Ephesians. Origen in the third century knew but did not accept this title. An appealing hypothesis suggests that this letter was a communication issued in several copies, each of them having the name of a church inserted. Marcion could have known of the copy sent to Laodicea. The Ephesian collectors of Paul's letters naturally made use of their copy and so started the belief that it was specifically addressed to the church in Ephesus.

If Paul wrote Ephesians, it must belong to the period of his Roman imprisonment, A.D. 60–62. Since it develops ideas found in

Colossians, it presumably follows the composition of that letter, somewhat as Galatians had treated ideas later developed systematically in Romans.

According to Thomas Henshaw, Ephesians is a theistic interpretation of the universe for Christians, written to counteract Epicurean materialism and Stoic pantheism. It goes beyond specific local cultic complications treated in Colossians in order to come to grips with wider aspects of the problems faced by Christians. Not a treatise, it is rather Paul's statement of his position than an exhaustive handling of the subject.

The theme of the letter is the act of God's mind and will in bringing all created things toward unity in Christ, the end to which the Church is the means. This concept grows naturally out of Paul's statement in Colossians that Christ is all sufficient. God is the universal Father from whom every family (*patria*) "in heaven and earth is named" (3:14–15). The tribal family, *patria,* obviously relates to *patēr* ("father"). The parallel to the clan or tribal ancestor was familiar to both Jew and Gentile. Jesus' debate with the Pharisees over the true children of Israel, which was later preserved in essence in John (6–8), had already been handled by Paul in Romans and, doubtless, had figured in Paul's oral discourses.

God as such a Father, Paul proceeded, chose us at the beginning of the world to be his holy and blameless sons. We lost our innocence through our own act. Through the agency of Christ, we have been bought out of the enslavement to sin which our act effected. Christ has made known to us the "mystery" of God's plan (a recurrence of the cultic jargon used in Colossians). Of this plan the design is to unite in Christ things in heaven and in earth. Recalling a metaphor used in Colossians, Paul called the Church the body of Christ who is its head (3:6). In 5:23–24 he combined this metaphor with his picture of the Christian family: the wife is to her husband as the Church is to Christ.

Ephesians divides into two nearly equal sections, the former ending with chapter 3. Part one is a series of prayers with intervening passages springing from these prayers. In it Paul illustrated what he meant in Colossians by his repeated admonitions (e.g., 4:2) to be constantly in prayer. He wrote in a state of reverie or mystical contemplation. The complicated expression of 3:1–12 reveals the free association characteristic of communication in such a prayerfully receptive state.

The translators of the KJV were hard put to present it to this communication within the limits of conventional syntax. Wisely, if not with strict regard to syntax, they broke it into two sentences after verse 7. The RSV, doing greater violence to Paul's Greek, seeks to bring order out of syntactical chaos by recasting the passage into five shorter sentences. What may be gained in logical statement is at the sacrifice of Paul's mood. If one must parse the passage, he must take "I Paul" in verse 1 as its subject. But it was speedily abandoned without a predicate, as related or suggested ideas thronged the writer's mind. The abandoned subject is resumed in verse 14, this time with a predicate. Actually such nit-picking insistence upon grammatical syntax obscures the nature of the passage as a contemplative prayer-reverie.

Within the passage one can follow the association of ideas without difficulty. Paul's current imprisonment "for you Gentiles" suggested to him his divinely directed mission as teacher of "the mystery of Christ." He then brooded over the strangeness of this new revelation. As a Jew by race, he marveled at its extension to the Gentiles—a new dimension added to a development of conservative Judaism. When he read over what he had dictated, he probably realized the anacoluthon following verse 1, which he partially corrected in verse 14. Reverie still gripped him, however. He went into more associated ideas that come to their height in perhaps the most loved benediction in the entire New Testament (3:20–21).

In part two (chapters 4–6), though Paul shifted from theory to application, the spell of his reverie lingered. He continued to write as "the prisoner of the Lord" (4:1 resumes the appositive of 3:1). Here, however, he marshaled his still-teeming ideas in a more orderly fashion. He besought his readers to follow worthily the calling to which life had fitted them both in daily affairs and in their service within the church. Each is to practice a humble, forbearing attitude toward other members in order to keep the church unified and at peace. By exercising their special gifts the members will build the church into a complete, firmly based edifice, a Body worthy of its Head. In particular, he warned them against being "carried about with every wind of doctrine, by the sleight of men, and cunning craftiness, whereby they lie in wait to deceive" (4:14). The fact that he did not, as in Colossians, spell out the nature of these dangers may be further indication that this letter was directed to various churches with unlike problems.

Although several sentences, especially those following 5:20, are long, their cumulatively admonitory form makes them readily intelligible. By chapter 6 his directions have become simple enough for tabulation. Metaphors now occupied his mind. His familiar image of the Christian as clad in new garments shifted here as he contemplated the opposition faced by the converts, and it assumed the form of defensive armor. He had started this image in 6:11 only to replace it in the next verse by his favorite image of the athlete—here a wrestler. The new military image speedily crowded this figure out, and he developed his most splendid detailed analogy.

Paul pictured the Christian as armed *cap a pie.* He wears the girdle of truth, the breastplate of righteousness, shoes of the gospel of peace (an echo of Isa. 52:7), the shield of faith, the helmet of salvation, and the sword of the spirit. The sword is used to parry blows, not to strike them. Paul's Christian soldier is not marching as to war. He uses quite other weapons, for he is "praying always with all prayer and supplication in the Spirit . . . [making] supplication for all saints" (6:18).

When Ephesians is read after Colossians, its nature and purpose become more readily apparent. Instead of a letter of suggestions to a particular congregation, Paul wrote a philosophical meditation on the newly revealed divine plan. From the literary approach, it appears to have grown out of his handling the cultic problems at Colossae; yet it is heavily indebted also to his wrestling with Judaizers and sectarians in earlier letters.

PSEUDONYMOUS PAULINE LETTERS

1–2 Timothy, Titus

Thomas Aquinas in A.D. 1274 referred to these three letters as pastoral Epistles, putting them thereby into the class made famous by Gregory the Great's *Cura Pastoralis*. This label became firmly fixed in 1726 when a prominent scholar, Paul Anton, delivered a series of lectures on them using this title. Being compositions long ascribed to Paul, they are properly treated as an appendix to his letters.

In the second century A.D., Marcion refused to count them as by Paul because they did not reveal his characteristics (in doctrine presumably). The Muratorian canon, on the other hand, accepted them as Pauline. Late in the fourth century Jerome included them in the Vulgate as by "the blessed Paul, the apostle," and twelve centuries later the KJV followed suit.

In modern times their Pauline authorship has been vigorously attacked. It is generally agreed that one author wrote all three letters. Paul's authorship is contested on three fronts. Striking differences from Paul's vocabulary in uncontested letters are noted. It is charged that their attitude toward faith is static rather than organic as Paul's was. It is charged that the letters imply a more highly developed Church organization than existed in Paul's day. Defenders of Paul's authorship deny any essential difference in vocabulary. They claim that the beginnings of the Church are too imperfectly known to justify dogmatic statements about its organization. They see the author's concept of faith as simply the reverse of the coin presented in Paul's other epistles. In these matters neither side has been able to finally confute its opponents.

From the literary point of view, Paul's authorship seems to be unlikely. The author impresses such readers as a man of authority in the Church buried in administrative problems to a degree that the Paul in the other letters would hardly have tolerated. He is occupied chiefly as an administrator and is a tireless worker in that field. He knows the moral and spiritual qualities which make Church leaders function properly. He lacks the vividness, the sparkle of Paul's accepted writings. Where evidence supports either position, August Boeckh declared that intuition must aid the experienced interpreter.

A compromise between these two schools has been offered that meets the approval of a number of critics. The author, its proponents hold, was an anonymous writer of the second century A.D. He was a follower of Paul, firmly grounded in his ideas, and quite possibly acquainted with nonextant letters by Paul. He embedded in these three letters excerpts or abstracts from Paul's letters available to him. He felt that his message was what Paul would have written if he had been in the writer's position. Following accepted practice, he presented his letters as by Paul, dispatched to Paul's co-workers Timothy and Titus. In this discussion such a situation is assumed to be the fact.

The author held that Christianity must square with Paul's teachings. To defend this position, he wrote to counter the attacks of heretical groups which showed pronounced Gnostic turns of thought. He could assume that "Timothy" and "Titus" knew the Church's organization and therefore—to our great loss today—did not outline it. He did, however, guide them in the choice of men for leadership in the Church.

In the first Christian century the terms *episkopos* ("bishop") and *presbyteros* ("elder") were apparently almost interchangeable. Paul, for example, addressed Philippians to the bishops and deacons of that congregation. The plural number of bishops here makes it practically certain that they were tantamount to elders—a title he did not use in his genuine letters. By the third century the two offices had become differentiated. In the early second century, the date of the Pastorals, the bishop (always in these letters used in the singular number) occupied a position above the elders. The Pastorals probably represent an intermediate stage of ecclesiastical organization between the first and third centuries.

The writer of the pastoral Epistles appears to have possessed powers analogous to the later metropolitan or archbishop. He could prescribe the duties of the bishop and could assign them to specific areas. Under his persona as Paul, he represents a man whose prestige without any exalted rank could have enabled him to direct such matters. One need not assume that the grade of archbishop had yet been created in the early second century.

The verisimilitude of these epistles as works by Paul is remarkably sustained. Timothy and Titus, Paul's helpers, are presented as bishops under his control. They in turn ordain elders. Even minute details about the apostle's personal needs are inserted as in the authentic letters. On a visit to Asia Minor, for instance, Paul has left his personal effects at Troas; he asks that these be forwarded. He is replacing Titus as bishop in Crete by either Tychicus or Artemas, and Titus is to report to Paul in Nicopolis, where he plans to winter. In 2 Timothy he bids his correspondent to hurry to him in Rome before winter puts an end to sailing. He is to bring Mark—Paul's rift with Mark reported in Acts 15:37–39 is pictured as closed. It is possible that the author drew these details from letters of Paul no longer extant. Whether they represent fact or are plausible fabrications, their verisimilitude is striking.

The author's criteria for church officials show eminent practical sense; in spite of changes in society since his day, many are still valid. That these leaders should be men of good moral reputation is obvious. Candidates for the bishopric must also be married, abstemious in use of wine, prudent, orderly in conduct, hospitable, good teachers, peaceable, generous, long suffering, and patient. They must govern their households and family conscientiously (if a man cannot control his own family, how can he direct the Church?) They shall not be recent converts, for such sudden elevation may generate deadly pride. Since each will be head of the Church in his area, he must bear a good reputation among non-Christians. Similar requirements hedge the eldership as well.

Deacons must possess some of the elders' qualities. They must be carefully examined about their handling of money. They must be married and must manage their households well. A surprisingly shrewd injunction follows: the deacon's wife must be serious minded, dependable, and not a gossip. An irresponsible woman who knows which members receive assistance from the Church could stir up endless bickering if she gossiped about these matters.

Financial problems loom large in the Church. The major problem in this area was apparently support of indigent members. The Church then as now evidently suffered from chiselers. Widows and orphans were left by relatives to the support of the congregation. The Church must enjoin upon pecuniarily able relatives that they must assume this responsibility. Young widows in particular had to be protected, for the sole means of support open to an unmarried woman was then prostitution. The Church must see to it that they remarry. Widows of sixty years and over are to be employed as lay assistants to the clergy. In such matters, the Church was pioneering in humanitarian concerns.

Both letters to Timothy urge the young bishop to vigorously oppose dangerous heresy within the Church. Although the author does not describe its nature, it was evidently Gnostic. The Church is to stand firm in Paul's teaching. To stand firm is not, as some commentators have assumed, to stand pat, to conserve without development. Paul had himself urged his readers to grow in the knowledge of Christ, and had admitted that he had not attained to its fullness (Phil. 3:10–14). He had also warned his readers (Rom. 16:17) to avoid those who caused division by heterodox doctrine. The writer of the Pastorals was simply following Paul's warning against the wolves who creep into the fold. He was not writing a treatise on faith, but advising on correctly handling immediate problems.

By the second century the Church was known as a vigorous minority movement. Many new movements wished to unite with it while preserving their own peculiar doctrines. Orthodoxy ran some danger of being swamped in these waves of alien ideas. To keep itself above water and intact, the Church had to maintain fiercely its own doctrines. It had to concern itself with holding its position rather than with developing its beliefs. Progress, however, sometimes results from such a contest.

The writer of the Pastorals realized that the Church was an outgrowth of both Hebrew and Hellenistic thinking and cultures. Occupying a position between these two, it had to ward off combinations of the two as well as extremists from both flanks. More than one set of ideas was probably arrayed against orthodoxy, but apparently all were Gnostic in their approach. The "fables" referred to in Titus 1:14 and the "endless genealogies" mentioned in 1 Timothy 1:4 apparently stem from chiefly Jewish origins. From both sides came a magical strain: the "evil men" mentioned in 2 Timothy 3:13 are *goētai* ("sorcerers").

Paul considered the faith practically, as a redeemed life; these heretics were concerned with a speculative philosophy. Such teaching is "vain [i.e., empty] jangling," "profane and vain babblings," "foolish and unlearned questions," a following after novelty by men with "itching ears" open to anything strange. They listen to "unruly and vain talkers and deceivers," who are "deceiving, and themselves deceived." They teach a knowledge "falsely so called" (*gnōsis*, which the KJV translates "science," is the special knowledge claimed by the Gnostics). The writer would have men keep in mind that "Jesus came into the world to save sinners" (1 Tim. 1:15), not to teach a misty philosophy. Christianity offers a practical goal, the attainment of eternal life.

Timothy and Titus are to concentrate their effort on teaching "the things which become sound doctrine," not on confuting Gnostic teachers. The surest way to maintain the true faith is to see that it is practiced without restraint. The Church occupies a strong position impregnable to attack so long as its members stand fast by the principles received by Paul from Jesus. Do not fight the enemy on a field of his choosing.

The author's talents are clearly not literary. The lack of order in these letters may possibly be excused by the informality of the epistolary genre. But the writer uses words as a rule simply to denote his meaning, rarely to illuminate it through imagery or telling figures. He appears to be unaware of the imaginative suggestiveness latent in words as the apostle used them. His metaphors are generally dead. He is earnest, intelligent, honest, and single-minded. He states concisely what is on his mind. He understands the problems facing the Church and has workable solutions for them. One can visualize the apostle as offering like suggestions in like circumstances, but Paul's advice was accompanied by principles accounting for it. This author simply states his directives. If, as Buffon declared, the style is the man, someone other than Paul composed these letters.

CHAPTER 9

THE GENERAL EPISTLES

The eight letters in this group have received the common designation of "general" (*katholikai*) because they are not addressed to individuals or readily definable regions. The sole exception, 3 John, which is addressed to someone named Gaius, was included here from its association with 1 and 2 John. Such other addresses are probably symbolical. The letters are of various authorship and probable date.

HEBREWS

Hebrews is unique among New Testament letters in bearing no address whatsoever. It begins like a treatise, but it concludes with personal messages like a letter. Such messages presume an addressee, but none is indicated. Outside the New Testament, its lack of address parallels that of 4 Maccabees in the Apocrypha and Barnabas and 2 Clement among the writings of the apostolic fathers. It shares with Luke and 1 John a carefully constructed rhetorical opening sentence such as letters seldom display. It is, in fact, so like a treatise that doubts have been expressed that chapter 12 with its messages was originally a part of it. Most scholars prefer to class it as a letter and to accept it as *sui generis*.

The title "To the Hebrews," which appeared as early as the second century A.D., was probably derived from its emphasis upon Jewish parallels and from the need for the reader to know a great deal about Judaism. The content does not otherwise warrant such a narrowing of readers. There exists no evidence that the Church did not include members versed in Jewish literature. In fact, the existence of the letter and its survival are proofs that readers in the Church were competent to follow its argument.

The date of Hebrews is nowhere clearly indicated. Its writer was a second-generation Christian who had received the gospel from men who had heard Christ (2:3). Since he wrote as a teacher, his readers were probably of the third or even fourth generation. He was concerned that the first flush of Christian enthusiasm had faded —another indication that the apostolic age had passed. Such indications point to composition fairly late in the first century. Hebrews was extensively quoted in 1 Clement (c. A.D. 96), an indication that it had already gained some acceptance. Internal evidence suggests that it was composed in anticipation of the persecutions under Domitian, who was Caesar A.D. 81–96. Its date presumably falls some two or three decades after Paul's death.

Its authorship was extensively debated in antiquity. Barnabas, Apollos, Aquila and Priscilla, Silas, Philip the deacon, Timothy, and Luke were suggested as its authors. Alexandrian scholars argued on internal grounds that Paul could not have written it. After the Roman church had begun to dominate in Christian affairs, Hebrews was authoritatively ascribed to Paul, and it is so classed in the Vulgate. Modern scholarship almost unanimously denies Paul's authorship and considers the writer of Hebrews to be anonymous.

The author's mind followed patterns quite unlike Paul's. Although his thought does not contradict that of the other New Testament writers, his emphasis upon Jesus as both final sacrifice and high priest is unique in this collection. The writer apparently took the principles in the Gospels and in Paul's letters as matters already established and built his argument upon them as a basis (6:1, cf. the translations of the RSV and NEB). It is not difficult to visualize him as a Jewish Christian teacher writing to readers deeply versed in the Old Testament and Apocryphal writings and receptive of their allegorical interpretation. Although he felt the need to correct a tendency in them to backslide into Judaism, his purpose was chiefly constructive.

His initial sentence reminds one in its length and structure of that in Luke. He presumably had in mind readers of an intellectual stature comparable to Luke's, but with a pervasive Jewish awareness along with their Hellenistic competence. The rhetorically constructed involutions of verses 1–4 would appeal to the trained Hellenist. Read in Greek and aloud, the passage immediately strikes the ear in the first verse with the alliteration of the plosive sound of *pi*. Five of the first eight words begin with *pi*. This alliteration continues in two words of verse 2 and three words of verse 3. Ten of the first sixty words begin with it, in one instance with the still more explosive *phi* (in Greek pronounced as a more forcible "p," not as "f"). Verse 1 is introduced by two resonant adverbs parallel in length and form: *polymerōs* and *polytropōs*. The whole sentence is basically periodic. In its subordinated phrases and clauses it indicates the major themes later to be discussed, thus almost subliminally suggesting them from the start.

Two comments need to be interposed here. First, the author's thought deals with priestly and sacrificial matters fairly familiar to his readers but alien to modern interests. These tend to shadow for us his logical reasoning. Second, he proceeds at times by association rather than by logical succession of ideas. The effect of the first sentence has already been mentioned. One idea may lead to another barely indicated there but used later. For example, after developing the concept of the superiority of Christian revelation to Mosaic law, he interpolated a warning. If those who disobeyed the Mosaic law perished in the wilderness, how much more serious is it to backslide from our profession of faith. This interruption in his argument is an idea which he interjects here but treats later.

The high level of style is maintained throughout the letter. Resonant words are carefully arranged to produce effective emphasis. The writer forcefully and frequently cited the Septuagint in support of his argument. To ensure the reader's notice of transition in argument, the word *therefore* is prominently inserted. He occasionally used words so rare in Koine Greek as to suggest that he may have coined them. Rhetorical question and answer appear on every page. Anaphora, alliteration, and accumulation effectively enforce his eloquent catalog in chapter 11. (Such devices can only rarely be satisfactorily reproduced in a translation.) The author shows mastery of the techniques of persuasive writing.

In conformity with his technique of suggestion, the author introduced his argument (4:14) in a subordinate participial phrase to substantiate an exhortation to stand by the faith: "Seeing then that we have a great high priest, that is passed into the heavens, Jesus Christ the Son of God . . . ." This concept was left to rest in the reader's mind for four chapters before he restated it (8:1–2) as his "head point" *(kephalaion)*: "We have such an high priest . . . ." To demonstrate this conclusion, he treated allegorically material from the Torah.

The author envisioned a two-story universe, in which the real existence is on the upper ideal plane. Of this the earthly plane is the symbol. This idea, familiar to American readers of Emerson's "Self-Reliance," came to the first century A.D. from Plato's diagram of the visible and intelligible world (*Republic* 595 C–E, 598 A). It had become a commonplace of first-century thinking, illustrated in Philo of Alexandria. Another echo of Plato, as first-century Hellenists would read it, is the writer's statement that the Mosaic law was "a shadow of good things to come" (10:1). It belongs with Plato's myth of the cave (*Republic* 514 E ff.). It had already gained a foothold in Christian expression in the letters of Paul (cf. 2 Cor. 4:18).

Less familiar to modern readers is the author's concept of priesthood and sacrifice. In the ancient world generally, sacrificial atonement for wrongdoing involved the shedding of blood as a symbolic substitute for the *lex talionis,* the right to retaliate in kind. Jewish religion involved the shedding of blood as acceptable worship of God, as the story of Cain and Abel symbolizes (Gen. 4:3–5). Even after the destruction of the Temple in A.D. 70, the laws of sacrifice continued to be an integral part of Jewish religious study. However repellent the subject may be to us, the author was here handling a matter of great moment to readers versed in Jewish law.

The Mosaic law of sacrifice, the author reminded his readers, came through angels and through Moses, who codified it. Moses' human limitations made his an imperfect revelation, a shadow of that to come through Christ. Jewish sacrifice, in atonement for sin, did not let a man enter into spiritual rest (3:11), for he must regularly repeat the sacrifice. This failure to attain the peace of God was due in part to the officiating priest's being a fallible human being. But Jesus the Son of God is the "great high priest" who officiates in heaven with God himself. Although as man he was "in every respect tempted as we are," he is sinless. He is paradoxically both priest and sacrifice. In his latter function he once and for all satisfied man's need for an atoning sacrifice.

The stickler for Jewish law might object that Jesus did not qualify as a priest. The priests were descendants of Aaron of the tribe of Levi, whereas Jesus came from Judah. The writer countered with a quotation from Psalm 110, which was taken allegorically to refer to the Messiah: "Thou art a priest for ever after the order of Melchizedek." Jesus as Messiah was not of the Aaronic priesthood at all.

The mythical Melchizedek provided a fertile field for Jewish speculation; both Philo and the Talmud treated of him. This priest-king of Jerusalem, as Genesis 14:17–20 relates, antedated by several centuries the institution of the Jewish law at Sinai. By giving him tithes of his booty taken in battle, Abraham indicated Melchizedek's superiority to him and, by implication, to all his descendants. Melchizedek, moreover, in being without genealogy foreshadows the priesthood of Christ, for he "abideth a priest continually," that is, without beginning or end. Ancient readers would consider this a valid argument in the case.

To clinch his argument, the author cited Jeremiah 31:31–34. The prophet here proclaimed a new covenant that, unlike the covenant of Sinai, cannot be degraded to a mere code of conduct but will be in the hearts of all men, not of Jews alone. This promised covenant, the author pointed out, clearly indicated that the former one was now passé; and "that which decayeth and waxeth old is ready to vanish away" (8:13). It need no longer concern men.

The author made clever use of ambiguity. *Diathēkē,* the Greek word for "covenant," signifies also a "last will and testament." Since a will becomes effective only at the death of the testator, he noted, Jesus' death made his atoning gift available to men. The blood sacrifices with which the Sinai covenant was ratified (Exod. 24:6–8), he added, foreshadowed the final blood sacrifice of Jesus which brought to an end this symbolic foreshadowing.

The remainder of Hebrews (10:19–end) is chiefly exhortation to readers to "hold fast the profession of our faith without wavering" (10:23). It is generally encouraging rather than censorious. The author recalled to them their patient, even joyful endurance of past "reproaches and afflictions" and, like Paul, reminded them of Habakkuk's declaration (2:4) that the just man shall live by his faith.

In the eleventh chapter, the best-known to modern readers, the author constructed an eloquent rhetorical pattern designed to move his readers to act on their assured faith. The pattern is best appreciated when read aloud, as the author meant it to reach his audience. The devices used are combined anaphora, alliteration, and accumulation. The anaphora consists in repetition of the phrase "by faith." In Greek this is a single explosive word, *pistei*. Repeated eighteen times, it alliteratively masses in the account many of the renowned and famous in Jewish history whose faith had produced right action.

The writer skillfully avoided overdoing the effect of his figures. After defining the concept of faith, he listed six instances, one referring to the Jewish belief in the divine act of Creation and the others adducing from Genesis men of outstanding faith when evidence was scant: Abel, Enoch, Noah, Abraham, and Sarah. (The KJV, fearing excessive alliteration, alters verse 11 to read "through faith"; no such fear was in the author's mind.) After the first two, he broke the iteration with a comment on the need of faith. The first three and Sarah receive one verse each; Abraham, three, as befitted his significant faith. So far the pattern of anaphora has been unobtrusive. The author did not wish to arrive at his full effect prematurely. Isaac, Jacob, and Joseph each receive one verse. Moses properly receives seven verses, with a list of his faithful acts. After Moses the items become more varied. The Hebrews as a body cross the Jordan and co-operate in the destruction of Jericho. Surprisingly, Rahab the harlot enters the list. Thereafter, the author lumped together in a rhetorical question individuals and groups until in a climactic moment he called them a cloud of witnesses (12:1) who even now surrounded the Christians to behold their achievement. All these, he added, sought a country, a kingdom, not attainable until Jesus gave entry into it; yet they did not waver in their purpose. It is up to us, with our clearer knowledge of God's plan, to fulfill their faith.

Skillful grouping of items in his catalog produces an overwhelming accumulation. The interspersed comments interrupt the iteration sufficiently to dispel any danger of monotony without lessening the pressure of multitude. The reader, as Longinus wrote, is overwhelmed by the combined figures and moved to acceptance of the argument which has previously been presented.

The author felt constrained to define his use of the term *faith.* To do so, he resorted to a metaphor which, though no doubt specific to his readers, no longer conveys a clear image. The word *hypostasis,* translated in the KJV (11:1), as "substance" and "evidence," basically means something underlying something else. (The KJV in using "substance" anglicized the Latin *substantia,* which literally translates *hypostasis.*) From its basic meaning, *hypostasis* could mean various things, from the sediment in a jar of liquid to the substructure of a building. Precisely which of its many meanings the author had in mind cannot now be determined.

One intriguing image conveyed by the term appears in the Oxyrhynchus papyrus (CCXXXVII vii.26), which was written at about the time of Hebrews. In it *hypostasis* means a title deed to property. According to this image, faith gives a clear title to the unseen "real" estate that is eternal. Lack of knowledge about the Koine, however, should not permit a tempting hypothesis to harden into a conviction.

Under the influence of the rhetorical *tour de force* in chapter 11, the reader is in a state of ecstasy (*ekstasis,* as Longinus called it)—the Greek word means literally getting out of a place where one is. In our century I. A. Richards saw the parallel poetic experience as producing action or readiness for action in the person "moved"; in Hebrews the intent was to produce both. The author introduced his appeal with a thundering "wherefore," using the sonorous

Greek *toigaroun* instead of the customary mild *oun*. He pictured the Christian as running in a stadium crowded with his "cloud of witnesses." The contest must be run by a racer who has shed every weight of sin and has the stamina to finish it. In order to win he must, as successful runners do, fix his eye on the goal, Jesus.

Once more (12:2) the translators face a dilemma. The author called Jesus the *archēgos* of faith, a word of many images. In despair the KJV settled for the colorless "author"; the RSV more picturesquely translates it "pioneer." Other meanings of *archēgos* included "founder" or "tutelary genius of a religious cult," "chief captain," "leader," or, less concretely, "first cause." The author, who was skilled at suggesting connotations as an artist in words must be, conceivably intended here to stir the speculative imagination of his readers by the ambiguity.

Besides the continuous grind of the lifelong race, the Christian must be ready for moments of special testing. The author shifts his metaphor (12:3-4) to resistance under attack. They have *not yet* resisted unto bloodshed, but the negative is itself a warning. Immediately he shifts the metaphor to the picture of a father wisely disciplining his sons. If he should neglect to do so, it would indicate that they are bastards, not sons in whom he takes affectionate interest and concern. In thus using three metaphors of one situation, the author followed what was evidently a common practice among rhetoricians.

The author added that those who act in faith will not cause friction within the Church. To develop this idea, he resorted to the enmity between Jacob and Esau (Gen. 25:29–34) and its consequences. Esau, who stood in line for the birthright from Isaac, thoughtlessly yielded it to Jacob and could not regain it. Those who backslide from the faith are a "root of bitterness" in the Church. This phrase, drawn from Deuteronomy 29:18, refers there to those who might introduce alien belief among the people of God.

Associated ideas once again control the author. The reference to Esau and to paganism recalled the picture of Israel in Hosea (4:12) as a wife deserting her husband Jahweh to go "awhoring from under her God." (Infidelity was the image used by the prophets for idolatry.) The contrast between the terrifying events at Sinai (Exod. 19:16, Deut. 9:19) and the delectable expectation of the heavenly country (11:14–16) suggested itself to him. The terrors of the Law could not keep the Jews from sinning, but the Christian is supported by an enthralling vision of "the city of the living God" (12:22) so that he remains true to his faith. The Judge in that city is "a consuming fire" to sinners, but with Jesus present as mediator those who do not backslide escape burning.

Backsliders occupied the author in his next image. In 12:10–15 he contrasted the new worship with that of the Tabernacle. In the Jewish ritual the bodies of sacrificial animals were burned outside the Hebrew camp (Lev. 16:27). This practice foreshadowed the crucifixion of Jesus "without the gate" of Jerusalem. If a man returns to the rites which foreshadowed Jesus, he thereby denies Jesus as having fulfilled them. This involved parallel is quite in keeping with the author's previous parallels. However inadequate it may seem to us, it was valid for the first century.

Admittedly, the modern reader finds the terms of the author's argument puzzling, partly because they are alien to his thinking. Once acquainted with the author's milieu and having absorbed his habit of thought, the reader finds himself rewarded by this masterly defense of the Christian faith. Although more closely attuned to Paul's thinking, modern readers ought not ignore the remarkable performance by the author of Hebrews. To work through it is to widen one's horizon on the varied scene of first-century Christianity.

JAMES

James sailed a stormy course before entering the haven of the New Testament canon. Origen's notation that it was "currently reported as by James" and Eusebius' calling it a disputed book "said to be by James" imply uncertainty about its author. Its canonicity for the Greek church was strengthened by the Easter letter of Athanasius (A.D. 367), which listed it without reservation as Scripture. In the Latin church its first extant mention occurred about the middle of the fourth century, but it was listed among tracts rather than in what was coming to be considered the canon. Around the end of this century, Jerome included it in the Vulgate, and shortly thereafter Augustine gave it the strong support of his acceptance as canonical.

Origen and Eusebius, without expressly stating it, appear to ascribe the letter to James the brother of Jesus. The first mention of it in Latin writing, noted above, assigns it to James the son of Zebedee. Jerome felt it to be pseudonymous. Augustine believed it to have been written by the brother of Jesus, and this ascription became the standard position of the Church for many centuries.

Modern scholars have found this ascription difficult to accept. Why, they ask, did the writer sign his name simply as, "a slave of God and of Lord Jesus Christ"? His letter would have gained great prestige if he had stated that he was the brother of Jesus and head of the church in Jerusalem. They also ask, How could a Galilean peasant have written such competent Koine Greek? Until at least the mid-fifties in the first century, James served as leader of the Jewish wing of the Church, a position which presumably did not require in him any skill in Greek. He, no doubt, had learned through practical experience the rhetorical devices used in this letter. But its writer uses some metaphors which seem to indicate knowledge of classical Greek prose as well. It is doubtful that the ideas used in some of his metaphors were still familiar to average readers in the first century. Even if they were, it is unlikely that this apostle would have known them. If James sent this letter, as he may well have done, one feels obliged to posit a man versed in Greek culture and with some knowledge of Greek tradition who composed it for him. Such a ghost-writer is not to be ruled out.

As the late William Barclay remarked, evidence for and against James's authorship balances so closely that a categorical judgment here is impossible. Whatever preponderance may exist weighs against his having personally composed it, though not against his having employed a ghost-writer.

The letter is directed to the twelve tribes in the Diaspora, ostensibly the Jews outside Palestine. Since both tone and content fit a letter directed to Christians, the address is clearly figurative. Seven hundred years earlier, with the fall of the Northern Kingdom, ten of the tribes had disappeared, assimilated by the peoples in the Assyrian Empire. Moreover, if it had been actually addressed to Jews, its entry into the canon would almost certainly have been denied. As Paul had demonstrated in Romans, and had doubtless been previously asserting, Christians could consider the Church as the genuine Israel. The term *Diaspora* ("people living outside their homeland") could also refer metaphorically to all Christians, who were citizens of the heavenly country and aliens in this world's life. Thus considered, the letter is a catholic or general epistle to all Christians.

There is evidence that James was executed in A.D. 62. If someone composed it out of his ideas, it could have been written somewhat later. Its exhortation to endure persecution lends some likelihood that it refers to a major persecution. The first one known occurred in Rome in A.D. 64–65. Whether this persecution spread to the provinces is not known, but its emergence in Rome undoubtedly made Christians apprehensive everywhere. It is possible, however, that the idea could have stemmed from James's own experiences under Jewish persecution in Jerusalem. Dating the letter is as insoluble a problem as determining its author.

The literary style of the letter shows characteristics common to both Jewish and Gentile teaching. Its rapid shift of subject was characteristic of rabbinical teaching in the first century. These teachers never dwelt long upon one topic but varied their themes so as to touch as many interests as possible. Such teaching was described as stringing pearls on a thread; the matters in a skilled teacher's discourse often had a central purpose. The so-called Sermon on the Mount in Matthew is of this genre. Such brief comment was also characteristic of Hellenistic philosophical teaching. The Stoics in particular had developed such a form of teaching in the marketplaces, where the constant ebb and flow of traffic dictated brief, pungent discussion or statement. A century earlier, Horace had combined it with earlier Roman forms in his *Satires* and *Epistles*. James is in form quite like the Stoic *parainesis*, exhortation to virtue and attack on loose living or irreligious conduct.

The indecisive evidence so far cited leaves linguistic evidence as the best clue to the man who wrote the letter. It is hardly conceivable, as already noted, that such fluency in Greek could have been attained by a Galilean. The letter could have been roughed out by a man like James, but he could hardly have composed it. The writer had available in the storehouse of Greek rhetoric the technique of *ēthopoiia,* through which he could reproduce James's mannerisms and habit of thought, but he could have added touches impossible for James himself while polishing it.

The suggestion of earlier Greek traces in James requires some amplification. It assumes a ghost-writer who used the Koine with facility but knew also the classical writers in Greek. Something of this earlier culture would unconsciously color what he wrote; for example, his words might at times carry classical overtones of meaning. This influence seems especially probable when the classical use of a word adds a pertinent figurative sense to what he has written. In interpreting modern literature one feels justified in indicating possible earlier literary relations; why should not the same practice apply to the New Testament? Once one has seen that many of the books were not composed by the men whose names they bear, such interpretation becomes valid.

A few instances from James will prove illuminating. In 1:3 one reads, "The trying of your faith worketh patience." *Dokimion,* "trying" ("testing" in the RSV), suggests the term *dokimasia,* the scrutiny which an Athenian candidate had to pass before running for office and at the end of his year of service if elected.[1] In verse 4, *holoklēroi,* "entire" ("complete" in the RSV), relates to *klēros,* which from Homer's day through the classical era had referred to one's share in an estate or to the plot of land offered as inducement to settle in a new colony. In James's day it often referred to physical soundness, but it had a number of specific meanings in common use, for example, the allotment made to a Roman legionary upon his retirement. A third such overtone is in verse 17, in which "variableness" and "shadow [cast] by turning" are astronomical terms.

[1] Lysias, the master of *ethopoiia,* had written a well-known speech for a young official on the latter occasion.

Parallagē ("variableness") is our astronomical term *parallax*. Such instances beyond James's probable scope are numerous.

The main tenor of the letter is couched in familiar, earthy, everyday terms. Its images are designed to clarify rather than to adorn. In 1:14 one sees a fish attracted by a lure and inexorably drawn in by the line. The next verse shifts to conception and birth. Desire becomes pregnant and gives birth to sin, which in its turn comes to term and brings forth death. In 3:1–12 there is a riot of images. The bit in a horse's mouth directs his huge body. The rudder of a ship steers its bulk. A well-bridled tongue controls the entire body. But what a forest fire starts from such a little spark as an unbridled tongue! Man can tame the universe of living things, but not his tongue; it is an uncontrollable evil, a vial of deadly poison.

James is at times colloquially informal; one is tempted to translate it on this level. Such colloquial style is impressive in 2:14–26: "What's the use [*ti ophelos* literally translated] if a man says he has faith but doesn't have works? His faith can't save him, can it? . . . Suppose a brother or sister Christian be bare and hungry, and you say, 'Bless you, keep warm and eat well,' but give him nothing he needs. What's the use? . . . You believe there is one God. Great! So do the devils—and it scares the wits out of them!"

Short ethical comments lead at times to tersely stated principles. One can recast 2:26 into a proportional metaphor: Spirit (i.e., breath) is to the body as faith is to works. A body without breath is dead; actions without spiritual faith are likewise dead. Granted; but where is faith without material embodiment in action?[2]

James admirably presents to the man in the street Christian principle and practice on a level he can readily grasp. It appeals to him more than a discussion by Paul. One can understand why theologians in the early Christian centuries hesitated to include it in the canon, for it was far different stylistically and linguistically, as well as logically, from the norm they had set up of Paul's letters. Looked at as popular expression of religious faith and practice, it is

[2] Luther, in his zeal for justification by faith, felt that James contradicted it, and called it "an epistle of straw." Far from contradicting Paul, as Luther thought, James actually supports him.

a masterpiece. Considered for religious content, it is in basic agreement with the other canonical books.

1 PETER

The authorship and date of 1 Peter are also debated. It is unlikely that Peter lived beyond the seventh decade of the first century A.D. If he did not write it, the date could be some three decades after his death, when a quotation from it appears in the Epistle of Barnabas (c. A.D. 95). Polycarp's brief Letter to the Philippians (c. A.D. 110) cites it ten times. Neither names the author. Irenaeus (c. A.D. 185) declared it to be by Peter. In the fourth century Eusebius, Jerome, and Augustine accepted it as by Peter. It was not, however, listed in the second-century Muratorian canon.

Supporters of Peter's authorship point to the author's intense interest in the imminent Parousia, a hope that dimmed as the century waned. They note also the simple Church government indicated in the letter: elders alone are mentioned. A third and stronger argument is in its conformity with the simple theology of the primitive Church: it fits the content of the *kērygma* presented in Acts.

Against Peter's authorship one strong argument is the superior quality of language and composition. Like James he could hardly have shown such literary mastery. A second objection is historical. The persecution implied as coming in 4:12–16 could not have happened, it is claimed, in Peter's day; the earliest-known mention of Christianity as a proscribed religion is in Pliny's correspondence with Trajan (c. A.D. 112). A third objection is that Peter could hardly have read Romans and Ephesians, to which 1 Peter is clearly indebted. Finally, Peter would surely have signed his letter as an apostle and not merely as an elder.

Defenders of Peter's authorship counter with the charge that Pliny's correspondence cannot be used to date the proscription of Christianity, it does not tell when the Church became outlawed. This status could have been implicit as soon as Judaism and Christianity were known to be different religions. As to the debt to Paul's epistles, Paul's ideas were, no doubt, widespread through his teaching and available to Peter from reports of his words. As to his calling himself simply an elder, he directed part of his letter (5:1–11) to elders. It was tactful to so designate himself without any higher claim.

Archibald Hunter has proposed a solution for the vexing question of who wrote 1 Peter. The credit given to Silvanus (5:12), he believes, indicates more than mere thanks to an amanuensis. In the Greek phrase referring to him, *dia Silouanou,* the preposition *dia* ("through") indicates assistance through active participation (cf. 2 Cor. 1:19, where it expresses agency). This Silvanus is almost certainly Paul's companion on his second journey (Acts uses his Jewish name Silas). Paul had found him congenial as a scholar who knew both the Jewish and Hellenistic worlds. He could readily express Peter's message in a style far superior to that characteristic of Peter; the special mention of him is probably inserted to account for the style to readers of 1 Peter. Incidentally, Silvanus could be the source of Peter's acquaintance with Paul's letters which has troubled many scholars. I have enlarged Hunter's hypothesis to apply to other books of the New Testament.

The nonevangelistic, literary style of 1 Peter strikes one with the first two sentences. In Greek, the first sentence contains thirty-two words, the second, fifty-four. Careful attention to 1:3–12 reveals that it is a continuous expression of a thought, essentially a single sentence by English principles. The KJV converted relative clauses into separate sentences while retaining the relative pronouns to show their close relation, as Milton was later to do in his essays. The passage illustrates the loose or running style of discourse which, though frowned on by Aristotle (*Rhetoric* III.9), is, nonetheless, well known in Greek prose. It tends to linger on a subject, piling up supplementary ideas. Such presentation of ideas, perhaps out of deference by Silvanus to Peter's rambling style, is characteristic of the letter as a whole.

Like James the author presents vivid images from daily life. The Christian's inheritance (1:4) is a *klēronomia,* a term used to describe the share of land given to the discharged Roman legionary who settled in a frontier region. It cannot be ravaged by enemies (*aphtharton*), nor defiled by impious conduct of others (*amianton*), nor caused to fade like a cut flower (*amaranton*)—all unattainable security for earthly property. Shortly after this the author in a metaphor like Jeremiah's (4:4) bade his readers to gird up the loins of their minds (1:13). The image is familiar to readers of Roman comedy: a man loops his long robe through his belt preparatory to running. They are (2:1–2) to disrobe themselves of "all malice, and all guile, and hypocrisies, and envies, and all evil speakings" (note the accumulation). Like newborn babes they are to yearn for the unadulterated spiritual milk of the Word. Through this food they are to grow (2:4) into stones for the edifice of God's temple. This bewildering aggregation of images, nonetheless, vividly conveys the author's intent.

The author continues his associative procedure. The image of the Christian as a building stone stems naturally from remembrance of Psalm 118:22, in which Christ is seen as the head cornerstone rejected by previous builders. A related image, from Isaiah 28:15, bids the scornful men in Jerusalem to look upon God's choice stone: whoever believes in Him will not be ashamed for having done so. (One can suspect the enjoyment with which Silvanus wrote this passage in a letter to be signed by Simon Peter, "the rock.")

The author provided practical advice about the Christian's conduct in a pagan society. He is to accept every social institution although he is himself a citizen of the heavenly kingdom. So far as his loyalty to that kingdom allows, he is to obey Caesar and the governors sent to preserve law and order. He is to respect all men, love the Christian brotherhood, and stand in obedient awe of God. His upright life is to quash all slanders against the Church. The principle governing his conduct is the imitation of Christ.

With respect to treatment of slaves, Peter's advice parallels Paul's. He adds some details to Paul's advice on the family. A pagan husband may be attracted to the Church by his Christian wife's chaste conduct and modest dress and adornment. Her true inner ornament is a gentle, quiet spirit like that of Sarah in obedience to Abraham—a startling characterization of her to the modern reader, who sees her in Genesis as the proverbial domineering Jewish mamma. Right conduct in the family leads to right conduct in the Christian community as a whole.

First Peter concludes with an appeal to elders (5:1–5). Remembering Jesus' thrice-repeated injunction to him (John 21:15–17), Peter admonishes them to tend God's flock like shepherds. They should act for the flock's benefit with no gain to themselves. They are examples, not lords. Their reward will come when the chief Shepherd comes. Those who are younger—a gentle pun on the title "elder"—are humbly to submit to the elders as to God, who in due time will reward their obedience.

Readers of the Gospels and Acts will recognize in 1 Peter the characteristics of the apostle that made him a colorful, competent leader in the new faith. They show through the writing of Silvanus and make the letter a moving, earnest appeal.

2 PETER

The plausible claim with respect to the author of 1 Peter cannot be advanced for 2 Peter. The first extant mention of the latter was made by Origen in the third century; he doubted that Peter had written it. Eusebius a century later listed it among accepted letters but also expressed skepticism about its writer: "It is disputed but accepted by the majority" (*Ecclesiastical History* III.iii.1). Later in the same century Athanasius, Augustine, and the Council of Carthage accepted it as canonical. Jerome mentioned that many doubted Peter's authorship of this second letter, but he included it in the Vulgate under his name. Contemporary scholars almost as one man view it as written after Peter's era, during the second century.

One contemporary argument against Peter's authorship is the fact that the author knew the Gospels and all the extant letters of Paul. These letters, it is generally believed, were collected about A.D. 90, and the Gospels some thirty-five years later. The author of 2 Peter apparently assumes these to be available to his readers. Moreover, the heretical movements which he condemned were pressing problems of the second century. Its ascription to Peter was quite in accord, as we have seen, with ancient practice, and Peter was so designated as author of seven works in the New Testament Apocrypha.

The author defends orthodoxy in the face of rising Gnostic tides that were eroding the doctrines of the Church. For him God's teachings presented by Jesus and transmitted by the apostles provide the sole pattern for the faith. These fill out the Old Testament with deeper significance. Any other interpretation perverts these truths and leads to improper conduct.

For various reasons the new beliefs offered in the second century proved attractive to many Christians. They played upon the deep-seated worry in the Church on account of the delay in the Parousia. This, hoped for in the lifetime of men living at the ascension of Jesus, had not occurred in an entire century. This worry led to doubt of those orthodox doctrines as taught by men who had believed the Parousia to be imminent. A second reason was a perverted interpretation of Paul's declaration that Christians were not under the Law but under grace—one of the teachings which the author of 2 Peter apparently found hard to understand. Some of the weaker Christian brethren took this as permission for licentious conduct, and Gnostic separation of soul from body, as we have seen, supported this notion. A third reason for the attractiveness of the Gnostic beliefs lay in the excessively allegorical approach to Scripture which they fostered. Allegorical interpretation was well known to pagan and Jewish scholars, and Paul himself had on occasion employed it. The Gnostics carried the practice to extremes.

The fourth and principal reason why Gnosticism was attractive was the special knowledge (*gnōsis*) claimed by the individual Gnostic. This egotistic self-confidence, always a temptation to thinkers, made the Gnostic feel restive in the trammels, as they seemed to him, of orthodox guidelines. Like Emerson he could declare that thinkers and apostles had persuaded men for generations: "Now they must persuade me." The Gnostic relied on his own inner light and felt free to abandon the tenets of Christianity as seemed good to him. He accepted ideas like Paul's doctrine of salvation through faith without observing what this faith entailed in action. In particular, his Gnostic severance of spirit from matter led to the belief that what one did with his body had no effect upon his soul: he could act licentiously as suited his desires. When this freedom is added to the mumbo-jumbo of secret knowledge and to the feeling that this was "the last word" in religion, the trap was cleverly baited for unwary Christians.

Second Peter was written to combat such powerful enticements. The true faith, the author declared, is based on fact supported by eyewitnesses; it is not sophistically devised fables (*sesophismenois mythois,* 1:16). Speaking in his persona as Peter, the author had himself seen and heard Jesus reveal the facts of the faith. Revelation gave the apostles clearer insight into prophecy than comes to any man through his own misleading powers.

The letter was designed to appeal to readers of better-than-average capacity who could appreciate the arts of language. The author could handle complex sentences—by no means the first attainment in writing—and he used an appropriately forceful vocabulary. He enjoyed euphonious, mouth-filling words arranged with an ear to delivery *ore rotundo.* He used competently also rhetorical devices to strengthen his message.

Amplification (*auxēsis*) is used with telling effect in 1:5–7. Here the successive waves of Christian qualities are reinforced by anaphora. In Greek the use of postpositive *de* instead of *kai* for "and" gives the effect almost of asyndeton. The verb *epichoregeō* ("add"), used instead of the more common *prostithēmi,* referred to service to the state beyond the average. It was a sort of surtax imposed on men of means. Here, however, the "additions" are made of the Christian's own volition. Such added service to the state was called a *leitourgia,* a term appropriated by the Church to designate a liturgy, a formal religious performance. The combined figures with the metaphorical verb were the product of a skilled rhetorician.

The author shocked his readers by shifts in the level of his discourse, but they had been carefully prepared for. The attack on Gnostic antinomians in chapter 2 charged them with greed and unlawful sexual desire (literally, going after *miasmos,* something ritually defiling). They speak evil of angelic beings, thereby showing their brutish understanding. They are dirty spots on the table at religious feasts. They leer adulterously and lure unstable souls through avarice and lust. They are like Balaam, whose greed led him from the right path; he was so stupid that a dumb ass, wiser than he, had to correct him.

The author's fury at antinomian corrupters leads at times to confused expression by reason of the outpouring of metaphorical epithets that crowd his mind. They are dry wells offering refreshment but giving none. They are mists driven by a tempest, and this misty darkness of mind presages the darkness reserved for them in hell. Their fate is more dire because they have deliberately slipped from the way of truth. Like Dante's souls in torment, their punishment parallels their sin.

The author shifts abruptly from the eschatological to the earthy. Their conduct supports the old proverb (Prov. 26:11) about the dog that eats its own vomit. They are—the crowning Jewish insult —like the sow that has been washed but returned to her miry wallow. This sudden lowering to the repulsive nadir of earthly life would jolt his readers and still powerfully shakes us.

Although the author was clearly infuriated, the crowded and occasionally confused images of this chapter do not necessarily represent a corresponding state of mind. Greek rhetoricians at times wrote deliberately in apparent confusion of mind as an added token of the speaker's sincerity. Under stress of overwhelming emotion, it would seem, he would be less likely to be calculating his effects, even less likely to fabricate an ingenious lie.

The author struck also at the root of the sensuality, the Gnostics' denial of the Parousia. Prophets and apostles had predicted that precisely such a condition as this would precede the second coming of Christ. Scoffers who deny his coming simply fulfill the prophecy. Their attitude indicates the earthy level of their thoughts. Christians should remember the Psalm (90:4): "A thousand years in thy sight are but as yesterday when it is past." What seems delayed to man is at hand to God. The end will come unexpectedly, and just as Noah's world was drowned in water, this one will perish in fire.

One source of Gnostic error, the writer hinted, lay in careless reading of Paul's letters. Paul explained matters "according to the wisdom given unto him" (3:15)—the author preserved in this patronizing phrase something of the coolness between Paul and Peter. Paul's letters are hard to understand by minds not well informed or firmly grounded. These the Gnostics have misinterpreted.

Careful examination of 2 Peter makes it evident that the author knew the personality of Peter and created a credible persona of the apostle. If Peter had been living at the time, one feels, this is the kind of message he would have delivered. There is no attempt to reproduce the nonliterary qualities of Peter's style, which probably would not have appealed to his readers. After reading it in the light of its milieu, one can understand why the letter gained entry into the canon. It met the Church's needs in its own day, and has stood the test of time ever since.

1–3 JOHN

These three letters, 1–3 John, along with the Fourth Gospel and the Apocalypse, have been traditionally regarded as written by the apostle John. The strong improbability that he composed the Fourth Gospel has already been presented. The tradition that these three letters were written by John has been as hotly contested. There is linguistic evidence linking the Fourth Gospel with 1 John. Notable parallels in emphasis also exist between the two; both look upon love as the final proof of true faith, and 1 John 1:1–3 condenses John 1:1–14. Opponents rejoin that the belief in love as the test of faith is also in the synoptic Gospels and in Paul's letters. No one denies that the author of 1 John knew the Fourth Gospel. None of the letters contain the Old Testament citations which appear in the Fourth Gospel; but the eminently practical intent of the three letters would not have been served by such quotation. The letters do not show the argumentative and mystical veins of the Fourth Gospel; but again these are alien to the purpose of the letters. These samples show that evidence of relation to the Fourth Gospel is indecisive.

The second and third letters appear to have been written by an author who did not compose the first. They are signed by an "elder." According to a second-century author, Papias, cited by Eusebius, in

Papias' day the term *elder* often was applied to men who had received the gospel from auditors of Jesus himself. In some instances they were presumably appointed by an apostle to be overseers of Christian work in their areas—a sort of presiding elder. They had a degree of ruling authority over the churches in their respective regions. These letters, like 1–2 Timothy and Titus written at about the same time, were directed toward regularizing procedure in such supervision with reference to Gnostic heretical inroads. The three taken together form a manual for such elders.

The situation common to these three documents may be plausibly reconstructed. The faith transmitted from Jesus through the Gospels and promulgated by the elders was under vigorous attack through infiltration of Gnostic ideas into some congregations. Orthodoxy was based on the Christian position concisely stated in John 3:16: "God so loved the world that he gave his only begotten Son, that whosoever believeth in him should not perish, but have everlasting life." To effectuate this gift, "The Word was made flesh, and dwelt among us" (John 1:14). Gnostic teaching struck at this basic principle of the faith.

During the second Christian century a tendency developed in local congregations in Asia Minor to break away from central supervision. In such congregations an individual like the Diotrephes of 3 John could wrest control from the former congregational officials. The elder could not easily come to their rescue through regular channels after such usurpation. Gnostic ideas were attractive to many members for their novelty, their complex and intriguing allegorization, and the license which Gnosticism allowed.

Whatever their origin, these three letters treat this problem skillfully. First John lays down the principles of orthodoxy as far as they concern the current Gnostic problem. Jesus once assumed a human yet sinless body in order as God to atone for the sins of other men by his death on the cross. All who believe this and accept his gift are thereby saved from eternal death. The author stresses this dual nature in Jesus because Gnosticism utterly denied its possibility.

Jesus came also through baptism in water when the Holy Spirit descended upon him.[3] Orthodoxy, the writer proceeds, is attested on earth by three witnesses: the Holy Spirit, the water, and the blood of Christ. The latter two, as Amos Wilder has shown, represent baptism and the Lord's Supper, in which members symbolically drink of the blood of Christ. To put it bluntly, if one has the Son in him, he has eternal life; if not, he has not (5:11–12).

The second letter was addressed to a congregation whose members included some who were holding fast to the faith. Its address "to the elect lady," employed a not uncommon metaphor for a congregation and by its general reference addressed others in a like situation. Four times in the first four verses the word *truth* is iterated to emphasize reliance upon the basic gospel. The author repeats the old yet new injunction to love one another. The rift in the congregation must not become permanent.

Next come specific directions for proper treatment of those members infected with Gnostic ideas. First, the sources of infection are to be removed. The congregation should not entertain or even speak to any Gnostic "walking delegate" who might come to it. The outside influence being cut off, the congregation should be able to win back its errant members. Exposure to the pure gospel is the best antidote to heresy. The elder adds that he hopes to visit them soon to take further steps to aid them. The letter reads almost like a form letter for such cases.

The third letter is a specimen of advice in a specific instance of Gnostic infection. The elder enlists the aid of a nearby orthodox congregation as his first step in handling a recalcitrant congregation. He addresses this letter to someone named Gaius whose reputation for active service to the Church has been glowingly commended to him. Gaius has assisted envoys of the elder sent to various congregations. In one congregation, however, a man named Diotrephes has gained control, rejected the elder's jurisdiction, and refused to accept a letter from him. He has ejected emissaries from the elder to the congregation. The elder plans to come and settle the case in person when he can. Meanwhile, he commends to Gaius'

[3] Strong evidence rejects 1 John 5:7 as a gloss upon early Greek and Latin manuscripts. Recent translations omit it.

care the bearer of this letter, his emissary Demetrius. The elder hopes to come soon to discuss the case with Gaius.

Without asking Gaius specifically to interfere in the other congregation's affairs, which would have been impolitic, the elder is setting up a base of operations in the neighborhood and keeping other congregations informed of the situation. Diotrephes, he adds, is speaking a lot of pernicious nonsense, presumably Gnostic. By implication the letter suggests that Gaius take action as he sees fit to prepare for the elder's meeting with the recalcitrant congregation.

These three letters inform us of the state of the Church in the second century, of the Gnostic problem, and of practical handling of it. The restatement of Christian doctrine indicates the orthodox position of the Church proclaimed in the face of heresy. It is not surprising that these letters seemed as a group to merit inclusion in the canon, and to regularize their status, they were ascribed to the apostle John.

JUDE

Jude purports to have been written by the brother of James, the influential leader of the church in Jerusalem. This ascription gives the letter greater weight as being written by one who was also the brother of Jesus. Like James the letter modestly omits mention of any special position: he is "the servant of Jesus Christ, and the brother of James." This brief letter is all but embodied in expanded form in 2 Peter 2. As a rule, the more expanded version of a document is later than that document itself. The letter is accordingly dated slightly earlier than 2 Peter, quite early in the second century. Such a date all but precludes Jude's having himself written it. In verse 17, moreover, the author reminds his readers of the words previously spoken (*proeirēmenon*) by the apostles—a fairly sure dissociation of himself from the time of Christ.

Jude was listed in the Muratorian canon (c. A.D. 190), cited by Tertullian (A.D. 197), and, during the same period, quoted by Clement of Alexandria as written by Jude. Cassiodorus, in his sixth-century Latin translation of Clement, states that Clement believed its author to be the Jude who was "brother to the sons of Joseph." Eusebius (c. A.D. 325) objects to Jude as spurious. Athanasius (A.D. 367), however, listed it as one of the canonical catholic epistles. Jerome, though aware of the charge that Jude had cited the apocryphal *Book of Enoch,* agreed with Athanasius.

Jude was an early lay figure in the synoptic Gospel and the Acts. Why should so short a letter ascribed to him gain admission to the canon? Aside from its supposedly being written by a brother of Jesus, Albert Barnett offers the plausible reason that it must have made its way by virtue of its content. He contends correctly that most of the New Testament books were written to aid the Church during early crises in its history. The more serious the problem, the more likely the preservation of a book that ably treated it. Jude is a forceful, orthodox resolution of Gnostic attacks upon basic Christian doctrine.

The best antidote to Gnostic heresy, Jude asserts, is the faith of the apostles, the "faith . . . once delivered unto the saints" (v. 3). Deviation from these principles is retreat from the truth. Gnostic teachers are dreamers (*enhypniazomenoi*) who pollute the body and blaspheme the truly angelic powers with their talk of other superior beings. To defend the true faith, Christians should build up their own belief and guard their posts in confident expectation of the mercy of God (vv. 20–21). Gnostic heretics have evidently gained a foothold within the Church. Some of them have previously been true believers and are twice dead as the result of their lapse. The prophets foretold their coming. (In verses 14–15, Jude cites passages from the *Book of Enoch* with evidence from Isaiah and books of the New Testament.) The writer refers bitingly to the Gnostic denial of the true nature of Christ, their dreamy notions, their denial of authority, and their permission of sexual license and perversion.

He expresses his detestation of this heresy in violent metaphors. Its followers are wind clouds without water, blown by the blasts. They are trees without fruit in their season. They are the wandering stars of Enoch's vision, which God imprisoned in chaotic darkness for their refusal to rise at appointed time. (He calls them planets, *planētai,* not necessarily through ignorance of planetary orbit, which was known generally, but to contrast their seemingly erratic course with the circling of the fixed stars.)

Gnostics, he continues, follow a life on the level of brute beasts. They attend the love feasts of the Church, but only to stuff themselves shamelessly. They are dirty spots (*spilades*) on the white tablecloth of the Church. He employs ambiguity here with telling force: *spilades* are also submerged reefs that wreck unwary mariners. This second meaning, which suggests Isaiah's metaphor (57:20), is repeated in the description of the wicked as "raging waves of the sea, foaming out their own shame" (v.13), a summary of Isaiah's longer figure.

Although verses 22–23 show textual uncertainty in the manuscripts, both KJV and RSV translate them as advice on proper treatment of those infected with heretical doctrine. They fall into three categories, carefully distinguished in the Greek. Some who are merely disturbed by these doctrines, you may treat compassionately. Your sympathetic help should restore their faith. Others more seriously infected you may save by the shock of sudden reproof. It will shake them emotionally like a sudden escape from fire. The third group, more hardened in their error, you should pity but handle fearfully, trying not to befoul yourselves from their soiled garb of belief as you try to rescue them. These last presumably have gone so far as to practice that licentiousness which Gnosticism sanctions.

Jude subtly flatters its readers by assuming that its readers are aware of the situation. In so doing it escapes the danger of boring them with explanations. These readers would agree to his vigorous images of the heresy and recognize the skill displayed in his invective. Gnostic heresies would run their course in time, but the human weaknesses which had spawned them are innate in mankind. They would bring forth other errant ideas, and the advice of Jude would be repeatedly applicable and effective.

CHAPTER 10

THE APOCALYPSE OF JOHN

John the Baptist inaugurated a revival of Jewish prophecy that continued in the Christian movement for the rest of that century. The Acts and several Epistles testify to its presence in the new religion; prophets held a respected position among the possessors of special gifts. In the New Testament canon, however, the Apocalypse is the sole specifically prophetic book; it fittingly closes the collection with its encouragement to Christians and its optimistic insights into the future of the Church. The reader has been partly prepared for a major apocalypse by three passages in the Gospels, Matthew 24, Mark 13, and Luke 21, but they have nothing comparable to the sustained insights presented by the author of the Apocalypse.

The term *apocalypse* is generally defined as a prophetic disclosure or revelation. As a literary term, it refers to a class of allegory which is called "vision." It may start with a dream, as in Bunyan's *Pilgrim's Progress* and Cicero's Vision of Scipio in the sixth book of his fragmentary *Republic*. In the Apocalypse the narrator is "in the Spirit," in an ecstatic state in which he perceives visions unveiling the course of the suffering Church through its change into the Church Militant and its apotheosis as the Church Triumphant. Such a work is not unorganized like the dream, but possesses a ritualistic ordering of events; the author gains insights into the future working of the divine plan until its fruition in a new heaven and a new earth. Such insights reveal realms which eye hath not seen nor ear heard. The author consequently is obliged to present them through symbol instead of explicit statement. Discussion of the author's symbolism, its origins, nature, and use forms a major part of any treatment of the Apocalypse, and so other matters will be considered first.

The author of the book is not agreed upon by scholars. Although other names, including that of Mark, who was also called John, were mentioned in early Christian centuries, two candidates soon stood out: John the son of Zebedee, the apostle long accepted as author of the Fourth Gospel and three Epistles, and John the presbyter, or elder, of Ephesus. At both beginning and end of the work the writer names himself as John, and there seems to be no reason why he should have assumed a pseudonym. According to Henry Barclay Swete, John in its Hebrew form "Johanan," was a fairly common Jewish name following the sixth-century B.C. Hebrew captivity in Mesopotamia. The Old Testament mentions some fifteen bearers of that name, Josephus refers to seventeen, and the New Testament shows at least five.

In his *Ecclesiastical History* (VII.25) Eusebius quotes at length from the work *On Promises* by Dionysius of Alexandria, a pupil of Origen, what is perhaps the most detailed discussion of the authorship of the Apocalypse. After rejecting the assertion that the heretic Cerinthus was its author, he modestly adds that he does not presume to reject the Apocalypse simply because he cannot fathom every passage. He suspects that some deeper, more wonderful meaning underlies its enigmatic utterances and wisely does not judge such matters by the standard of his own capacities. "I do not refuse to accept what I have not comprehended." Dionysius then subjects the book to exhaustive linguistic examination and concludes that while the book is unquestionably written by a man named John, it cannot be John the apostle, whom he believes to have written the Fourth Gospel and the three Epistles. He adduces a variety of evidence. First, in his accepted works the apostle never claims his authorship by name as the writer does here, nor does he use here any of the periphrases used in the Gospel (e.g., "that disciple whom Jesus loved"), nor does he ever claim to have seen and heard Christ while He lived on earth. The writer identifies himself as a Christian brother who shares the trials and sufferings of his intended readers. Second, Dionysius notes that while the Fourth Gospel and the first

Johannine epistle have similar beginnings and many expressions in common, they are not noticeable in the Apocalypse. Third, he notes among stylistic differences the far superior Greek usage in the Gospel and the Epistles. Their author had both the word of knowledge and the word of speech. The writer of the Apocalypse as a prophet had the word of knowledge but was woefully deficient in the word of speech. Some of his words are barbarous and his constructions include outright solecisms. Dionysius, in short, presents the earliest extant critical treatment of style as a criterion of New Testament authorship.

Modern criticism has, on the whole, refused to accept the apostle's authorship of either the Fourth Gospel or the Epistles, and in so doing has undermined the basis from which Dionysius argued. It introduces the vague possibility that John the apostle died with his brother James in Herod's persecution in A.D. 43.[1]

Stronger support for the argument against Johannine authorship of the Apocalypse has followed that linguistic path indicated by Dionysius of Alexandria. Perhaps one of the most objective surveys is offered in a ten-page summary of the problem by Swete.[2] Swete reports that the book contains 871 Greek words exclusive of 51 proper names. Of these, 108 words—about one-eighth—are found only in the Apocalypse. Mark, which is slightly longer, shows about one-sixteenth of its words as peculiar to it. Comparison of the vocabulary of the Apocalypse with that of the Fourth Gospel is inconclusive about authorship. Both show, however, a number of peculiar constructions in common. In style, as Dionysius had asserted, the Fourth Gospel is far removed from the eccentricities and roughness of the Apocalypse. Taking the linguistic and stylistic characteristics of the Fourth Gospel and the Apocalypse as a whole, Swete finds the evidence of authorship to be inconclusive.

Swete and Austin Farrer, who have immersed themselves in the

[1] Evidence for this supposition comes from George Hamartolus, a ninth-century writer who says that Papias had made such a statement. The manuscripts of Acts do not support such a supposition, and commentators on the whole have received it skeptically.

[2] *The Apocalypse of St. John*, cxx–cxxx.

study of Johannine literature, agree in believing the whole of it to have been written by the apostle John. The intuitive awareness of such men, as August Boeckh declared, is itself evidence not to be ignored. Linguistic and stylistic differences are at least partly explicable on the difference in theme and literary genre between the Apocalypse and the other works ascribed to John. While I am strongly of the opinion that the apostolic authorship for any of the Johannine works is extremely doubtful, I am also strongly swayed by the intuitions of the two scholars mentioned to accept the possibility of common authorship for all five of these works.

The place from which the Apocalypse emanated was almost certainly some Christian center in the eastern third of Asia Minor, the Roman province of Asia. The Ephesian beginning of Christian work in Asia, and the outstanding position of that city, make Ephesus, which tradition claims as its origin, a highly probable site.

The date of the work must be settled partly from internal evidence, though nothing in it fixes dates as do certain references in the Acts. The situation described fits the reign of Domitian as Caesar, between A.D. 81 and 96. He was active in the development of the imperial cult beyond the earlier Caesars, who since about A.D. 40 had not been greatly interested in it. Since the writer of the Apocalypse could not have written at this earlier date, Domitian's reign best fits the situation described in the book; and since the writer sees persecution as imminent rather than present, the earlier part of Domitian's reign seems the more probable time of writing. The energy with which the imperial cult was developed in Asia is incidental evidence also of the book's place of origin.

The multitude of Old Testament echoes in the Apocalypse could hardly have come from any but a Jewish author steeped in the Scriptures. According to Swete, 278 of its 404 verses derive from Old Testament passages. The author rarely quotes from it verbatim; rather, he blends two or more passages, sometimes drawn from the same book, often from different books. He follows a like practice in employing Old Testament scenes or episodes. Only intimate familiarity with these sources could enable him to make such use of them. He uses 24 of the 39 Old Testament books: the Torah, Judges,

Samuel and Kings, Psalms, Proverbs, the Song of Solomon, the three major prophets, Daniel, and seven of the twelve minor prophets. References to Daniel, not surprisingly, appear forty-five times; others chiefly cited are the Psalms, Isaiah, Ezekiel, and Zechariah. He is acquainted with the Septuagint, but some Old Testament renderings appear to be from nonextant traditions of the Septuagint or other translations, or, perhaps, are his own. He makes use of some sayings of Christ and knows his teachings, but he never clearly refers to the New Testament epistles. Due, perhaps, to the nature of his work and purpose, the Old Testament was clearly far more impressive than such books by Christian writers as may have been available to him. Little influence of extant extracanonical Jewish books can be traced, though he shares some of their common fund of imagery, along with what he has found in the Old Testament.

Our fragmentary knowledge of Jewish and Christian extracanonical writing prevents identification of images that belong specifically to the author. Interpreters have often succumbed to the temptation to treat every image used as symbolically intended. Much of his imagery is clearly symbolical, some is less clearly so, and some is used, like parts of the classical epic simile, to add decoration or vividness to the picture presented. As the threefold classification in the preceding sentence indicates, there is room for scholarly disagreement about whether an image is symbolic or not.

Swete also warns against the practice of attempting to see in the images specific references to future persons and events.[3] Swete cites an earlier commentator, A. B. Davidson, who wrote, "There is much prophecy but there are few predictions in the Apocalypse"—a truth which has been too often ignored or unrealized.

If one correctly views the images in the Apocalypse as belonging to the philosophical field of prophecy rather than to the closer references of prediction, he is ready to accept Emerson's assertion of "the manifold meaning of every sensuous fact" and his parallel assertion that the visible world is as a whole and in its parts the symbol of

[3] In my lifetime the number of beasts was enthusiastically interpreted as referring in 1917 to the Kaiser and in 1941 to Hitler.

the ideal, intelligible world indicated in Plato's *Republic*. Austin Farrer, though perhaps unduly under the sway of Carl Jung and his acolyte Maud Bodkin, points out that the Old Testament images were not strictly invariable in significance. Their earlier meanings had to be remade, even reborn, into a new liberation for Christian use. While one must interpret the images of the Apocalypse in the light of their previous Old Testament use, they are not bound by that use. The freedom of the New Testament images is in the Gospels and Epistles to some degree fettered by their expository or persuasive application. In the Apocalypse the images are simply there, presented without this immediate application, and therefore free.

This free application could result in near meaninglessness if each image stood alone. In the Apocalypse the images are presented in clusters, and their concatenation tends to clarify their meaning. One must, however, rightly appreciate their connection. Further clarification, as has already been shown, is afforded by knowledge of their situation in the life and ideas of their time, even in their physical, geographical situation.

Farrer feels that the author started his book with the purpose of heartening the Christians of Asia in the face of imminent peril from paganism and, in particular, from the growing influence of the imperial cult of worship. As his insights increased, he became aware of the book's possible future role as a Christian philosophy of the world's fate. His symbolic images accordingly developed from their immediate reference to cover the widest possible earthly scope from the present time to the beginning of eternity. Such subject matter cannot be analyzed as can the data of history; it can only be presented. The symbolic presentation through visions such as the author beheld, making due allowance for the variability of the symbols, is still the appropriate vehicle through which to communicate it.

It is reasonable to assume that the audience to whom John's book was first read would understand his symbols in the light of their situation. Readers like ourselves from later times and cultures and other situations need to seek their interpretation. Scholars are familiar with such difficulties in trying to interpret allusions to contemporary matters in the plays of Aristophanes. Such references are at times quite opaque, while others need skilled interpretation. To perform this work is a delicate operation. It requires not only adequate scholarly training but demands that the interpreter, as Friedrich Schlegel showed a century and a half ago, enter into the very personality of his author and, so far as possible, reconstruct his career mentally and emotionally as he prepared for and executed the work. The two students of the Apocalypse, Swete and Farrer, to whom this account is deeply indebted, were thus prepared to interpret John's book. Before detailed consideration of John's symbolism, however, something should be said about the organization of the Apocalypse, which in point of fact belongs also to its symbolism.

The Apocalypse falls into two nearly equal parts, the point of cleavage being in chapter 11, verse 19. It is as if the author at this point, after finishing the report of his visions regarding the imminent perils of the Church in Asia, came to view his theme in longer perspective. As a result of this enlarged vision, he developed on a new scale the theme which he had already treated in the preceding part. He employed new protagonist figures as symbolic agents, inserted near the end of the first section transitional material to unite the two parts, and so achieved a unified whole. The two parts are similarly but not identically constructed; to make them completely parallel would have violated the enlarged scope of the second part.

Swete finds that the book breaks down into 42 minor sections, 21 in each of the major parts. These 42 sections cluster in 14 larger headings, 6 in part one, 8 in part two. Farrer, who in the main follows a similar outline, is perhaps more interested in the differences than in the parallels. He notes that in the first eleven chapters there are visions arranged in three series of sevens: messages, unsealings, trumpet blasts, each series elaborating and modifying the preceding pattern without exact repetition. Each of the three series is treated in roughly the same space. The number 7 evidently is partly suggested by the beginning of the visions on "the Lord's day" (1:10), which suggests the seven-day week instituted at the Creation (Gen. 1). The consummation of the new heaven and new earth (Rev.

21:1) occupies several series of events analogous to the creation of that which is passing away.

Swete sees part one as a unit complete in itself: if part two had never been written, we should not have noticed any lack of unity in the shorter work. When he projected part two, John naturally inserted transitions. Farrer evidently sees at least two links: first, the series of seven thunders which John was forbidden to describe (10:1–4), and second, the command to John that he must "prophesy again before many peoples, and nations, and tongues, and kings" (10:11). The first link indicates that John still has more visions to report. The second, one is tempted to believe, indicates the universal significance which John has come to see in the vision which had at first seemed to him of merely local import. With these transitions, the reader can proceed with no realization that a juncture has been effected.

The first grouping of seven, symbolized by the seven candlesticks (chaps. 1–3), is in serial order. W. J. McKnight has suggested that the seven churches, which are located in a narrow-based triangle with Ephesus and Laodicea at the western and eastern ends of its base and Pergamum at its apex to the north, occupy geographical positions in an order which a circuit-riding evangelist from Ephesus, the mother church, would follow in his regular visitations. The second grouping, the seven unsealings (5:1–8:6), reports also a series, four figures upon four different-colored horses. The fourth symbolizes Death followed by Hell, after which appear the souls of the martyrs beneath the throne of God who are given white robes and encouraged to await through persecution of their fellow worshipers. The sixth unsealing reveals a cosmic earthquake heralding the end of earth and heaven as now constituted and the ruin of the great men on earth.

The final unsealing follows an interval during which the rescued martyrs of the ideal twelve tribes who truly worship God receive their reward of blissful existence. The breaking of the seventh seal reveals the seven angels with trumpets whose soundings (8:2–11:19) symbolize the third series and conclude part one of the book. These trumpets first presumably sound together, then the serial order is resumed. The first four soundings release cosmic and earthly ruin, the latter reminding one of the plagues visited upon Egypt. The fifth sounding announces a plague of locusts with stings like scorpions, bodies like horses armored for battle, and heads like the mythical Babylonian sphinxes. Their leader is Apollyon. The sixth sounding releases four angels from the river Euphrates who should with their myriad forces annihilate a third of mankind. The final sounding introduces the adoration of the Church before God for his victory and the impending final judgment of mankind.

It is conceivable that this passage constituted the conclusion of the earlier plan for the Apocalypse, before its wider scope was revealed to the writer. It includes the appearance of the temple of God opened in heaven, which resembles the appearance of the new Jerusalem in chapter 21. It was retained in the final, amplified version as a foreshadowing of the new Jerusalem, but is not the sign of final victory as presented here, for with its appearance "there were lightnings, and voices, and thunderings, and an earthquake, and great hail" (11:19). A place for God's worship is available now; but in the final heavenly city God and Christ the Lamb are everywhere.

In the interval between the sixth and seventh trumpet blasts, which presumably serves also as a transition, John hears seven thunders utter their voices, but he is forbidden to report their message. Instead, he is given a book from the hands of "a mighty angel" and bidden to eat it, that is, to digest its contents. Thereupon he is advised that he must prophesy again to a far wider audience (10:11). He is next given a reed and bidden to measure with it "the temple of God,"[4] apparently an edifice not unlike the Temple of Herod in Jerusalem. (The vagueness of reference here will not surprise any reader familiar with the way in which dream pictures present themselves.) Since John has been admonished that he must continue to prophesy, it seems reasonable to assume that the second part of his revelation constitutes the carrying out of these admonitions. It has been made clear (10:4) that he has been writing down what he has

[4] The term *kalamos* ambiguously signifies a measuring stick and also a pen made out of a small sharpened reed.

already seen. There is no reason to assume that his subsequent prophecies will not also be written, or that his abruptly concluded writing at 10:4 is not continued in part two. The effect of the book he has eaten is to widen and deepen the scope of his insights.

With the series of trumpet-soundings, the enumeration of visions is briefly interrupted, perhaps to indicate the shift from messages referring to Asia to those on a more elevated universal plane. Somewhat surprisingly, the unnumbered group of visions with which part two opens (chaps. 12–14) contains seven sequential visions. It is followed (chaps. 15–16) by a numbered series of seven plagues—a reminder of that significant numeral—and the book concludes with a final unnumbered group of seven more visions. As both Swete and Farrer point out, the Apocalypse is composed of six series of seven visions; and Farrer notes that each of the series receives approximately the same space.

The preceding observations amply testify to the orderly plan in John's mind which he worked out in his book. He envisaged a progression of groupings of seven items which are not identical in form but differ in a variety of ways as one succeeds another. It is necessary to emphasize this orderly underlying structure because the reader not uncommonly feels that the book is a chaotic mass of visions.

The symbolism of the so-called Letters to the Seven Churches (1–3) has been worked out in detail by McKnight, who develops hints in the earlier work of Swete. Since these letters particularly refer to identifiable sites about which ancient history and geography provide valuable details, he properly refers each "letter" to the known conditions of that specific church. With equal propriety, he sees in each message something of wider, perennial significance. These data will now be briefly considered to demonstrate one aspect of John's symbolism.

Access to the high plains of Anatolia in central Asia Minor was provided by river valleys which carried water down to the Aegean Sea. Of these, one of the most easily traversed was that of the Cayster River, which entered the sea at Ephesus. Anatolia produced a large part of the wheat needed by the Mediterranean area as well as hides and naval stores; such commerce made the city a flourishing center of commerce and travel. It had been shrewdly selected by Paul as his base of operations in the province, and it had grown to be the leading force in the new religion. It gained in prestige politically from the fact that the Roman proconsul regularly entered Asia through its port. But while Ephesus owed its prosperity to the Cayster River, that river was also its greatest source of danger. Flowing westward down a valley constricted by mountain ridges, it dropped as much as 4,000 feet within a hundred miles or so. When flooded by heavy rains, it carried with it silt, gravel, and stones in great quantity which were deposited at its mouth. Ephesus could maintain its harbor and its commercial position only by constant, alert dredging. A like constant, alert activity is required of the Christian congregation.

Careful attention to the tenses in this message is enlightening. Jesus says, in effect, to the "angel" of the church in Ephesus: I know your actions and your exhausting toil and your perseverance. I know that you cannot endure evil men, and that you tested men who falsely claimed to be apostles and found them to be deceitful. You keep persevering in action, and you did stand up under pressure through my name, and you have not yet become exhausted. But I hold it against you that you did abandon your first love. Keep in mind, therefore, whence you have fallen, and repent and act as you did in your first works. (These two aorist imperatives—*metanoēson* and *poiēson*—have the force of our colloquial "Snap to it.") If you do not, I am now coming, and I shall remove (*kinēsō,* compare our "kinetic") your candlestick from its position. The church, like the city, went about its task without the spirited concentration which vital problems require. Ephesus ultimately lost its harbor and its position, and so did the church.

The other six churches likewise receive topically symbolical messages. Smyrna was a peculiarly active center of emperor worship, and failure to participate brought severe punishment, even death. Followers of Satan (Domitian?), both Jewish and Gentile, persecute offenders severely. They may even die for their faith; but those who resist temptation will receive the victor's wreath of eternal life. Such an award far excels the wreaths won by victors in the athletic games in honor of the Caesar.

Pergamum was the political capital of Asia and the official center of the imperial religion; this church exists "where Satan's seat is." It has become infected with the imperial cult and with other false faiths. Jesus orders it to "repent"—*metanoēson* again. Its reward will be far greater than the secret passwords and insignia of these cults.

Thyatira was a garrison city defending the frontier between Mysia and Lydia, a defense to be held to the last in the face of attack. Although wars between these two former kingdoms were a thing of the past, the citizens kept alive their pride in the city's former significance. It had developed into an industrial center with active laboring men's guilds, roughly equivalent to our trade unions. These guilds were also social clubs with pagan deities as patrons. If the Christian was to find employment, he would be forced to join a guild. In doing this, he recognized the worship of a pagan deity and, in effect, participated in it, for to share in the guild dinners was "to eat things sacrificed to idols." The reference to the woman Jezebel, who seduces men, may follow the ancient practice of Jewish prophets in calling idolatry fornication.

For the church at Sardis, John dips into earlier history. Sardis had an acropolis like Athens, almost impregnable to attack, yet it had several times been captured by enterprising besiegers because it was too complacent in its security. The church is like the history of the city: it seems to be alive, but is dead. It must wake up and stay alert; it must prop up its moribund remaining powers (the aorist imperative, *stērison*). If it does not keep alert, Jesus will come like a thief in the night as the conquerors had gotten into the city.

The topical allusion in the message to Philadelphia is less clear than the others. It seems possible that frequent earthquakes leveled that area and made prosperous life extremely difficult. The Philadelphians have few resources but persist in surviving, as does the church there. Perhaps the reward that he who perseveres will be made "a pillar in the temple of my God" points to the overthrown temples to pagan deities in Philadelphia.

The seventh church is in Laodicea, which was at once a watering place with medicinal baths, a manufacturing center for bleaches, and a purveyor of an ointment for the eyes. People were prosperous and religiously indifferent. Unlike the baths they were lukewarm and therefore act upon Jesus like an emetic. They need true whiteness of character and an eye salve that will truly restore their vision.

Several local allusions in these messages are no longer meaningful to us, though, doubtless, they were intelligible to John's readers. The messages themselves, however, are clear enough when read in the light of their topical allusions. As John's vision assumed universal scope, these messages, for all their local allusions, were directed, as McKnight intimates, to elemental problems faced by Christian churches for all time. John had no need to alter them to fit them into his wider purpose.

With chapter 4 the topical allusions give way to the imagery familiar to the first-century Christian from Apocalyptic and prophetic visions in the Old Testament, as well as in apocryphal Jewish writings. John's free adaptations of this imagery and uninhibited combinations of sources, as well as his own contributions, keep the reader alert to discover nuances and novelties in his composition. It will be sufficient to indicate instances of his practice; to exhaust the body of his vision would prolong this chapter out of all proportion.

The opening verses in chapter 4 illustrate clearly John's practice with imagery. Ezekiel 1:1 states that the prophet saw the heavens opened and received visions of God. John's vision is more specific: he saw a door opened in heaven. Immediately a throne appeared with a radiantly hued person sitting upon it. Not until verse 26 does the "likeness of a throne" with "the likeness as the appearance of a man upon it" appear to Ezekiel. He has first seen a whirlwind, cloud, and fire out of which came "the likeness of four living creatures" resembling the composite winged figures of Mesopotamian mythology. John also includes four composite figures (vv. 6–8) but, unlike Ezekiel's beasts who say nothing, these, like the six-winged seraphim of Isaiah's vision (6:2–3), constantly sing to God in praise almost identical with that sung by the seraphim. From his own store of imagery, John has meanwhile (v. 4) supplied a chorus of twenty-four elders—possibly symbolizing the twelve Jewish patriarchs and the twelve apostles—sitting on lower seats and singing a chorus of praise to God. He has included also seven lamps burning before the throne "which are the seven spirits of God." Presumably these are the previously mentioned "seven spirits which are before his throne" (1:4). The lightning, fire, and storm, which in Ezekiel 1:4 come before the appearance of the throne, in the Apocalypse proceed out of the throne itself.

John's cluster of images in this brief chapter incorporates into a closely knit scene features from Isaiah and Ezekiel with images apparently his own. Every detail is made to center in the throne of God revealed in his vision. Ezekiel's beasts were clearly related to recent and current events, not organized into an artistic unit with other images as are John's.

Chapter 9 further indicates the variable reference of symbols. In chapter 13 the beast that comes out of the sea is evil and deadly. Ezekiel's composite beasts, which in face are like John's in chapter 4, take their character from the stormy tumult from which they appear. Whereas they represent God's retributive justice, John's typify Nature's best attributes. Their wings symbolize the velocity of Nature. Their eyes within and without symbolize the vigilant alertness of Nature and her inner, secret energies. John employs beasts to represent both good and evil and freely changes their punitive force in Ezekiel to the love of God for man. John has added to the talents from the prophets the product of his own efforts.

The concluding vision of chapters 21 and 22 further shows John's practice in combining his symbols. He is indebted to Second Isaiah for his concept of new heavens and new earth, and a new Jerusalem (Isa. 65:17–18).[5] The City of God, the new Jerusalem, prefigured in Apocalypse 3:12, symbolizes the ideal Church, the Bride of the Lamb, who has already been mentioned in 19:7–8 as arrayed in fine linen which is the righteousness of saints. The image of the City-Church was apparently by this time a Christian commonplace. Galatians 4:26 and Hebrews 11:10, 13:14 are evidence. So is Philippians 3:20, where "conversation" should be "commonwealth." By

[5] Related matter from the *Book of Enoch* is mentioned by Swete.

the end of the first century, Paul's successes in urban centers and perhaps the work of other Christians had firmly established the Church as urban rather than village or rural—a pattern that was to prevail throughout most of the first Christian millennium.

Another instance of shift in symbolic significance is attached to the statement "I am Alpha and Omega." In 1:8 and in 21:6, the terms apply to God the Father; in 22:13, to Christ who comes quickly. This shift in reference indicates that full divine quality belongs also to the Son.

John continues his practice of fusing old and new images into a new concept in his description of the new Jerusalem. The twelve gates named for the twelve tribes of Israel come from Ezekiel 48:30–34, the closing vision of that prophetic book. To them John adds the twelve foundations named for the twelve apostles. The measuring of the city is also found in Ezekiel beginning 40:3. The cubic—"foursquare"—dimensions of the city come from the proportions of the altars in the primitive Tabernacle (Exod. 27:1, 30:1) and from those of Ezekiel's new city and temple (41:21, 43:16, 45:1, 48:20). The latter, however, are square but not cubical. In Solomon's Temple (1 Kings 6:19–20), the holy of holies, the peculiar site of the divine Presence, was cubical. The inference from the cubic shape of the new Jerusalem is inescapable. First, it is itself the holy of holies—the entire city is the temple of God. Second, the cube conveyed by its shape the concept of steadfastness and permanence; like Jesus Christ, it is the same yesterday, today, and forever.

The garniture of precious stones on the foundations is also adapted from two lists in the Old Testament: from the description of Aaron's breastplate (Exod. 28:17–20), and from the "covering" of the king of Tyre (Ezek. 28:13). The two lists in the Old Testament contain eight stones in common; the four stones substituted here are unnamed in the Septuagint. How far one should go in attempting to find symbolic significance in the choice of stones, it is difficult to say. This may well be one of the instances in which John has simply embellished his picture with no symbolic intent. One item it is hard not to see as symbolic: The great pearl which forms each gate and so gives entry to the city-temple inescapably calls to mind the "pearl of great price" in Jesus' parable of the kingdom of heaven.

The reader of the Apocalypse can hardly be unaware of the pervasive influence of astrology which it shares with other apocalypses and with Hellenistic and Hebrew thought of its day. Without being a devotee of this pseudoscience, John frequently indicates his awareness of it. More significant is his concern with numbers, which to him convey symbolic if not occult significance.

John's preoccupation with the numbers 7 and 12 has already been mentioned. The reason for his interest in the number 12 is partly Jewish history, but he uses also various multiples of it up to 144,000. The number 7 is encountered 54 times. There are nine instances of 3, eight of 9, twelve of 8, six of 2, and five of 3. The number 4 occurs in repeated references to angels, beasts, winds, and the quarters of the earth. Frequently appearing numbers were peculiarly significant in Semitic thinking, but they may or may not be symbolic.

Two less-expected numbers are 3½ (11:9) and 666 (13:18). The former presumably is the sum of the "time, and times, and half a time" in 12:14, which is taken from Daniel (7:25, 12:7). In Daniel the number probably represents the time when Jerusalem was occupied by the Syrians. Here, too, it no doubt indicates a period of persecution. The numeral 666 (in the codex of Ephraim it is 616) has given rise to many fanciful references, none of which resolves its significance. In view of the prophetic rather than predictive nature of the Apocalypse, it is risky to attempt to account for a solitary numeral symbol which lacks the accompanying cluster of symbols needed for interpretation.

The Apocalypse is alien to Western habits of thought and, thus, is especially a mystery in our day. Nonetheless, partly for its mistily evident grandeur of vision, it amply repays careful, cautious study. It reminds modern man that the mystic's vision transcends ours yet is valid. Truth may be apprehended by other than rational or imaginative means as ordinarily experienced. Pictures present what words cannot express—which is incidentally one reason why artists paint pictures. Why should not symbols operate upon us in the Apocalypse as effectively, if less specifically, as they do in the plastic arts?

THE CONCLUSION OF THE MATTER

I recall vividly my dissatisfaction many years ago upon first reading William DeWitt Hyde's *The Five Great Philosophies of Life*. Having been reared as an orthodox Christian, I found this treatment of Jesus as a teacher of ethics incomplete and lifeless. Several years later I encountered Goethe's critical question, "What was the author trying to do?" Response to this question enabled me to appraise Hyde's excellent statement "with the same spirit that the author writ." Some readers of this book may feel a similar deficiency. It is hoped that they will consider it in the light of Goethe's question.

The extensive ancient disagreement as to the authors of several New Testament books has already been noted. Their scarcity of literary and stylistic criteria in reaching decisions on the authorship of several New Testament books indicates a gap in the data used through which modern scholarship has not been slow to enter. The above-mentioned criterion points to writers with far superior literary talent and training than the putative authors in several cases were at all likely to have possessed. Aside from Luke and Paul, who were competent literary artists, they had doubtful qualifications. The presumption that Silvanus, a man congenial to the apostle Paul, was a ghost-writer for Peter in 1 Peter opens the way to further justifiable speculation. Along with 1 Peter, the literary quality of Matthew, John, Hebrews, and the Apocalypse—and perhaps other books—indicates that their authors were men of superior literary qualifications.

Such a probability opens significant linguistic vistas. The New Testament was composed for and by users of Koine Greek, it is true. Literary artists of the first Christian century were not limited to knowledge of their own century. Those with Hellenistic training were trained in schools in which Greek literature from Homer's day down was studied. Many of them knew also the Latin writers, particularly Virgil, whose poems were used in schools even during his own lifetime. In particular, they knew the works of Greek and Roman oratory and some at least of the many treatises on the art of rhetoric. These latter were also filtered down to them through the popular teachers of rhetoric whom they almost daily encountered in the marketplaces. To what extent the classical Greek vocabulary had filtered down to them in the spoken Greek, our limited acquaintance with the Koine mades it impossible to determine. The number of such survivals noted in this book point sharply to such a carry over.

The mention of oratory and works on rhetoric leads to a fundamental principle of this study. The prevalence of rhetorical concerns, reinforced as it is by the Christian's concept of his contract to spread his gospel within a few decades, makes the art of persuasion a prime consideration in his activity. The Epistles and the Apocalypse have always been considered documents of propaganda. The same concept is here applied in detail to the Gospels and the Acts. These books conform far more closely to the requirements of documents of propaganda than to those of the biographical or historical genres.

The approach to literature, as the late Richard Blackmur repeatedly asserted, is to be made along all available avenues. Criticism he once described as the "formal discourse of an amateur." It is formal in the sense that it shows the form of the work studied and applies to it the forms of critical study established by long practice. The critic is an amateur, that is, a lover of the work studied, who does not let his formal approaches be limited to the unconcerned analysis of the professional. As Plato declared, the critic and reader must be actuated by a love which animates insights and directs to ever higher levels of perception.

When writing the Preface to his edition of Shakespeare, Samuel Johnson wrote, "I am almost frighted at my own temerity." He had ventured to question traditional ideas and realized that his approach to the great dramatist's work would be considered presumptuous. With more justifiable trepidation, yet with equal assurance, I echo his words.

APPENDIX

Below is a brief account of the establishment of the New Testament canon, its medieval translations and renderings until the invention of printing, Continental and English efforts culminating in the King James Version, and mention of subsequent influential versions in English. For the first four Christian centuries, information and documents are in many instances fragmentary, and most dates given are approximate. For more detailed information, see relevant books by Robert M. Grant, Sir Frederic Kenyon, and Bruce M. Metzger, listed in the bibliography.

I. DEVELOPMENTS PRIOR TO THE ESTABLISHMENT OF THE CANON.

From the start of the Christian movement, early Christians used the Old Testament books as canonical. Probably before the end of the first century, collections of Paul's letters were read in churches. The Gospels and Acts were soon accepted as authoritative, though there was some local disagreement about accepting all these. Many churches also accepted 1 Peter, 1 John, and the Revelation in the second century. Nearly three centuries were to elapse before general acceptance of our New Testament took place, and some local disagreement continued for decades thereafter.

Circa A.D. 144, a leader named Marcion, feeling that the Church had become too Hebraic, withdrew from it and formed a separate sect. His list of authoritative books omitted all that did not focus attention upon Paul: Luke, Galatians, 1 and 2 Corinthians, 1 and 2 Thessalonians, Ephesians, Colossians, Philippians, and Philemon. His heretical activity probably contributed to interest among the more orthodox in the problem of canonicity.

Circa A.D. 150, a Latin version appeared, probably in Africa, and subsequently another Latin version appeared in Italy. Their history is obscure, but an Old Latin Version continued in use until the eighth century as a rival to the Vulgate. Versions in other languages also appeared at various times.

Circa A.D. 170, Tatian, a Syrian from Mesopotamia, made a sort of Harmony of the four Gospels, by combining sections from all four into one continuous account. Known as the *Diatessaron,* it is aptly termed by Metzger a cento of short passages from the Gospels so far as the sole surviving fragment indicates. Scholars speculate that Tatian's Harmony may have exerted some influence upon later manuscripts of the Gospels.

Circa A.D. 185, Irenaeus, Bishop of Lyons, made a list of New Testament books which he called "scripture": the four Gospels, Acts, thirteen Pauline epistles (he included 1 and 2 Timothy and Titus), 1 John, 1 Peter, the Revelation, and perhaps 2 John and James.

Circa A.D. 200, the Muratorian Canon, a fragmentary manuscript written in the ninth century, listed the following books as used at Rome at the end of the second century: four Gospels, Acts, nine of Paul's epistles, Philemon, Titus, 1 and 2 Timothy, Jude, 1 and 2 John, and the Revelation. (This fragment is translated in Robert M. Grant, *A Historical Introduction to the New Testament*, pp. 38–40).

In the early third century, the Chester Beatty Papyri included four Gospels, Acts, ten Pauline epistles, and the Revelation. Nonextant papyri perhaps included more books. Scholarly effort was brought to bear on the question of canonicity, especially among Alexandrian scholars, among whom Clement, Origen, and Didymus were noteworthy scholars.

In the fourth century, the question of canonicity was settled. Circa A.D. 330, Bishop Eusebius of Caesarea listed in his *Historia Ecclesiastica* as generally accepted books four Gospels, Acts, Paul's epistles (not numbered or listed), 1 John, and 1 Peter. He could not decide about the Revelation. He listed as disputed books James, Jude, 2 Peter, 2 and 3 John, and did not make clear the position of Hebrews.

A.D. 367, in his Easter letter, the widely influential Bishop Athanasius of Alexandria gave a list of New Testament books identical with ours, and declared these to be the official Scriptures. In spite of minor local disagreement which sporadically appeared, this became the generally accepted list throughout the Church. There is no record of any Church Council's having taken official action on the question.

II. MEDIEVAL VERSIONS PRIOR TO THE INVENTION OF PRINTING

Circa A.D. 400, the Vulgate, Jerome's scholarly translation of the Bible, appeared. It became in time the authoritative Bible of the Latin-speaking Church.

For this section the field is narrowed to translations into English.

Circa A.D. 670, an Anglo-Saxon priest named Caedmon made versified paraphrases of narratives from both Old and New Testaments in his native language.

A.D. 735, the Venerable Bede died after finishing a translation of the Fourth Gospel into Old English.

Circa A.D. 950, an Old English version of the Gospels became necessary for priests who could no longer read Latin. Copies of this version were used in the Church for the next two centuries by less literate priests.

Thirteenth century. Stephen Langton, a doctor at the University of Paris and later Archbishop of Canterbury, divided the books of the Bible into chapters.

Circa 1215, the Ormulum appeared, a versified translation of the daily services of the Church. It included passages from the New Testament.

Circa 1380, John Wycliffe translated the New Testament into English. A revision of it was completed c. 1400. Along with Wycliffe's translation of the Old Testament, this was the first complete English Bible.

III. FROM THE INVENTION OF PRINTING TO THE KING JAMES VERSION

A.D. 1456, Johann Gutenberg issued the first printed book in Europe, St. Jerome's Vulgate.

A.D. 1466, a German version of the Bible was issued by Mentelin. It was followed by others.

Circa A.D. 1478, a French version was issued at Lyons. Another followed circa 1487.

A.D. 1514–17, under the auspices of Francisco Ximenes, Cardinal Primate of Spain, the first Greek New Testament was printed. It was not circulated until circa 1522. It formed part of the Complutensian Polyglot Bible; both Greek and Latin texts of the New Testament were printed.

A.D. 1516, in order to publish a Greek Testament before the appearance of the Complutensian, Erasmus printed his Greek Testament from readily available manuscripts, not first-class sources. A second edition appeared in 1519, and a third in 1527. For this third edition, the Complutensian text was consulted.

A.D. 1522, Martin Luther's German version appeared.

A.D. 1525, William Tyndale printed in Germany the first English New Testament directly translated from the Greek text. He used the text of Erasmus. A revised translation appeared in 1534 at Antwerp. King Henry VIII and the English Church authorities tried unsuccessfully to prevent its being read in England. He translated also the Old Testament from Genesis through 2 Chronicles. Tyndale's translation is the beginning of the English Bible.

A. D. 1535, Myles Coverdale published a complete English Bible with the Apocrypha. Instead of translating from the Greek text, he used as his bases Latin and German translations along with Tyndale's English version. Its second edition in 1537 was printed in London with the King's license.

A.D. 1537, John Rogers published an English Bible, for some unknown reason using the name Thomas Matthew. He used Tyndale's translation and took from Coverdale the Old Testament section which Tyndale had left unfinished.

A.D. 1539, the "Great Bible," so-called from its bulk, was a revision of that by Rogers. It was produced under the auspices of the King's minister Thomas Cromwell. In 1540 a second edition carried a preface by Thomas Cranmer, the Archbishop of Canterbury, with the notation that it was "the Bible appointed to be read in the Churches."

A.D. 1546–57, Robert Estienne (Latinized form Stephanus) issued four editions of the Greek New Testament. Though they were based on the text of Erasmus, the third edition (1550) was the first to contain a critical apparatus noting readings from fifteen Greek manuscripts of late date. Forced to move from Paris to Geneva, he issued in 1557 the first edition divided into verses. His divisions are still followed. His third edition is substantially the accepted or "received text" (*Textus Receptus*) for Greek testaments in England that was so regarded for three centuries.

A.D. 1557–60, English scholars in Geneva, Switzerland, prepared an English translation on the basis of Tyndale's final revision but revised with careful scholarship. It used Estienne's division into verses. It was second only to Tyndale's Bible in its influence upon the translators of the King James Version.

A.D. 1568, Matthew Parker, Archbishop of Canterbury, directed the preparation of the so-called "Bishops' Bible." Parker, a scholarly textual critic, personally reviewed its editing. It superseded the Great Bible in English churches.

A.D. 1582–1609, scholars of the English Roman Catholic Seminary at Douai, France, translated the Vulgate into English. The Seminary was temporarily at Douai when the New Testament translation appeared in 1582, but had returned to its former site at Rheims by 1609, when its Old Testament appeared. Its phraseology exerted some influence upon the translators of the King James Version.

A.D. 1604–11, the translation authorized by King James was prepared. James, himself a competent scholar, laid down rules for the work. It was to be a revision of the Bishop's Bible with the aid of earlier translations. It was not to alter familiar terminology. Proper names were as far as possible to retain their popularly known forms. From a list submitted to him, James selected from forty-eight to fifty of the leading British scholars, drawn mostly from the faculties of Oxford and Cambridge and distinguished graduates of these institutions. These were divided into six committees, each having a part of the task. As each committee completed the translation of a book, it passed its results for review to another; and conferences were held to decide disagreements. When the work was finished in 1610, a committee of twelve reviewed the work and prepared a final draft for the printer. Notes on this committee's deliberations kept by John Bois have recently been printed with facsimiles by Ward Allen,

Translating for King James (1969). The surviving notes concern the ten Pauline epistles, 1 and 2 Timothy, Titus, Hebrews, James, 1 and 2 Peter, 1, 2, and 3 John, Jude, and the Revelation. These notes testify to the scrupulous attention of these competent scholars to minute details. Though the translation was criticized by some for its "low" style, it was on the whole favorably received and remained unchallenged until well into the nineteenth century.

IV. DEVELOPMENTS AFTER THE KING JAMES VERSION

A.D. 1628, the Patriarch of Constantinople presented Codex Alexandrinus to King Charles I.

A.D. 1658, The Polyglot Bible of Brian Walton, Bishop of Chester, included some readings from Codex Alexandrinus (A) and started the interest in manuscripts which was to grow with the centuries. The search for such manuscripts culminated with G. F. C. Tischendorf's discovery in 1844 of Codex Sinaiticus (Aleph), which was to become a leading source for the New Testament text.

A.D. 1870–85, the Revised Version of the Bible was produced, in which basic manuscripts unknown to earlier scholars were used to prepare a Greek text.

A.D. 1901, the American Standard Revision of the Revised Version appeared. In it the style of the Revised Version was adapted for American use.

A few of the outstanding twentieth-century versions are added.

A.D. 1913, The Holy Bible: A New Translation, by James Moffatt, stimulated wide interest through the occasionally daring practices of its scholarly author.

A.D. 1946, The Revised Standard Version of the New Testament appeared after nine years of careful, scholarly work in which the latest discoveries, including the papyri, were used.

A.D. 1961, the New Testament of The New English Bible appeared, in which the scholarly translators have attempted to present in our modern idiom "what we believed the author to be saying in his." The two last mentioned translations have been favorably received.

A.D. 1966, *Good News for Modern Man,* is a scholarly version of the New Testament in popular language. It was later republished as *Today's English Version of the New Testament.*

GLOSSARY
OF LITERARY AND BIBLICAL TERMS

Allegory: literally, saying one thing but meaning another; an account in which the meaning intended is other than the literal sense.

Amplification: elaboration of a scene by dwelling upon it; addition of details so as to overwhelm the auditor or reader.

Anacoluthon: literally, not following; failure to finish a sentence in accord with the beginning structure.

Analogy: clarification or elaboration of an idea or object through a usually extended comparison with something more familiar. Ex.: *Ephesians* 6:13–17.

Anaphora: repetition of a word or phrase at the beginnings of successive clauses or phrases. Ex.: *Philippians* 4:8.

Antinomianism: belief that faith in the gospel's message frees the believer from obedience to the moral law.

Antithesis: sharp contrast of ideas by balancing opposed expressions in parallel structure. Ex.: *Romans* 6:23.

Apocrypha (Old Testament): books included in the Greek Septuagint but not in the scriptural canon.

(New Testament): Christian writings from the second century A.D. or later, imitating or echoing books in the New Testament canon.

Aposiopesis: the sudden breaking off of a sentence, leaving it unfinished.

Asyndeton: literally, not bound together, omission of conjunctions that would normally be expected. Ex. *Romans* 12:9–13.

Atonement, The: the reconciliation between sinful man and God effected through the sacrificial death of Jesus.

Caesar-worship: deification of the Roman Caesars, a rapidly extending cult during the first century A.D., especially in the Near East.

Canon: literally, a measuring rod; a list of books established or accepted as authoritative.

Circumcision: removal of the male prepuce or foreskin, a rite widely practiced in the ancient Near East but in the Bible generally associated with the Hebrews. In *Genesis* 17:10–14 it is recorded as a sign of Jahweh's covenant with Abraham.

Corban: something dedicated to Jahweh by a Hebrew. It could not thereafter be used by its donor for other purposes.

Covenant: a binding agreement or contract between two or more parties. In the Bible, it refers principally to such an agreement between God and the Hebrews or their successors the Christians.

Dead Sea Scrolls: see "Essenes."

Dialectic: reasoning through conversational question and answer as a method of investigation, a procedure characteristic of Greek philosophy.

Diaspora: literally, seed sown broadcast; the settling of Jews outside of Palestine in the centuries following the fall of Jerusalem in 587/6 B.C. to the Babylonians; also the Jews living outside of Palestine.

Dilemma: in debate or argument, the placing of an opponent in a position in which he may choose one or two responses, either of which will embarrass him. Ex., *Matthew* 21:23–26 and 22:16–22.

Docetism: denial that Christ had a human body, from Greek *dokein*, to seem, a characteristic Gnostic doctrine combated in the Fourth Gospel.

Epicureanism: a Greek philosophical system founded by Epicurus (341–270 B.C.). The belief that gods exist but wish no service from or contact with man. Escape from religious fears makes possible human happiness, the chief end of man. Epicurus taught an atomic materialism and a world without design in which man is a free agent.

Eschatology: a term developed during the nineteenth century to denote religious theories concerning the end of this world and events connected with this catastrophe.

Essenes: an ascetic Jewish sect that flourished until its monastery at Qumran, near the Dead Sea, was destroyed by the Romans between 66 and 70 A.D. Discovery of the Dead Sea Scrolls, manuscripts belonging to this sect, in 1947 and later has stimulated interest in them.

Ethopoiia: literally, delineation of character; the preparation of a speech or letter by a rhetorician for its nominal author, in which his mannerisms, vocabulary, idioms, and ideas are carefully copied. Lysias, a fifth century B.C. Attic orator, developed this art and illustrated it by some 30 extant speeches.

Gloss: a comment written by a reader in the margin or between the lines of an early manuscript. Later copyists of such a manuscript sometimes confused it with a proofreader's correction and incorporated it into the author's text.

Glossolalia: in the New Testament, articulate but generally unintelligible speech by Christians in a state of religious ecstasy. It is first reported at Pentecost (*Acts* 2), and is discussed at length by Paul in I *Corinthians* 14.

Gnosticism: see text pp. 179–81.

Grace: literally, something given gratis. In the New Testament, it is God's gift of his saving but unmerited love for mankind. It is a distinctively Christian doctrine.

Hagiographa: literally, holy writings; the third and final section of the Hebrew Bible, finally canonized in 90 A.D. along with the Law and the Prophets. It was accepted as authoritative in Christ's day.

Hasidim: (also called Hasideans). A Jewish religious community, whose origin is unknown, referred to in I and II *Maccabees*, who fought on the side of Maccabees in the second century B.C. wars of liberation from the Syrians. They were probably the parent organization from which came the later Pharisees and Essenes.

Hellenism: in the New Testament times, the Greek culture spread throughout the Near East through the fourth-century conquests of Alexander the Great. It combined with local cultures either as an amalgam or a veneer to produce what is called Hellenistic culture as distinct from the earlier Greek or Hellenic culture.

Herod: the name of a family which ruled Palestine under the Romans. The following members of this dynasty are mentioned in the New Testament: Herod the Great, who ruled all Palestine 40–c. 4 B.C.

His sons: Archelaus, ruler of Judea 4 B.C.–6 A.D., when Augustus banished him to France.

Philip, ruler of northeastern areas, died 34 A.D.

Antipas, ruler of Galilee and Perea 6 A.D.–39 A.D.

Agrippa I, Herod's grandson, succeeded Philip 37 A.D. and Antipas 40 A.D.; king of most of Palestine 41–44 A.D.

Agrippa II, son of Agrippa I, ruled a large area of Palestine after 53 A.D.

Herodians: a group of Jews opposed to Caesar. Their name suggests that they were a political rather than a religious party, but little is known about them.

Hyperbole: exaggerated statement employed for rhetorical effect, not to be taken literally. Ex., *Matthew* 19:24.

Incarnation, The: The doctrine that the second Person of the Trinity, the divine Son, entered into a human body in the person of Jesus of Nazareth, who was thus both God and man.

Intuition: the faculty of obtaining knowledge immediately, without intervention of any rational process.

Irony: communication of a meaning opposed to the literal meaning expressed. Ex., *Luke* 16:1–10. *Luke* and *Acts* furnish abundant examples of irony.

Jahweh: (also Jahwe or Yahweh). The name of God introduced in the revelation from the burning bush. *Exodus* 3:13–14. It is in Hebrew JHWH. Later addition of vowels produced the word Jahweh or Jehovah as written occasionally in the KJV. (In Hebrew, consonants only are written, the vowels being indicated by small signs or "points.")

Jihad: The Moslem equivalent of the Christian Crusades. A jihad may occur whenever a fanatical revivalist succeeds in inflaming his followers to attack non-Moslems. Minor wars arising from such fanaticism were fairly numerous in the nineteenth century.

Judaizers: Jewish Christians who asserted that all Christians, whether Jewish or Gentile in origin, must become circumcised and obey the Jewish Law. Much of *Galatians* is Paul's retort to them.

Kerygma: a general term for Christian preaching. More specifically, it denoted the proclamation of the basic Christian message, as contrasted with *didachē*, a discourse designed primarily to teach.

Koinē: *koinē dialektos*, the Greek spoken as a means of communication throughout the Hellenistic world. The New Testament is a specimen of this speech.

"L": the symbol used to denote material in *Luke* which does not appear in *Matthew* or *Mark*.

"Law and the Prophets, The": the two canonical collections of sacred Jewish literature in Jesus' day. The Law had been canonized prior to 400 B.C., and the Prophets about 200 B.C. See Hagiographa.

Levirate: (from the Latin *levir*, a husband's brother). In ancient Hebrew practice, when a man died without leaving a son, his brother was expected to beget a son with the widow, and this son was legally the son of the dead man. See *Deut.* 25:5–10 for the law, and *Ruth* 4:5–17 for a possibly older variant of the practice. The custom was called levirate marriage.

Logia, The: collections of Jesus' sayings no longer extant except in a few fragments but available to and no doubt drawn upon by the Gospel-writers.

Logos, The: see pp. 179–80.

"M": the symbol used to denote material in *Matthew* which does not appear in *Mark* or *Luke*.

Maccabees, The: leaders and kings of the Palestinian Jews c.168 B.C.–63 B.C. They liberated their race from Seleucid domination and established a dynasty that ruled Palestine until the intervention of the Romans under Pompey.

Marcion: a second-century heretical Christian leader who c.150 A.D. formed a canon of Christian writings which was centered on Paul.

Metaphor: an imaginative partial identification of two objects. These do not fully coincide, but overlap. Successful use of metaphor requires deep insights in the author.

Mystery: in the New Testament, secret rites, often dramatically expressed, through which pagan religious cults celebrated their faith and instructed neophytes; also the secret teachings themselves.

Mysticism: the belief in immediate personal communication with God.

Myth: a story, historical or not, that serves to illustrate a people's view of the world, or accounts for a custom, a belief, or a natural phenomenon.

Nazirite vow: Originally a Nazirite was a man who had won a special sanctity through a vow made to God, in token of which he let his hair grow and abstained from alcoholic beverages. The vow could be for life-long observance or for a stipulated period. When his vow was finished, he could cut his hair short and offer the hair to God. In some cases, apparently, the head might be shaved as a part of the religious undertaking at the beginning instead of at the end (*Acts* 18:18; 21:23–24).

Paleography: the study and editing of ancient manuscripts. Epigraphy, the study of ancient inscriptions, is a part of paleography.

Palimpsest: a parchment from which previous writing has been erased in order to write on it a second time.

Parable: a brief narrative used for teaching. It is an extended metaphor or simile.

Paradox: a statement which seems to contradict fact, which upon examination proves to be true.

Parousia: literally, presence or coming; the return of Jesus Christ to usher in a new age. In the New Testament age, many Christians believed that this return would come quickly, even within the span of a man's life.

Pentateuch: the Greek term for the Torah, the first five books of the Old Testament.

Pentecost; literally, fiftieth; the Jewish Feast of Weeks, celebrated seven weeks (fifty days by ancient computation) following the feast of the barley sheaf during the Passover. The Christian Church calendar has named it Whitsunday.

Pharisees: a Jewish religious party, an outgrowth of the Hasidim (Jews loyal to the Law who supported the Maccabean uprising in the second century B.C.) They supported both the written Mosaic law and the Oral law of the scribes.

Proselytes: literally, newcomers; in the New Testament, Gentile converts to Judaism.

Proto-Luke: A hypothetical "first edition" of *Luke*, which the author subsequently expanded into the extant *Luke* by adding about one-half of *Mark* and *Luke* 1–2.

"Q": the initial letter of *Quelle*, the German word for "source." With a few exceptions, "Q" denotes material common to both *Matthew* and *Luke* but not found in *Mark*. This source material, whether one document or several, may have been written within perhaps two decades following the Crucifixion.

Sadducees: a Jewish religious sect whose name was derived from Zadok, the high priest under David and Solomon who established the Temple priesthood in the tenth century B.C. This sect appeared during the second century B.C. after the successful revolt of the Maccabees from Syria. In Christ's day, they centered their concern in the Temple priesthood and ritual, which they controlled. After the destruction of the Temple in 70 A.D., they diminished in significance.

Samaritans: inhabitants of Samaria, the district between Judea and Galilee. They were regarded by Jews as descendants of various peoples moved into the region to replace the ten Jewish tribes deported by the Assyrians after the fall of Samaria in 722/721 B.C. They claimed to be Jews who were descendants of Jews repatriated during the seventh century B.C. by the Assyrians. They constituted a distinct Jewish sect founded during the fourth century B.C. and totally unrelated with orthodox Judaism.

Sanhedrin: a word transliterated into Hebrew from the Greek word *synedrion*, a body of men in deliberative session. In Jesus' day, the internal government of Roman Judea was largely controlled by it, though the limits of its power are not clear. Its religious influence was recognized by many Jews outside of Judea.

Scribes: *sopherim*, persons able to reckon in numbers and so more highly educated than the average Jew. In Jesus' day, and for some four centuries previously, they functioned as teachers and interpreters of the Law.

Sentence: a readily quotable utterance of the nature of an adage or proverb; a sententious expression. Ex., *Luke* 10:7.

Septuagint: literally, "seventy," from the mistaken notion that seventy translators collaborated in it; the Greek translation of the Hebrew Old Testament, with some extra-canonical books. The Pentateuch was translated probably in the early third century B.C., followed by the other books over an undetermined period of time.

Shema: the first Hebrew word of *Deuteronomy* 6:4, the beginning of the Hebrew confession of faith. To it verse 5 was added, together with other passages. To these two verses Jesus added from *Leviticus* 19:18 the clause, "thou shalt love thy neighbor as thyself," an addition in *Luke* 10:25, amplified by the parable of the good Samaritan.

Sinaiticus: The only surviving complete manuscript of the New Testament written in capital letters. It originally contained both Old and New Testaments, but parts of the Old Testament are lost. Written near the middle of the fourth century B.C., it was edited by scholars working in Caesarea, whose corrections are believed to come from a still older manuscript. It was discovered in 1853. Until the discovery and editing of the New Testament papyri, modern translations based their text chiefly on *Sinaiticus and Vaticanus.*

Stoicism: a Greek philosophical system founded in the fourth-third century by Zeno. It spread with Hellenism and became the dominant philosophy of the Roman Empire. It shows certain parallels with Paul's principles, notably in *Philippians* 4:11–12, but in its self-reliance did not agree with verse 13.

Symbolism: in religious practice, the representation of something invisible by means of something visible—a device peculiarly necessary to express the ideas in a revealed religion. The term has complex ramifications.

Syncretism: the attempt to combine differing religious beliefs.

Synoptic Problem, The: the consideration of similar and differing materials and their arrangement in *Matthew, Mark,* and *Luke*.

Torah: in general, divine guidance and instruction in the Law; also the Hebrew term for the Pentateuch.

Trinity: the New Testament doctrine of the coexistence of Father, Son, and Holy Spirit in God as one being.

Urmarkus: (German for "the original *Mark*"). A hypothetical "first edition" of *Mark,* which subsequent writers expanded into the extant *Mark*.

Vaticanus: One of the two oldest surviving parchment manuscripts (*Sinaiticus,* q.v., is the other) of the New Testament. It has been in the Vatican Library since before 1475 A.D. It was written near the middle of the fourth century B.C., perhaps in Egypt. It originally contained both the Old and New Testaments. Most of *Genesis* and about thirty Psalms are lost, as is the part of the New Testament following *Hebrews* 9:14.

Vulgate: Jerome's Latin version of the Bible, dating from the end of the fourth and beginning of the fifth centuries A.D.

Zealots: certain radical and warlike elements among the Jews, hostile to Roman rule. They felt themselves to be God's agents to combat idolatry and other Law-breaking that aroused God's anger at failure to respect God's divine prerogatives.

BIBLIOGRAPHY

After some forty-five years of teaching the New Testament as literature in both Greek and English, it has become sometimes difficult to assign each specific bit of information to its specific source. The matters treated in this book can all be documented, but behind them lies a mass of reading experience which has blended into fairly clear but unidentifiable memory. In this bibliography I try to include such works as I have in the past several years consulted. The General Bibliography lists works dealing with the New Testament as a whole or in large segments. These more inclusive works provide a better perspective at times on a book in relation to the entire collection than special studies may furnish. In so doing, they may balance judgments made by the specialist in the study of a single book or subject. The reader, therefore, is referred to them in addition to the special studies cited in the chapter bibliographies.

The works in the General Bibliography will be mentioned in the chapter bibliographies by author's name and a brief title. Since most of these books are well indexed, the notes will not as a rule supply page references to them. Some matters relevant but not closely connected to the account in the text are treated in brief notes.

GENERAL BIBLIOGRAPHY

Two indispensable works must be first mentioned:

The Interpreter's Dictionary of the Bible, 12 vols. Nashville, Tenn., Abingdon Press, 1951–57. Volumes 7–12 treat the New Testament. Articles in it (hereafter *IB*) are listed in the chapter bibliographies.

BIBLIOGRAPHY

The Interpreter's Bible Dictionary, 4 vols. Nashville, Tenn., Abingdon Press, 1962. Probably the most nearly complete collection of information relevant to the Bible.

The text consulted for the Septuagint is *Vetus Testamentum Graecum iuxta Septuaginta Interpretes*, edited by Leander Van Ess, (Leipzig, Ernest Bredt, 1908). Three editions of the Greek New Testament were consulted: *The New Testament in the Original Greek*, edited by Brooke F. Westcott and Fenton J. A. Hort (1882); *Novum Testamentum Graece*, edited by Eberhard Nestle; twenty-fifth edition revised by Erwin Nestle and Kurt Aland (Stuttgart, Wuerttembergische Bibelanstalt, 1963); and *The Greek New Testament*, edited by Kurt Aland, Matthew Black, Carlo M. Martini, Bruce M. Metzger, and Allen Wikgren; second edition (New York, American Bible Society, 1968). For the Vulgate the edition used is *Bibliorum Sacrorum iuxta Vulgatam Clementinam Nova Editio*, edited by Aloisius Grammatica (Rome, Vatican Press, 1946).

Studies of the New Testament as a whole:

Clarke, W. K. Lowther. *Concise Bible Commentary*. New York, Macmillan, 1953.

Davies, W. D. *Invitation to the New Testament: A Guide to Its Main Witnesses*. New York, Doubleday, 1966.

Feine, Paul, and Johannes Behm. *Introduction to the New Testament*. 14th rev. ed. Ed. by Werner Georg Kuemmel. Trans. by A. J. Mattill, Jr. Nashville, Tenn., Abingdon Press, 1966.

Grant, Robert M. *A Historical Introduction to the New Testament*. New York, Harper and Row, 1963.

Henshaw, Thomas. *New Testament Literature in the Light of Modern Scholarship*. London, Allen and Unwin, 1952.

Kee, Howard Clark, Franklin W. Young, and Karlfried Froelich. *Understanding the New Testament*. 2nd ed. Englewood Cliffs, N.J., Prentice-Hall, 1965.

McNeile, A. H. *An Introduction to the Study of the New Testament*. 2nd ed. Revised by C. S. C. Williams. Oxford, Clarendon Press, 1953.

Marxsen, Willi. *Introduction to the New Testament: An Approach to Its Problems*. Trans. by Geoffrey Buswell. Philadelphia, Fortress Press, 1968.

Mould, Elmer W. K. *Essentials of Bible History*. Revised by H. Neil Richardson and Robert F. Berkey. New York, Ronald Press, 1966.

Moule, Charles Francis Digby. *The Phenomenon of the New Testament*. London, S. C. M. Press, 1967.

Price, James L. *Interpreting the New Testament*. New York, Holt, Rinehart, and Winston, 1961.

Spivey, Robert A., and D. Moody Smith, Jr. *Anatomy of the New Testament*. London, Macmillan, 1969.

Source materials consulted:

Eusebius. *The Ecclesiastical History*. 2 vols. Vol. I ed. and trans. by Kirsopp

Lake; Vol. II trans. by J. E. R. Oulton. Cambridge, Harvard University Press, 1926, 1932.

James, Montague Rhodes, ed. and trans. *The Apocryphal New Testament.* 1st ed. corrected. Oxford, Clarendon Press, 1953.

Lake, Kirsopp, ed. and trans. *The Apostolic Fathers.* 2 vols. Cambridge, Harvard University Press, 1912–13.

Studies of the first-century A.D. world:

Brehier, Émile. *The Hellenistic and Roman Age.* Trans. by Wade Baskin. Chicago, University of Chicago Press, 1965.

Cochrane, Charles Morris. *Christianity and Classical Culuture.* Rev. ed. New York, Oxford, 1944.

DeWitt, Norman Wentworth. *Epicurus and His Philosophy.* Minneapolis, University of Minnesota Press, 1954.

Fowler, W. Warde. *The Religious Experience of the Roman People.* London, Macmillan, 1911.

Grant, Frederick C. *Ancient Judaism and the New Testament.* New York, Harper's, 1959.

———. *Roman Hellenism and the New Testament.* Edinburgh, Oliver and Boyd, 1962.

Harshberger, Luther H., and John A. Mourant. *Judaism and Christianity: Perspectives and Traditions.* Boston, Allyn and Bacon, 1968.

Howerth, Ira W. "What Is Religion?" *International Journal of Ethics,* Vol. XIII (Jan. 1903), 185–206. The definition cited by Fowler occurs on page 205.

Sherwin-White, Adrian Nicholas. *Roman Society and Roman Law in the New Testament.* Oxford, Clarendon Press, 1963.

Tarn, William Woodthorpe. *Hellenistic Civilization.* 3rd. ed. Revised by the author and G. T. Griffith. London, St. Martin's Press, 1952.

Two valuable atlases:

Negenman, Jan H. *New Atlas of the Bible.* Trans. by Hubert Hoskins and Richard Beckley; ed. by Harold H. Rowley. New York, Doubleday, 1969.

Wright, George Ernest, and Floyd Vivian Filson. *The Westminster Atlas of the Bible.* Rev. ed. Philadelphia, Westminster, 1956.

CHAPTER BIBLIOGRAPHIES

Introduction

THE LITERARY APPROACH TO THE NEW TESTAMENT

Auerbach, Erich. *Mimesis: The Representation of Reality in Western Literature.* Trans. by Willard Trask. Princeton, Princeton University Press, 1953.

Boeckh, August Wilhelm. *Encyclopaedie und Methodologie der philologischen*

Wissenschaften. Ed. by Ernst Bratuscheck; re-ed. by Rudolf Klussmann. Berlin, B. G. Teubner, 1886.

———. *On Interpretation and Criticism*. Trans. and ed. by John Paul Pritchard. Norman, University of Oklahoma Press, 1968. Translation of the theoretical part of the *Encyclopaedie*.

Cook, Albert Stanburrough. *The Authorized Version of the Bible and Its Influence*. New Haven, Yale University Press, 1910.

Fletcher, Angus. *Allegory: The Theory of a Symbolic Mode*. Ithaca, N.Y., Cornell University Press, 1964.

Frye, Northrop. *Anatomy of Criticism*. Princeton, Princeton University Press. 1957.

Longinus. *Longinus on Great Writing*. Trans. by G. M. A. Grube. New York, Liberal Arts Press, 1957.

Lowes, John Livingston. "The Noblest Monument of English Prose." In D. G. Kehl, *Literary Style of the Old Bible and the New*, pp. 8–17. Indianapolis, Bobbs-Merrill, 1970. From Lowes's *Essays in Appreciation* (Boston, Houghton Mifflin, 1936), pp. 3–31.

Moulton, Richard G. *The Literary Study of the Bible*. Rev. ed. New York, Heath, 1899.

Philo Judaeus. *Works*. 12 vols. Trans. by F. H. Colson and G. H. Whitaker, Cambridge, Harvard University Press, 1929–62.

Underhill, Evelyn. *Mysticism: A Study in the Development of Man's Spiritual Consciousness*. 12th ed. New York, Meridian Books, 1955.

Wilder, Amos N. *Early Christian Rhetoric: The Language of the Gospel*. Cambridge, Harvard University Press, 1971. An expanded issue of *The Language of the Gospel* (New York, Harper and Row, 1964).

THE PROBLEM OF THE LANGUAGE

Allen, Ward. *Translating for King James: Notes Made by a Translator of King James's Bible*. Nashville, Tenn., Vanderbilt University Press, 1969. John Bois, a member of the revising committee for the KJV, kept notes of the discussions and suggestions. The surviving notes beginning with Romans show the committee to have been alert, well-informed scholars.

Cadbury, Henry J. "The New Testament and Early Christian Literature." *IB* 7 (1951), 32–44.

Metzger, Bruce M. "The Language of the New Testament." *IB* 7 (1951). 43–59.

THE NEW TESTAMENT AS PROPAGANDA

Several ancient rhetorical works treat of the art of persuasion, which is readily adaptable for propaganda:

Caplan, Harry, ed. and trans. *Cicero ad C. Herennium de Ratione Dicendi*.

Cambridge, Harvard University Press, 1954. This pseudo-Ciceronian treatise contains the practical knowledge of rhetoric which filtered down in the Hellenistic first century A.D.

Cooper, Lane, trans. *The Rhetoric of Aristotle: An Expanded Translation . . .* New York, Appleton, 1932.

Longinus on Great Writing.

Quintilian. *The Institutio Oratoria,* 4 vols. Trans. by H. E. Butler. New York, Putnams, 1922.

Clarke, M. L. *Rhetoric at Rome.* London, Cohen and West, 1962. A good treatment of rhetoric in the Roman world.

Among the studies which indicate the author's awareness of propaganda purposes in the New Testament without developing its implications, are the following:

Cadbury, Henry J. "The New Testament and Early Christian Literature." *IB* 7 (1951), 32–44 (see p. 33).

Filson, Floyd Vivian. "Thinking with the Biblical Writer," *Biblical Research,* Vol. XI (1966), 5–16 (see especially pp. 8–9).

Neill, Stephen. *The Interpretation of the New Testament: 1861–1961.* New York, Oxford University Press, 1966. Chapter 5, "Greeks and Christians" (pp. 137–90), touches repeatedly on this matter. Neill's extensive quotations from Edwin Hatch, *The Influence of Greek Ideas on Christianity* (1889) indicate that Hatch was also aware of the propaganda.

Votaw, Clyde Wever. *The Gospels and Contemporary Biographies in the Greco-Roman World.* Philadelphia, Fortress Press, 1970. It first appeared as an article in the *American Journal of Theology,* Vol. XIX (1915), 45–73, 217–49. In spite of his different major concern, Votaw clearly states the propaganda nature of the Gospels.

CRITICISM OF THE NEW TESTAMENT

Textual criticism:

Birt, Theodor. *Kritik und Hermeneutik.* Munich, C. H. Beck, 1913.

Boeckh, August. *Encyclopaedie* and *On Interpretation* (tr. and ed. by John Paul Pritchard).

Kenyon, Frederic C. *Handbook to the Textual Criticism of the New Testament.* 2nd ed. London, Macmillan, 1926.

———. *Our Bible and the Ancient Manuscripts.* Revised by A. W. Adams. New York, Harper and Row, 1958.

Metzger, Bruce M. *The Text of the New Testament.* 2nd ed. New York, Oxford, 1968.

Neill. *Interpretation.* Chapter 2, "The New Testament and History" (pp. 33–61), and chapter 3, "What the New Testament Says, and What It Means" (pp. 61–103), include much textual information.

Thompson, Edward Maunde. *An Introduction to Greek and Latin Palaeography*. Oxford, Oxford University Press, 1912.

Literary criticism:

Beardslee, William A. *Literary Criticism of the New Testament*. Philadelphia, Fortress Press, 1970.

Braaten, Carl E. *History and Hermeneutics*. Philadelphia, Westminster, 1966.

Boeckh. *Encyclopaedie* and *On Interpretation*.

The KJV (in addition to references already given):

Daiches, David. *The King James Version of the Bible*. Chicago, University of Chicago Press. 1942.

Eppstein, Victor. "The New English Bible of 1970," *Midstream* (Oct. 1970), 50–66.

Pollard, Alfred W., ed. *Records of the English Bible*. London, H. Frowde, 1911. The "Preface to the Version of 1611" is printed on pages 340–77.

Form criticism:

Bultmann, Rudolph, and Karl Kundsin. *Form Criticism: Two Essays on New Testament Research*. Trans. by Frederick C. Grant. New York, Harper and Row, 1962.

Kee, Young, and Froelich. *Understanding the New Testament*. Favorable to the school.

McKnight, Edgar V. *What is Form Criticism?* Philadelphia, Fortress Press, 1969.

McNeile. *Introduction*. Hostile to the school.

Moule, Charles Francis Digby. *The Birth of the New Testament*. New York, Harper and Row, 1962. Favorable to the school.

Muilenburg, James. "Form Criticism and Beyond," *Journal of Biblical Literature*, Vol. LXXXVIII (March 1969), 1–18.

Price, James L. *Interpreting the New Testament*. Judicious.

Redaction criticism:

Perrin, Norman. *What Is Redaction Criticism?* Philadelphia, Fortress Press, 1969.

Symbolic criticism:

Auerbach. *Mimesis*.

Boeckh. *Encyclopaedie* and *On Interpretation*.

Fletcher. *Allegory*.

Philo Judaeus. *Works*.

Sayers, Dorothy. *Dante: The Divine Comedy*. Baltimore, Penguin Books, 1949, Vol. I, pp. 10–16.

Underhill. *Mysticism*.

Source criticism: The introductions to the New Testament already listed are ample.

Chapter 1: The Gospel according to Mark

Barclay, William. *The Gospel of Mark*. Translated with an Introduction and Interpretation. 2nd ed. Philadelphia, Westminster, 1956. Barclay's commentaries on the books of the New Testament are devotional rather than scholarly. They show at the same time a well-informed, keenly probing mind, and are useful for scholarly interpretation.

Grant, Frederick C. "The Gospel according to St. Mark: Introduction and Exegesis," *IB* 7 (1951), 629–917.

Streeter, Burnett Hillman. *The Four Gospels: A Study of Origins*. New York, Macmillan, 1924.

Traditional accounts of Mark and the Gospel ascribed to him are to be found in *The Ecclesiastical History* of Eusebius, II. xv. 1–16.1; II. xxiv; III. xxxix. 14–16; V. viii. 3; VI. xiv. 6; VI. xxv. 5.

Chapter 2: The Gospel according to Matthew

Barclay, William. *The Gospel of Matthew*. 2 vols. Philadelphia, Westminster, 1958.

Johnson, Sherman E. "The Gospel according to Matthew: Introduction and Exegesis," *IB* 7 (1951), 231–625.

Perowne, Stewart. *The Life and Times of Herod the Great*. London, Hodder and Stoughton, 1957. Fills out the picture of the astute but unscrupulous ruler of Palestine when Christ was born.

Richards, Ivor A. *Science and Poetry*. London, Kegan Paul, 1926.

Streeter. *The Four Gospels*.

Traditional accounts of *Matthew* are reported by Eusebius, *The Ecclesiastical History*, III. xxiv. 5–9, xxxix. 4, xxxix. 16; V. viii. 1–2; VI. xxv. 3–4.

Chapter 3: The Gospel according to Luke

Barclay, William. *The Gospel of Luke*. 2 vols. Philadelphia, Westminster, 1956.

Gilmour, S. MacLean. "The Gospel according to St. Luke: Introduction and Exegesis," *IB* 8 (1952), 3–434.

Streeter, *The Four Gospels*. Neill, *Interpretation*, pp. 122–27, writes of Streeter and his theory of Proto-Luke.

Traditional accounts of Luke and his Gospel are reported by Eusebius, *The Ecclesiastical History*, III. iv. 6–7, xxxviii. 2; VI. xiv. 2–3, xxv. 6.

Chapter 4: The Acts of the Apostles

Barclay, William. *The Acts of the Apostles*. 2nd ed. Philadelphia, Westminster, 1955.

MacGregor, G. H. C. "The Acts of the Apostles: Introduction and Exegesis," *IB* 9 (1954), 3–352.

Scott, Ernest F. "The History of the Early Church: The Beginnings," *IB* 7 (1951), 176–86.

Torrey, Charles Cutler. *The Composition and Date of Acts.* Cambridge, Harvard University Press, 1916.

The fact that the Acts of the Apostles focuses upon Paul, phases out Peter at an early date, and mentions the career of no other apostle may have been one reason for the spate of later books relating the doings of other apostles. In *The New Testament Apocrypha,* M.R. James lists and translates five such works: *The Acts of John,* of about the same length as *Matthew,* was composed before A.D. 150. *The Acts of Paul,* of about twice the length apparently of the part of the canonical *Acts* devoted to Paul, was composed about A.D. 160–170. *The Acts of Peter,* slightly shorter than the entire canonical Acts, may date from about A.D. 200. *The Acts of Andrew,* surviving in fragments and in a Latin abstract made by Gregory of Tours (6th century A.D.), may date from A.D. 260. *The Acts of Thomas* is the only one of these documents to survive as a whole. Composed probably in Syriac, it was translated into Greek and dates from some time in the third century A.D. The Manichaean heretics made a volume of these which they substituted for the canonical Acts. Other *Acts,* written apparently in Egypt, later appeared in considerable numbers. "The Gospel of Thomas," a Gnostic document discovered some twenty-five years ago, has been published with explanatory essays by R. M. Grant and David Noel Freedman in *The Secret Sayings of Jesus* (Garden City, N.Y., Doubleday, 1960). The translation is by William R. Schoendel.

Chapter 5: The Fourth Gospel

Barclay, William. *The Gospel of John.* 2nd ed. 2 vols. Philadelphia, Westminster, 1956.

Brown, Raymond E. *The Gospel according to John.* 2 vols. New York, Doubleday, 1966, 1970. This work contains an extremely valuable introduction.

Dods, Marcus. "Introduction to the Gospel according to John," *Expositor's Greek Testament.* Grand Rapids, Mich., W. B. Eerdmans, n.d., Vol. I, pp. 655–81.

Grant, Robert McQueen. *Gnosticism and Early Christianity.* 2nd ed. New York, Columbia University Press, 1966.

Howard, Wilbert F. "The Gospel according to St. John: Introduction and Exegesis," *IB* 8 (1952), 437–811.

Lightfoot, R. H. *St. John's Gospel: A Commentary.* ed. by C. F. Evans. Oxford, Clarendon Press, 1956.

Martyn, J. Louis. *History and Theology in the Fourth Gospel.* New York, Harper and Row, 1968.

Streeter. *The Four Gospels.*

Chapter 6: The Letters of Paul

PAUL OF TARSUS

Conybeare, W. J., and J. S. Howson. *The Life and Epistles of St. Paul.* London, Longmans, Green, 1898. An old but still valuable work.

Deissmann, Adolf. *Paul: A Study in Social and Religious History*. 2nd ed. Trans. by William E. Wilson. 1927. Reprint. New York, Harper's, 1957.

Hatch, William H. P. "The Life of Paul," *IB* 7 (1951), 187–99.

Machen, J. Gresham. *The Origin of Paul's Religion*. New York, Macmillan, 1923.

Minear, Paul S., "The History of the Early Church: Paul the Apostle," *IB* 7 (1951), 200–13.

See also the discussions on Paul in the works on his epistles, Chapter 7.

1 AND 2 THESSALONIANS

Bailey, John W. "The First and Second Epistles to the Thessalonians," *IB* 11 (1955), 245–339.

Chapter 7: The Letters of Paul, Group 2

GALATIANS

Barclay, William. *The Letters to the Galatians and Ephesians*. 2nd ed., pp. 1–70. Philadelphia, Westminster, 1958.

Stamm, Raymond L. "The Epistle to the Galatians: Introduction and Exegesis," *IB* 10 (1953), 429–593.

Robert Browning's "Soliloquy of the Spanish Cloister" refers to "a great text in Galatians" which mentions "twenty-nine distinct damnations." Three hardy scholars in English literature ventured into the higher criticism more than a decade ago in order to discover precisely what list of damnations Browning had in mind. Their findings, which were inconclusive, are in the following articles:

Cutts, John Paul. "Browning's Soliloquy of the Spanish Cloister," *Notes and Queries*, Vol. CCIII (Jan. 1958), 17–18.

Goyne, Grover C., Jr. "Browning and the Higher Criticism," *Dissertation Abstracts* 28. 4128 A (Vanderbilt). 1968.

Waters, D. Douglas, Jr. "Does Browning's 'Great Text in Galatians' Entail Twenty-Nine Distinct Damnations?" *Modern Language Review*, Vol. LV (April, 1960), 243–44.

1 AND 2 CORINTHIANS

Craig, Clarence Tucker. "The First Epistle to the Corinthians: Introduction and Exegesis," *IB* 10 (1953), 3–262.

Filson, Floyd Vivian. "The Second Epistle to the Corinthians: Introduction and Exegesis," *IB* 10 (1953), 265–425.

ROMANS

Barclay, William. *The Letter to the Romans.* 2nd ed. Philadelphia, Westminster, 1957.

Knox, John. "The Epistle to the Romans: Introduction and Exegesis," *IB* 9 (1954), 355–668.

Chapter 8: The Letters of Paul, Group 3

PHILIPPIANS

Scott, Ernest F. "The Epistle to the Philippians: Introduction and Exegesis," *IB* 11 (1955), 3–129.

COLOSSIANS

Beare, Francis W. "The Epistle to the Colossians: Introduction and Exegesis," *IB* 11 (1955), 133–241.

Grant, Robert McQueen. *Gnosticism and Early Christianity.*

Johnston, G. "Colossians," *Interpreter's Bible Dictionary,* Vol. I, pp. 658–62.

PHILEMON

Barclay, William. "The Letters to Timothy, Titus, and Philemon," in his book bearing the same title. pp. 309–24. Philadelphia, Westminster, 1957.

Knox, John. "The Epistle to Philemon: Introduction and Exegesis," *IB* 11 (1955), 555–73.

EPHESIANS

Barclay, William. *The Letters to the Galatians and Ephesians.* 2nd ed. pp. 71–219. Philadelphia, Westminster, 1958.

Beare, Francis W. "The Epistle to the Ephesians: Introduction and Exegesis," *IB* 10 (1953), 597–749.

1 AND 2 TIMOTHY AND TITUS

Barclay, William. *The Letters to Timothy, Titus, and Philemon.* 2nd ed. Philadelphia, Westminster, 1960.

Gealy, Fred D. "The First and Second Epistles to Timothy: Introduction and Exegesis," *IB* 11 (1955), 343–522.

———. "The Epistle to Titus: Introduction and Exegesis," *IB* 11 (1955), 522–51.

Shepherd, Massey H., Jr. "The History of the Early Church: The Post-Apostolic Age," *IB* 7 (1951), 214–27.

Chapter 9: The General Epistles

HEBREWS

Barclay, William. *The Letter to the Hebrews.* 2nd ed. Philadelphia, Westminster, 1957.

Purdy, Alexander C. "The Letter to the Hebrews: Introduction and Exegesis," *IB* 11 (1955), 577–763.

JAMES

Barclay, William. *The Letters of James and Peter.* 2nd ed., pp. 1–159. Philadelphia, Westminster, 1960.

Easton, Burton Scott. "The Epistle of James: Introduction and Exegesis," *IB* 12 (1957), 3–74.

1 PETER

Barclay, William. *The Letters of James and Peter.* 2nd ed. pp. 163–333. Philadelphia, Westminster, 1960.

Hunter, Archibald M. "The First Epistle of Peter: Introduction and Exegesis," *IB* 12 (1957), 77–159.

2 PETER

Barclay, William. *The Letters of James and Peter.* 2nd ed., pp. 335–415. Philadelphia, Westminster, 1960.

Barnett, Albert E. "The Second Epistle of Peter: Introduction and Exegesis," *IB* 12 (1957), 163–206.

1, 2, AND 3 JOHN

Wilder, Amos N. "The First, Second, and Third Epistles of John: Introduction and Exegesis," *IB* 12 (1957), 209–313.

JUDE

Barnett, Albert E. "The Epistle of Jude: Introduction and Exegesis," *IB* 12 (1957), 317–43.

Chapter 10: The Apocalypse

Caird, George Bradford. *The Revelation of St. John the Divine.* New York, Harper and Row, 1966.
Farrer, Austen. *A Rebirth of Images: The Making of St. John's Apocalypse.* London, Dacre Press, 1949.
McKnight, William J. *The Apocalypse of Jesus Christ: A Reappearance.* Boston, Hamilton Brothers, 1927.
Rist, Martin. "The Revelation of St. John the Divine: Introduction and Exegesis," *IB* 12 (1957), 347–551.
Swete, Henry Barclay. *The Apocalypse of St. John.* 3rd ed. London, Macmillan, 1922.
Also to be studied in connection with the Apocalypse are the following:
Fletcher, Angus. *Allegory: The Theory of a Symbolic Mode.* Ithaca, N.Y., Cornell University Press, 1964.
Frye, Northrop. *Anatomy of Criticism.* Princeton, Princeton University, 1957.

INDEX

University of Oklahoma Press

Norman